Chinese Link

中文天地

Zhōng Wén Tiān Dì

Intermediate Chinese

Level 2	Part 1

吴素美 Sue-mei Wu

于月明 Yueming Yu

張燕輝 Yanhui Zhang

Carnegie Mellon University

PEARSON Prentice Hall

world Languages

Upper Saddle River, New Jersey 07458

Acquisitions Editor: Rachel McCoy
Editorial Assistant: Alexei Soma
Director of Marketing: Kristine Suárez
Director of Editorial Development: Julia Caballero
Production Supervision: Nancy Stevenson
Project Manager: Margaret Chan, Graphicraft
Assistant Director of Production: Mary Rottino
Supplements Editor: Meriel Martínez
Senior Media Editor: Samantha Alducin
Prepress and Manufacturing Buyer: Brian Mackey
Prepress and Manufacturing Manager: Nick Sklitsis
Interior and Cover Design: Wanda España/Wee Design Group
Senior Marketing Manager: Denise E. Miller
Marketing Coordinator: William J. Bliss
Assistant Development Editor/Editorial Supervisor: Debbie King
Publisher: Phil Miller
Cover Image: Richard Nowitz Photography

This book was set in 12/15 Sabon by Graphicraft Ltd., Hong Kong, and was printed and bound by Courier – Westford. The cover was printed by Phoenix Color Corp.

Printed in the United States of America
10 9 8 7 6 5 4 3

ISBN 0-13-194766-4
978-013-194766-5

Pearson Education LTD., *London*
Pearson Education Australia PTY, Limited, *Sydney*
Pearson Education Singapore Pte. Ltd
Pearson Education North Asia Ltd., *Hong Kong*
Pearson Education Canada, Ltd., *Toronto*
Pearson Educación de México, S.A. de C.V.
Pearson Education-Japan, *Tokyo*
Pearson Education Malaysia, Pte. Ltd
Pearson Education, *Upper Saddle River*, New Jersey

目錄 (目录) CONTENTS

範圍和順序 (范围和顺序)
Scope and Sequence (Lessons 1–10)

Lessons & Topics 課程 & 主題 (课程 & 主题)	Objectives & Communications 教學目標 & 交際活動 (教学目标 & 交际活动)	Grammar 語法要點 (语法要点)	Idiom Story 成語故事 (成语故事)	Culture Link 文化知識 (文化知识)
1 I Parked the Car on the Side 我把車停在旁邊(我把车停在旁边) *p. 1*	■ Move into an apartment/ a house ■ Describe the result of an action	1. Resultative complement (RC) 結果補語 (结果补语) 2. 把(把) sentences and the resultative complement	The fox makes use of the tiger's majesty 狐假虎威 (狐假虎威)	**Culture Notes:** Moving celebrations and taboos 中國人的搬家誌慶和禁忌(中国人的搬家志庆和禁忌) **Fun with Chinese:** Idiom: 喬遷之喜 (乔迁之喜) **Let's Go:** Residential area 住宅區(住宅区)
2 There Is a Picture Hanging on the Wall 牆上掛著一張照片 (墙上挂着一张照片) *p. 31*	■ Describe an event ■ Talk about experiences	1. Two 了 (and review 了) 2. The aspect 著(着) 3. The experiential aspect 過(过)	*Dongshi* frowns to imitate *Xishi* 東施效顰 (东施效颦)	**Culture Notes:** Four great classical Chinese novels 中國四大古典小說 (中国四大古典小说) **Fun with Chinese:** Idiom: 隔牆有耳 (隔墙有耳) **Let's Go:** Signs in the airport 機場入境/出境的告示(机场入境/出境的告示)

Lessons & Topics 課程 & 主題 (课程 & 主题)	Objectives & Communications 教學目標 & 交際活動 (教学目标 & 交际活动)	Grammar 語法要點 (语法要点)	Idiom Story 成語故事 (成语故事)	Culture Link 文化知識 (文化知识)
3 Go Straight from Here 從這兒往前走(从这儿往前走) *p. 63*	■ Ask and give directions ■ Take a cab ■ Pay money and give change	1. (有)多 + Adjective (How *Adjective*?) 2. Ask and give directions: 往(向) + direction/location + V. 3. V. 起來(起来)	Yugong (the foolish old man) removed the mountains 愚公移山(愚公移山)	**Culture Notes:** China's new economic development zones 中國的新經濟開發區(中国的新经济开发区) **Fun with Chinese:** Idiom: 拐彎抹角(拐弯抹角) **Let's Go:** Airport arrivals guidelines and procedures 機場入境須知及流程(机场入境须知及流程)
4 You Are the Same As Before 你們跟以前一樣(你们跟以前一样) *p. 97*	■ Present gifts and be a courteous guest ■ Receive guests and express hospitality ■ Eat with manners and courtesy ■ Express similarity and comparison	1. 比較(比较) Comparison (1): Simple Comparison Sentences 2. Comparison: relative, superlative and emphatic degree 比較，最，更(比较，最，更) 3. 一天比一天 4. 比 + ... 多了	Inconsistent; self-contradictory 自相矛盾(自相矛盾)	**Culture Notes:** Chinese hospitality: being a good host and a courteous guest 中國人的好客，請客和做客(中国人的好客，请客和做客) **Fun with Chinese:** Slang: 人逢喜事精神爽(人逢喜事精神爽) **Let's Go:** Airport departure guidelines and procedures 機場出境須知及流程(机场出境须知及流程)

Lessons & Topics 課程 & 主題 (课程 & 主题)	Objectives & Communications 教學目標 & 交際活動 (教学目标 & 交际活动)	Grammar 語法要點 (语法要点)	Idiom Story 成語故事 (成语故事)	Culture Link 文化知識 (文化知识)
5 My Trip to China – Review 我的中國行–復習(我的中国行–复习) *p. 135*	■ Make a report ■ Recall memories and past experiences	Grammar Review: 語法復習 (语法复习) 1. Resultative complement (RC) 2. 把(把) sentences and the resultative complement 3. The aspects 了(了), 著(着) and 過(过) 4. (有)多 + Adjective (How Adjective?) 5. Ask and give directions 6. Comparison (1): Simple Comparison Sentences 7. Comparison: Relative, Superlative and Emphatic degree	Waiting for hares by the tree 守株待兔 (守株待兔)	**Culture Notes:** Transportation in China 中國的交通 (中国的交通) **Fun with Chinese:** Slang: 趕鴨子上架 (赶鸭子上架) **Let's Go:** Hotel guest satisfaction survey 北京酒店賓客滿意程度調查表(北京酒店宾客满意程度调查表)
6 I Am Going to the Bank to Open an Account 我要去銀行開一個帳戶 (我要去银行开一个账户) *p. 169*	■ Open a bank account ■ Talk about interest rates and exchange rates	1. Various kinds of phrases A. Juxtaposed phrases B. Endocentric phrases C. Subj. + V. phrases D. V. + Obj. phrases 2. Ways to express percentage and proportion 3. Decimals 4. Noun/Pronoun + 這兒/那兒 (这儿/那儿)	A frog in a well 井底之蛙 (井底之蛙)	**Culture Notes:** China's banking industry 中國的銀行業(中国的银行业) **Fun with Chinese:** Slang: 三百六十行，行行出狀元。(三百六十行，行行出状元。) **Let's Go:** Bank deposit slip 銀行存款單 (银行存款单)

Lessons & Topics 課程 & 主題 (课程 & 主题)	Objectives & Communications 教學目標 & 交際活動 (教学目标 & 交际活动)	Grammar 語法要點 (语法要点)	Idiom Story 成語故事 (成语故事)	Culture Link 文化知識 (文化知识)
7 I Can't Find My Phone Book 我的電話簿找不到了 (我的电话簿找不到了) *p. 205*	■ Talk about possibility and feasibility ■ Book plane tickets	1. Potential complement 可能補語 (可能补语) 2. Questions with structural particles 嗎/呢(吗/呢)	Covering one's ears while stealing a bell 掩耳盜鈴 (掩耳盗铃)	**Culture Notes:** China: a multi-ethnic country 中國：一個多民族的國家(中国：一个多民族的国家) **Fun with Chinese:** Proverb: 四海之內皆兄弟(四海之内皆兄弟) **Let's Go:** 1. Airline ticket price list 機票價格表 (机票价格表) 2. Bus guide 大巴指南 (大巴指南)
8 You Are Much Busier Than Before 你比以前忙得多(你比以前忙得多) *p. 235*	■ Describe contrast ■ Express personal opinion	1. Comparison (2) I. A 比 B + V. + degree of complement II. 比(比) + quantifier 2. Emphatic pattern: 連……都/也……(连……都/也……) 3. Preposition 對(对)	Feeling complacent or extremely proud 得意揚揚 (得意扬扬)	**Culture Notes:** The movie industry in China 中國的電影事業 (中国的电影事业) **Fun with Chinese:** Idiom: 比上不足，比下有餘(比上不足，比下有余) **Let's Go:** Movie and opera tickets 電影票和戲票(电影票和戏票)

Lessons & Topics 課程 & 主題 (课程 & 主题)	Objectives & Communications 教學目標 & 交際活動 (教学目标 & 交际活动)	Grammar 語法要點 (语法要点)	Idiom Story 成語故事 (成语故事)	Culture Link 文化知識 (文化知识)
9 You Are Getting More and More Energetic 你越來越精神了(你越来越精神了) *p. 273*	■ Talk about fitness ■ Make comparisons	1. Comparison (3): 比 and the emphatic degree 更(要)，還(要) [更(要)，还(要)] 2. Progressive change 越來越…… (越来越……) 3. 越……越…… (越……越……) pattern	To add feet to a snake while drawing it 畫蛇添足 (画蛇添足)	**Culture Notes:** The culture of slimness and beauty in China 中國的瘦身美容業 (中国的瘦身美容业) **Fun with Chinese:** Proverb: 人不可貌相 (人不可貌相) **Let's Go:** Weight loss advertisement 瘦身廣告(瘦身广告)
10 My Plan for the Winter Vacation – Review 我的寒假計畫–復習(我的寒假计划–复习) *p. 301*	■ Make an oral report ■ Discuss plans	Grammar Review: 語法復習 (语法复习) 1. Phrases 2. Percentage and proportion 3. Complements 4. Comparison 5. Progressive change 越來越…… (越来越……) 6. 越……越…… (越……越……) pattern	The arrogance of Yelang 夜郎自大 (夜郎自大)	**Culture Notes:** The Great Wall of China 中國的長城 (中国的长城) **Fun with Chinese:** Idiom: 滿載而歸 (满载而归) **Let's Go:** Visa application form 簽證申請表 (签证申请表)

Appendices

前言（前言） PREFACE

CHINESE LINK: Zhongwen Tiandi 中文天地 (Intermediate Chinese) serves as the intermediate level in the *Chinese Link*: 中文天地 program. This series systematically emphasizes and integrates the "5Cs" principles of the National Standards for Foreign Language Education—Communication, Cultures, Comparisons, Connections, and Communities—throughout the program.

The intermediate curriculum encompasses 20 lessons. It is designed to be completed in an academic year of college-level study. This intermediate level program is designed to be well linked to the elementary level program by continuing to provide a practical, learner-centered, and enjoyable language and culture learning experience for intermediate level Chinese learners, as well as an efficient and comprehensive teaching resource for instructors.

While learners of Chinese at the intermediate level need to continue to build their mastery of commonly used vocabulary and grammatical structures, they also need to begin to train for advanced level language usage. Thus, there are two main goals for the intermediate level program:

1. The first goal is to continue to systematically build learners' abilities in the four skills of listening, speaking, reading, and writing so that they can reach the intermediate level of competence. The content and exercises in the second-year program build upon what has been studied in the first-year program, gradually adding more sophisticated vocabulary and grammatical structures. Frequent consolidation and review exercises are included.
2. The second goal is to help the learners to get ready for advanced Chinese study by introducing formal and written expressions and increasing students' "media literacy." This is accomplished by providing exposure to common Chinese idioms and the stories behind them, and by including texts written in the style of newspaper, magazines, and Internet news articles.

Features of CHINESE LINK: 中文天地 (Intermediate Chinese)

- As with the first-year program, the **5Cs (National Standards)** principles are addressed consistently throughout the content, exercises, and homework in the second-year program.
- **Clearly and systematically linked** to the elementary level program. This helps Chinese learners to reuse and review what they have learned, as well as to continue to develop their skills in listening, speaking, reading, and writing for daily communication.
- **Topics** are selected to be **interesting and practical** from the students' point of view. Topics in the second-year program are expanded to **more abstract** and **more societal phenomena** to help learners better understand current Chinese society and be able to discuss, compare, and analyze cultural differences. Learners will also be exposed to various communicative situations that require them to develop and use skills such as basic summary, description, discussion, debate, and report.
- While equal emphasis is still given to both vocabulary and grammatical structures, students are guided to write **longer and more cohesive essays** in Chinese.

- From the beginning of the text, we help students build from words and phrases to sentences and cohesive passages and then to application in **communicative tasks.**
- The **grammar points** and **core vocabulary** are presented naturally in the main texts. The main texts, in turn, provide model situations in which the grammar and vocabulary for each lesson are integrated into **realistic** communicative situations.
- Care has been taken to indicate regional differences in Chinese societies in expressions, pronunciation, and culture notes.

Highlights of the Differences Between the Elementary and Intermediate Level Programs

Much of the lesson structure and pedagogical strategy of the elementary program has been incorporated in the intermediate level program. Key similarities and differences between these programs are summarized below:

- In the intermediate level textbook the texts and examples are provided in both traditional and simplified characters in order to accommodate different users' needs and preferences.
- In order to help the learners become accustomed to reading Chinese characters without phonetic transliteration, in the intermediate level textbook the Pinyin has been removed from under the characters in the core lesson texts. However, the texts with Pinyin are placed in an appendix for reference.
- The vocabulary and sentence patterns introduced before the core texts are still supplemented with Pinyin. This allows learners to familiarize themselves with the core vocabulary and sentence patterns before they progress to the core text, which is presented without Pinyin.
- As in the elementary level textbook, each lesson in the intermediate textbook will include a supplementary text that is written in a different format from the main text, but these supplementary texts are longer. An idiom story passage is also provided in this section as an interesting way to introduce Chinese history and traditions and expose learners to important formal and written expressions. Exercises are provided and are designed to link the learner's comprehension of the text to his/her personal experiences and opinions.
- Review lessons follow every five lessons; these are specifically designed as summary, review, and consolidation lessons. They require learners to apply what they have learned to various interesting and practical communicative situations.
- In-class exercises and homework provide more varied and longer listening passages to help build solid listening ability for communication. Related media materials are carefully selected for the exercises and homework.
- The poem readings for tones and rhythm in the elementary level textbook focus on *Tang Shi*, famous poems of the Tang dynasty (618–907 A.D.). In the intermediate level textbook this section has switched to the lyric poems, *Song Ci*, of the Song dynasty (960–1279 A.D.) for the first part and the songs, *Yuan Qu*, of the Yuan dynasty (1260–1368 A.D.) in the second part. This will help expose learners to varied Chinese literature traditions.
- The **Let's Go!** section in the elementary level textbook focused on survival skills, such as reading street signs, shop signs, and receipts. In the intermediate level textbook the section is expanded to include realistic artifacts that have more content.

- Media literacy is promoted in the intermediate level textbook through various channels such as idiom stories and articles written in the style of newspapers, magazines, and the WWW.

Organization of the Textbook

The intermediate level program is divided into two volumes: Level 2, Part 1 (Lesson 1 to Lesson 10) and Level 2, Part 2 (Lesson 11 to Lesson 20). Both volumes contain the **Core lessons** and **Appendices.**

Core Lessons:

- **Lesson opener:** Lesson objectives and lesson photos
- **Vocabulary: Core vocabulary** and **supplementary vocabulary**
- **Language Link: Sentence Patterns, Language in Use** (main text), **Language Notes,** and **Supplementary Practice, Idiom Story,** and **Media Literacy**
  - **Sentence Patterns** provided before the core texts are designed in dialogue format so that learners can form pairs to practice the dialogue. This provides a convenient way to practice listening and speaking skills with the new vocabulary and patterns before progressing to the **Language in Use** reading.
  - **Language in Use** presents a broader variety of expressions and complicated sentence structures so that students can carry on conversations related to various topics in modern Chinese society. The intermediate level program also emphasizes frequent **consolidation, summarization,** and **analysis** of **vocabulary** and **grammatical structures** throughout the content and exercises.
  - **Supplementary Practice** texts are carefully designed to enhance and consolidate the core elements of the **Language in Use** text. They are written in a different format from the main texts in order to expose learners to different genres of communication.
  - **Idiom Story** is carefully chosen and written to consolidate the core grammar points of that lesson. Its purpose is to introduce students to the rich Chinese cultural and literary tradition while reviewing what they have learned in another interesting way.
  - **Media Literacy** texts, which are incorporated into Lessons 11–20, are short texts written in the style of newspapers, magazines, and Internet news articles. These texts introduce students to the formal grammatical structures common in these written genres. **Exercises** in this section include text skimming, comparing written and spoken expressions, translation, and finding examples of the lesson's grammar points in the article. This section will not only promote students' media literacy skills but will also give them motivation and confidence toward becoming life-long independent readers of Chinese.
- **Grammar:** A broad variety of more advanced grammar points and expressions is introduced in order to strengthen students' ability to express themselves in Chinese. The **Grammar** section contains many examples and summary tables to organize the information for students. The second-year program also emphasizes frequent and systematic review, summarization, and consolidation of grammatical structures throughout the content and exercises.

- **Culture Link:** This section contains three components.
  - **Culture Notes:** This section links the lesson themes together and is relevant to both traditional culture and current societal changes. Authentic photos are provided to create a vivid and pleasing learning experience. The discussion questions are designed to encourage students to provide opinions and to discuss and compare culture differences.
  - **Fun with Chinese:** Common slang expressions, idioms, and proverbs that are related to the lesson vocabulary or theme are introduced. Discussion questions and exercises related to the slang expression, idiom, or proverb are provided to encourage students to perform cultural comparisons. The exercises also encourage students to use Chinese to explain the slang expression, idiom, or proverb. This is a challenge that can help students enhance their speaking and expression skills.
  - **Let's Go!:** This section provides exposure to authentic artifacts of Chinese society, and aims to train the students to be more confident and comfortable getting around in Chinese societies. These items are carefully chosen from real situations related to the lesson theme. New vocabulary and exercises are also provided to reinforce comprehension of the authentic artifact.
- **Activities:** Listening, character, grammar, media literacy, and communicative exercises are contained in the textbook. The exercises progress from drills and practice to content-based communicative tasks. They also provide rich opportunities for summary and consolidation.
- **Appendices:** Rich and helpful appendices are provided as a resource for in-class exercises, self-study, and review.

Other Program Components:

Workbook: Homework and Character Book

The **Homework** portion contains a homework assignment for each lesson in the main textbook. A typical assignment is around 5–6 pages in length, including space for students to write their responses. Homework activities include listening, character consolidation, grammar, media literacy (for Lessons 11–20), and communicative tasks.

The **Character** portion provides reference information for the new Chinese characters in the Core Vocabulary of every lesson. It shows the following for each character:

1. Character with its stroke order indicated by numbers
2. Traditional form of the character
3. Simplified form of the character
4. Pinyin pronunciation, grammatical usage, and a sample sentence or phrase
5. Stroke order illustrated by writing the character progressively
6. Radical of the character with its Pinyin pronunciation and meaning

Blank boxes are also included for students to practice writing the character. As a handy reference, three types of indices are provided in the Character Book: (1) by number of strokes; (2) by lesson number; (3) alphabetic by Pinyin.

Instructor's Resource Manual

The **Instructor's Resource Manual** provides the instructional samples, sample syllabi (for semester and quarter systems), daily schedules, the answer key for in-class and homework exercises, and sample test questions (for each lesson and by every two lessons).

Audio Materials

Audio recordings for all vocabulary, **Language Link** items, listening exercises, and lyric poems, as well as the listening exercises in the **Homework** portion of the **Workbook** are provided on audio CDs. The audio program is also available on the **Companion Website™** and, with permission, can be uploaded to a school's server and/or lab server.

Companion Website, <www.prenhall.com/chineselink>

This open-access Web site will provide useful tools that will allow students to further their learning of the Chinese language and culture, and includes the audio materials.

致謝 (致谢) ACKNOWLEDGMENTS

We are very happy to complete the *Chinese Link*: 中文天地 (Intermediate Chinese) project. We would like to take this opportunity to thank many individuals who offered us support, suggestions, and encouragement, all of which led to the improvement and development of this project.

We would like to thank Mark Haney for his assistance with English proofreading of our manuscript as well as his valuable suggestions from the learner's point of view. Thanks also to our manuscript illustrators, Chi-chen Wu, Chung-ning Lu, and Yi-ju Chen.

Many thanks to our friends and families in Taiwan and Mainland China who have helped provide photos. Special thanks to Tsan-lung Wu, Mark Haney, David L. Forney, and Andi Hermawan.

We are especially grateful to the folks at Prentice Hall whose faith in Chinese Link, innovative ideas, and professional publishing experience have helped guide this project to a successful conclusion: Rachel McCoy, Senior Acquisitions Editor, for her professional guidance, enthusiasm, and tireless dedication to the Chinese Link program, and to Phil Miller, Publisher, for his commitment to and confidence in Chinese Link. Alex Soma, Editorial Assistant, for helping we authors make the final changes before the manuscript could enter the production stage. Nancy Stevenson, Senior Production Editor, and Mary Rottino, Assistant Director of Production, for their mindful supervision of every detail of the production process. Meriel Martinez, Supplements Editor, for carefully overseeing the production of the Workbook, Instructor's Resource Manual, and Audio Program. Thanks to Samantha Alducin, Media Editor, for her skillful management of the excellent media products that have been incorporated into Chinese Link, and to Wanda Espana, of Weedesign, whose creativity resulted in a wonderful cover design.

Our sincere appreciation goes to Margaret Chan, Project Manager, and her Graphicraft team members. Their hard work and dedication helped this project to reach final production.

And finally, we wish to thank our families, without whose love and support this project would not have been possible. Many thanks to our husbands, Mark, Denny, and Dejun, for their patience and support. Thanks also to the first author's children, Carrie and Marion, for their love and for giving up a lot of time with their mom so that this project could be completed.

We extend our sincere thanks and appreciation to the colleagues who reviewed the manuscript and provided valuable input. Their detailed comments and insightful suggestions helped us to further refine our manuscript.

Doris Chun – City College of San Francisco
Hsiu-hsien Chan – Harvard University
Cindy Lee Shih – University of Arizona, Tucson
Yun Xiao – University of Massachusetts
Pei-Chia Chen – University of California, San Diego
Alexander C. Y. Huang – Pennsylvania State University
Zheng-sheng Zhang – San Diego State University
Kitty Shek – San Joaquin Delta College

I-Ping Fu – Radford University & Virginia Tech
Wen-Chao Li – San Francisco State University
Matthew B. Christensen – Brigham Young University
Hua-Fu Liu – San Jose City College
Jean Wu – University of Oregon
Weihsun Mao – Ohlone College

Sue-mei Wu
Yueming Yu
Yanhui Zhang

第一課
LESSON

1

我把車停在旁邊 (我把车停在旁边) I Parked the Car on the Side

教學目標 (教学目标) OBJECTIVES

- Move into an apartment/a house
- Describe the result of an action

A sign for 房屋租賃(房屋租赁) ([fángwū zū lìn]: house for rent), 租售(租售) ([zū shòu]: rent or sale). What is the contact phone number and address? The apartment is on which floor?

生詞 (生词) VOCABULARY

核心詞 (核心词) Core Vocabulary

TRADITIONAL	SIMPLIFIED	PINYIN		
1. 倒	倒	dào	V.	to move backwards, to reverse
2. 别	别	bié	Aux.	don't
3. 房東	房东	fángdōng	N.	landlord
4. 樹	树	shù	N.	tree
5. 撞	撞	zhuàng	V.	to collide with, hit, strike
6. 壞	坏	huài	Adj.	bad
7. 呀	呀	ya	Part.	(used at the sentence end to soften the tone)
8. 小心	小心	xiǎoxīn	Adj. V.	careful, cautious to be careful
9. 鏡子	镜子	jìngzi	N.	mirror
10. 破	破	pò	Adj.	broken
11. 分工合作	分工合作	fēngōnghézuò		to collaborate by dividing up the work
12. 主意	主意	zhǔyi	N.	idea
13. 負責	负责	fùzé	V.	to be responsible for
14. 行李	行李	xíngli	N.	luggage, baggage
15. 放	放	fàng	V.	to put, place

TRADITIONAL	SIMPLIFIED	PINYIN		
16. 裝	装	zhuāng	V.	to install, assemble; to load, pack
17. 掃	扫	sǎo	V.	to clean, sweep
18. 整理	整理	zhěnglǐ	V.	to arrange, sort out
19. 箱子	箱子	xiāngzi	N.	box, case
20. 衣服	衣服	yīfu	N.	clothes
21. 掛	挂	guà	V.	to hang
22. 累	累	lèi	Adj.	tired, get tired of
23. 請客	请客	qǐngkè		to act as the host, to treat
24. 死	死	sǐ	Adj. V.	dead to die
25. 附近	附近	fùjìn	N.	nearby
26. 忘	忘	wàng	V.	to forget
27. 門	门	mén	N.	door
28. 窗	窗	chuāng	N.	window
29. 關上	关上	guānshàng	V.C.	to close
30. 外套	外套	wàitào	N.	coat
31. 咱們	咱们	zánmen	N.	we, us, when used by the speaker to include him/herself and the person(s) being spoken to

補充詞 (补充词) Supplementary Vocabulary

TRADITIONAL	SIMPLIFIED	PINYIN		
1. 鑰匙	钥匙	yàoshi	N.	key
2. 地下室	地下室	dìxiàshì	N.	basement
3. 樓梯	楼梯	lóutī	N.	stair
4. 層	层	céng	M.W.	floor; layer
5. 地毯	地毯	dìtǎn	N.	carpet, rug
6. 地板	地板	dìbǎn	N.	(wooden) floor
7. 整齊	整齐	zhěngqí	Adj.	tidy
8. 方便	方便	fāngbiàn	Adj.	convenient
9. 乾淨	干净	gānjìng	Adj.	clean, tidy
10. 亂	乱	luàn	Adj.	messy
11. 髒	脏	zāng	Adj.	dirty
12. 亮	亮	liàng	Adj.	bright

語文知識 (语文知识) LANGUAGE LINK

The Sentence Patterns provide models that will help you with the Language in Use section. In both sections, pay attention to the grammar points, vocabulary, and expressions.

句型 (句型) Sentence Patterns

A: 讓我把車停在旁邊。
让我把车停在旁边。
Ràng wǒ bǎ chē tíng zài pángbiān.

B: 我先把我的車開走，你再把車開過來。
我先把我的车开走，你再把车开过来。
Wǒ xiān bǎ wǒ de chē kāi zǒu, nǐ zài bǎ chē kāi guò lái.

A: 我負責把行李搬下來、放好。
我负责把行李搬下来、放好。
Wǒ fùzé bǎ xínglǐ bān xiàlái, fàng hǎo.

B: 我來掃地、整理客廳，再把書放好。
我来扫地、整理客厅，再把书放好。
Wǒ lái sǎodì, zhěnglǐ kètīng, zài bǎ shū fàng hǎo.

A: 這次搬家把你們累壞了。你們一定餓了！
这次搬家把你们累坏了。你们一定饿了！
Zhè cì bānjiā bǎ nǐmen lèi huài le. Nǐmen yídìng è le!

B: 對呀！我快餓死了！
对呀！我快饿死了！
Duì ya! Wǒ kuài è sǐ le!

課文: 我把車停在旁邊 (繁體字)
Language in Use: Traditional Character Version

謝進學: 我們到了, 讓我把車停在旁邊。

常天: 等一會兒, 我先把我的車開走, 你再把車開過來。

夏中明: 你在倒車的時候, 我幫你看看, 別把房東的樹撞壞了。

常天: 對呀! 上次我們搬進來的時候, 不小心把房東的鏡子打破了, 真不好意思。

謝進學: 我們先把床和書桌搬到樓上去, 然後再分工合作, 怎麼樣?

夏中明: 好主意, 我負責把行李搬下來、放好, 我也會把電腦裝好。

謝進學: 好, 我來掃地、整理客廳, 再把書放好。

常天: 我來洗碗, 把箱子打開, 再把衣服掛好。

謝進學: 謝謝你們幫我的忙, 這次搬家把你們累壞了。今天晚上想吃什麼? 我請客!

常天: 好極了! 我快餓死了。

夏中明: 這附近有一家很不錯的中國飯館, 可是我把地址忘了。

常天: 沒關係, 我有。你們看, 我找到了。

謝進學: 太好了, 讓我把門窗關上。

夏中明: 別忘了把外套穿上, 咱們走吧!

课文: 我把车停在旁边 (简体字)
Language in Use: Simplified Character Version

谢进学: 我们到了，让我把车停在旁边。

常天: 等一会儿，我先把我的车开走，你再把车开过来。

夏中明: 你在倒车的时候，我帮你看看，别把房东的树撞坏了。

常天: 对呀！上次我们搬进来的时候，不小心把房东的镜子打破了，真不好意思。

谢进学: 我们先把床和书桌搬到楼上去，然后再分工合作，怎么样?

夏中明: 好主意，我负责把行李搬下来、放好，我也会把电脑装好。

谢进学: 好，我来扫地、整理客厅，再把书放好。

常天: 我来洗碗，把箱子打开，再把衣服挂好。

谢进学: 谢谢你们帮我的忙，这次搬家把你们累坏了。今天晚上想吃什么？我请客！

常天: 好极了！我快饿死了。

夏中明: 这附近有一家很不错的中国饭馆，可是我把地址忘了。

常天: 没关系，我有。你们看，我找到了。

谢进学: 太好了，让我把门窗关上。

夏中明: 别忘了把外套穿上，咱们走吧！

注釋 (注释) LANGUAGE NOTES

1. 等一會兒 (等一会儿)

一會兒 means "a moment." 等一會兒 means "Wait a moment." It means the same as "等一下兒."

2. 對呀! (对呀!)

"Right!": a colloquial expression used to show agreement.

3. 不好意思 (不好意思)

不好意思 means "embarrassing" or "embarrassed." The phrase is used to comment on an occasion or behavior which makes people feel embarrassed. It is also commonly used to be courteous when someone has done something for the speaker or the speaker has inconvenienced someone in some way.

4. 咱們 (咱们)

咱們 is a very colloquial way to express "we," used by the speaker to include him/herself and the person(s) being spoken to.

語法 (语法) GRAMMAR

1. 結果補語 (结果补语) Resultative complement (RC)

The resultative complement (RC) indicates the result, extent or goal of an action. It is formed by attaching an adjective or a verb directly to another verb. The RC should be regarded as a unit, and usually does not allow the insertion of another element.

Verb +	adjective/verb	→	resultative complement (RC)
看	錯 (wrong)	→	看錯 (wrong seeing)
看	错 (wrong)	→	看错 (wrong seeing)
	完 [wán] (finish)	→	看完 (finish seeing)
	完 [wán] (finish)	→	看完 (finish seeing)
	見 (perceive)	→	看見 (see)
	见 (perceive)	→	看见 (see)

- The first verb 看 indicates the means. The following adjective (or verb) tells the result or goal of the first verb.
- The object and the aspect particle 了 usually occur after the complement. 沒(有) is used for its negation.

Subject + RC + (Object) + (了)

Positive	**Negative**
我看錯了。 我看错了。 I saw it wrong.	我沒(有)看錯。 我没(有)看错。 I didn't see it wrong.
我看完書了。 我看完书了。 I finished reading the book.	我沒(有)看完書。 我没(有)看完书。 I didn't finish reading the book.
我看見他了。 我看见他了。 I saw him.	我沒(有)看見他。 我没(有)看见他。 I didn't see him.

The following adjectives (or words) are commonly used as the complement in the RC structure.

Adj./Verb	Features	Examples
完 [wán] 完	Indicates some work is finished by some action	看完 做完 寫完 看完 做完 写完
好 好	Indicates the desired state of an action or completion of an action	坐好 拿好 放好 坐好 拿好 放好 收好 搬好 做好 收好 搬好 做好
到 到	Indicates the continuation of an action to a certain point or a certain time	找到 看到 回到 找到 看到 回到
在 在	Indicates that a person or thing ends up at a place as the result of an action. The 在 RC is followed by a place.	放在 坐在 站在 住在 放在 坐在 站在 住在
上 上	Indicates the completion of an action has brought about a certain result such as coming together or being closed up.	接[jiē](to connect)上 穿上 接上 穿上 關上 蓋[gài](to cover)上 关上 盖上

Adj./Verb	Features	Examples
開 开	Indicates the result of an action that moves an object away from its original position.	打開 拿開 拉[lā](to pull)開 跑開 打开 拿开 拉开 跑开
成 成	Indicates that the items have become, become treated as, or become regarded in a certain way.	換[huàn](to exchange)成 看成 换成 看成 當[dàng](to treat as)成 当成 翻譯[fānyì](to translate into)成 翻译成
Aspect 了 了	Usually indicates a change of state but is also commonly associated with the 把 structure.	開了 看了 寫了 吃了 开了 看了 写了 吃了

2. 把字句和結果補語的搭配 (把字句和结果补语的搭配)
把 sentences and the resultative complement

Since the resultative complement indicates the result or influence of an action, it is often used with the 把 structure. Note that when the object is definite, the 把 structure is preferred. For example,

Group A	Group B (with a definite object)
我找到孩子了。 我找到孩子了。	我把你的孩子找到了。 我把你的孩子找到了。 I found your children.
孩子都搬到北京去了。 孩子都搬到北京去了。	我把我的孩子都搬到北京去了。 我把我的孩子都搬到北京去了。 I moved my children to Beijing.
我打破了杯子。 我打破了杯子。	我把你的杯子打破了。 我把你的杯子打破了。 I broke your cup.
我洗完衣服了。 我洗完衣服了。	我把你的衣服洗完了。 我把你的衣服洗完了。 I washed your clothes.

Group A	Group B (with a definite object)
我寫錯地址了。 我写错地址了。	我把他家的地址寫錯了。 我把他家的地址写错了。 I wrote the wrong address for his house.
我裝好電腦了。 我装好电脑了。	我把弟弟的電腦裝好了。 我把弟弟的电脑装好了。 I installed my younger brother's computer.

- The 把 structure is usually compulsory in the following situations:

把 Object + verb 在/到 place

For example:

我把床搬到樓下。 I moved the bed downstairs.
我把床搬到楼下。

我把車停在河[hé](river)邊。 I parked my car by the river.
我把车停在河边。

我把他們送到機場了。 I took them to the airport.
我把他们送到机场了。

補充課文 (补充课文) SUPPLEMENTARY PRACTICE

This section will help you test your comprehension of the grammar and vocabulary you have learned in this lesson. Be prepared to answer questions about the meaning of the passage.

搬家 Moving to a New Home (繁體字 Traditional Character Version)

親愛的小文:

怎麼樣? 忙不忙? 上個星期我搬到一個新的地方, 我們三個人分工合作, 已經把搬家的事處理好了。我們還把室內的擺設重新安排了一下。本來一進門是一個大沙發, 小謝說這樣不方便, 有點兒窄, 風水也不太好, 所以我們就一起把那個大沙發搬到裡邊, 還買了幾個盆栽放在窗戶的旁邊。

我們也把臥室裡邊的音響和電視都搬到客廳了。小謝說他還有幾張中國的山水畫, 明天要把那些畫掛上去, 那麼, 我們的客廳看起來就會寬敞舒服多了。

雖然搬家把我們累壞了, 可是看到我們的新家, 又整齊、又乾淨, 心裡就覺得很高興, 我們的辛苦是值得的。常天提議我們來一個新居誌慶, 這是一個好主意, 我們想邀請你來參加。以下是我們的邀請函,

祝

好

中明

九月三日

補充課文 (补充课文) SUPPLEMENTARY PRACTICE

This section will help you test your comprehension of the grammar and vocabulary you have learned in this lesson. Be prepared to answer questions about the meaning of the passage.

搬家 Moving to a New Home (简体字 Simplified Character Version)

亲爱的小文:

怎么样? 忙不忙? 上个星期我搬到一个新的地方, 我们三个人分工合作, 已经把搬家的事处理好了。我们还把室内的摆设重新安排了一下。本来一进门是一个大沙发, 小谢说这样不方便, 有点儿窄, 风水也不太好, 所以我们就一起把那个大沙发搬到里边, 还买了几个盆栽放在窗户的旁边。

我们也把卧室里边的音响和电视都搬到客厅了。小谢说他还有几张中国的山水画, 明天要把那些画挂上去, 那么, 我们的客厅看起来就会宽敞舒服多了。

虽然搬家把我们累坏了, 可是看到我们的新家, 又整齐、又干净, 心里就觉得很高兴, 我们的辛苦是值得的。常天提议我们来一个新居志庆, 这是一个好主意, 我们想邀请你来参加。以下是我们的邀请函,

祝

好

中明

九月三日

Useful words and expressions:

親愛的(亲爱的) [qīn'àide]: dear
處理(处理) [chǔlǐ]: to deal with
室內(室内) [shìnèi]: indoor
擺設(摆设) [bǎishè]: articles for interior decoration
重新(重新) [chóngxīn]: anew, afresh
安排(安排) [ānpái]: to arrange; arrangement
沙發(沙发) [shāfā]: sofa
不方便(不方便) [bùfāngbiàn]: inconvenient
窄(窄) [zhǎi]: narrow
風水(风水) [fēngshuǐ]: geomancy, Fengshui
盆栽(盆栽) [pénzāi]: potted plant
音響(音响) [yīnxiǎng]: musical entertaining equipment
山水畫(山水画) [shānshuǐhuà]: landscape painting
寬敞(宽敞) [kuānchǎng]: spacious
辛苦(辛苦) [xīnkǔ]: great care or effort, laborious
值得(值得) [zhíde]: to be worth it
提議(提议) [tíyì]: to make a proposal, suggest
新居誌慶(新居志庆) [xīnjū zhìqìng]: celebrations on moving to a new home
邀請(邀请) [yāoqǐng]: to invite; invitation
以下(以下) [yǐxià]: (written expression) below
函(函) [hán]: (written expression) letter

練習 (练习) Exercises

1. 他們是怎麼把室內的擺設重新安排一下的呢?
   他们是怎么把室内的摆设重新安排一下的呢?

2. 找出有下面語法的句子: the directional complement (DC), resultative complement (RC) and the 把 structure.

   找出有下面语法的句子: the directional complement (DC), resultative complement (RC) and the 把 structure.

3. 用你自己的話再把這封信說一遍。
   用你自己的话再把这封信说一遍。

邀請函 Invitation Letter (繁體字 Traditional Character Version)

誠摯地邀請您　　　　歡迎攜伴參加

時間: 九月八日　星期日　下午五點
地點: 大學路23號
事由: 新居誌慶
活動內容: 吃飯、包餃子、聽音樂、唱卡拉OK、跳舞、聊天、玩遊戲等等。
聯絡電話: (一四二) 二六八 三五八八
手機號碼: (一四二) 二六八 六七九九
電子郵件: banxinjia@zhongwen.edu

謝進學、常天和夏中明　敬邀

邀请函 Invitation Letter (简体字 Simplified Character Version)

诚挚地邀请您　　　　欢迎携伴参加

时间：九月八日　星期日　下午五点
地点：大学路23号
事由：新居志庆
活动内容：吃饭、包饺子、听音乐、唱卡拉OK、跳舞、聊天、玩游戏等等。
联络电话：(一四二) 二六八 三五八八
手机号码：(一四二) 二六八 六七九九
电子邮件：banxinjia@zhongwen.edu

谢进学、常天和夏中明　敬邀

Useful words and expressions:

誠摯(诚挚) [chéngzhì]: sincere, cordial
攜伴(携伴) [xiébàn]: (written expression) to bring company/friends
地點(地点) [dìdiǎn]: (written expression) place, address
事由(事由) [shìyóu]: (written expression) subject, purpose
聊天(聊天) [liáotiān]: to chat
遊戲(游戏) [yóuxì]: game
聯絡(联络) [liánluò]: to come into contact; contact
敬邀(敬邀) [jìngyāo]: (written expression) to invite respectfully

練習 (练习) Exercises

Translate the invitation letter into English.

____

____

____

____

____

____

____

成語故事 (成语故事) IDIOM STORY

狐假虎威 (狐假虎威) [hú jiǎ hǔ wēi]

Meaning: The fox makes use of the tiger's majesty

Usage: This is used to describe somebody who bullies the weak by flaunting his/her powerful connections

Example: 他“狐假虎威”，以為他爸爸是校長，搬新家的時候，就叫老師們去幫忙。
他“狐假虎威”，以为他爸爸是校长，搬新家的时候，就叫老师们去帮忙。

Pay special attention to the directional complement (DC), resultative complement (RC) and the 把 structure.

(繁體字 **Traditional Character Version**)

有一隻老虎肚子餓了，牠走過來走過去，要找東西吃，可是都找不到。後來牠看到有一隻狐狸走過來了，牠很快地跳上去，把狐狸抓住了，牠要把狐狸吃掉。

狐狸：你不可以吃我。

老虎：我為什麼不能吃你？

狐狸：天帝派我下來管理所有的動物，你要是把我吃了，那就是不聽天帝的命令，天帝是會把你殺死的。

老虎：你把我當成笨蛋啊！我才不相信你說的話！

狐狸：要是你不相信，你讓我起來，然後走在我的後面，你會看到很多動物都很怕我。

老虎聽了就把狐狸放開，走在狐狸的後面。牠們走進森林裡面，狐狸很威風地走在老虎的前面，所有的動物一看到老虎就嚇壞了，都很快地跑開了。老虎以為那些動物是真的怕狐狸，所以都跑開了。狐狸就對老虎說：「現在你應該相信了吧！」老虎就把狐狸放了，自己走開了。

(简体字 **Simplified Character Version**)

有一只老虎肚子饿了，它走过来走过去，要找东西吃，可是都找不到。后来它看到有一只狐狸走过来了，它很快地跳上去，把狐狸抓住了，它要把狐狸吃掉。

狐狸：你不可以吃我。

老虎：我为什么不能吃你？

狐狸：天帝派我下来管理所有的动物，你要是把我吃了，那就是不听天帝的命令，天帝是会把你杀死的。

老虎：你把我当成笨蛋啊！我才不相信你说的话！

狐狸：要是你不相信，你让我起来，然后走在我的后面，你会看到很多动物都很怕我。

老虎听了就把狐狸放开，走在狐狸的后面。它们走进森林里面，狐狸很威风地走在老虎的前面，所有的动物一看到老虎就吓坏了，都很快地跑开了。老虎以为那些动物是真的怕狐狸，所以都跑开了。狐狸就对老虎说：「现在你应该相信了吧！」老虎就把狐狸放了，自己走开了。

Useful words and expressions:
成語(成语) [chéngyǔ]: idiom
故事(故事) [gùshi]: story
假(假) [jiǎ]: to make use of
威(威) [wēi]: prestige, majesty; 威(威) is an abbreviation for 威風(威风)
老虎(老虎) [lǎohǔ]: tiger
肚子(肚子) [dùzi]: belly
牠(它) [tā]: it (the 3rd. person pronoun for an animal)
後來(后来) [hòulái]: later
狐狸(狐狸) [húli]: fox
抓住(抓住) [zhuāzhù]: to catch
吃掉(吃掉) [chīdiào]: to eat up, devour
天帝(天帝) [Tiāndì]: the Lord of Heaven
派(派) [pài]: to send, dispatch
管理(管理) [guǎnlǐ]: to rule, manage
所有的(所有的) [suǒyǒude]: all of...
動物(动物) [dòngwù]: animal
命令(命令) [mìnglìng]: order
殺死(杀死) [shāsǐ]: to kill
笨蛋(笨蛋) [bèndàn]: idiot
相信(相信) [xiāngxìn]: to believe
怕(怕) [pà]: to be afraid of, fear
森林(森林) [sēnlín]: forest

嚇壞(吓坏) [xiàhuài]: scared
以為(以为) [yǐwéi]: to think, to regard . . . as
那些(那些) [nàxiē]: those
對……說(对……说) [duì...shuō]: to tell, to talk to
放(放) [fàng]: to let go, to release

練習 (练习) Exercises

1. 找出有下面語法的句子: the directional complement (DC), resultative complement (RC) and the 把 structure.

   找出有下面语法的句子: the directional complement (DC), resultative complement (RC) and the 把 structure.

2. 用你自己的話說說"狐假虎威"的故事。
   用你自己的话说说"狐假虎威"的故事。

3. 請用"狐假虎威"造一個句子或者說一個"狐假虎威"的例子。
   请用"狐假虎威"造一个句子或者说一个"狐假虎威"的例子。

4. "狐假虎威"的故事，告訴了我們什麼?
   "狐假虎威"的故事，告诉了我们什么?

練習 (练习) ACTIVITIES

I. 聽力練習 (听力练习)

1-1 In the blanks provided, write the Pinyin for the words you hear:

1. 我們 ______ ______ ______ ______，把房子 ______ ______ ______ ______ 。
   我们 ______ ______ ______ ______，把房子 ______ ______ ______ ______ 。

2. 好 ______ ______，我 ______ ______ 把 ______ ______ ______ 好，
   也把 ______ ______ ______ 乾淨。

   好 ______ ______，我 ______ ______ 把 ______ ______ ______ 好，
   也把 ______ ______ ______ 干净。

3. 我 ______ 他家的 ______ ______ ______ ______ 了。
   我 ______ 他家的 ______ ______ ______ ______ 了。

4. 天氣 ______ 了，______ 把外 ______ ______ ______ 。
   天气 ______ 了，______ 把外 ______ ______ ______ 。

1-2 Listen to the following passages and answer the questions:

第一段(第一段) ([dìyī duàn]: Passage 1):

Useful words and expressions:

其它(其它) [qítā]: other
家具(家具) [jiājù]: furniture
方便(方便) [fāngbiàn]: convenient
碰(碰) [pèng]: to hit, strike
花瓶(花瓶) [huāpíng]: vase
生氣(生气) [shēngqì]: to be angry

第一段問題(第一段问题):

1. 他們前天做什麼了?
   他们前天做什么了?
2. 他們先搬什麼? 然後再搬什麼?
   他们先搬什么? 然后再搬什么?
3. 小謝的房間在哪兒? 搬東西的時候方便嗎?
   小谢的房间在哪儿? 搬东西的时候方便吗?
4. 小謝的床大嗎? 發生 ([fāshēng]: to happen) 了什麼事?
   小谢的床大吗? 发生 ([fāshēng]: to happen) 了什么事?
5. 房東太太生氣了嗎?
   房东太太生气了吗?

第二段(第二段) ([dì'èr duàn]: Passage 2):

Useful words and expressions:

地毯(地毯) [dìtǎn]: carpet
乾淨(干净) [gānjìng]: clean
外賣(外卖) [wàimài]: (food) delivery
匹薩(匹萨) [pǐsà]: pizza
雞翅膀(鸡翅膀) [jīchìbǎng]: chicken wing
開始(开始) [kāishǐ]: to start
直到(直到) [zhídào]: until
半夜(半夜) [bànyè]: midnight

第二段問題(第二段问题):

1. 他們這次幫小謝搬家，累不累？餓不餓？
   他们这次帮小谢搬家，累不累？饿不饿？
2. 他負責做什麼？
   他负责做什么？
3. 小謝請他們吃飯了嗎？吃什麼？
   小谢请他们吃饭了吗？吃什么？
4. 他們整理到什麼時候才回家？
   他们整理到什么时候才回家？

1-3 Read the following lyric, paying special attention to the tones and the rhythm:

Wū Yè Tí	烏夜啼 乌夜啼
(Lǐ Yù)	(李煜) (李煜)
Wúyán dúshàng xīlóu,	無言獨上西樓， 无言独上西楼，
Yuè rú gōu.	月如鈎。 月如钩。
Jìmò wútóng shēnyuàn suǒ qīngqiū.	寂寞梧桐深院鎖清秋。 寂寞梧桐深院锁清秋。
Jiǎn bú duàn,	剪不斷， 剪不断，
Lǐ hái luàn,	理還亂， 理还乱，
Shì líchóu,	是離愁， 是离愁，
Bié yǒu yìfān zīwèi zài xīntóu.	別有一番滋味在心頭。 别有一番滋味在心头。

To the tune of **Wu Ye Ti**
(Li, Yu)

Silently and alone, I climb the western tower.
The moon is like a hook.
The firmiana tree stands lonely. The clear Autumn is locked in the deep garden.
My efforts cannot stop it, nor control it, this sorrow of parting.
There is also a kind of particular mood in my heart.

Practice: What are the rhyming words in this lyric? Write them out in Pinyin:

押 ________ 韻，押韻的字有：________________________________ 。
押 ________ 韵，押韵的字有：________________________________ 。

In the first year text we learned about 詩(诗) ([shī]: poems). In this second year text we will learn about 詞(词) ([cí]: lyrics or song-words). 詞(词) is one of the major poetic genre in the Chinese literary tradition. 詞(词) began as lyrics set to existing musical tunes and their titles always indicate the tune, or 詞牌(词牌) [cípái], for which the lyrics were composed. There are around 825 forms of 詞牌(词牌) which are considered distinct verse patterns.

We may consider 詞(词) as songs for which the melody has been lost. Poets still write to these tune patterns without knowing the original melodies. Thus 詞(词) composition is referred to as 填詞(填词) ([tiáncí]: filling out a pattern). The rhyming scheme and the tonal arrangement of the longer patterns have become very complicated.

詞(词) poetry is characterized by lines of unequal length, in contrast to 律詩(律诗) ([lǜshī]: regulated verse). 詞(词) is usually associated with 宋朝(宋朝) ([Sòngcháo]: the Song Dynasty, 960–1279 A.D.) because the genre reached the height of its literary status during this period. Famous 詞(词) poets include 李煜(李煜) [Lǐ Yù] (937–978 A.D.), 蘇軾(苏轼) [Sū Shì] (1037–1101 A.D.), 韋莊(韦庄) [Wěi Zhuāng] (836–910 A.D.) and a female 詞(词) poet, 李清照(李清照) [Lǐ Qīngzhào] (1084–1151 A.D.).

II. 漢字練習 (汉字练习)

1-4 Read the following words, phrases, and sentences:

壞 坏	關 关
撞壞了 撞坏了	關上 关上
把房東的樹撞壞了 把房东的树撞坏了	把門窗關上 把门窗关上
別把房東的樹撞壞了 别把房东的树撞坏了	讓我把門窗關上 让我把门窗关上

Now try to use the following characters to make words, phrases, and then sentences:

1. 撞 撞	2. 鏡 镜	3. 破 破	4. 合 合	5. 主 主	6. 責 责	7. 裝 装	8. 箱 箱
9. 掃 扫	10. 整 整	11. 掛 挂	12. 累 累	13. 餓 饿	14. 忘 忘	15. 窗 窗	16. 套 套

1-5 Write down the traditional forms for the following simplified characters:

1. 房东 ______ ______
2. 树木 ______ ______
3. 镜子 ______ ______
4. 挂好 ______ ______
5. 饿死 ______ ______
6. 装坏 ______ ______
7. 负责扫地 ______ ______ ______ ______

1-6 Form groups of three and create phrases with the following words (pay attention to the various usages of each word):

Example: 塊：十五塊
块：十五块
一塊鏡子，一塊麵包，一塊蛋糕
一块镜子，一块面包，一块蛋糕

1. 開：
   开：
2. 客：
   客：
3. 近：
   近：
4. 停：
   停：
5. 分：
   分：
6. 床：
   床：
7. 意：
   意：
8. 地：
   地：
9. 洗：
   洗：

III. 語法練習 (语法练习)

1-7 Rewrite the following sentences using "把":

1. 他寫完第三課的作業了。
   他写完第三课的作业了。
2. 他送一件襯衫給他女朋友。
   他送一件衬衫给他女朋友。
3. 媽媽洗了衣服。
   妈妈洗了衣服。

4. 弟弟打破鏡子了。
   弟弟打破镜子了。
5. 我的中文書忘在宿舍了。
   我的中文书忘在宿舍了。
6. 妹妹吃了藥了。
   妹妹吃了药了。
7. 姐姐穿上新裙子。
   姐姐穿上新裙子。
8. 哥哥幫我裝好電腦了。
   哥哥帮我装好电脑了。
9. 弟弟吃了我的蛋糕。
   弟弟吃了我的蛋糕。
10. 我室友洗好我的碗了。
    我室友洗好我的碗了。
11. 他打開那個箱子了。
    他打开那个箱子了。
12. 他餓死小狗了。
    他饿死小狗了。

1-8 Picture talk: 去公園烤肉(去公园烤肉)

With the help of the clues provided, use directional complements, resultative complements and the 把 structure to describe the picture below. (Work in groups of two to three. Try to make at least eight sentences.)

Useful words and expressions:
烤肉(烤肉) [kǎoròu]: to grill, barbecue
烤肉醬(烤肉酱) [kǎoròu jiàng]: barbecue sauce
烤爐(烤炉) [kǎolú]: barbecue grill
夾(夹) [jiā]: to pick up (with clips/tongs)
盤子(盘子) [pánzi]: plate
吃完(吃完) [chīwán]: to eat up
端(端) [duān]: to hold something level with both hands
收拾(收拾) [shōushi]: to tidy up

乾淨(干净) [gānjìng]: clean
垃圾(垃圾) [lājī]: trash (pronounced as [lèsè] in Taiwan)
垃圾桶(垃圾桶) [lājītǒng]: trash can (pronounced as [lèsètǒng] in Taiwan)

上個星期天，我們去烤肉，爸爸把車停在河邊……
上个星期天，我们去烤肉，爸爸把车停在河边……

(1)

(2)

(3)

(4)

(5)

IV. 交際活動 (交际活动)

Situational dialogue:

Situation 1:

One of your friends is concerned about you. She/he tends to use a demanding tone to tell you what to do. (Perfom this situation in groups of two to three. Each person should try to say at least five sentences.)

Use 把 sentences and the directional and resultative complements to form commands such as: 整理房間, 收拾 ([shōushi]: to tidy up) 好廚房, 洗衣服, 別看電視, 穿上大衣, 洗碗, 書放好, 搬好桌子, 吃了午飯, 吃飯, 吃藥…

整理房间, 收拾 ([shōushi]: to tidy up) 好厨房, 洗衣服, 别看电视, 穿上大衣, 洗碗, 书放好, 搬好桌子, 吃了午饭, 吃饭, 吃药…

Situation 2:

You live with your younger brother in an apartment. Tomorrow the parents of your girlfriend/boyfriend are coming to see her/him. She/he will bring them over to meet you. You want your younger brother to help clean up the apartment so that they will have a better impression of you. (Use 把 sentences, resultative complements and directional complements.)

Scene one:	You and your younger brother are discussing the assigned tasks.
Scene two:	You are talking while cleaning up.
Scene three:	Two hours later, you and your younger brother are checking around the apartment.
Scene four:	The next day, the visitors arrive.

文化點滴 (文化点滴) CULTURE NOTES

中國人的搬家誌慶和禁忌 (中国人的搬家志庆和禁忌)
[Zhōngguórén de bānjiā zhìqìng hé jìnjì]
Moving Celebrations and Taboos

There are many traditional Chinese customs and practices related to moving. Their purpose is to avoid bad luck and to bring good fortune to the new home.

First of all, it is very important to choose an auspicious date on which to move. People planning a move usually consult the lunar calendar, which indicates the dates that are good for performing certain activities such as weddings, funerals, moves and travel. In general, moving and other auspicious events are not recommended during the lunar month of July, which is known as "ghost month." It is believed that in ghost month the ghosts are released and wander about. To appease them, people will offer food and sacrifices.

A pregnant woman should avoid moving into a new home or moving/repairing any furniture in her bedroom if possible, because Chinese believe that the spirit of a fetus is not yet settled and might be scared by the move. In the event that a pregnant woman has to move or repair furniture, some Chinese believe that the area around the furniture should be swept with a broom before the move or repair in order to avoid scaring the spirit.

Another important belief is that the first person to enter the new home should be the head of the household. Also, the home should always be entered from the front, not the back. When first entering the home, a broom should be carried inside not only to help sweep out dirt, but also to sweep out bad luck and anything old to make room for the new things that will be placed inside. Moreover, each time a person enters the new home they should carry something in with them. Stoves are another important item for a move. Often, small clay stoves will be lit and carried around the home in order to ward off evil spirits. The stove should be kept burning for a while to symbolize growth. The sparkle given off by the stove also represents the growing of wealth. Finally, before everything is arranged in the new home, the owner may sometimes consult with a Feng Shui master

The banquet is frequently held in a tent in front of the new house. Lots of food is prepared for the guests to enjoy.

Firecrackers are commonly available in street-side shops. The sparkle, fire, and sound from setting off the firecrackers can help scare away bad spirits, and add an auspicious atmosphere for Chinese holidays, and happy occasions, such as a moving celebration.

to help determine the ideal arrangement of furniture in the home to maximize good fortune.

The owner of the new home will also pick a lucky day to host a celebration banquet. They will invite friends and family over to help celebrate moving into the new home. These celebrations are similar to holiday celebrations. Lots of food is prepared for the guests to eat. Tables are covered with red cloth, since red represents happiness, fortune, and prosperity. The guests generally bring red envelopes with cash or other gifts. Incense is often lit and firecrackers are set off to celebrate the move and to scare away any bad spirits that may be around the house.

問題討論 (问题讨论) Discussion Questions

1. 在你們的文化或者其他文化中有沒有一些搬家誌慶和禁忌? 請舉出一些例子。

   在你们的文化或者其他文化中有没有一些搬家志庆和禁忌? 请举出一些例子。

   Are there any moving celebrations or taboos in your culture or other cultures? Please provide some examples.

2. 你會想送你朋友什麼樣的搬家誌慶禮物 ([lǐwù]: gift)?
你想收到什麼樣的搬家誌慶禮物? 為什麼?
你会想送你朋友什么样的搬家志庆礼物 ([lǐwù]: gift)?
你想收到什么样的搬家志庆礼物? 为什么?
What kind of moving celebration gifts would you prefer to give to or receive from your friends? Why?

趣味中文 (趣味中文) FUN WITH CHINESE

喬遷之喜
乔迁之喜
best wishes for your move to a new home

qiáo	qiān	zhī	xǐ
喬	遷	之	喜
乔	迁	之	喜
tall	move	(Particle)	happy event

問題討論 (问题讨论) Discussion Questions

Are there similar sayings in English or other languages used to congratulate people who have moved to a new home?

行動吧! (行动吧!) LET'S GO!

住宅區 (住宅区) Residential Area

常天 is visiting his friend's house in Shenzhen, Guangdong Province. This is a sign at the entrance of the residential community where his friend lives.

Useful words and expressions:

住宅區(住宅区) [zhùzhái qū]: residential area
蔚藍(蔚蓝) [wèilán]: sky blue
海岸(海岸) [hǎi'àn]: seashore
棕櫚(棕榈) [zōnglǚ]: palm
棟(栋) [dòng]: ridgepole (here it is used as a measure word for buildings)
社區(社区) [shèqū]: community
中心(中心) [zhōngxīn]: center
會所(会所) [huìsuǒ]: room, chamber
社康(社康) [shèkāng]: an abbreviation of 社區康樂 (社区康乐) [shèqū kānglè] community entertainment
幼兒園(幼儿园) [yòu'ér yuán]: kindergarten

問題討論 (问题讨论) Discussion Questions

1. Translate the following signs into English:
   (1) 2號會所 社康中心 (2号会所 社康中心)
   (2) 社區服務中心 (社区服务中心)
   (3) 棕櫚園 1-3 棟 (棕榈园 1-3 栋)
2. What is this residential community called? What facilities are provided for the community?

第二課
LESSON
2

牆上掛著一張照片 (墻上挂着一张照片) There Is a Picture Hanging on the Wall

教學目標 (教学目标) OBJECTIVES

- Describe an event
- Talk about experiences

Use the aspect particles 了(了), 著(着) and 過(过) to talk about your experiences with Chinese performing arts. Then try to use your own words to describe this stage.

生詞 (生词) VOCABULARY

核心詞 (核心词) Core Vocabulary

TRADITIONAL	SIMPLIFIED	PINYIN		
1. 牆	墙	qiáng	N.	wall
2. 著	着	zhe	Part.	(indicates continuous or stationary status)
3. 照片	照片	zhàopiàn	N.	photograph, picture
4. 服裝	服装	fúzhuāng	N.	clothes
5. 舞台	舞台	wǔtái	N.	(performance) stage
6. 擺	摆	bǎi	V.	to place, put
7. 各種	各种	gèzhǒng	Adj.	various, all kinds of
8. 樂器	乐器	yuèqì	N.	musical instrument
9. 演員	演员	yǎnyuán	N.	actor or actress, performer
10. 表演	表演	biǎoyǎn	N. V.	performance to perform
11. 樂師	乐师	yuèshī	N.	musician
12. 打	打	dǎ	V.	to play (the drum); to hit
13. 鼓	鼓	gǔ	N.	drum
14. 拉	拉	lā	V.	to play (stringed musical instrument); to pull
15. 胡琴	胡琴	húqín	N.	two-stringed bowed instruments

TRADITIONAL	SIMPLIFIED	PINYIN		
16. 彈奏	弹奏	tánzòu	V.	to play, pluck, strike
17. 自己	自己	zìjǐ	N.	oneself
18. 齣	出	chū	M.W.	measure word (classifier) for Chinese theatre performances
19. 戲	戏	xì	N.	play, drama
20. 畫	画	huà	V. N.	to paint, draw painting
21. 臉	脸	liǎn	N.	face
22. 拿	拿	ná	V.	to hold, take
23. 把	把	bǎ	M.W.	measure word (classifier) for an utensil which has a handle
24. 刀	刀	dāo	N.	knife
25. 神氣	神气	shénqì	Adj.	energetic, high-spirited, proud
26. 座位	座位	zuòwèi	N.	seat
27. 滿	满	mǎn	Adj.	full
28. 觀眾	观众	guānzhòng	N.	audience
29. 站	站	zhàn	V.	to stand
30. 一言為定	一言为定	yì yán wéi dìng		It's a deal.

專名 (专名) Proper Nouns

TRADITIONAL	SIMPLIFIED	PINYIN		
1. 李訪	李访	Lǐ Fǎng	N.	(name) Fang Li
2. 關明遠	关明远	Guān Míngyuǎn	N.	(name) Mingyuan Guan
3. 關公	关公	Guān Gōng	N.	(name), a famous general in the Three Kingdoms
4. 北京	北京	Běijīng	N.	Beijing, the capital of China
5. 長城	长城	Chángchéng	N.	the Great Wall

補充詞 (补充词) Supplementary Vocabulary

TRADITIONAL	SIMPLIFIED	PINYIN		
1. 敲鑼	敲锣	qiāo luó	V.O.	to play the gong
2. 吹笛子	吹笛子	chuī dízi	V.O.	to play the flute
3. 鋼琴	钢琴	gāngqín	N.	piano
4. 小提琴	小提琴	xiǎotíqín	N.	violin
5. 吉他	吉他	jítā	N.	guitar
6. 專心	专心	zhuānxīn	Adj.	be attentive, absorbed
7. 欣賞	欣赏	xīnshǎng	V.	to enjoy, appreciate
8. 關於	关于	guānyú	Prep.	about

語文知識 (语文知识) LANGUAGE LINK

The Sentence Patterns provide models that will help you with the Language in Use section. In both sections, pay attention to the grammar points, vocabulary, and expressions.

句型 (句型) Sentence Patterns

A: 你學中文學了多久了(or 你學中文學了多長時間了)?
你学中文学了多久了(or 你学中文学了多长时间了)?
Nǐ xué Zhōngwén xuéle duō jiǔ le? (or Nǐ xué Zhōngwén xuéle duō cháng shíjiān le?)

B: 我學中文學了兩年了。
我学中文学了两年了。
Wō xué Zhōngwén xuéle liǎngnián le.

–多久 ([duō jiǔ]: How long (duration of time)?)
–多長時間(多长时间) ([duō cháng shíjiān]: How long (duration of time)?)

A: 演員正忙著表演，旁邊還坐著幾個樂師。
演员正忙着表演，旁边还坐着几个乐师。
Yǎnyuán zhèng mángzhe biǎoyǎn, pángbiān hái zuòzhe jǐge yuèshī.

B: 人真不少啊！有的觀眾還得站著。
人真不少啊！有的观众还得站着 。
Rén zhēn bùshǎo a! Yǒude guānzhòng hái děi zhànzhe.

A: 你在中國的時候去過哪兒?
你在中国的时候去过哪儿?
Nǐ zài Zhōngguó de shíhòu qù guo nǎr?

B: 我只去過上海，可是沒去過北京和長城。
我只去过上海，可是没去过北京和长城。
Wō zhǐ qù guo Shànghǎi, kěshì méi qù guo Běijīng hé Chángchéng.

課文: 牆上掛著一張照片 (繁體字)
Language in Use: Traditional Character Version

李訪： 那邊牆上掛著一張照片。那是誰? 我好像沒見過。
關明遠： 那是我姐姐照的照片。
李訪： 她現在在哪兒?
關明遠： 她現在正在北京留學, 她在那兒學中文, 已經在那兒住了一年多了。
李訪： 她學中文學了多久了?
關明遠： 她學了三年了。
李訪： 那是京劇的服裝吧!
關明遠： 是的。這是她上個月去看京劇的時候照的照片。以前她沒看過京劇, 現在看到了, 她很高興。
李訪： 舞台上面擺著什麼? 好像是中國的各種樂器。
關明遠： 沒錯! 你看台上京劇演員, 正忙著表演呢。旁邊還坐著幾個樂師, 有的在打鼓, 有的在拉胡琴, 他們都忙著彈奏自己的樂器。
李訪： 這齣戲說的是什麼? 好像很不錯。
關明遠： 這齣戲說的是關公。你看關公他畫著紅臉, 手上拿著一把大刀, 真神氣!
李訪： 人真不少啊! 你看, 座位都坐滿了, 有的觀眾還得站著。對了, 你看過京劇嗎?
關明遠： 我看過兩次, 都是在上海看的。
李訪： 你在中國的時候去過上海, 還去過哪兒?
關明遠： 我只去過上海。那時候, 我每天都忙著上課, 所以沒有機會去北京和長城。
李訪： 我聽說上海的小籠包很好吃, 你吃過嗎?
關明遠： 吃過, 我還學過做小籠包呢!
李訪： 真有意思! 我也想去中國看看。
關明遠： 我下個月要去中國, 你跟我去吧! 我們可以一起去看京劇, 怎麼樣?
李訪： 好, 一言為定!

课文: 墙上挂着一张照片 (简体字)
Language in Use: Simplified Character Version

李访： 那边墙上挂着一张照片。那是谁？我好像没见过。
关明远： 那是我姐姐照的照片。
李访： 她现在在哪儿？
关明远： 她现在正在北京留学，她在那儿学中文，已经在那儿住了一年多了。
李访： 她学中文学了多久了？
关明远： 她学了三年了。
李访： 那是京剧的服装吧！
关明远： 是的。这是她上个月去看京剧的时候照的照片。以前她没看过京剧，现在看到了，她很高兴。
李访： 舞台上面摆着什么？好像是中国的各种乐器。
关明远： 没错！你看台上京剧演员，正忙着表演呢。旁边还坐着几个乐师，有的在打鼓，有的在拉胡琴，他们都忙着弹奏自己的乐器。
李访： 这出戏说的是什么？好像很不错。
关明远： 这出戏说的是关公。你看关公他画着红脸，手上拿着一把大刀，真神气！
李访： 人真不少啊！你看，座位都坐满了，有的观众还得站着。对了，你看过京剧吗？
关明远： 我看过两次，都是在上海看的。
李访： 你在中国的时候去过上海，还去过哪儿？
关明远： 我只去过上海。那时候，我每天都忙着上课，所以没有机会去北京和长城。
李访： 我听说上海的小笼包很好吃，你吃过吗？
关明远： 吃过，我还学过做小笼包呢！
李访： 真有意思！我也想去中国看看。
关明远： 我下个月要去中国，你跟我去吧！我们可以一起去看京剧，怎么样？
李访： 好，一言为定！

注釋 (注释) LANGUAGE NOTES

1. 沒錯 (没错)

沒錯(没错) means "correct!" or "what you said was correct." It is commonly used in a conversation to express agreement with what someone else has just said.

2. 樂 (乐) [lè, yuè]

樂(乐) has two pronunciations which have two different meanings:
快樂(快乐) [kuàilè]: happy, happiness 音樂(音乐) [yīnyuè]: music

3. 有的 (有的)

有的(有的) means "some part (of a group)."

e.g.: 中文課的學生都得學漢字，
中文课的学生都得学汉字，
All students in the Chinese class have to learn Chinese characters.

有的(人)喜歡學繁體字，有的(人)喜歡學簡體字。
有的(人)喜欢学繁体字，有的(人)喜欢学简体字。
Some like learning traditional characters, some like learning simplified characters.

4. 關公 (关公)

關公(关公) is one of the main characters in the well-known ancient Chinese historical novel 三國演義(三国演义) [Sānguó Yǎnyì] (The Romance of the Three Kingdoms). 關公(关公) is known for his bravery, loyalty, and righteousness. He is also referred to as 關羽(关羽) [Guān Yǔ] or 關雲長(关云长) [Guān Yúncháng].

5. 過 (过)

過(过) has the following different usages:

1. As a verb, it means "to pass,"
   e.g.: 現在是三點過五分。 It is 3:05 now.
   現在是三点过五分。
2. As a verb, it means "to celebrate,"
   e.g.: 我昨天過生日。 I celebrated my birthday yesterday.
   我昨天过生日。
3. As an aspect, it indicates past experience,
   e.g.: 我去過長城。 I have been to the Great Wall.
   我去过长城。

6. 長城 (长城)

長城(长城) is the Great Wall, one of the greatest projects in world history. It was started during the Qin Dynasty (221–206 B.C.) and completed in the Ming Dynasty (1368–1644) to defend China from invasions by the Mongolians. It is reputed to be the only man-made structure on earth that can be seen from the moon.

語法 (语法) GRAMMAR

1. Two 了 (and review 了)

– 了 indicates completed action. It is placed after a verb or at the end of the sentence.

	Structure	Examples
Question:	了嗎/了沒有	你吃飯了嗎?/你吃飯了沒有? 你吃饭了吗?/你吃饭了没有?
Affirmative Answer:	V. + 了/sentece-end + 了	我吃了。 我吃了。
Negative Answer:	(還)沒有……呢	我還沒有吃呢。 我还没有吃呢。

– When two 了 co-occur, it usually indicates that the action is still ongoing at the moment of speaking.

For example:

她學中文學了三年了。
她学中文学了三年了。
She has been studying Chinese for three years. (Note: She is still studying Chinese at the moment of speaking.)

他已經在這兒住了一年多了。
他已经在这儿住了一年多了。
He has lived here for over a year. (Note: He still lives here.)

我看了三本書了。
我看了三本书了。
I have read three books. (Note: It implies that I have read three books and there are more books for me to read.)

2. The aspect 著 (着)

著(着) is an aspect particle that is added to a verb to describe a state which is continuous or stationary.

For example:

他穿著一件外套。
他穿着一件外套。
He is wearing a jacket. (He has a jacket on.)

牆上掛著一張照片。
墙上挂着一张照片。
There is a picture hanging on the wall.

台上坐著幾個樂師。
台上坐着几个乐师。
There are a few musicians sitting on the stage.

V. + 著(着) is also used to provide a background in which an action is carried out.

For example:

媽媽忙著做飯。 妈妈忙着做饭。	Mother is busy cooking.
觀眾站著看戲。 观众站着看戏。	The audience is standing watching the play.
他們都忙著彈奏自己的樂器。 他们都忙着弹奏自己的乐器。	They are all busy playing their own instruments.

Note: The difference between 在 + V. and V. + 著(着) is that 在 indicates a dynamic action while 著(着) is stative. See the following examples:

他在穿外套。 他在穿外套。	He is putting a coat on.
他穿著外套。 他穿着外套。	He has a coat on.

3. The experiential aspect 過 (过)

The aspect 過 is added to a verb to indicate past experience (ever . . . before).

Pattern:	V. + 過(过)
Negation:	沒(有) + V. + 過(过)
Question:	V. + 過(过) ...... 沒有? V. + 過(过) ...... 嗎(吗)?

For example:

A: 你看過京劇沒有?
你看过京剧没有?
Have you (ever) seen Peking Opera?

B: 我看過京劇。
我看过京剧。
I have seen it.

A: 你去過長城嗎?
你去过长城吗?
Have you been to the Great Wall?

B: 我沒(有)去過長城。
我没(有)去过长城。
I have never been to the Great Wall.

Since V. + 過(过) indicates past experience, it often co-occurs with time phrases that indicate the past, such as 以前(以前), 去年(去年), 上個星期(上个星期), etc.

我以前看過那本小說。
我以前看过那本小说。
I have read that novel before.

他兩年以前去過中國。
他两年以前去过中国。
He went to China two years ago.

我上個星期吃過他做的菜。
我上个星期吃过他做的菜。
I ate what he cooked last week.

補充課文 (补充课文) SUPPLEMENTARY PRACTICE

This section will help you test your comprehension of the grammar and vocabulary you have learned in this lesson. Be prepared to answer questions about the meaning of the passage.

姐姐的信 My Sister's Letter (繁體字 Traditional Character Version)

親愛的明遠:

怎麼樣? 最近好嗎? 我已經在北京住了一年多了，一切都很好，請放心。

以前我沒有看過京劇，上個月我和我的中國朋友去看了一齣，很棒! 我們看的戲叫"關公"，這些照片是在戲院照的。你看，台上京劇演員穿著戲服忙著表演；上面坐著幾個樂師，他們都忙著彈奏自己的樂器。因為這齣戲特別有名，所以來了很多觀眾，座位都坐滿了，有的觀眾還得站著看戲呢!

你聽說過關公嗎? 你可以在《三國演義》的小說裡找到很多他的故事。其中有一個很有名的故事叫"桃園三結義"，書中寫著關公、劉備和張飛他們三個人結拜成為兄弟的故事。他們本來不認識，後來遇見了，他們一面喝著酒一面討論著國家大事，談得非常高興。他們互相欣賞著對方的才能和志氣，後來決定要成為結拜兄弟。所以他們一起來到桃花園中，手上拿著香，跪在地上，一起發誓說"不能同年同月同日生，但願同年同月同日死"。從此以後他們三個人就一起打天下。這一個故事非常感人，你有機會應該看看。

爸爸媽媽好嗎? 請代我向他們問好。

祝

學業進步

姐 明華

二零零七年九月六日

補充課文 (补充课文) SUPPLEMENTARY PRACTICE

This section will help you test your comprehension of the grammar and vocabulary you have learned in this lesson. Be prepared to answer questions about the meaning of the passage.

姐姐的信 My Sister's Letter (简体字 Simplified Character Version)

亲爱的明远:

怎么样? 最近好吗? 我已经在北京住了一年多了, 一切都很好, 请放心。

以前我没有看过京剧, 上个月我和我的中国朋友去看了一出, 很棒! 我们看的戏叫 "关公", 这些照片是在戏院照的。你看, 台上京剧演员穿着戏服忙着表演; 上面坐着几个乐师, 他们都忙着弹奏自己的乐器。因为这出戏特别有名, 所以来了很多观众, 座位都坐满了, 有的观众还得站着看戏呢!

你听说过关公吗? 你可以在《三国演义》的小说里找到很多他的故事。其中有一个很有名的故事叫 "桃园三结义", 书中写着关公、刘备和张飞他们三个人结拜成为兄弟的故事。他们本来不认识, 后来遇见了, 他们一面喝着酒一面讨论着国家大事, 谈得非常高兴。他们互相欣赏着对方的才能和志气, 后来决定要成为结拜兄弟。所以他们一起来到桃花园中, 手上拿着香, 跪在地上, 一起发誓说 "不能同年同月同日生, 但愿同年同月同日死"。从此以后他们三个人就一起打天下。这一个故事非常感人, 你有机会应该看看。

爸爸妈妈好吗? 请代我向他们问好。

祝

学业进步

姐 明华

二零零七年九月六日

Useful words and expressions:

一切(一切) [yíqiè]: everything
放心(放心) [fàngxīn]: to feel relieved
故事(故事) [gùshi]: story
有名(有名) [yǒumíng]: famous
小說(小说) [xiǎoshuō]: fiction
桃園三結義(桃园三结义) [táoyuán sān jiéyì]: three men, Liu Bei, Guan Yu and Zhang Fei, have sworn to be brothers in a peach orchard
劉備(刘备) [Liú Bèi]: Liu Bei, who later became ruler of the 蜀 [Shǔ] State (221–263 A.D.)
結拜(结拜) [jiébài]: to pledge a sworn brotherhood
成為(成为) [chéngwéi]: to become
兄弟(兄弟) [xiōngdì]: brothers
本來(本来) [běnlái]: originally, initially
遇見(遇见) [yùjiàn]: to run into
討論(讨论) [tǎolùn]: to discuss
國家大事(国家大事) [guójiā dàshì]: important affairs of state
結拜兄弟(结拜兄弟) [jiébài xiōngdì]: sworn brothers
互相(互相) [hùxiāng]: each other
欣賞(欣赏) [xīnshǎng]: to admire, appreciate
才能(才能) [cáinéng]: talent, ability
志氣(志气) [zhìqì]: ambition
桃花園(桃花园) [táohuā yuán]: peach orchard
香(香) [xiāng]: incense
跪(跪) [guì]: to kneel
發誓(发誓) [fāshì]: to swear
但願(但愿) [dànyuàn]: to wish
從此以後(从此以后) [cóngcǐyǐhòu]: from now on
天下(天下) [tiānxià]: the world, under heaven
感人(感人) [gǎnrén]: moving, touching
代我向……問好(代我向……问好) [dài wǒ xiàng . . . wènhǎo]: send my regards to . . . , say hello to . . . for me
學業(学业) [xuéyè]: schoolwork

練習 (练习) Exercises

1. 這封信是誰寫給誰的? 信上分成幾段 ([duàn]: passage, paragraph)? 每一段的大意 ([dàyì]: outline) 是什麼?

   这封信是谁写给谁的? 信上分成几段 ([duàn]: passage, paragraph)? 每一段的大意 ([dàyì]: outline) 是什么?

2. 照片上有什麼?
   照片上有什么?

3. 用你自己的話，說說桃園三結義的故事。
   用你自己的话，说说桃园三结义的故事。

成語故事 (成语故事) IDIOM STORY

東施效顰 (东施效颦) [Dōngshī xiào pín]

Meaning: *Dongshi* frowns to imitate *Xishi*

Usage: It is used to describe somebody who imitates poorly, making the imitator appear even more awkward and unpleasant.

Example: 很多人喜歡小王的室友，小王想只要他室友做什麼，他就做什麼，他以為這樣，大家就會喜歡他了。結果"東施效顰"，沒有一個人喜歡小王。

很多人喜欢小王的室友，小王想只要他室友做什么，他就做什么，他以为这样，大家就会喜欢他了。结果"东施效颦"，没有一个人喜欢小王。

Pay attention to the aspects of two 了(了), 著(着) and 過(过)

(繁體字 **Traditional Character Version**)

中國古代有一個美女叫西施。人人都喜歡看她，都稱讚她很美。她有一個鄰居叫東施，東施長得很醜，沒有一個人稱讚過東施漂亮。她們倆都在同一個村莊住了十幾年了。東施很羨慕西施，常常看著西施，模仿她。她以為這樣她就能跟西施一樣漂亮了。她常模仿西施，模仿了三年了，可是還是沒有人說過她漂亮。

西施以前得過心病。有一天，她的心很痛，她穿著一件很普通的衣服，摸著胸口，皺著眉頭，走出去看大夫。東施沒看過西施這樣做過，她覺得西施今天皺著眉頭的樣子特別好看，就想到一個好主意。她快快地跑回家去，換了一件跟西施一樣普通的衣服，然後她也學著西施摸著胸口，皺著眉頭，裝著心痛的樣子走在路上。可是，東施本來就不好看，她再皺著眉頭，裝著心痛的樣子就更醜了。別人看到她都嚇壞了，都快快地躲開她。

(简体字 **Simplified Character Version**)

中国古代有一个美女叫西施。人人都喜欢看她，都称赞她很美。她有一个邻居叫东施，东施长得很丑，没有一个人称赞过东施漂亮。她们俩都在同一个村庄住了十几年了。东施很羡慕西施，常常看着西施，模仿她。她以为这样她就能跟西施一样漂亮了。她常模仿西施，模仿了三年了，可是还是没有人说过她漂亮。

西施以前得过心病。有一天，她的心很痛，她穿着一件很普通的衣服，摸着胸口，皱着眉头，走出去看大夫。东施没看过西施这样做过，她觉得西施今天皱着眉头的样子特别好看，就想到一个好主意。她快快地跑回家去，换了一件跟西施一样普通的衣服，然后她也学着西施摸着胸口，皱着眉头，装着心痛的样子走在路上。可是，东施本来就不好看，她再皱着眉头，装着心痛的样子就更丑了。别人看到她都吓坏了，都快快地躲开她。

Useful words and expressions:
東施(东施) [Dōngshī]: name of an ugly female in ancient China
效(效) [xiào]: to imitate
顰(颦) [pín]: to frown (used in Classical Chinese); its counterpart in Modern Chinese is 皺眉頭(皱眉头) [zhòu méitóu]: to frown
古代(古代) [gǔdài]: ancient times
西施(西施) [Xīshī]: name of a famous beauty in the Spring and Autumn period (around 722 B.C. to 484 B.C.)
稱讚(称赞) [chēngzàn]: to praise
鄰居(邻居) [línjū]: neighbor
醜(丑) [chǒu]: ugly
村莊(村庄) [cūnzhuāng]: village
羨慕(羡慕) [xiànmù]: to envy
模仿(模仿) [mófǎng]: to imitate
心(心) [xīn]: heart (note: a heart as an organ is called 心臟(心脏) [xīnzàng])
普通(普通) [pǔtōng]: common
摸著胸口(摸着胸口) [mōzhe xiōngkǒu]: (a state of) to touch the chest
皺著眉頭(皱着眉头) [zhòuzhe méitóu]: (a state of) to frown
大夫(大夫) [dàifu]: doctor
裝著(装着) [zhuāngzhe]: (a state of) to pretend
本來(本来) [běnlái]: originally, initially
嚇(吓) [xià]: frighten, scare
躲開(躲开) [duǒkāi]: to dodge, avoid

2-3 Read the following lyric, paying special attention to the tones and the rhythm:

Shuǐ Diào Gē Tóu (**Shàng Què**)	水調歌頭 (上闕) 水调歌头 (上阙)
(Sū Shì)	(蘇軾) (苏轼)
Míngyuè jǐshí yǒu?	明月幾時有? 明月几时有?
Bǎ jiǔ wèn qīngtiān.	把酒問青天。 把酒问青天。
Bùzhī tiānshàng gōngquè,	不知天上宮闕, 不知天上宫阙,
Jīnxī shì hé nián?	今夕是何年? 今夕是何年?
Wǒ yù chéngfēng guīqù,	我欲乘風歸去, 我欲乘风归去,
Yòu kǒng qiónglóu yùyǔ,	又恐瓊樓玉宇, 又恐琼楼玉宇,
Gāochù bù shēng hán.	高處不勝寒。 高处不胜寒。
Qǐwǔ nòng qīngyǐng,	起舞弄清影, 起舞弄清影,
Hésì zài rénjiān?	何似在人間? 何似在人间?

To the tune of **Shui Diao Ge Tou** (Part 1)
(Su, Shi)

"How many times will we have the bright moon?"
Holding our wine we ask the heavens.
Who knows what year this is in the heavenly palace?

I would like to ride there on the wind,
But I fear it will be too cold up in the beautiful palace.
Why not dance and play with our shadows as if we were in the human world?

Practice: What are the rhyming words in this lyric? Write them out in Pinyin:

押 ________ 韻，押韻的字有：______________________________。
押 ________ 韵，押韵的字有：______________________________。

II. 漢字練習 (汉字练习)

2-4 Read the following words, phrases, and sentences:

擺 摆	齣 出
擺著 摆着	一齣戲 一出戏
上面擺著樂器 上面摆着乐器	一齣關公的戲 一出关公的戏
舞台上面擺著各種樂器 舞台上面摆着各种乐器	這是一齣說關公的戲 这是一出说关公的戏

Now try to use the following characters to make words, phrases, and then sentences:

1. 牆 墙	2. 照 照	3. 表 表	4. 鼓 鼓	5. 拉 拉	6. 琴 琴	7. 彈 弹	8. 已 已
9. 畫 画	10. 刀 刀	11. 滿 满	12. 拿 拿	13. 眾 众	14. 站 站	15. 神 神	16. 臉 脸

2-5 Write down the traditional forms for the following simplified characters:

1. 摆各种乐器 ______ ______ ______ ______ ______

2. 观众 ______ ______

3. 看过 ______ ______

4. 神气 ______ ______

2-6 Form groups of three and create phrases with the following words (pay attention to the various usages of each word):

Example: 塊：十五塊
块：十五块
一塊鏡子，一塊麵包，一塊蛋糕
一块镜子，一块面包，一块蛋糕

1. 過：
   过：
2. 裝：
   装：
3. 公：
   公：
4. 自：
   自：

III. 語法練習 (语法练习)

2-7 Form groups of two to ask / answer the following questions (remember to switch roles):

– 多久 ([duō jiǔ]: How long (duration of time)?)
– 多長時間(多长时间) [duō cháng shíjiān]: How long (duration of time)?
– 漢字(汉字) [hànzì]: Chinese character

1. 你在這兒住了多久了? (or 你在這兒住了多長時間了)?
   你在这儿住了多久了? (or 你在这儿住了多长时间了)?
2. 你學了多久的中文了? (or 你學了多長時間的中文了?)
   你学了多久的中文了? (or 你学了多长时间的中文了?)
3. 你今天上了多久的課了? (or 你今天上了多長時間的課了?)
   你今天上了多久的课了? (or 你今天上了多长时间的课了?)
4. 你已經學了多少漢字了?
   你已经学了多少汉字了?

2-8 Picture talk:

With the help of the clues provided, use V. + 著(着) to describe 小李's love story. (Work in groups. Try to make at least eight sentences. Be creative!)

Useful words and expressions:
聊(聊) [liáo]: to chat
躺(躺) [tǎng]: to lie down
情書(情书) [qíngshū]: love letter

(1)

(2)

(3)

(4)

2-9 Use "V. + 過(过)" to conduct a conversation.

Pattern: V. + 過(过)
Negation: 沒(有) + V. + 過(过)
Question: V. + 過(过)...... 沒有?
V. + 過(过)...... 嗎(吗)?

Example:

A: 你看過京劇沒有?
你看过京剧没有?

B: 我看過，我已經看過三次京劇了。你呢?
我看过，我已经看过三次京剧了。你呢?

A: 我沒有看過京劇......
我没有看过京剧......

(去過中國、上海、北京、長城；做過中國菜；包過小籠包；看過中國小說、電影......)

(去过中国、上海、北京、长城；做过中国菜；包过小笼包；看过中国小说、电影......)

2-10 Talk about your experiences:

Ask your friends about their previous experiences. Form groups to discuss the following questions:

Useful words and expressions:
漂亮(漂亮) [piàoliang]: pretty, beautiful
帥(帅) [shuài]: handsome
報告(报告) [bàogào]: report

你吃過的最好吃的菜是什麼菜? (你看過的最好的電影；你見過的最漂亮的女人/最帥的男人；你去過的最好玩的地方；寫過的最難的報告；上過的最有意思的課，etc.)

你吃过的最好吃的菜是什么菜? (你看过的最好的电影；你见过的最漂亮的女人/最帅的男人；你去过的最好玩的地方；写过的最难的报告；上过的最有意思的课，etc.)

IV. 交際活動 (交际活动)

2-11 Work in groups of two-three. Use two 了, V. + 過(过), and V. + 著(着) to create a story:

(1) (2) (3) (4)

2-12 報告(报告) ([bàogào]: report):

Use two 了, V. + 過(过), V. + 著(着) to report on your previous experiences (such as the most tasty dish you have ever had, most interesting novel you have ever read, most unforgettable person/event, etc.)

For example:

吃過的最好吃的菜，這是我看過的最有意思的小說，
見過的最好的人

吃过的最好吃的菜，这是我看过的最有意思的小说，
见过的最好的人

(Each person should come up with at least 12 sentences)

文化知識 (文化知识) Culture Link

文化點滴 (文化点滴) CULTURE NOTES

中國四大古典小説 (中国四大古典小说) [Zhōngguó sì dà gǔdiǎn xiǎoshuō] Four Great Classical Chinese Novels

1. 三國演義(三国演义) [Sānguó Yǎnyì]: The Romance of the Three Kingdoms
2. 水滸傳(水浒传) [Shuǐhǔ Zhuàn]: Water Margin
3. 西遊記(西游记) [Xīyóujì]: Journey to the West
4. 紅樓夢(红楼梦) [Hónglóu Mèng]: Dream of the Red Chamber

Chinese has a long and rich literary tradition. The Four Great Classical Novels, 三國演義 [Sānguó Yǎnyì], 水滸傳 [Shuǐhǔ Zhuàn], 西遊記 [Xīyóujì], and 紅樓夢 [Hónglóu Mèng], are written in vernacular Chinese and are well known to most Chinese. They have had a great influence on Chinese literature and society. Their plots are commonly told over and over again through Chinese drama, theater, storytelling, folk performances, TV series, and movies.

三國演義 [Sānguó Yǎnyì] was written by 羅貫中 [Luó Guànzhōng] (1330–1440) during the 明 [Míng] Dynasty. It is based on actual events that happened during 220–280 A.D., near the end of the 漢 [Hàn] Dynasty. During this period, three kingdoms, 魏 [Wèi], 蜀 [Shǔ] and 吳 [Wú], and their respective leaders, 曹操 [Cáo Cāo], 劉備 [Liú Bèi] and 孫權 [Sūn Quán], contended for the throne of *Han*, each claiming direct lineage from the last *Han* emperor. The novel begins with 劉備, 關羽 [Guān Yǔ] and 張飛 [Zhāng Fēi] forming a brotherhood.

The characters of 三國演義 (The Romance of the Three Kingdoms) are well known among Chinese. These are the hand puppet figures of 諸葛亮 (in the front, with his famous fan), 關羽 and 張飛 (back row in the center and on the right).

They promise to enjoy happiness and endure hardship together. The novel includes many well known stories, including accounts of the strategic brilliance of 劉備's minister 諸葛亮 [Zhūgě Liàng] and tales of 關羽's loyalty, courage, and bravery.

水滸傳 [Shuǐhǔ Zhuàn] is generally believed to be written by 施耐庵 [Shī Nài'ān] (ca. 1296–1370). Set at the end of the North Song period (around the thirteen century), it tells the stories of a group of heroes, 105 men and three women in all, daring to struggle against evil. The heroes, who are thought to stand for different classes of people, are oppressed by corrupt and unjust officials and then rise up. They do lots of good deeds, helping the poor and fighting evil. But later, they surrender to the officials and work with them to fight invaders. In the end, most of them die or are badly hurt.

西遊記 [Xīyóujì] was written by 吳承恩 [Wú Chéngēn] (around 1500–1582) during the Ming Dynasty. It tells the story of 唐三藏 [Táng Sānzàng], a monk who undertakes a journey to India to retrieve Buddhist holy texts. He is joined by three disciples along the way, namely 孫悟空 [Sūn Wùkōng] (the Monkey King), 豬八戒 [Zhū Bājiè] (a pig-headed fellow), and 沙悟淨 [Shā Wùjìng] (a reincarnated water creature). They encounter many adventures and together overcome 81 hardships. 孫悟空 uses his talents and skills to protect his master. At the end of the novel all four companions are honored and became gods.

西遊記 (Journey to the West) hand puppet theater figures: 唐三藏 (the monk, front row on the left), 沙悟淨 (front row in the center), and 孫悟空 (back row on the left).

紅樓夢 [Hónglóu Mèng], an outstanding classic novel of the 清 [Qīng] Dynasty, was written by 曹雪芹 [Cáo Xuěqín] (1715–1763). It is generally assumed that the author drew on his own experiences and that his hero, 賈寶玉 [Jiǎ Bǎoyù], is a self-portrait. The novel chronicles the fall of the wealthy 賈 clan, and the relationship of the clan's heir, 賈寶玉, with two ladies, 薛寶釵 [Xuē Bǎochāi] and 林黛玉 [Lín Dàiyù]. 賈寶玉's family believes that his marriage with 薛寶釵 has been predetermined. 賈寶玉 and 薛寶釵 both wore the same jade pendant at birth, and 薛寶釵 has great social tact and would make a very good traditional Chinese wife. 賈寶玉, however, is actually in love with 林黛玉, who is temperamental, sickly, and generally the opposite of 薛寶釵. After much coercion from his family, 賈寶玉 enters into a very unhappy arranged marriage with 薛寶釵. 林黛玉, hearing the bad news, falls ill and dies soon after. 賈寶玉 is so distraught by this event that he goes off to be a monk.

問題討論 (问题讨论) Discussion Questions

1. 在西方小說中有沒有和四大中國小說相似的故事?
   在西方小说中有没有和四大中国小说相似的故事?
   Are there any Western novels which have similar stories to these Four Classic Chinese Novels?

2. 在這四大古典小說中，哪一個故事是你最感興趣的? 為什麼?
   在这四大古典小说中，哪一个故事是你最感兴趣的? 为什么?
   Which story sounds most interesting to you? Why?

趣味中文 (趣味中文) FUN WITH CHINESE

隔牆有耳
隔墙有耳
(Literally) There are ears on the other side of the wall – it's difficult to keep a secret.

gé	qiáng	yǒu	ěr
隔	牆	有	耳
隔	墙	有	耳
partition	wall	have	ear

問題討論 (问题讨论) Discussion Questions

Are there similar sayings in English or other languages? Please provide some examples.

行動吧! (行动吧!) LET'S GO!

機場入境/出境的告示 (机场入境/出境的告示)
Signs in the Airport

Following are common signs in airports. Let's study them together.

(1)

(2)

(3)

(4)

(5)

(6)

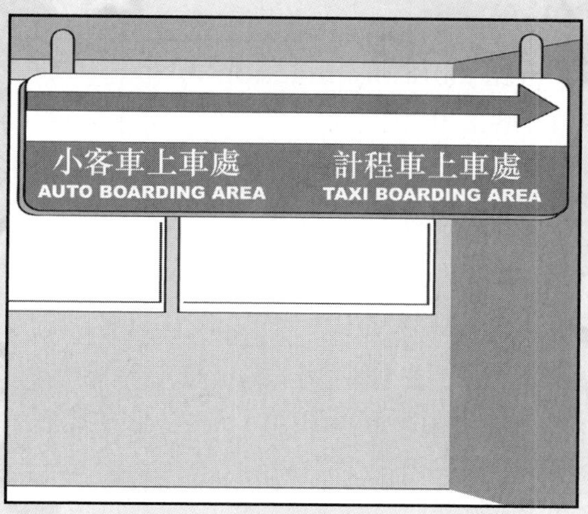

(7)

Useful words and expressions:

(1) 入境(入境) [rùjìng]: arrival
轉機(转机) [zhuǎnjī]: switch flights

(2) 證照查驗(证照查验) [zhèngzhào cháyàn]: document check
提領行李(提领行李) [tílǐng xíngli]: baggage claim

(3) 等待線(等待线) [děngdài xiàn]: waiting line

(4) 育嬰室(育婴室) [yùyīng shì]: nursery room
淋浴室(淋浴室) [línyù shì]: shower room
盥洗室(盥洗室) [guànxǐ shì]: toilet, restroom

(5) 外幣兌換(外币兑换) [wàibì duìhuàn]: foreign currency exchange

(6) 登機門(登机门) [dēngjī mén]: boarding gate

(7) 小客車(小客车) [xiǎokèchē]: van
上車處(上车处) [shàngchēchù]: automobile boarding area
計程車(计程车) [jìchéngchē]: taxi

復習 (复习) Review

LESSON 1 TO LESSON 2

1. Use 把 and the following resultative complements to make sentences

For example: 看完 → 我昨天把你借給我的那本英文小說看完了。
看完 → 我昨天把你借给我的那本英文小说看完了。

Adj./Verb	Features	Examples
完 完	Indicates some work is finished by some action	看完　做完　寫完 看完　做完　写完
好 好	Indicates the desired state of an action or completion of an action	坐好　拿好　放好 坐好　拿好　放好 收好　搬好　做好 收好　搬好　做好
到 到	Indicates the continuation of an action to a certain point or a certain time	找到　看到　回到 找到　看到　回到
在 在	Indicates that a person or thing ends up at a place as the result of an action. The 在 RC is followed by a place.	放在　坐在　站在　住在 放在　坐在　站在　住在
上 上	Indicates the completion of an action has brought about a certain result such as coming together or being closed up.	接上　穿上　關上　蓋上 接上　穿上　关上　盖上
開 开	Indicates the result of an action that moves an object away from its original position.	打開　拿開　拉開　跑開 打开　拿开　拉开　跑开
成 成	Indicates that the items have become, become treated or become regarded a certain way.	換成　看成　當成　翻譯成 换成　看成　当成　翻译成
了 了	Usually indicates a change of state but is also commonly associated with the 把 structure.	開了　看了　寫了　吃了 开了　看了　写了　吃了

2. Form groups to conduct the following dialogue

Topic: How did you clean up your apartment (with your roommate(s), or by yourself) last night (at least six sentences.) Remember to switch roles!

Useful words and expressions:

拿走，搬過來，搬進去，搬到，負責，裝好，掃地，整理，洗碗，打開，衣服，公寓，

拿走，搬过来，搬进去，搬到，负责，装好，扫地，整理，洗碗，打开，衣服，公寓，

放好，門窗，關上，分工合作，自己，乾淨，亂，髒

放好，门窗，关上，分工合作，自己，干净，乱，脏

A： 昨天晚上你做什麼了？
昨天晚上你做什么了？

B： 昨天晚上我和我的室友把我們的公寓整理乾淨了。
昨天晚上我和我的室友把我们的公寓整理干净了。

A： 你們是怎麼整理你的房間的？
你们是怎么整理你的房间的？

B： 我們把……
我们把……

3. 会话 (會話) Conversation: Form groups to ask/reply to the following questions

For example: **A：** 你看過京劇沒有？
你看过京剧没有？

B： 我沒看過。你呢？
我没看过。你呢？

A： 我看過，很不錯。
我看过，很不错。

1. 你在這兒住了多久了？
   你在这儿住了多久了？
2. 你學了多久的中文了？
   你学了多久的中文了？
3. 你今天上了多久的課了？
   你今天上了多久的课了？

4. 你已經學了多少漢字了?
   你已经学了多少汉字了?
5. 你們吃過餃子嗎? 怎麼樣? 你包過餃子沒有?
   你们吃过饺子吗? 怎么样? 你包过饺子没有?
6. 你吃過最好吃的中國菜是什麼?
   你吃过最好吃的中国菜是什么?
7. 你上過最有意思的課是哪一門?
   你上过最有意思的课是哪一门?
8. 你去過最好玩的地方是哪兒?
   你去过最好玩的地方是哪儿?
9. 誰是你見過最難忘 ([nánwàng]: unforgettable) 的人? 為什麼 ([wèishénme]: why)?
   谁是你见过最难忘 ([nánwàng]: unforgettable) 的人? 为什么 ([wèishénme]: why)?
10. 什麼是你碰到 ([pèngdào]: encounter) 過最難處理 ([chǔlǐ]: to deal with) 的一件事?
    什么是你碰到 ([pèngdào]: encounter) 过最难处理 ([chǔlǐ]: to deal with) 的一件事?

4. 看图说故事 Picture description: Apply 了 (了), 著 (着) and 過 (过) to create a story

5. Traditional and Simplified Characters 繁體字/簡體字

Read each character aloud. Write its traditional form. Then make a phrase and a sentence using the character.

For example: 学 → 學 → 學生 → 我是學生

树 ( ) 坏 ( ) 挂 ( ) 墙 ( ) 着 ( )
摆 ( ) 种 ( ) 戏 ( ) 长 ( )

第三課
LESSON
3

從這兒往前走
(从这儿往前走)
Go Straight from Here

教學目標 (教学目标) OBJECTIVES

- Ask and give directions
- Take a cab
- Pay money and give change

A taxi stand in China

生詞 (生词) VOCABULARY

核心詞 (核心词) Core Vocabulary

TRADITIONAL	SIMPLIFIED	PINYIN		
1. 往	往	wǎng/wàng	Prep.	toward
2. 各位	各位	gèwèi	Pron.	everybody (a term used to address people)
3. 旅客	旅客	lǚkè	N.	traveler, passenger
4. 降落	降落	jiàngluò	V.	to land, descend
5. 安全帶	安全带	ānquándài	N.	seat belt, safety belt
6. 繫上	系上	jìshàng	V.C.	to tie, fasten, buckle up
7. 計算機	计算机	jìsuànjī	N.	computer
8. 電子	电子	diànzǐ	N.	electronics
9. 用品	用品	yòngpǐn	N.	product
10. 搭乘	搭乘	dāchéng	V.	to take (a means of transportation)
11. 航空	航空	hángkōng	N.	aviation, airline
12. 出租	出租	chūzū	V.	to rent
13. 旅館	旅馆	lǚguǎn	N.	hotel, hostel
14. 路人	路人	lùrén	N.	passerby
15. 棟	栋	dòng	M.W.	(measure word for buildings)
16. 交叉口	交叉口	jiāochākǒu	N.	intersection
17. 左	左	zuǒ	N.	left side
18. 拐	拐	guǎi	V.	to turn
19. 一直	一直	yìzhí		straight
20. 路口	路口	lùkǒu	N.	block, diverging point of a road
21. 司機	司机	sījī	N.	driver

TRADITIONAL	SIMPLIFIED	PINYIN		
22. 假日	假日	jiàrì	N.	holiday
23. 公里	公里	gōnglǐ	N.	kilometer
24. 後車箱	后车箱	hòuchēxiāng	N.	trunk (of a car)
25. 發展	发展	fāzhǎn	V. N.	to develop development
26. 變化	变化	biànhuà	V. N.	to change change
27. 本來	本来	běnlái	Adv.	originally
28. 農田	农田	nóngtián	N.	farmland; cropland
29. 變成	变成	biànchéng	V.C.	to become
30. 馬路	马路	mǎlù	N.	road, avenue, street
31. 喔	喔	ō	Int.	(used to indicate realization)
32. 公尺	公尺	gōngchǐ	N.	meter (measurement of length)
33. 紅綠燈	红绿灯	hónglǜdēng	N.	traffic light
34. 向	向	xiàng	Prep.	toward
35. 右	右	yòu	N.	right side
36. 轉	转	zhuǎn	V.	to turn
37. 小吃店	小吃店	xiǎochīdiàn	N.	snack shop
38. 彎兒	弯儿	wār	N.	turn, detour
39. 車費	车费	chēfèi	N.	car fare
40. 人民幣	人民币	Rénmínbì	N.	RMB (name of currency used in Mainland China)
41. 找	找	zhǎo	V.	to seek, look for; to give (change)

專名 (专名) Proper Nouns

TRADITIONAL	SIMPLIFIED	PINYIN		
1. 浦東	浦东	Pǔdōng	N.	a place in Shanghai
2. 中山路	中山路	Zhōngshānlù	N.	Zhongshan Road

補充詞 (补充词) Supplementary Vocabulary

TRADITIONAL	SIMPLIFIED	PINYIN		
1. 載	载	zài	V.	to carry, transport
2. 方向	方向	fāngxiàng	N.	direction
3. 雙行道	双行道	shuāngxíngdào	N.	two-way road
4. 單行道	单行道	dānxíngdào	N.	one-way road
5. 超車	超车	chāochē	V.O.	to overtake another car
6. 出差	出差	chūchāi	V.O.	to go on a business trip
7. 橋	桥	qiáo	N.	bridge

語文知識 (语文知识) LANGUAGE LINK

The Sentence Patterns provide models that will help you with the Language in Use section. In both sections, pay attention to the grammar points, vocabulary, and expressions.

句型 (句型) Sentence Patterns

A: 坐出租汽車去有多快?
坐出租汽车去有多快?
Zuò chūzū qìchē qù yǒu duō kuài?

B: 很快,不到十分鐘就可以到了。
很快,不到十分钟就可以到了。
Hěnkuài, búdào shí fēnzhōng jiù kěyǐ dào le.

A: 請問，到出租汽車站怎麼走?
请问，到出租汽车站怎么走?
Qǐngwèn, dào chūzū qìchē zhàn zěnme zǒu?

B: 你從這兒往前走，走到前面的交叉口，
你从这儿往前走，走到前面的交叉口，
Nǐ cóng zhèr wǎng qián zǒu, zǒu dào qiánmiàn de jiāochākǒu,
往左拐。
往左拐。
wǎng zuǒ guǎi.

A: 中國看起來發展得很快。
中国看起来发展得很快。
Zhōngguó kàn qǐlái fāzhǎn de hěnkuài.

B: 是呀! 這兒變得太快了!
是呀! 这儿变得太快了!
Shì ya! Zhèr biàn de tài kuài le!

A: 車费多少錢?
车费多少钱?
Chēfèi duōshǎo qián?

B: 司機: 一共是二十八塊人民幣。
司机: 一共是二十八块人民币。
Yígòng shì èrshíbā kuài Rénmínbì.

A: 給你三十塊。
给你三十块。
Gěi nǐ sānshí kuài.

B: 司機: 找你兩塊，謝謝。
司机: 找你两块，谢谢。
Zhǎo nǐ liǎngkuài, xièxie.

課文: 從這兒往前走 (繁體字)
Language in Use: Traditional Character Version

SCENE 1: (在飛機上)

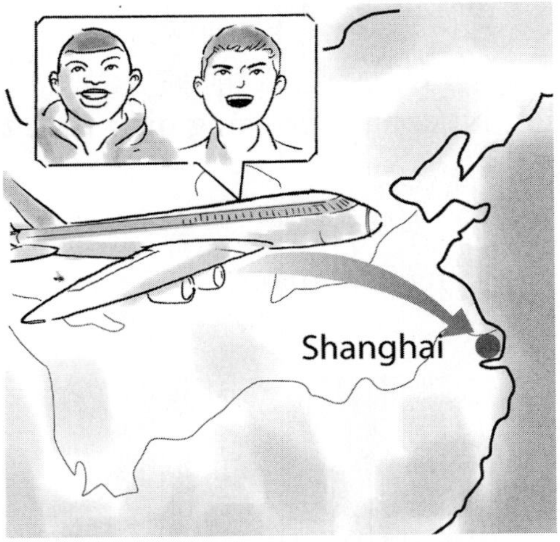

各位旅客，飛機再過二十分鐘就要降落了，我們就要到上海的浦東機場了。請您回到您的座位坐好，把安全帶繫上。請您也把計算機等電子用品關上。謝謝您的合作。再次感謝您搭乘中國航空。

SCENE 2: (在機場)

關明遠： 我們到了，我們搭出租汽車去旅館吧！搭出租汽車去快多了。

李訪： 搭出租汽車去有多快?

關明遠： 我想，不到十分鐘就可以到了。

李訪： 好的。我們來問路吧!

關明遠： 先生，對不起，請問，出租汽車站在哪兒?

路人： 出租汽車站在那棟樓的後邊。你從這兒往前走，走到前面的交叉口，往左拐。從那兒再往前一直走，過兩個路口，你就能看到出租汽車站了。

關明遠： 謝謝。

路人： 不客氣。

SCENE 3: (在出租汽車站)

司機： 請問，兩位先生要搭車，是嗎?

關明遠： 是的，我們要去假日旅館，離這兒有多遠?

司機： 有三公里，不太遠，請上車。來，我先把行李放到後車箱去。

……

Continued on page 70

课文: 从这儿往前走 (简体字)
Language in Use: Simplified Character Version

SCENE 1: (在飞机上)

各位旅客，飞机再过二十分钟就要降落了，我们就要到上海的浦东机场了。请您回到您的座位坐好，把安全带系上。请您也把计算机等电子用品关上。谢谢您的合作。再次感谢您搭乘中国航空。

SCENE 2: (在机场)

关明远： 我们到了，我们搭出租汽车去旅馆吧！搭出租汽车去快多了。

李访： 搭出租汽车去有多快？

关明远： 我想，不到十分钟就可以到了。

李访： 好的。我们来问路吧！

关明远： 先生，对不起，请问，出租汽车站在哪儿？

路人： 出租汽车站在那栋楼的后边。你从这儿往前走，走到前面的交叉口，往左拐。从那儿再往前一直走，过两个路口，你就能看到出租汽车站了。

关明远： 谢谢。

路人： 不客气。

SCENE 3: (在出租汽车站)

司机： 请问，两位先生要搭车，是吗？

关明远： 是的，我们要去假日旅馆，离这儿有多远？

司机： 有三公里，不太远，请上车。来，我先把行李放到后车箱去。

……

Continued on page 71

課文: 從這兒往前走 (繁體字) — 接第六十八頁
Language in Use: Traditional Character Version

李訪：　中國看起來發展得很快。

關明遠：是呀！這兒變得太快了！

司機：　聽起來你好像來過上海。

關明遠：是的。我兩年前來過，可是現在有很多路我都想不起來了。

司機：　沒錯！上海變化得非常快，你看，本來這兒還都是農田，現在都變成大樓和大馬路了。

李訪：　你看，那棟樓真高，不知道有多高?

司機：　喔！那棟樓是新的，聽說有九十公尺高。

關明遠：對了，我想起來了，那條是中山路。以前我常在那個紅綠燈等著過馬路，過了馬路以後我就向右轉，再走兩三分鐘，就到了上海小吃店。那兒的東西好吃極了！

司機：　假日旅館就在前面，可是我不能在這兒往左轉，我得多拐幾個彎兒。

李訪：　行，沒問題。

……

司機：　好，我們到了。

李訪：　車費多少錢?

司機：　一共是二十八塊人民幣。

關明遠：給你三十塊。

司機：　找你兩塊，謝謝！

课文: 从这儿往前走 (简体字) — 接第六十九页

Language in Use: Simplified Character Version

李访: 中国看起来发展得很快。

关明远: 是呀! 这儿变得太快了!

司机: 听起来你好象来过上海。

关明远: 是的。我两年前来过, 可是现在有很多路我都想不起来了。

司机: 没错! 上海变化得非常快, 你看, 本来这儿还都是农田, 现在都变成大楼和大马路了。

李访: 你看, 那栋楼真高, 不知道有多高?

司机: 喔! 那栋楼是新的, 听说有九十公尺高。

关明远: 对了, 我想起来了, 那条是中山路。以前我常在那个红绿灯等着过马路, 过了马路以后我就向右转, 再走两三分钟, 就到上海小吃店。那儿的东西好吃极了!

司机: 假日旅馆就在前面, 可是我不能在这儿往左转, 我得多拐几个弯儿。

李访: 行, 没问题。

……

司机: 好, 我们到了。

李访: 车费多少钱?

司机: 一共是二十八块人民币。

关明远: 给你三十块。

司机: 找你两块, 谢谢!

注釋 (注释) LANGUAGE NOTES

1. 我們到了 (我们到了)

我們到了: literally means "We've arrived!" It can also be used colloquially to mean "Here we go!"

2. 搭, 乘, 坐 (車) (搭, 乘, 坐 (车))

搭, 乘, and 坐 are verbs meaning "to take (a means of transportation)." 搭 and 坐 are commonly used in spoken Chinese, while 乘 and 搭乘 are more formal.

3. 棟 (幢) (栋 (幢))

棟 as a noun means "the main-beam of a house." It is also used as a measure word (classifier) for buildings. For buildings, the measure word 幢 [zhuàng] can also be used. (幢 as a noun means "a large beam used in a building of more than one story").

4. 小吃 (小吃)

小吃 refers to snacks, including noodles, wonton, dumplings, scallion pancakes, etc., which are readily available at small restaurants or food stands.

5. 找 (錢) (找 (钱))

找 as a verb has two meanings: "to seek, to look for" and "to give (change)." "找你兩塊錢" means "give you two dollars change."

語法 (语法) GRAMMAR

1. (有) 多 + Adjective (How *Adjective*?)

(有) 多 + Adjective is a pattern used to ask about the degree of distance, length, speed, size, etc. It is similar to the English pattern "How + Adjective" (for example "How far?" or "How fast?"). 有 is optional.

- Common adjectives for length, height, distance, speed, weight and size:

length:	長(长) [cháng] (long)	短(短) [duǎn] (short)	height:	高(高) [gāo] (tall)	矮(矮) [ǎi] (short)
Distance:	遠(远) [yuǎn] (far)	近(近) [jìn] (close)	speed:	快(快) [kuài] (fast)	慢(慢) [màn] (slow)
weight:	輕(轻) [qīng] (light)	重(重) [zhòng] (heavy)	size:	大(大) [dà] (big)	小(小) [xiǎo] (small)

- Common standard measures

公里(公里) [gōnglǐ] (kilometer)	公尺(公尺) [gōngchǐ] (meter) 米(米) [mǐ]	公分(公分) [gōngfēn] (centimeter) 厘米(厘米) [límǐ]
英哩(英里) [yīnglǐ] (mile)	英呎(英尺) [yīngchǐ] (foot)	英吋(英寸) [yīngcùn] (inch)
公斤(公斤) [gōngjīn] (kilogram)	磅(磅) [bàng] (pound)	

How Adj.?	(有)多 + Adj.	Example	English
How long? (length)	(有)多長? (有)多长?	長城(有)多長? 长城(有)多长? 長城有五千公里。 长城有五千公里。	How long is the Great Wall? The Great Wall is five thousand kilometers long.
How long? (duration of time)	(有)多久? (有)多久?	你來這兒有多久了? 你来这儿有多久了? 我來這兒有兩年了。 我来这儿有两年了。	How long have you been here? I have been here for two years.
How tall?	(有)多高? (有)多高?	這棟大樓(有)多高? 这栋大楼(有)多高? 這棟大樓(有)五十英呎高。 这栋大楼(有)五十英尺高。	How tall is the building? This building is 50 feet tall.
How far?	(有)多遠? (有)多远?	這兒離飛機場(有)多遠? 这儿离飞机场(有)多远? 這兒離飛機場有十英哩。 这儿离飞机场有十英里。	How far is it from here to the airport? It is 10 miles from here to the airport.
How fast?	(有)多快? (有)多快?	他開車開得(有)多快? 他开车开得(有)多快? 他開時速八十五英哩。 他开时速八十五英里。 – 時速(时速) [shísù]: speed per hour	How fast does he drive? He drives 85 miles per hour.
How heavy?	(有)多重? (有)多重?	這個包裹(有)多重? 这个包裹(有)多重? 這個包裹(有)三十磅。 这个包裹(有)三十磅。 – 包裹 [bāoguǒ]: package	How heavy is this package? This package weighs 30 pounds.

How Adj.?	(有)多 + Adj.	Example	English
How big?	(有)多大? (有)多大?	你的車(有)多大? 你的车(有)多大?	How big is your car?
		我的車可以坐七個人。 我的车可以坐七个人。	My car can carry seven people.

Note: 多 pronounced as [duō] may function as an adjective meaning "many." In the pattern of (有)多 + Adjective (How *Adjective*?) 多 can be pronounced as either [duó] or [duō].

2. Ask and give directions: 往 (向) + direction/location + V.

The common expressions for asking and giving directions are as follows:

往(向) +	direction/location	+	V.
	(e.g. 東，前，右/市中心，飛機場，那棟大樓) (e.g. 东，前，右/市中心，飞机场，那栋大楼)		(e.g. 拐，轉，走，跑，開) (e.g. 拐，转，走，跑，开)

Examples: i) A: 請問，到火車站去怎麼走?
请问，到火车站去怎么走?

B: 你從這兒往前走，再向左拐就到了。
你从这儿往前走，再向左拐就到了。

ii) A: 請問，假日旅館在哪兒?
请问，假日旅馆在哪儿?

B: 你往市中心方向開二十分鐘就到了。
你往市中心方向开二十分钟就到了。

– 市中心 [shìzhōngxīn] (downtown)
– 方向 [fāngxiàng] (direction)

Notes:
– 往 can be pronounced as either [wǎng] or [wàng]
– 往 and 向 used as prepositions both mean "in the direction of."
– For most of the directional words, such as 東邊, 右邊, the suffix 邊 is usually omitted when the directional word occurs after 往 or 向.

3. V. 起來 (看起來, 聽起來; 想起來; 說起來容易, 做起來難)

V. + 起來 is a compound directional complement. It combines with certain verbs to give a sense of an action beginning unexpectedly, or a gradual change. It is also used in a few idiomatic expressions.

1. An action that begins unexpectedly

Examples: i) 我們才遲到一分鐘，他就生起氣來了。
我们才迟到一分钟，他就生起气来了。
We were just one minute late, and he started to get angry.

– 遲到(迟到) [chídào]: to be late
– 生氣(生气) [shēngqì]: to get angry

ii) 他又吸起煙來了。 He has started to smoke again.
他又吸起烟来了。

Note: the verb is placed between 起 and 來 in the pattern V. + 起 + Obj. + 來.

2. A gradual change

Examples: i) 他開始胖起來了。 He is getting chubby.
他开始胖起来了。

– 胖(胖) [pàng]: chubby, fat

ii) 春天就要來了，天氣暖和起來了。
春天就要来了，天气暖和起来了。
Spring is coming, the weather is getting warm.

3. Idomatic expressions

想起來: to recall

Example: 我想起來了！你是我小學的同學，王大中。
我想起来了！你是我小学的同学，王大中。
I remember! You are my elementary school classmate, Dazhong Wang.

想不起來: cannot recall

Example: 對不起，我真的想不起來在哪兒見過你。
对不起，我真的想不起来在哪儿见过你。
Sorry! I really cannot recall where I have seen you before.

看起來: to look

Example: 你今天看起來很累。 You look very tired today.
你今天看起来很累。

聽起來: to sound

Example: 這首歌聽起來真美。 This song sounds beautiful.
这首歌听起来真美。

– 首 [shǒu]: measure word (classifier) for songs
– 歌 [gē]: song

說起來: to say
做起來: to do

Example: 說起來容易，做起來難。 To say it is easy, to do it is hard.
说起来容易，做起来难。

補充課文 (补充课文) SUPPLEMENTARY PRACTICE

This section will help you test your comprehension of the grammar and vocabulary you have learned in this lesson. Be prepared to answer questions about the meaning of the passage.

上海動物園 Shanghai Zoo (繁體字 Traditional Character Version)

(在動物園的售票處)

售票員：歡迎光臨！請問你們要買幾張票？

王先生：我們全家一共要買四張票。兩張全票，兩張兒童票。謝謝。

售票員：一共二十塊。這是動物園的地圖，今天有特別的海豚表演，在海洋世界那兒。

王先生：海洋世界離這兒有多遠？

售票員：不太遠，你看，這是入口，你們從這兒往前走，走到前面的交叉口，再往右拐，過了獅子大象區，就是海洋世界了。海豚表演每兩個小時一次。

王先生：聽起來好像很不錯，謝謝。

補充課文 (补充课文) SUPPLEMENTARY PRACTICE

This section will help you test your comprehension of the grammar and vocabulary you have learned in this lesson. Be prepared to answer questions about the meaning of the passage.

上海动物园 Shanghai Zoo (简体字 Simplified Character Version)

(在动物园的售票处)

售票员：欢迎光临！请问你们要买几张票？

王先生：我们全家一共要买四张票。两张全票，两张儿童票。谢谢。

售票员：一共二十块。这是动物园的地图，今天有特别的海豚表演，在海洋世界那儿。

王先生：海洋世界离这儿有多远？

售票员：不太远，你看，这是入口，你们从这儿往前走，走到前面的交叉口，再往右拐，过了狮子大象区，就是海洋世界了。海豚表演每两个小时一次。

王先生：听起来好像很不错，谢谢。

Useful words and expressions:

動物園(动物园) [dòngwùyuán]: zoo
售票處(售票处) [shòupiàochù]: ticket booth
歡迎光臨(欢迎光临) [huānyíng guānglín]: welcome
全票(全票) [quánpiào]: full ticket
兒童(儿童) [értóng]: children
海豚(海豚) [hǎitún]: dolphin
海洋世界(海洋世界) [hǎiyáng shìjiè]: sea world
入口(入口) [rùkǒu]: entrance
獅子(狮子) [shīzi]: lion
大象(大象) [dàxiàng]: elephant
區(区) [qū]: district

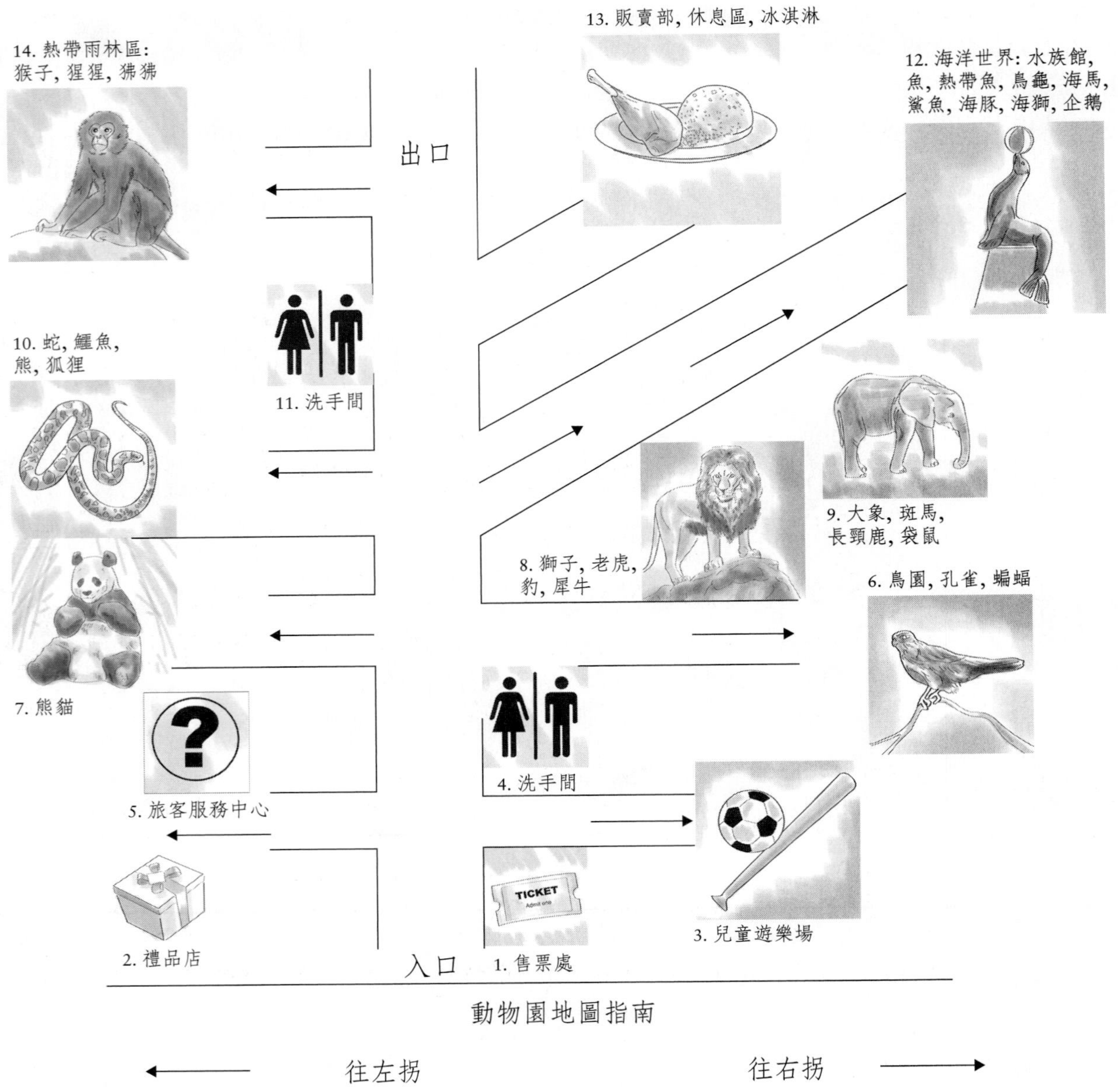

區域(区域) [qūyù]: area
1. 售票處(售票处) [shòupiàochù]: ticket booth
2. 禮品店(礼品店) [lǐpǐndiàn]: gift shop
3. 兒童遊樂場(儿童游乐场) [értóng yóulèchǎng]: children's playground
4. 洗手間(洗手间) [xǐshǒujiān]: restroom
5. 旅客服務中心(旅客服务中心) [lǚkè fúwù zhōngxīn]: visitor service, (information) center
6. 鳥園(鸟园) [niǎoyuán]: aviary
   孔雀(孔雀) [kǒngquè]: peacock
   蝙蝠(蝙蝠) [biānfú]: bat
7. 熊貓(熊猫) [xióngmāo]: panda
8. 獅子(狮子) [shīzi]: lion
   老虎(老虎) [lǎohǔ]: tiger
   豹(豹) [bào]: leopard
   犀牛(犀牛) [xīniú]: rhinoceros

9. 大象(大象) [dàxiàng]: elephant
   斑馬(斑马) [bānmǎ]: zebra
   長頸鹿(长颈鹿) [chángjǐnglù]: giraffe
   袋鼠(袋鼠) [dàishǔ]: kangaroo
10. 蛇(蛇) [shé]: snake
    鱷魚(鳄鱼) [èyú]: crocodile
    熊(熊) [xióng]: bear
    狐狸(狐狸) [húli]: fox
11. 洗手間(洗手间) [xǐshǒujiān]: restroom
12. 海洋世界(海洋世界) [hǎiyángshìjiè]: sea world
    水族館(水族馆) [shuǐzúguǎn]: aquarium
    魚(鱼) [yú]: fish
    熱帶魚(热带鱼) [rèdàiyú]: tropical fish
    烏龜(乌龟) [wūguī]: turtle
    海馬(海马) [hǎimǎ]: sea horse
    鯊魚(鲨鱼) [shāyú]: shark
    海豚(海豚) [hǎitún]: dolphin
    海獅(海狮) [hǎishī]: sea lion
    企鵝(企鹅) [qǐ'é]: penguin
13. 販賣部(贩卖部) [fànmàibù]: food shops
    休息區(休息区) [xiūxiqū]: rest area
    冰淇淋(冰淇淋) [bīngqílín]: ice cream
14. 熱帶雨林區(热带雨林区) [rèdài yǔlínqū]: tropical forest district
    猴子(猴子) [hóuzi]: monkey
    猩猩(猩猩) [xīngxing]: gorilla
    狒狒(狒狒) [fèifei]: baboon

練習 (练习) Exercises

1. 小王在兒童遊樂場，他想去看熊貓，要怎麼走呢？
   小王在儿童游乐场，他想去看熊猫，要怎么走呢？

2. 看了獅子老虎以後，他想吃冰淇淋，怎麼去呢？
   看了狮子老虎以后，他想吃冰淇淋，怎么去呢？

3. 在這個動物園，你最喜歡什麼動物？你要怎麼走才能看到你要看的動物呢？

   在这个动物园，你最喜欢什么动物？你要怎么走才能看到你要看的动物呢？

成語故事 (成语故事) IDIOM STORY

愚公移山 (愚公移山) [Yúgōng yí shān]

Meaning: Yugong (the Foolish Old Man) removed the mountains

Usage: This implies that a determined effort can help accomplish things. That is, "Where there is a will, there is a way."

Example:

A: 上海變化得太快了，我們已經走了兩個小時，可是還是找不到以前的上海小吃店。
上海变化得太快了，我们已经走了两个小时，可是还是找不到以前的上海小吃店。

B: 沒關係，我們要學"愚公移山"的精神，再問問看，說不定上海小吃店就在那個路口。
没关系，我们要学"愚公移山"的精神，再问问看，说不定上海小吃店就在那个路口。

Pay attention to the usages of (有)多 + Adjective; 往(向) + Direction/location 拐(轉); V. + 起來

Pay attention to the usages of (有)多 + Adjective; 往(向) + Direction/location 拐(转); V. + 起来

(繁體字 **Traditional Character Version**)

中國從前有一個老人叫愚公，他家前面有兩座大山。每次他們要到對面的村莊去的時候，都要拐很多的彎兒，走了很多天的路才能到，很不方便。有一天，愚公把家人找來，討論要移山的事情：

愚公問他的家人：我們已經在這兒住了多久了?

大兒子說：我們在這兒住了幾十年了。

愚公又問：現在我們要到對面的村莊去，有多遠?

大兒子說：本來不太遠，可是我們一定要轉很多彎兒。有時候應該向左拐的時候，拐錯了，向右拐了，常常會迷路，很不方便。

愚公問：如果我們把前邊的兩座大山搬走，那麼離對面的村莊會有多近?

二兒子說：很近，馬上就可以到了。

愚公說：太好了，我們來把這兩座大山移走，怎麼樣? 雖然聽起來，好像不可能，可是，俗話說"有志者，事竟成"。我們有子子孫孫，總有一天我們一定可以把這兩座大山移走，到時候，我們的子孫就可以往前一直走，不用辛苦地拐那麼多的彎了。

最後，他們全家都動起來了。大家一起分工合作，決定要把那兩座大山搬走。後來天帝聽到了，很感動，就命令大神把那兩座山移到別的地方去了。這樣一來，愚公和他家人只要往前一直走，就可以到對面的村莊，方便多了。

(简体字 **Simplified Character Version**)

中国从前有一个老人叫愚公，他家前面有两座大山。每次他们要到对面的村庄去的时候，都要拐很多的弯儿，走了很多天的路才能到，很不方便。有一天，愚公把家人找来，讨论要移山的事情：

愚公问他的家人：我们已经在这儿住了多久了?

大儿子说：我们在这儿住了几十年了。

愚公又问：现在我们要到对面的村庄去，有多远?

大儿子说：本来不太远，可是我们一定要转很多弯儿。有时候应该向左拐的时候，拐错了，向右拐了，常常会迷路，很不方便。

愚公问：如果我们把前边的两座大山搬走，那么离对面的村庄会有多近?

二儿子说：很近，马上就可以到了。

愚公说：太好了，我们来把这两座大山移走，怎么样? 虽然听起来，好像不可能，可是，俗话说"有志者，事竟成"。我们有子子孙孙，总有一天我们一定可以把这两座大山移走，到时候，我们的子孙就可以往前一直走，不用辛苦地拐那么多的弯了。

最后，他们全家都动起来了。大家一起分工合作，决定要把那两座大山搬走。后来天帝听到了，很感动，就命令大神把那两座山移到别的地方去了。这样一来，愚公和他家人只要往前一直走，就可以到对面的村庄，方便多了。

Useful words and expressions:

愚公(愚公) [Yúgōng]: name of the old person
移(移) [yí]: to move
山(山) [shān]: mountain
座(座) [zuò]: a measure word for mountains
村莊(村庄) [cūnzhuāng]: village
討論(讨论) [tǎolùn]: to discuss, discussion
迷路(迷路) [mílù]: to get lost
有志者，事竟成(有志者，事竟成) [yǒuzhìzhě, shìjìngchéng]: Where there is a will, there is a way.
子孫(子孙) [zǐsūn]: children and grandchildren, descendants
總有一天(总有一天) [zǒngyǒuyìtiān]: there will be one day, eventually
辛苦(辛苦) [xīnkǔ]: painstaking, hardship
天帝(天帝) [tiāndì]: The Emperor of the Heaven
感動(感动) [gǎndòng]: to be moved, inspired
大神(大神) [dàshén]: a giant god

練習 (练习) Exercises

1. 找出有下面語法的句子: (有) 多 + Adjective; 往 (向) + Direction/location 拐 (轉); V. + 起來

   找出有下面语法的句子: (有) 多 + Adjective; 往 (向) + Direction/location 拐 (转); V. + 起来

2. 用你自己的話說說 "愚公移山" 的故事。
   用你自己的话说说 "愚公移山" 的故事。

3. 請用 "愚公移山" 造一個句子或者說一個愚公移山的例子。
   请用 "愚公移山" 造一个句子或者说一个愚公移山的例子。

4. "愚公移山" 的故事, 告訴了我們什麼?
   "愚公移山" 的故事, 告诉了我们什么?

練習 (练习) ACTIVITIES

I. 聽力練習 (听力练习)

3-1 In the blanks provided, write the Pinyin for the words you hear.

1. 感 ____ 您搭 ____ 我們的出 ____ 汽 ____。
   感 ____ 您搭 ____ 我们的出 ____ 汽 ____。

2. 飛 ____ 就要 ____ 落了, ____ 把安 ____ 帶 ____ 好。
   飞 ____ 就要 ____ 落了, ____ 把安 ____ 带 ____ 好。

3. 你 ____ 這兒 ____ 前 ____, ____ 往左 ____, 就到了。
   你 ____ 这儿 ____ 前 ____, ____ 往左 ____, 就到了。

4. 一 ____ 十四塊 ____, ____ 你六 ____, 謝謝。
   一 ____ 十四块 ____, ____ 你六 ____, 谢谢。

3-2 Listen to the following passages and answer the questions:

Useful words and expressions:

告訴(告诉) [gàosu]: to tell
牌子(牌子) [páizi]: sign
春捲(春卷) [chūnjuǎn]: spring roll
蘿蔔糕(萝卜糕) [luóbo gāo]: turnip cake

問題(问题):

1. 他要告訴我們什麼?
   他要告诉我们什么?
2. 那家店離這兒遠嗎，開車要多久?
   那家店离这儿远吗，开车要多久?
3. 我們要從這兒往哪兒開，過了什麼以後向右轉?
   我们要从这儿往哪儿开，过了什么以后向右转?
4. 那家店的牌子是什麼顏色 ([yánsè]: color) 的? 上面寫著什麼?
   那家店的牌子是什么颜色 ([yánsè]: color) 的? 上面写着什么?
5. 那家店的什麼東西很好吃?
   那家店的什么东西很好吃?

3-3 Read the following lyric, paying special attention to the tones and the rhythm:

Shuǐ Diào Gē Tóu (Xià Què)	水調歌頭 (下闕) 水调歌头 (下阙)
(Sū Shì)	(蘇軾) (苏轼)
Zhuǎn zhūgé,	轉朱閣， 转朱阁，
Dī yǐhù,	低綺戶， 低绮户，
Zhào wúmián.	照無眠。 照无眠。
Bùyīng yǒuhèn,	不應有恨， 不应有恨，
Héshì chángxiàng biéshí yuán?	何事長向別時圓? 何事长向别时圆?
Rén yǒu bēihuān líhé,	人有悲歡離合， 人有悲欢离合，
Yuè yǒu yīnqíng yuánquē,	月有陰晴圓缺， 月有阴晴圆缺，
Cǐshì gǔ nánquán.	此事古難全。 此事古难全。
Dànyuàn rén chángjiǔ,	但願人長久， 但愿人长久，
Qiānlǐ gòng chánjuān.	千里共嬋娟。 千里共婵娟。

To the tune of **Shui Diao Ge Tou** (Part 2)
(Su, Shi)

The red windows are turning,
The delicate door becomes lower,
The bright moon illuminates the sleepless.
There shouldn't be regrets.
Is there anything which is perfect and smooth all the time?

People encounter sorrow, happiness, departure and reunion,
Just like the moon has her time of shadow, brightness, waxing and waning.
This is a fact from an ancient time.
Wishing everybody could live forever,
And though separated by a thousand miles share watching the bright moon.

Practice: What are the rhyming words in this lyric? Write them in Pinyin:

押 ________ 韻，押韻的字有：________________________。
押 ________ 韵，押韵的字有：________________________。

II. 漢字練習 (汉字练习)

3-4 Read the following words, phrases, and sentences:

往 往	搭 搭
往右拐 往右拐	搭乘出租汽車 搭乘出租汽车
到前面的交叉口，再往右拐。 到前面的交叉口，再往右拐。	搭乘出租汽車，有多快? 搭乘出租汽车，有多快?
往東走到前面的交叉口， 再往右拐。 往东走到前面的交叉口， 再往右拐。	搭乘出租汽車去旅館會有多快? 搭乘出租汽车去旅馆会有多快?

Now try to use the following characters to create words, phrases, and then sentences:

1. 降	2. 全	3. 繫	4. 品	5. 航	6. 棟
降	全	系	品	航	栋
7. 直	8. 變	9. 農	10. 叉	11. 拐	12. 落
直	变	农	叉	拐	落

3-5 Write down the traditional forms for the following simplified characters:

1. 系上安全带 _____ _____ _____ _____ _____
2. 后车箱 _____ _____ _____
3. 人民币二十块 _____ _____ _____ _____ _____ _____
4. 农田和马路 _____ _____ _____ _____ _____
5. 在红绿灯那儿往右拐 ____ ____ ____ ____ ____ ____ ____ ____ ____

3-6 Form groups of three and create phrases with the following words (pay attention to the various usages of each word):

Example: 塊: 十五塊
塊: 十五块
一塊鏡子，一塊麵包，一塊蛋糕
一块镜子，一块面包，一块蛋糕

1. 租:
   租:
2. 找:
   找:
3. 感:
   感:
4. 起:
   起:
5. 過:
   过:

III. 語法練習 (语法练习)

3-7 Form groups of two to ask/answer the following questions (remember to switch roles):

1. 你家離學校有多遠?
   你家离学校有多远?
2. 你有多久沒回家了?
   你有多久没回家了?
3. 你有多高 ([gāo]: tall)?
   你有多高 ([gāo]: tall)?
4. 你有多重 ([zhòng]: heavy)?
   你有多重 ([zhòng]: heavy)?
5. 你今年多大?
   你今年多大?
6. 你常打字 ([dǎzì]: to type) 吧! 你打英文字打得有多快? 中文字呢?
   你常打字 ([dǎzì]: to type) 吧! 你打英文字打得有多快? 中文字呢?

3-8 Interpretation:
Use the pattern: 往(向) + direction/location + V. to translate the following sentences orally.

The points of the compass:

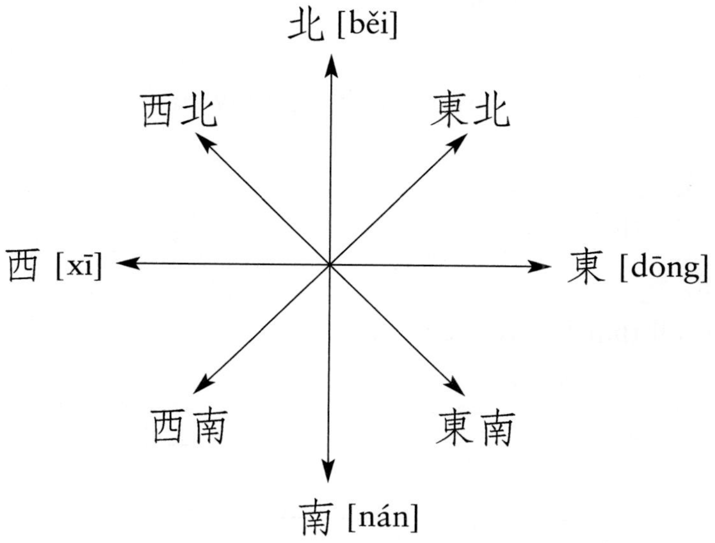

Useful words and expressions:

單行道(单行道) [dānxíngdào]: one-way street

1. You first go south, and then turn left at the second traffic light. You will see the taxi station.
2. After crossing the road, then you turn right. You will arrive at a Chinese restaurant.
3. You go northeast from here, then go straight.
4. This is an one-way street. I cannot turn right here. I have to make few more turns.
5. You go north from here, go to that intersection, then turn left.
6. You go southwest from that big building, keep going, pass two intersections, then you will soon see the hotel.

3-9 Fill in the blanks to complete the following dialogues. (pay attention to the V. + 起來 pattern)

New words:

剛剛(刚刚) [gānggāng]: just now
累(累) [lèi]: tired
公尺(公尺) [gōngchǐ]: meter
跑步(跑步) [pǎobù]: to run
胖(胖) [pàng]: fat, chubby
減肥(减肥) [jiǎnféi]: to lose weight

Dialogue (1)

A: 小姐，__________ (sorry)，我剛剛在這兒買了東西，____________________ ____________ (you forgot to give me my change)。

小姐，__________ (sorry)，我刚刚在这儿买了东西，____________________ ____________ (you forgot to give me my change)。

B: 是嗎？我怎麼 ____________________________ (cannot recall that I have seen you; use "V. + 起來")？

是吗？我怎么 ____________________________ (cannot recall that I have seen you; use "V. + 起来")？

A: 你再想想，________________________ (you will recall; use "V. + 起來")，我剛剛在這兒買了一瓶可樂。

你再想想，________________________ (you will recall; use "V. + 起来")，我刚刚在这儿买了一瓶可乐。

B: 對了，________________ (I remember; use "V. + 起來")，你給了我十塊錢，________________ (I should give you $8 change)。

对了，________________ (I remember; use "V. + 起来")，你给了我十块钱，________________ (I should give you $8 change)。

Dialogue (2)

A: 你 ________________ (You look very tired; use "V. + 起來")。

你 ________________ (You look very tired; use "V. + 起来")。

B: 是呀！我剛剛跑了五千公尺。

是呀！我刚刚跑了五千公尺。

A: 怎麼現在開始 ________________ (start running; use "V. + 起來")?

怎么现在开始 ________________ (start running; use "V. + 起来")?

B: 我姐姐說我胖了，我也覺得我開始 ________ (start getting chubby; use "V. + 起來")，就想跑步，________ (start losing weight; use "V. + 起來")。

我姐姐说我胖了，我也觉得我开始 ________ (start getting chubby; use "V. + 起来")，就想跑步，________ (start losing weight; use "V. + 起来")。

A: 這個主意 ________________ (sounds good; use "V. + 起來")。

这个主意 ________________ (sounds good; use "V. + 起来")。

B: 是呀！可是很多事情常常是 ________________ (to say it is easy, but to do it is hard; use "V. + 起來")。

是呀！可是很多事情常常是 ________________ (to say it is easy, but to do it is hard; use "V. + 起来")。

IV. 交際活動 (交际活动)

問路(问路): Form groups. Look at the map, and then take turns asking and answering the following questions:

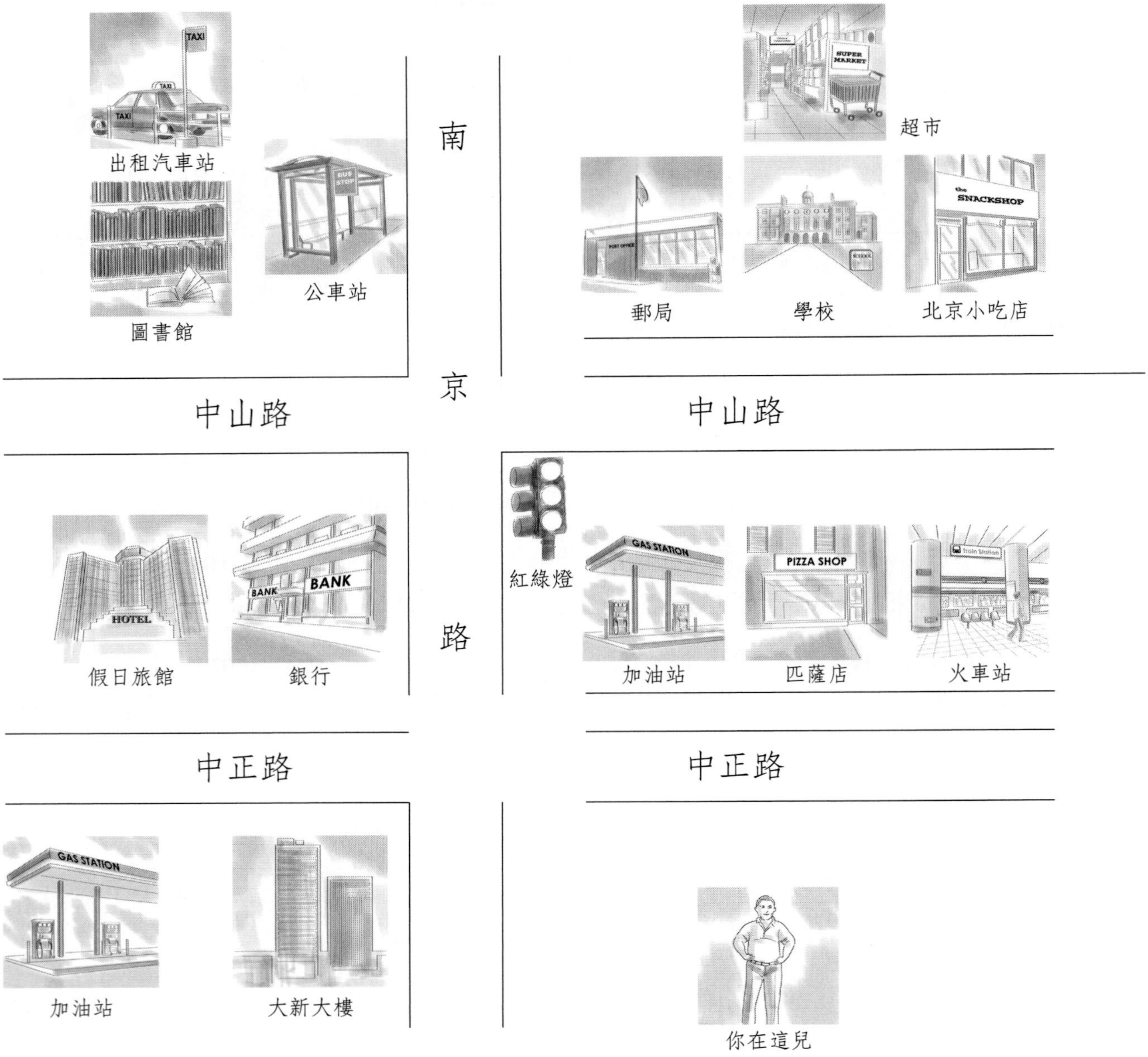

問題(问题):

1. 我要去超市 ([chāoshì]: supermarket), 請問怎麼走?
   我要去超市 ([chāoshì]: supermarket), 请问怎么走?
2. 小王的車快沒有油 ([yóu]: gas) 了, 請告訴他加油站 ([jiāyóuzhàn]: gas station), 在哪兒? 怎麼走?

   小王的车快没有油 ([yóu]: gas) 了, 请告诉他加油站 ([jiāyóuzhàn]: gas station), 在哪儿? 怎么走?
3. 我想坐公車去吃匹薩 ([pǐsà]: pizza), 怎麼走?
   我想坐公车去吃匹萨 ([pǐsà]: pizza), 怎么走?
4. 我想吃小籠包, 要去哪兒吃? 怎麼走?
   我想吃小笼包, 要去哪儿吃? 怎么走?
5. 請問出租汽車站在哪兒? 怎麼走?
   请问出租汽车站在哪儿? 怎么走?
6. 從火車站到假日旅館遠嗎? 要怎麼走?
   从火车站到假日旅馆远吗? 要怎么走?
7. 圖書館在哪條路上? 從假日旅館去圖書館要怎麼走?
   图书馆在哪条路上? 从假日旅馆去图书馆要怎么走?
8. 中正路上有銀行 ([yínháng]: bank) 嗎? 從郵局 ([yóujú]: post office) 到銀行去怎麼走?

   中正路上有银行 ([yínháng]: bank) 吗? 从邮局 ([yóujú]: post office) 到银行去怎么走?
9. 我在銀行, 要去寄 ([jì]: to send) 一個包裹 ([bāoguǒ]: package), 要去哪兒寄? 從這兒到那兒怎麼走呢?

   我在银行, 要去寄 ([jì]: to send) 一个包裹 ([bāoguǒ]: package), 要去哪儿寄? 从这儿到那儿怎么走呢?
10. 學校離大新大樓遠嗎? 要怎麼走?
    学校离大新大楼远吗? 要怎么走?

文化知識 (文化知识) Culture Link

文化點滴 (文化点滴) CULTURE NOTES

中國的新經濟開發區 (中国的新经济开发区)
[Zhōngguó de xīn jīngjì kāifāqū]
China's New Economic Development Zones

China's economy is growing and improving rapidly. One of the major features of China's economic growth has been the establishment of new economic development zones.

Since the late 1970s, China has worked to reform its economy. One of the biggest changes in China has been the opening up of its vast economy to foreign countries. During the 1980s, China established economic development zones (also known as special economic zones) to encourage foreign investment in China. Currently, there are economic development zones in Shenzhen, Zhuhai and Shantou in Guangdong Province, in Xiamen in Fujian Province, and the entire province of Hainan. They have flourished and have also stimulated growth in other areas of China.

The new economic development zones receive special treatment under China's economic laws. The government grants these zones special policies and flexible measures. They are especially preferred by foreign investors because they offer significant tax concessions for foreign direct investment during the early stage of company's operations. They have benefited the Chinese economy by bringing jobs, technical knowledge and future tax revenues to the country.

In addition to the new economic development zones, China has also opened several coastal cities and areas to foreign investment, including the Pudong zone in Shanghai.

These economic development zones are crucial to the development of the Chinese economy. They open up free trade and foreign investment as well as inspiring market-oriented business and an entrepreneurial spirit in China.

Shenzhen, one of the pioneer special economic zones established in the 1980s, is now a well established metropolitan city with a stock exchange, high rise buildings and many foreign enterprises.

問題討論 (问题讨论) Discussion Questions

1. 你對現在中國的經濟發展有什麼看法?
   你对现在中国的经济发展有什么看法?
   What do you think about China's current economic development?

2. 如果你去中國，你想去新經濟開發區還是去偏遠 ([piānyuǎn]: remote) 地區?
   如果你去中国，你想去新经济开发区还是去偏远 ([piānyuǎn]: remote) 地区?
   If you visit China, would you prefer to visit the economic development zones or the more remote areas of China?

趣味中文 (趣味中文) FUN WITH CHINESE

拐 彎 抹 角
拐 弯 抹 角
a roundabout way of talking

guǎi	wān	mò	jiǎo
拐	彎	抹	角
拐	弯	抹	角
turn	curve	bypass	corner

問題討論 (问题讨论) Discussion Questions

1. Do you like people to be straightforward or to use a roundabout way of talking? Why?
2. Are there any expressions in your language which are similar to 拐彎抹角?
3. Try to use your own words to explain 拐彎抹角 in Chinese.

行動吧! (行动吧!) LET'S GO!

機場入境須知及流程 (机场入境须知及流程) Airport Arrivals Guidelines and Procedures

明明 is helping his American friend get ready to teach English in Taipei, Taiwan. Below is the information he found from the CKS International Airport website. Let's help translate the information into English.

中正國際機場入境須知及流程
入境必備證件: (1) 護照 (2) 入境旅客申報單 (3) 外籍旅客: 簽證，機票，入境登記表
入境流程: 第一步驟: 填寫入境申請表，入境旅客申報單 第二步驟: 證照查驗 第三步驟: 領取行李 第四步驟: 動植物檢疫 第五步驟: 海關行李檢查
* 第一航廈出境動畫 Terminal I Departure (Flash animation movie) * 第二航廈入境動畫 Terminal II Arrival (Flash animation movie)

Useful words and expressions:

國際(国际) [guójì]: international
入境(入境) [rùjìng]: arrival
須知(须知) [xūzhī]: guidelines, information
及(及) [jí]: and
流程(流程) [liúchéng]: procedures in order
必備(必备) [bìbèi]: necessary, require
證件(证件) [zhèngjiàn]: documents
護照(护照) [hùzhào]: passport
旅客(旅客) [lǚkè]: traveler

申報單(申报单) [shēnbàodān]: declaration form
外籍(外籍) [wàijí]: foreign
登記表(登记表) [dēngjìbiǎo]: registration form
步驟(步骤) [bùzhòu]: step
填寫(填写) [tiánxiě]: to fill in
申請表(申请表) [shēnqǐngbiǎo]: application form
證照(证照) [zhèngzhào]: documents
查驗(查验) [cháyàn]: examination, inspection
領取(领取) [lǐngqǔ]: draw, receive, collect
動植物(动植物) [dòngzhíwù]: plants and animals
檢疫(检疫) [jiǎnyì]: quarantine
海關(海关) [hǎiguān]: customs
檢查(检查) [jiǎnchá]: check up
航廈(航厦) [hángshà]: terminal building
動畫(动画) [dònghuà]: animation movie

Translation Exercise: Translate the form into English. Fill in the following blanks:

中正國際機場入境須知及流程 (CKS international airport: The Procedures & Regulations for Arrival)
入境必備證件 (Essential documents for arrival): (1) ( ) (2) ( ) (3) ( )
入境流程 (Arrival procedures in order): Step 1: ( ) Step 2: ( ) Step 3: ( ) Step 4: ( ) Step 5: ( )
* 第一航廈(出境，動畫) Terminal Building I (Departure, Flash animation movie) * 第二航廈(入境，動畫) Terminal Building II (Arrival, Flash animation movie)

第四課
LESSON

4

你們跟以前一樣
(你们跟以前一样)
You Are the Same As Before

教學目標 (教学目标) OBJECTIVES

- Present gifts and be a courteous guest
- Receive guests and express hospitality
- Eat with manners and courtesy
- Express similarity and comparison

For Chinese, it is very common for guests to **敬酒** *([jìngjiǔ]: toast) the host with some courteous words to show their appreciation.*

生詞 (生词) VOCABULARY

核心詞 (核心词) Core Vocabulary

TRADITIONAL	SIMPLIFIED	PINYIN		
1. 師母	师母	shīmǔ	N.	(a honorific term used when addressing the teacher's wife)
2. 些	些	xiē	M.W.	some
3. 維生素	维生素	wéishēngsù	N.	vitamin
4. 永遠	永远	yǒngyuǎn	Adv.	forever
5. 健康	健康	jiànkāng	Adj.	healthy
6. 年輕	年轻	niánqīng	Adj.	young
7. 破費	破费	pòfèi	V.O.	(a common courteous expression used by the gift receivers) to spend money, go to expenses
8. 小意思	小意思	xiǎoyìsi		not a big deal
9. 難得	难得	nándé	Adv.	seldom, rarely
10. 特地	特地	tèdì	Adv.	specially
11. 拿手菜	拿手菜	náshǒucài	N.	best cooking
12. 涼	凉	liáng	Adj.	cool, cold
13. 精神	精神	jīngshen	Adj.	energetic, high-spirited
14. 白頭髮	白头发	báitóufa	N.	gray or white hair
15. 眼睛	眼睛	yǎnjīng	N.	eye
16. 花	花	huā	Adj. N.	blurred eyesight flower

TRADITIONAL	SIMPLIFIED	PINYIN		
17. 適應	适应	shìyìng	V.	to get used to
18. 時差	时差	shíchā	N.	time difference, jetlag
19. 白天	白天	báitiān	N.	day time
20. 睏	困	kùn	Adj.	sleepy, dozy
21. 睡不著	睡不着	shuìbuzháo		unable to sleep
22. 街道	街道	jiēdào	N.	street
23. 習慣	习惯	xíguàn	V.	to be used to
24. 長	长	zhǎng	V.	to grow
25. 年糕	年糕	niángāo	N.	new-year cake, rice cake
26. 味道	味道	wèidao	N.	taste
27. 地道	地道	dìdao	Adj.	original, genuine, authentic
28. 香	香	xiāng	N. Adj.	aroma aromatic, good-smelling
29. 俱全	俱全	jùquán		all included, altogether
30. 飽	饱	bǎo	Adj.	full
31. 只是	只是	zhǐshì	Adv.	just, simply
32. 家常便飯	家常便饭	jiāchángbiànfàn	N.	homemade meal
33. 相聚	相聚	xiāngjù	V.	to be together, get together
34. 乾杯	干杯	gānbēi	V.O.	to toast, cheers
35. 有朋自遠方來，不亦樂乎?	有朋自远方来，不亦乐乎?	Yǒu péng zì yuǎnfāng lái, bú yì yuè hū?		Isn't it pleasant to have friends coming from afar?

專名 (专名) Proper Nouns

TRADITIONAL	SIMPLIFIED	PINYIN		
1. 匹兹堡	匹兹堡	Pǐzībǎo	N.	Pittsburgh

補充詞 (补充词) Supplementary Vocabulary

TRADITIONAL	SIMPLIFIED	PINYIN		
1. 藥草	药草	yàocǎo	N.	medicinal herbs
2. 失眠	失眠	shīmián	N. V.	insomnia to be unable to fall asleep
3. 燙	烫	tàng	Adj.	burning hot

語文知識 (语文知识) LANGUAGE LINK

The Sentence Patterns provide models that will help you with the Language in Use section. In both sections, pay attention to the grammar points, vocabulary, and expressions.

句型 (句型) Sentence Patterns

A: 來了就好，怎麼還帶東西來呢！讓你破費了。
来了就好，怎么还带东西来呢！让你破费了。
Lái le jiù hǎo, zěnme hái dài dōngxi lái ne! Ràng nǐ pòfèi le.

B: 沒什麼，小意思。
没什么，小意思。
Méi shénme, xiǎoyìsi.

A: 你們還是跟以前一樣。
你们还是跟以前一样。
Nǐmen háishì gēn yǐqián yíyàng.

B: 我們是一天比一天老了，做事也沒有以前那麼快了。
我们是一天比一天老了，做事也没有以前那么快了。
Wǒmen shì yìtiān bǐ yìtiān lǎo le, zuòshì yě méiyǒu yǐqián nàme kuài le.

A: 你做的飯真好吃。
你做的饭真好吃。
Nǐ zuò de fàn zhēn hǎochī.

B: 哪裡，哪裡！只是家常便飯。
哪里，哪里！只是家常便饭。
Nǎli, nǎli! Zhǐshì jiāchángbiànfàn.

A: 你太客氣了，好吃極了！色香味俱全。
你太客气了，好吃极了！色香味俱全。
Nǐ tài kèqi le, hǎochī jí le! Sè xiāng wèi jù quán.

課文: 你們跟以前一樣 (繁體字)
Language in Use: Traditional Character Version

老師: 歡迎, 歡迎, 請進!

關明遠: 李訪, 來, 我給你們介紹一下, 這是王老師, 這是師母。

李訪: 你們好。

關明遠: 老師, 這是一些您喜歡的美國文學書。師母, 這些維生素是給您和老師吃的, 祝你們永遠健康年輕。

師母: 來了就好, 怎麼還帶東西來呢! 讓你破費了。

關明遠: 沒什麼, 小意思。

老師: 你們難得來上海, 師母特地做了一些拿手菜。來, 來, 快上座, 菜都要涼了!

關明遠: 老師, 師母, 你們倆還是跟以前一樣, 看起來真精神。

師母: 不行了! 我們是一天比一天老了, 白頭髮比以前多了, 眼睛也花了, 做事也沒有以前那麼快了。

老師: 李訪, 第一次來中國, 適應嗎?

李訪: 還可以, 現在還有一點兒時差。白天覺得很睏, 晚上就睡不著。不過, 今天比昨天好多了。

關明遠: 李訪說這兒的天氣比匹茲堡熱。還有, 這兒的人也比匹茲堡多, 街道上到處都是人, 他還不太習慣。

李訪: 我長這麼大, 第一次看到這麼多人。

師母: 你們倆誰比較大?

關明遠: 我跟李訪一樣大, 都是二十四歲。

師母: 對了, 不要只說話, 忘了吃菜。來, 來, 來, 多吃一點兒。

老師: 這是師母做的年糕, 味道很地道, 你們嚐嚐。

……

關明遠: 師母您做的飯真好吃。

李訪: 是啊! 色香味俱全, 我吃了很多, 現在已經很飽了。

師母: 哪裡, 哪裡! 只是家常便飯。

老師: 難得我們相聚, 來, 一起來乾一杯。今天真高興, "有朋自遠方來, 不亦樂乎!"

老師、師母、關明遠、李訪: 乾杯!

课文: 你们跟以前一样 (简体字)

Language in Use: Simplified Character Version

老师: 欢迎, 欢迎, 请进!
关明远: 李访, 来, 我给你们介绍一下, 这是王老师, 这是师母。
李访: 你们好。
关明远: 老师, 这是一些您喜欢的美国文学书。师母, 这些维生素是给您和老师吃的, 祝你们永远健康年轻。
师母: 来了就好, 怎么还带东西来呢! 让你破费了。
关明远: 没什么, 小意思。
老师: 你们难得来上海, 师母特地做了一些拿手菜。来, 来, 快上座, 菜都要凉了!
关明远: 老师, 师母, 你们俩还是跟以前一样, 看起来真精神。
师母: 不行了! 我们是一天比一天老了, 白头发比以前多了, 眼睛也花了, 做事也没有以前那么快了。
老师: 李访, 第一次来中国, 适应吗?
李访: 还可以, 现在还有一点儿时差。白天觉得很困, 晚上就睡不着。不过, 今天比昨天好多了。
关明远: 李访说这儿的天气比匹兹堡热。还有, 这儿的人也比匹兹堡多, 街道上到处都是人, 他还不太习惯。
李访: 我长这么大, 第一次看到这么多人。
师母: 你们俩谁比较大?
关明远: 我跟李访一样大, 都是二十四岁。
师母: 对了, 不要只说话, 忘了吃菜。来, 来, 来, 多吃一点儿。
老师: 这是师母做的年糕, 味道很地道, 你们尝尝。

……

关明远: 师母您做的饭真好吃。
李访: 是啊! 色香味俱全, 我吃了很多, 现在已经很饱了。
师母: 哪里, 哪里! 只是家常便饭。
老师: 难得我们相聚, 来, 一起来干一杯。今天真高兴, "有朋自远方来, 不亦乐乎!"
老师、师母、关明远、李访: 干杯!

注釋 (注释) LANGUAGE NOTES

1. 維生素 (維他命) (维生素 (维他命))

維生素(维生素) means vitamin. In Taiwan, vitamins are referred to as 維他命(维他命) [wéitāmìng].

2. 小意思 (小意思)

小意思(小意思) is a common courteous expression used by guests when presenting a gift to the hosts. It implies that the gift is small and just serves as a small token of appreciation. It helps to make the receiver more comfortable in receiving the gift.

3. 請上座 (請坐) (请上座 (请坐))

請上座(请上座) is a common and courteous way for the host to invite guests to be seated. 上座(上座) means "the seat at the head of the table reserved for the guest of honor." Note that "please sit down; please be seated" can be also expressed as 請坐(请坐) but 請上座(请上座) is more formal and courteous.

4. 應 (应) [yīng, yìng]

應 has two pronunciations. When it means "should" it is pronounced as [yīng] as in 應該(应该); when it means "to suit," it is pronounced as [yìng] as in 適應(适应).

5. 長 (长) [zhǎng, cháng]

Note that the word 長(长) has two different pronunciations and functions: When it is a verb pronounced as [zhǎng], it means "to grow;" as an adjective, it is pronounced as [cháng], and means "long."

6. 地道 (道地) (地道 (道地))

地道(地道) means "genuine, authentic." It is also sometimes expressed as 道地(道地). The expression is commonly used to describe and pay compliments to tasty food dishes.

7. 哪裡, 哪裡 (哪里, 哪里)

哪裡，哪裡(哪里，哪里) is a relatively old courteous expression used in reply to compliments. It could be translated as "not at all, not at all."

語法 (语法) GRAMMAR

1. 比較 (比较) Comparison (1): Simple Comparison Sentences 簡單的比較句 (简单的比较句)

- Indicate similarity or sameness

Patterns	Negatives
A 像 B (A is like B) e.g. 他像他爸爸。 (He is like his father.)	A 不像 B (A is not like B) e.g. 他不像他爸爸。 (He is not like his father.)
像 A 跟 B 一樣(一样) (A is the same as B) 和 e.g. 他長得跟他爸爸一樣。 他长得跟他爸爸一样。 He looks the same as his father.	A 跟 B 不一樣(不一样) 和 (A is different from B) e.g. 他長得跟他爸爸不一樣。 他长得跟他爸爸不一样。 He looks different from his father.

- Compare certain qualities of A and B

Patterns	Negatives
A 比 B Adjective (A is more [adjective] than B) e.g. 這兒比上海暖和。 这儿比上海暖和。 It is warmer here than in Shanghai.	A 不比 B Adjective (A is not more [adjective] than B) e.g. 這兒不比上海暖和。 这儿不比上海暖和。 It is not any warmer here than in Shanghai. (both places are about the same)

Patterns	Negatives
A 有 B (這麼/那麼) Adjective (这么/那么) (A is as [adjective] as B) e.g. 這兒有上海(那麼)熱嗎? 这儿有上海(那么)热吗? Is it as warm here as it is in Shanghai?	A 沒有 B (這麼/那麼) Adjective (这么/那么) (A is as not as [adjective] as B) e.g. 這兒沒有上海(那麼)熱。 这儿没有上海(那么)热。 It is not as warm here as it is in Shanghai.
Note: 這麼/那麼(这么/那么) is optional. It is used for emphasis. 這麼(这么) indicates that B is near the speaker, while 那麼(那么) indicates that B is distant from the speaker.	

2. Comparison: Relative, Superlative and Emphatic degree 比較, 最, 更 (比较, 最, 更)

Patterns	Examples
比較(比较) + Verb – indicates the "relative" degree of comparison	春夏秋冬我比較喜歡秋天。 春夏秋冬我比较喜欢秋天。 Out of spring, summer, autumn and winter, I prefer autumn.
最(最) [zuì] (the most) + Verb/adjective . . . 了 – indicates the superlative degree in comparisons – 了 can occur at the end of a sentence to indicate a sense of finality or strong conviction	春夏秋冬我最喜歡秋天了。 春夏秋冬我最喜欢秋天了。 Out of spring, summer, autumn and winter, I like autumn the most.
更(更) [gèng] + Verb/adjective – indicates "even more so" or "even less so"	這兒春天很美，秋天更美。 这儿春天很美，秋天更美。 It is beautiful in spring here. It is even more beautiful in autumn.

3. 一天比一天

一天比一天 is an adverbial expression indicating gradual change. 一次比一次 and 一年比一年 are similar expressions.

For example:	我們是一天比一天老了。 我们是一天比一天老了。	We are getting older day by day.
	他說得一次比一次好。 他说得一次比一次好。	He speaks better each time.
	房租一年比一年貴。 房租一年比一年贵。	The rent is getting more expensive year by year.

4. 比 + . . . 多了

比 comparisons are commonly followed by the complement 多了 for emphasis.

For example:	今天<u>比</u>昨天冷<u>多了</u>。 今天<u>比</u>昨天冷<u>多了</u>。	Today is much colder than yesterday.
	他<u>比</u>以前胖<u>多了</u>。 他<u>比</u>以前胖<u>多了</u>。	He is much more chubbier than before.
	她<u>比</u>她姐姐漂亮<u>多了</u>。 她<u>比</u>她姐姐漂亮<u>多了</u>。	She is much more beautiful than her older sister.

補充課文 (补充课文) SUPPLEMENTARY PRACTICE

This section will help you test your comprehension of the grammar and vocabulary you have learned in this lesson. Be prepared to answer questions about the meaning of the passage.

在中國 In China (繁體字 Traditional Character Version)

十月二日 星期六 天氣：晴

這次很高興去拜訪了老師和師母，他們跟以前一樣，非常健康、好客。師母特地做了一些拿手菜請我們吃，我們真有口福。她做的菜很道地，色香味俱全，其中我最喜歡的是年糕和蘿蔔糕，好吃極了！

我們還去看了幾個中國朋友，他們比以前瘦了，也比以前忙多了。他們看到我們都很高興，堅持要帶我們出去打牙祭。他們知道我比較喜歡吃辣的，所以就帶我們去一家新開的四川飯館。聽說這家的四川菜很好吃，價錢也很便宜，所以生意一天比一天好。以下是他們的幾個招牌菜：

酸辣湯 [suānlà tāng]: hot and sour soup
擔擔麵 [dàndàn miàn]: spicy noodles
水煮牛 [shuǐzhǔ niú]: hot and spicy beef
麻婆豆腐 [mápó dòufu]: spicy tofu
回鍋肉 [huíguō ròu]: double sauteed sliced pork
甜酸肉 [tiánsuān ròu]: sweet and sour pork
宮保雞丁 [gōngbǎo jīdīng]: Gongbao (Kung Po) chicken
椒鹽炸蝦 [jiāoyán zháxiā]: hot pepper fried shrimp

以上的菜，我們都嚐過了，真不錯！

李訪還有一些時差，白天還會覺得很睏，希望他今晚能睡著。已經是十一點十五分了，該上床睡覺了，明天我們還要出去逛逛呢！晚安！

補充課文 (补充课文) SUPPLEMENTARY PRACTICE

This section will help you test your comprehension of the grammar and vocabulary you have learned in this lesson. Be prepared to answer questions about the meaning of the passage.

在中国 In China (简体字 Simplified Character Version)

十月二日　　　星期六　　　天气：晴

这次很高兴去拜访了老师和师母，他们跟以前一样，非常健康、好客。师母特地做了一些拿手菜请我们吃，我们真有口福。她做的菜很道地，色香味俱全，其中我最喜欢的是年糕和萝卜糕，好吃极了！

我们还去看了几个中国朋友，他们比以前瘦了，也比以前忙多了。他们看到我们都很高兴，坚持要带我们出去打牙祭。他们知道我比较喜欢吃辣的，所以就带我们去一家新开的四川饭馆。听说这家的四川菜很好吃，价钱也很便宜，所以生意一天比一天好。以下是他们的几个招牌菜：

酸辣汤 [suānlà tāng]: hot and sour soup
担担面 [dàndàn miàn]: spicy noodles
水煮牛 [shuǐzhǔ niú]: hot and spicy beef
麻婆豆腐 [mápó dòufu]: spicy tofu
回锅肉 [huíguō ròu]: double sauteed sliced pork
甜酸肉 [tiánsuān ròu]: sweet and sour pork
宫保鸡丁 [gōngbǎo jīdīng]: Gongbao (Kung Po) chicken
椒盐炸虾 [jiāoyán zháxiā]: hot pepper fried shrimp

以上的菜，我们都尝过了，真不错！

李访还有一些时差，白天还会觉得很困，希望他今晚能睡着。已经是十一点十五分了，该上床睡觉了，明天我们还要出去逛逛呢！晚安！

Useful words and expressions:
晴(晴) [qíng]: a fine day
拜訪(拜访) [bàifǎng]: to visit
口福(口福) [kǒufú]: luck in having good food
蘿蔔糕(萝卜糕) [luóbo gāo]: turnip cake
瘦(瘦) [shòu]: thin
堅持(坚持) [jiānchí]: to insist
打牙祭(打牙祭) [dǎ yájì]: to have a rare and sumptuous meal
辣(辣) [là]: spicy hot
價錢(价钱) [jiàqián]: price
生意(生意) [shēngyì]: business
以下(以下) [yǐxià]: below
招牌菜(招牌菜) [zhāopái cài]: house specialties
以上(以上) [yǐshàng]: above
睡著(睡着) [shuìzháo]: to fall asleep
逛逛(逛逛) [guàngguang]: to take a stroll
晚安(晚安) [wǎn'ān]: good night

練習 (练习) Exercises

1. 四川飯館有那些招牌菜?
   四川饭馆有那些招牌菜?

2. 找出有下面語法的句子: (比, 跟(像)……一樣, 最, 有……那麼, 比 + …… 多了)

   找出有下面语法的句子: (比, 跟(像)……一样, 最, 有……那么, 比 + …… 多了)

3. 用你的話再說說每一段的內容。
   用你的话再说说每一段的内容。

成語故事 (成语故事) IDIOM STORY

自相矛盾 (自相矛盾) [zì xiāng máo dùn]

Meaning: inconsistent; self-contradictory

Usage: use to indicate someone's words or behavior is self-contradictory

Example: 你昨天說不知道王先生是誰，現在說你以前吃過他做的飯，色香味俱全，好吃極了。那不是"自相矛盾"嗎?
你昨天说不知道王先生是谁，现在说你以前吃过他做的饭，色香味俱全，好吃极了。那不是"自相矛盾"吗?

Pay special attention to (比，跟(像)……一样，最，有……那麼，比 + ……多了)

(繁體字 **Traditional Character Version**)

古時候，有一個人，他賣矛也賣盾。他把他的盾拿起來說：我的盾是世界上最好的盾，跟石頭一樣堅固，世界上沒有任何東西可以把它戳破。

然後，他又把他的矛拿起來說：我的矛非常鋒利，世界上沒有任何東西像它一樣鋒利。它比別的矛鋒利多了，可以刺穿世界上任何的東西。

旁邊的人問他：你的矛和盾真的有你說的那麼好嗎？你說你的矛和盾都是最好的。你的矛可以刺穿任何東西，你的盾可以擋住任何東西。現在你用你的矛來刺你的盾，讓我們看看吧！

那個賣矛和盾的人不知道要怎麼回答。

(简体字 **Simplified Character Version**)

古时候，有一个人，他卖矛也卖盾。他把他的盾拿起来说：我的盾是世界上最好的盾，跟石头一样坚固，世界上没有任何东西可以把它戳破。

然后，他又把他的矛拿起来说：我的矛非常锋利，世界上没有任何东西像它一样锋利。它比别的矛锋利多了，可以刺穿世界上任何的东西。

旁边的人问他：你的矛和盾真的有你说的那么好吗？你说你的矛和盾都是最好的。你的矛可以刺穿任何东西，你的盾可以挡住任何东西。现在你用你的矛来刺你的盾，让我们看看吧！

那个卖矛和盾的人不知道要怎么回答。

Useful words and expressions:
自(自) [zì]: self
相(相) [xiāng]: each other
矛盾(矛盾) [máodùn]: contradiction
古時候(古时候) [gǔshíhòu]: ancient times
賣(卖) [mài]: to sell
矛(矛) [máo]: a spear
盾(盾) [dùn]: a shield
世界上(世界上) [shìjièshàng]: in the world
石頭(石头) [shítóu]: stone, rock
堅固(坚固) [jiāngù]: solid, strong
任何(任何) [rènhé]: any
戳破(戳破) [chuōpò]: to be broken by jabbing or poking
鋒利(锋利) [fēnglì]: sharp
刺穿(刺穿) [cìchuān]: to be broken by piercing or stabbing
擋住(挡住) [dǎngzhù]: to block
回答(回答) [huídá]: to reply

練習 (练习) Exercises

1. 找出有下面語法的句子: (比, 跟(像)……一樣, 最, 有……那麼, 比 + ……多了)。

   找出有下面语法的句子: (比, 跟(像)……一样, 最, 有……那么, 比 + ……多了)。
2. 用你自己的話說說"自相矛盾"的故事。
   用你自己的话说说"自相矛盾"的故事。
3. 請用"自相矛盾"造一個句子或者說一個自相矛盾的例子。
   请用"自相矛盾"造一个句子或者说一个自相矛盾的例子。
4. "自相矛盾"的故事, 告訴了我們什麼?
   "自相矛盾"的故事, 告诉了我们什么?

練習 (练习) ACTIVITIES

I. 聽力練習 (听力练习)

4-1 In the blanks provided, write the Pinyin for the words you hear.

1. _____ 你們 _____ 遠 _____ 康年 _____。
   _____ 你们 _____ 远 _____ 康年 _____。
2. 師母特地 _____ 了一 _____ 拿手 _____ 給你們嚐 _____。
   师母特地 _____ 了一 _____ 拿手 _____ 给你们尝 _____。
3. 我有一點兒時 _____, 白天 _____ 得很 _____, 晚上 _____ 睡不 _____。

   我有一点儿时 _____, 白天 _____ 得很 _____, 晚上 _____ 睡不 _____。

4. 來乾一 _____，今天真高 _____，"有朋 _____ 遠方來，不 _____ 樂乎!"
来干一 _____，今天真高 _____，"有朋 _____ 远方来，不 _____ 乐乎!"

4-2 Listen to the following passages and answer the questions.

Useful words and expressions:

招待(招待) [zhāodài]: to treat, treat
麻煩(麻烦) [máfan]: to trouble
打擾(打扰) [dărăo]: to bother
做客(做客) [zuòkè]: to be a guest
文化(文化) [wénhuà]: culture
做東(做东) [zuòdōng]: to play the host; to host

問題(问题):

1. 他是剛到王家，還是要走了?
他是刚到王家，还是要走了?
2. 他說了哪些感謝的話?
他说了哪些感谢的话?
3. 他在王家作客學到了什麼?
他在王家作客学到了什么?
4. 他送王家什麼東西了?
他送王家什么东西了?
5. 他請王家以後做什麼?
他请王家以后做什么?

4-3 Read the following lyric, paying special attention to the tones and the rhythm:

Pú Sà Mán	菩薩蠻 菩萨蛮

4-6 Form groups of three to create phrases with the following words (pay attention to the various usages of each word):

Example: 應：應該；適應
应：应该；适应

1. 生：
   生：
2. 年：
   年：
3. 道：
   道：
4. 長：
   长：
5. 花：
   花：

III. 語法練習 (语法练习)

4-7 Form groups. Based on the information given, provide at least two types of comparison.

- Simple Comparison:
  A 像 B; A 像/跟/和 B 一樣; A 比 B; A (沒)有 B (這麼/那麼)
  A 像 B; A 像/跟/和 B 一样; A 比 B; A (没)有 B (这么/那么)
- Comparison: Relative, Superlative and Emphatic degree 比較，最，更
  比较，最，更
- 比 + ……多了
  比 + ……多了

Examples:

日文書四十五元。 日文书四十五元。	日文書比英文書貴。 日文书比英文书贵。
英文書四十元。 英文书四十元。	中文書沒有日文書那麼貴。 中文书没有日文书那么贵。

中文書 三十元。
中文书 三十元。

中文書很貴，英文書更貴，日文書最貴。
中文书很贵，英文书更贵，日文书最贵。

日文書比中文書貴多了。
日文书比中文书贵多了。

我覺得日文書比較貴。
我觉得日文书比较贵。

1. 王先生今年五十二歲。
   王先生今年五十二岁。

   王太太今年五十二歲。
   王太太今年五十二岁。

   張先生今年四十六歲。
   张先生今年四十六岁。

   張太太今年三十六歲。
   张太太今年三十六岁。

2. 紐約今天華氏 63 度。
   纽约今天华氏 63 度。

   洛杉磯今天華氏 72 度。
   洛杉矶今天华氏 72 度。

3. 爸爸一米七三。
   爸爸一米七三。

   一米七三 ([yìmǐ qīsān]: 173 cm in height)

   哥哥一米七八。
   哥哥一米七八。

   弟弟一米八。
   弟弟一米八。

4. 我室友七點起床。
   我室友七点起床。

   我八點半起床。
   我八点半起床。

5. 媽媽一百四十八磅。
   妈妈一百四十八磅。

   姐姐一百三十磅。
   姐姐一百三十磅。

   妹妹一百三十磅。
   妹妹一百三十磅。

4-8 Form groups to talk about the gradual changes in 小李:
(Use the pattern 一 Noun 比一 Noun, e.g.: 一天比一天，一年比一年，一次比一次)

Example:

小李看書：星期一看了一本，星期二看了兩本，星期三看了三本。
小李看书：星期一看了一本，星期二看了两本，星期三看了三本。

A: 小李看書看得怎麼樣？
小李看书看得怎么样？

B: 小李看書看得一天比一天多。
小李看书看得一天比一天多。

Useful words and expressions:

年齡(年龄) [niánlíng]: age
身高(身高) [shēngāo]: height
體重(体重) [tǐzhòng]: weight
磅(磅) [bàng]: pound
考試(考试) [kǎoshì]: exam
報告(报告) [bàogào]: report
分(分) [fēn]: points

年齡：一九九五年(十歲) 一九九六年(十一歲) 一九九七年(十二歲)
年龄：一九九五年(十岁) 一九九六年(十一岁) 一九九七年(十二岁)

二〇〇二年(十七歲) 二〇〇三年(十八歲)
二〇〇四年(十九歲)

二〇〇二年(十七岁) 二〇〇三年(十八岁)
二〇〇四年(十九岁)

身高：二〇〇二年(一米六三) 二〇〇三年(一米六八)
二〇〇四年(一米七二)

身高：二〇〇二年(一米六三) 二〇〇三年(一米六八)
二〇〇四年(一米七二)

體重: 二〇〇二年 (一百三十五磅) 二〇〇三年 (一百四十磅)
二〇〇四年 (一百四十五磅)

体重: 二〇〇二年 (一百三十五磅) 二〇〇三年 (一百四十磅)
二〇〇四年 (一百四十五磅)

考試: 第一課 (八十分) 第二課 (八十八分) 第三課 (九十三分)
考试: 第一课 (八十分) 第二课 (八十八分) 第三课 (九十三分)

報告: 第一次 (八十五分) 第二次 (九十分) 第三次 (九十四分)
报告: 第一次 (八十五分) 第二次 (九十分) 第三次 (九十四分)

IV. 交際活動 (交际活动)

4-9 猜猜他/她是誰? (猜猜他/她是谁?) (Play "Guess the classmate")

Divide the class into groups. Each group secretly decides on a classmate whose identity the other groups will attempt to guess. Each member of the group gives one or two sentences to describe the person.

Useful expressions:

– Simple Comparison:
A 像 B; A 像/跟/和 B 一樣; A 比 B; A (沒)有 B (這麼/那麼)
A 像 B; A 像/跟/和 B 一样; A 比 B; A (没)有 B (这么/那么)

– Comparison: Relative, Superlative and Emphatic degree
比較, 最, 更
比较, 最, 更

– 比 + ...多了
比 + ...多了

– 穿, 戴 [dài]: to put on, to wear
穿, 戴

– 猜 [cāi]: to guess
猜

e.g.: 他/她比我高, 他沒有我那麼胖 ([pàng]: fat), 他今天穿一件白襯衫, 一條黑褲子, 戴一頂 ([dǐng]: measure word for hats) 黃帽子 ([màozi]: hat)......

他/她比我高, 他没有我那么胖 ([pàng]: fat), 他今天穿一件白衬衫, 一条黑裤子, 戴一顶 ([dǐng]: measure word for hats) 黄帽子 ([màozi]: hat)......

你們猜猜他/她是誰?
你们猜猜他/她是谁?

4-10 You and your roommates are looking for a new apartment. Below is information about apartments. Discuss and compare these choices.

Useful expressions:

– Comparison: Relative, Superlative and Emphatic degree
  比較，最，更
  比较，最，更
– 比 + …… 多了
  比 + …… 多了

公寓地址：中國北京北三環中路 公寓地址：中国北京北三环中路	房租/月 房租/月 (2006年)	房租/月 房租/月 (2007年)	水電費 水电费	離學校 离学校	超市 超市	公車站 公车站	車庫 车库	寵物(貓，狗) 宠物(猫，狗)
A: 三環公寓 三环公寓	$400 $400	$430 $430	$40 $40	半英哩 半英里	有 有	沒有 没有	沒有 没有	可以 可以
B: 北京公寓 北京公寓	$400 $400	$430 $430	$50 $50	一英哩 一英里	有 有	有 有	沒有 没有	不可以 不可以
C: 長春公寓 长春公寓	$500 $500	$530 $530	$50 $50	一英哩 一英里	有 有	有 有	有 有	可以 可以

4-11 You and your roommates cook a lot of Chinese food. You invite your friends to come over to enjoy it with you.

Group one: hosts Group two: guests

Useful words and expressions:

破費 小意思 難得 特地
破费 小意思 难得 特地

拿手菜 涼 地道 香 味 俱全
拿手菜 凉 地道 香 味 俱全

飽 家常便飯 相聚 乾杯 有朋自遠方來，不亦樂乎
饱 家常便饭 相聚 干杯 有朋自远方来，不亦乐乎

文化知識 (文化知识) Culture Link

文化點滴 (文化点滴) CULTURE NOTES

中國人的好客, 請客和做客 (中国人的好客, 请客和做客) [Zhōngguórén de hàokè, qǐngkè hé zuòkè] Chinese Hospitality: Being a Good Host and a Courteous Guest

In Chinese culture, being a good host or a courteous guest are important matters. Not only are they ways to show kindness and appreciation to others, but also to keep face 面子 [miànzi] and build relationships 關係(关系) [guānxi]. For example, when a friend comes from out of town, Chinese usually offer to host the friend and show them around. In addition, a Chinese guest who is being treated at a restaurant will usually make an attempt to pay for the meal. In fact, it is common to see the parties fighting for the privilege of paying the check.

A common way that Chinese show hospitality is to invite someone to their house for lunch or dinner. Chinese like to serve guests with the best food they have, and often serve a dish that they are particularly good at cooking and are particularly proud of. Regardless of the quality of the food, however, the host will usually humbly claim that it is just plain common food, and that they are a poor cook. It is best not to agree with such humble statements!

Instead of picking up each dish and passing it around as in Western culture, the typical Chinese way is to place the dishes at the center of the table. Each guest will generally serve themselves from the dishes that are closest to them. The host usually helps the guests by continually serving them more food (especially those dishes that are relatively distant from them). On some newer design there is a circular platform in the center of the table that rotates so that each guest can reach each dish. Even if a guest has indicated that he/she is full, the host will usually keep adding food to his/her plate and inviting him/her to eat and drink more. The host will perceive any protestations of being full as just polite talk. It is the host's responsibility to make sure that guests are constantly served food and drink.

Drinking is an important part of Chinese culture and social occasions. The drinking usually begins after the host offers a short toast with an invitation to the group. Toasting tends to be done with two hands. The host will lift his cup toward the guests with two hands, say some polite words, and then say 乾杯(干杯) [gānbēi], which literally means "dry cup," or "bottoms up." The guests will join in the drinking by raising their cups to the center, gently touching each other's cups or nodding to acknowledge each other. Then each guest will empty their glass or take a small sip. It is a good idea for the guest to return the toast with some courteous words later in the evening or after a few more courses have been served. The toasts usually occur back and forth from host to guest, guest to host, and guest to guest many times during a meal.

Following are some tips for being a courteous guest:

- At a dinner party, don't begin eating until the host picks up his or her chopsticks.
- It is the Chinese way to decline gifts two or even three times before accepting them.

Food plays an important role in Chinese social occasions. Chinese like to invite friends to their houses to and serve them the best food they have to show their hospitality.

The hosts and guests usually toast each other several times during a meal.

- Don't stick your chopsticks upright in your rice. This is considered impolite since it resembles an offering to the dead.
- When you are finished eating, place your chopsticks in parallel across your dish or bowl. Bones are often placed directly on the table alongside your dish.
- Guests should sample all of the dishes and leave some food on their plate at the end of the meal. A clean plate indicates that you are still hungry and is a signal for the host to continue to serve you.
- Refusing food may be considered impolite. If you do not want to eat something, just leave it on the side of your dish.
- Respect elders by acts of kindness like pouring a drink or holding a door open for them.
- Gifts of food are not recommended at dinner parties or other occasions where food is served, since such a gift may imply insufficiency on the part of the hosts. The guests can bring candy, tea, beverages or fruit to the host as a thank-you gift.
- If possible, it is a good idea for the guests to invite the host to be their guest the next time.

問題討論 (问题讨论) Discussion Questions

1. 你去過中國人的家做客嗎？說說你的經驗。
   你去过中国人的家做客吗？说说你的经验。
   Have you ever been invited to eat at a Chinese person's house? Share your experience.

2. 你看過哪些電影中(例如《喜宴》)有描述中西文化的差異？
   你看过哪些电影中(例如《喜宴》)有描述中西文化的差异？
   Have you seen any movies (such as "The Wedding Banquet") which show some differences between Chinese and Western culture?

趣味中文 (趣味中文) FUN WITH CHINESE

人逢喜事精神爽
人逢喜事精神爽
When encountering good news or a joyful occasion, he/she will be in high spirits and look pleased.

rén	féng	xǐ	shì	jīng	shén	shuǎng
人	逢	喜	事	精	神	爽
人	逢	喜	事	精	神	爽
people	meet	happy	event	spirit	spirit	pleased

問題討論 (问题讨论) Discussion Questions

1. What kinds of happy events make you feel pleased? Please give some examples in Chinese.
2. Are there any expressions in your language which are similar to 人逢喜事精神爽(人逢喜事精神爽)?
3. Try to use your own words to explain 人逢喜事精神爽 (人逢喜事精神爽) in Chinese.

行動吧! (行动吧!) LET'S GO!

機場出境須知及流程 (机场出境须知及流程)
Airport Departure Guidelines and Procedures

Below is some information from an international airport regarding departure guidelines and procedures. Let's translate the information into English.

(繁體字 **Traditional Character Version**)

出境
您必須在起飛前二個小時到機場等候並辦理一些手續。
出境必備證件: (1) 護照 (2) 機票 (3) 出境登記表。
出境流程: 步驟 1. 辦理報到 步驟 2. 托運行李 步驟 3. 證照查驗 步驟 4. 安全檢查及候機 步驟 5. 登機

(简体字 **Simplified Character Version**)

出境
您必须在起飞前二个小时到机场等候并办理一些手续。
出境必备证件：(1) 护照 (2) 机票 (3) 出境登记表。
出境流程： 步骤 1. 办理报到 步骤 2. 托运行李 步骤 3. 证照查验 步骤 4. 安全检查及候机 步骤 5. 登机

Useful words and expressions:

出境(出境) [chūjìng]: departure
起飛(起飞) [qǐfēi]: to take off
等候(等候) [děnghòu]: to wait
辦理(办理) [bànlǐ]: to handle
手續(手续) [shǒuxù]: procedures
報到(报到) [bàodào]: to check in
托運(托运) [tuōyùn]: to transport, ship
安全(安全) [ānquán]: security
登機(登机) [dēngjī]: to board

Translation Exercise: Fill in the blanks below by translating the airport form above into English.

Departure
( )
( ) (1) (2) (3)
Departure procedures in order: Step 1: ( ) Step 2: ( ) Step 3: ( ) Step 4: ( ) Step 5: ( )

復習 (复习) Review

LESSON 3 TO LESSON 4

1. Form groups to portray the following situation

A: You invite your friends to attend your party which will be held this weekend at your place. Tell them how to get to your place.
B: You are excited. You will attend the party. You would like to ask when, where, distance and directions . . .

Useful words and expressions:

你住在哪兒，怎麼走，如果 ([rúguǒ]: if)，週末 ([zhōumò]: weekend)
你住在哪儿，怎么走，如果 ([rúguǒ]: if)，周末 ([zhōumò]: weekend)

(有) 多 + Adjective (How *Adjective*?)

往(向)	+ direction / location	+ V.
往(向)	+ (e.g. 東，前，右) / (e.g. 市中心，飛機場，那棟大樓)	+ (e.g. 拐，轉，走，跑，開)
往(向)	+ (e.g. 东，前，右) / (e.g. 市中心，飞机场，那栋大楼)	+ (e.g. 拐，转，走，跑，开)

V. + 起來
起来

2. Form groups to read aloud the following passage and ask or reply to the questions

Situation: 小英今年二十八歲，可是還沒有男朋友，她的同事給她介紹了三個男孩子。

小英今年二十八岁，可是还没有男朋友，她的同事给她介绍了三个男孩子。

	李先生 李先生	王先生 王先生	關先生 关先生
年齡 年龄	二十八歲 二十八岁	二十八歲 二十八岁	三十歲 三十岁
身高 身高	一米七〇 一米七〇	一米七〇 一米七〇	一米七六 一米七六
體重 体重	一百六十八磅 一百六十八磅	一百七十八磅 一百七十八磅	一百七十八磅 一百七十八磅
大學成績 大学成绩	**C** **C**	**B** **B**	**A** **A**
去健身房鍛煉 去健身房锻炼	一週三次 一周三次	一週三次 一周三次	一週三次 一周三次
運動愛好 运动爱好	游泳，打籃球 游泳，打篮球	游泳，打籃球 游泳，打篮球	打籃球，跑步 打篮球，跑步

Useful words and expressions:

年齡(年龄) [niánlíng]: age
選(选) [xuǎn]: to choose
如果(如果) [rúguǒ]: if
那麼(那么) [nàme]: then
帥(帅) [shuài]: handsome
愛好(爱好) [àihào]: hobby
適合(适合) [shìhé]: suitable
一米七六(一米七六) [yìmǐ qīliù]: 176 cm in height
當(当) [dāng]: to serve as, to be
成績(成绩) [chéngjì]: grades, academic performance
我覺得(我觉得) [wǒ juéde]: I think
次數(次数) [cìshù]: the number of times
條件(条件) [tiáojiàn]: criteria

Below are her notes. Listen and then answer the questions in Chinese.

1. 我的同事：老李、老王和老關給我介紹了他們的兒子，要我跟他們當朋友。我跟他們吃過飯，也看過電影。他們看起來都還不錯。可是我不知道要選李先生，王先生還是關先生當我的男朋友。

   我的同事：老李、老王和老关给我介绍了他们的儿子，要我跟他们当朋友。我跟他们吃过饭，也看过电影。他们看起来都还不错。可是我不知道要选李先生，王先生还是关先生当我的男朋友。

2. 李先生和王先生都跟我一樣大，我們都是二十八歲，關先生三十歲。

   李先生和王先生都跟我一样大，我们都是二十八岁，关先生三十岁。

3. 李先生跟王先生一樣高，可是沒有關先生那麼高，關先生最高。我覺得，李先生比王先生帥，也比關先生帥，可是李先生的大學成績最不好，王先生還可以，關先生的成績最好。

   李先生跟王先生一样高，可是没有关先生那么高，关先生最高。我觉得，李先生比王先生帅，也比关先生帅，可是李先生的大学成绩最不好，王先生还可以，关先生的成绩最好。

4. 他們三個都喜歡鍛煉，他們去健身房鍛煉的次數一樣多。李先生游泳游得不錯，可是王先生游泳游得更好，關先生不會游泳。他們三個都跟我一樣喜歡打籃球，其中關先生籃球打得最好。我的愛好是打籃球，看籃球比賽和游泳，可是我不太喜歡跑步。他們三個人的條件都不錯，不知道哪一個比較適合我，我很難做最後的決定！

   他们三个都喜欢锻炼，他们去健身房锻炼的次数一样多。李先生游泳游得不错，可是王先生游泳游得更好，关先生不会游泳。他们三个都跟我一样喜欢打篮球，其中关先生篮球打得最好。我的爱好是打篮球，看篮球比赛和游泳，可是我不太喜欢跑步。他们三个人的条件都不错，不知道哪一个比较适合我，我很难做最后的决定！

問題(问题):

1. 小英的問題是什麼?
小英的问题是什么?

____

2. 李先生、王先生和關先生誰最大?
李先生、王先生和关先生谁最大?

____

3. 李先生、王先生和關先生誰比較高?
李先生、王先生和关先生谁比较高?

____

4. 小英覺得誰最帥?
小英觉得谁最帅?

____

5. 他們三個人的大學成績怎麼樣? 誰最好?
他们三个人的大学成绩怎么样? 谁最好?

____

6. 小英的爱好是什麼?
小英的爱好是什么?

____

7. 關先生會不會游泳? 誰游泳游得最好?
关先生会不会游泳? 谁游泳游得最好?

____

8. 如果你是小英，你會選誰? 為什麼?
如果你是小英，你会选谁? 为什么?

____

3. Picture description: Form groups to talk about 小李's story. (Be creative!)

Useful words and expressions:

出租汽車(出租汽车) 變化(变化) 車費(车费) 人民幣(人民币)
找(找) 維生素(维生素) 健康(健康) 年輕(年轻) 破費(破费)
小意思(小意思) 難得(难得) 特地(特地)
拿手菜(拿手菜) 精神(精神) 白頭髮(白头发) 眼睛(眼睛)
花(花) 地道(地道) 色香味俱全(色香味俱全) 吃飽(吃饱)
家常便飯(家常便饭) 相聚(相聚) 乾杯(干杯)
有朋自遠方來，不亦樂乎(有朋自远方来，不亦乐乎)

(1)

(2)

(3)

(4)

4. 寫感謝卡 (写感谢卡) Write thank-you cards

____

____

____

____

____

5. Simplified and Traditional Characters 簡體字/繁體字 (简体字/繁体字)

Read each character aloud. Write its traditional form. Then create a phrase and a sentence using the character.

For example: 学 → 學 → 學生 → 我是學生

L3: 系 ( ) 栋 ( ) 变 ( ) 农 ( ) 灯 ( )
转 ( ) 弯 ( ) 费 ( ) 币 ( )

L4: 轻 ( ) 发 ( ) 适 ( ) 困 ( )
味 ( ) 俱 ( ) 饱 ( ) 干 ( )

第五課
LESSON

5

我的中國行–復習
(我的中国行–复习)
My Trip to China – Review

教學目標 (教学目标) OBJECTIVES

- Make a report
- Recall memories and past experiences

China is both an old and a young country. Looking out from the ancient buildings, one can spot the outlines of a modern city.

生詞 (生词) VOCABULARY

核心詞 (核心词) Core Vocabulary

TRADITIONAL	SIMPLIFIED	PINYIN		
1. 陰	阴	yīn	Adj.	cloudy
2. 終於	终于	zhōngyú	Adv.	finally, at last
3. 本來	本来	běnlái	Adv.	originally, at first, initially
4. 飛行	飞行	fēixíng	N.	flight, flying
5. 轉機	转机	zhuǎnjī	N.	change planes, transfer
6. 誤點	误点	wùdiǎn	N. V.O.	delay to delay
7. 趕上	赶上	gǎnshàng	V.C.	to catch, catch up with
8. 班機	班机	bānjī	N.	flight
9. 熱情	热情	rèqíng	Adj.	warm-hearted, enthusiastic
10. 好客	好客	hàokè	Adj.	hospitable
11. 津津有味	津津有味	jīnjīnyǒuwèi		with relish, with keen pleasure
12. 大開眼界	大开眼界	dàkāiyǎnjiè		be exposed to many great new things
13. 團	团	tuán	N.	group
14. 方向	方向	fāngxiàng	N.	direction
15. 鬧	闹	nào	V.	to make, cause, induce
16. 笑話	笑话	xiàohuà	N.	joke
17. 繁榮	繁荣	fánróng	Adj.	prosperous
18. 大廈	大厦	dàshà	N.	large and high building
19. 雖然	虽然	suīrán	Conj.	although
20. 别人	别人	biérén	N.	other people
21. 小吃	小吃	xiǎochī	N.	snack
22. 挺	挺	tǐng	Adv.	very
23. 值得	值得	zhídé	Adj.	worthwhile

語文知識 (语文知识) LANGUAGE LINK

The Sentence Patterns provide models that will help you with the Language in Use section. In both sections, pay attention to the grammar points, vocabulary, and expressions.

句型 (句型) Sentence Patterns

這次飛機誤點把我跟李訪累壞了。
这次飞机误点把我跟李访累坏了。
Zhècì fēijī wùdiǎn bǎ wǒ gēn Lǐ Fǎng lèi huài le.

他們看起來都很精神。
他们看起来都很精神。
Tāmen kànqǐlái dōu hěn jīngshen.

他們還是跟以前一樣非常熱情。
他们还是跟以前一样非常热情。
Tāmen háishì gēn yǐqián yíyàng fēicháng rèqíng.

現在的京劇票比以前貴了。
现在的京剧票比以前贵了。
Xiànzài de jīngjù piào bǐ yǐqián guì le.

我們手裡拿著地圖，忙著問路。
我们手里拿着地图，忙着问路。
Wǒmen shǒu lǐ ná zhe dìtú, máng zhe wènlù.

他去過中國，看過京劇。
他去过中国，看过京剧。
Tā qù guo Zhōngguó, kàn guo jīngjù.

課文: 我的中國行 (繁體字)
Language in Use: Traditional Character Version

十月二十日　　星期三　　天氣: 陰

我們坐了三十多個小時的飛機，終於回到美國來了。從中國到美國本來十幾個小時就到了，但是在日本轉機的時候，因為我們的飛機誤點了，所以沒趕上我們的班機。我們在機場等了五個小時以後，才坐上了飛機。這次飛機誤點把我跟李訪累壞了。在飛機上，我們一把行李放好，就一直睡覺，睡到飛機降落以後才起來。

不過這次很高興能在上海和老師再次相聚。老師和師母看起來都很精神，他們還是跟以前一樣非常熱情、好客。師母還特地做了幾樣很地道的上海菜，讓我們嚐嚐，其中我最喜歡的是上海年糕。真好吃!

我還帶李訪去看了京劇，我們看得津津有味，他也覺得大開眼界。不過，我聽說現在的京劇劇團比以前少了，所以票也比以前貴了。

上海真的變得很快，有些路都很難找到了。我們手裡拿著地圖，忙著問路、找方向。常常應該向左拐的時候，我們轉錯了，往右拐了，鬧了不少笑話。

中國真的是一天比一天繁榮、進步了。在大城市裡，高樓大廈跟美國的一樣高，到處都能看到外國人。

這次在中國的時間雖然很短，可是我們都玩得很高興。李訪說他現在可以跟別人說他去過中國、看過京劇了。還有，他也嚐了很多中國的小吃，都很棒!

我們倆都覺得這次去中國旅行，挺不錯的，也非常值得。下次有機會，我們還要再去。

课文: 我的中国行 (简体字)

Language in Use: Simplified Character Version

十月二十日　　星期三　　天气: 阴

我们坐了三十多个小时的飞机，终于回到美国来了。从中国到美国本来十几个小时就到了，但是在日本转机的时候，因为我们的飞机误点了，所以没赶上我们的班机。我们在机场等了五个小时以后，才坐上了飞机。这次飞机误点把我跟李访累坏了。在飞机上，我们一把行李放好，就一直睡觉，睡到飞机降落以后才起来。

不过这次很高兴能在上海和老师再次相聚。老师和师母看起来都很精神，他们还是跟以前一样非常热情、好客。师母还特地做了几样很地道的上海菜，让我们尝尝，其中我最喜欢的是上海年糕。真好吃!

我还带李访去看了京剧，我们看得津津有味，他也觉得大开眼界。不过，我听说现在的京剧剧团比以前少了，所以票也比以前贵了。

上海真的变得很快，有些路都很难找到了。我们手里拿着地图，忙着问路、找方向。常常应该向左拐的时候，我们转错了，往右拐了，闹了不少笑话。

中国真的是一天比一天繁荣、进步了。在大城市里，高楼大厦跟美国的一样高，到处都能看到外国人。

这次在中国的时间虽然很短，可是我们都玩得很高兴。李访说他现在可以跟别人说他去过中国、看过京剧了。还有，他也尝了很多中国的小吃，都很棒!

我们俩都觉得这次去中国旅行，挺不错的，也非常值得。下次有机会，我们还要再去。

注釋 (注释) LANGUAGE NOTES

1. 中國行 (中国行)

中國行(中国行) is an idiomatic expression meaning "trip to China." 我的中國行(我的中国行) means "My trip to China." 行(行) is a short form of "旅行(旅行)."

2. 一直 (一直)

一直(一直) has two meanings as illustrated below:

(1) from beginning to the end; always; constantly

For example: 我們上飛機以後就一直睡覺。
我们上飞机以后就一直睡觉。
After we boarded the airplane, we slept from beginning to end (of the flight).

(2) (to go) straight ahead

For example: 從那兒往前一直走。
从那儿往前一直走。
From there, go straight ahead.

3. 好 (好) [hǎo, hào]

好(好) has two pronunciations which have different meanings and functions. When 好(好) is used as an adjective which means "good" as in 好吃(好吃), the pronunciation is [hǎo]; when 好(好) is used as a verb, it is pronounced as [hào] as in 好客(好客).

4. 挺 (很, 非常) (挺 (很, 非常))

挺(挺) is an adverb meaning "very, quite." It is a relatively more colloquial form than 很(很) "very" and 非常(非常) "extraordinary."

語法 (语法) GRAMMAR

(Review: The main Grammar Points from Lesson 1 to Lesson 4)

1. 結果補語 (结果补语) Resultative complement (RC)

The resultative complement (RC) indicates the result, extent or goal of an action.

Verb	+ adjective / verb	→	resultative complement (RC)
看	錯 (wrong)	→	看錯 (wrong seeing)
看	错 (wrong)	→	看错 (wrong seeing)
	完 (finish)	→	看完 (finish seeing)
	完 (finish)	→	看完 (finish seeing)
	見 (perceive)	→	看見 (see)
	见 (perceive)	→	看见 (see)

2. 把字句和結果補語的搭配 (把字句和结果补语的搭配) 把 sentences and the resultative complement

Since the resultative complement indicates the result or influence of an action, it is often used with the 把 structure. Note that when the object is definite, the 把 structure is preferred.

Subject	把 Object + RC (e.g. 看完，收好，找到，放在，穿上，打開，換成)
	把 看完，收好，找到，放在，穿上，打开，换成

For example: 我把那本小說看完了。
我把那本小说看完了。

3. The aspects 了 (了), 著 (着) and 過 (过)

- 了 indicates completed action.

  For example: 我吃藥了。
  我吃药了。
  I have taken the medicine.

  When two 了(了) co-occur, it usually indicates that the action is still ongoing at the moment of speaking.

  For example: 她學中文學了三年了。
  她学中文学了三年了。
  She has been studying Chinese for three years.
  (She is still studying Chinese at the moment of speaking.)

- 著(着) describes a state which is continuous or stationary.

  For example: 牆上掛著一張照片。
  墙上挂着一张照片。
  There is a picture hanging on the wall.

- 過(过) indicates past experience (ever . . . before).

  For example: 我去過長城。
  我去过长城。
  I have been to the Great Wall.

4. (有) 多 + Adjective (How *Adjective*?)

(有)多 + Adjective is a pattern used to ask about the degree of distance, length, speed, size, etc. It is similar to the English pattern "How + Adjective" (for example "How far?" or "How fast?").

For example: 有多長，多高，多遠，多快，多重，多大 and 多久。
有多长，多高，多远，多快，多重，多大 and 多久。

5. Ask and give directions:

往(向) + direction / location + V.

往(向)	東(东)	轉(转)
	前(前)	走(走)
	右(右)	跑(跑)
	城裡(城里)	開(开)
	飛機場(飞机场)	拐(拐)

For example: 從這兒往前走，再向左拐就到了。
从这儿往前走，再向左拐就到了。
Go straight ahead, then turn left and it's right there.

6. 比較 (比较) Comparison (1): Simple Comparison Sentences 簡單的比較句 (简单的比较句)

A 像(像) B	A is like B
A 跟(跟) B 一樣(一样)	A is the same as B
A 比(比) B Adjective	A is more [adjective] than B
A 有(有) B (這麼(这么) / 那麼(那么)) Adjective	A is as [adjective] as B

7. Comparison: Relative, Superlative and Emphatic degree 比較 (比较), 最 (最), 更 (更)

比較(比较): indicates the "relative" degree of comparison
最(最): the superlative degree of comparisons
更(更): even more so

補充課文 (补充课文) SUPPLEMENTARY PRACTICE

This section will help you test your comprehension of the grammar and vocabulary you have learned in this lesson. Be prepared to answer questions about the meaning of the passage.

旅行日記 Travel Diary (繁體字 Traditional Character Version)

關明遠：高飛，你看，我的旅行日記《我的中國行》在校報上登出來了，上面還登了幾張我在中國照的照片呢！

高飛：是嗎？快讓我看看！…… 嗯，你的文章寫得真不錯，快講講，你這次到中國旅行，去了哪些地方？

關明遠：我們先從美國坐飛機到上海去看了老師和師母，然後從上海搭船沿著長江往西走，一路上到了南京、武漢和長江三峽，再從重慶坐飛機到北京，最後從北京飛回美國。

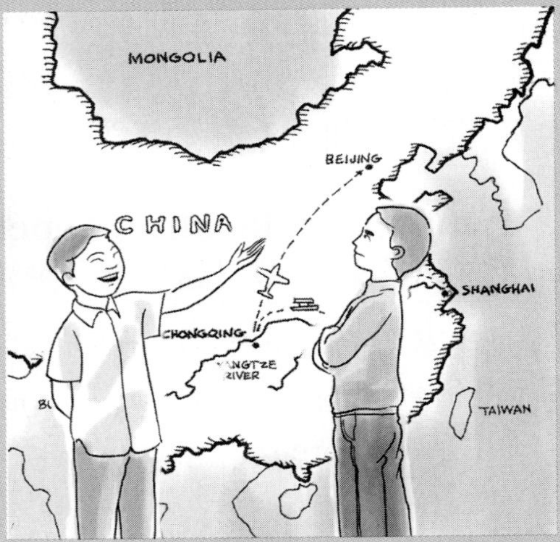

高飛：聽起來你們好像玩得很開心。

關明遠：是的，我們這次真的是大開眼界，挺不錯的。

高飛：這第一張照片是上海的外灘吧！那兒的建築跟歐洲的一些建築風格一樣，真漂亮！難怪人們還把上海叫做"東方巴黎"呢。

關明遠：沒錯，上海是一個很國際化的大城市。你看，這張照片就是外灘對面有名的浦東新區。聽說國際上很多有名的大公司都把它們的分公司設在浦東新區，他們還要把他們的工廠搬到中國去呢。來，你看，這張照片上的兩個人就是王老師和師母。

高飛：他們看起來真精神。

關明遠：他們每天都去公園打太極拳，比我們年輕人還有活力呢。

高飛：嗯。…… 啊！這張照片有山有水，是長江三峽吧！

Continued on page 146

補充課文 (补充课文) SUPPLEMENTARY PRACTICE

This section will help you test your comprehension of the grammar and vocabulary you have learned in this lesson. Be prepared to answer questions about the meaning of the passage.

旅行日记 Travel Diary (简体字 Simplified Character Version)

关明远：高飞，你看，我的旅行日记《我的中国行》在校报上登出来了，上面还登了几张我在中国照的照片呢！

高飞：是吗？快让我看看！……嗯，你的文章写得真不错，快讲讲，你这次到中国旅行，去了哪些地方？

关明远：我们先从美国坐飞机到上海去看了老师和师母，然后从上海搭船沿着长江往西走，一路上到了南京、武汉和长江三峡，再从重庆坐飞机到北京，最后从北京飞回美国。

高飞：听起来你们好像玩得很开心。

关明远：是的，我们这次真的是大开眼界，挺不错的。

高飞：这第一张照片是上海的外滩吧！那儿的建筑跟欧洲的一些建筑风格一样，真漂亮！难怪人们还把上海叫做"东方巴黎"呢。

关明远：没错，上海是一个很国际化的大城市。你看，这张照片就是外滩对面有名的浦东新区。听说国际上很多有名的大公司都把它们的分公司设在浦东新区，他们还要把他们的工厂搬到中国去呢。来，你看，这张照片上的两个人就是王老师和师母。

高飞：他们看起来真精神。

关明远：他们每天都去公园打太极拳，比我们年轻人还有活力呢。

高飞：嗯。……啊！这张照片有山有水，是长江三峡吧！

Continued on page 147

旅行日記 Travel Diary —— 接第一百四十四頁

關明遠：是的。長江三峽美麗極了，我們的船走在水上，就好像走在山水畫裡一樣。對了，這張照片是我在北京的王府井大街前面照的。去過王府井大街的人都說那兒曾經是一條很窄的老街，現在已經是一條寬敞的商業街了。

高飛：嗯，聽起來很有意思，有機會我也要去中國看看。

關明遠：我的數碼相機裡還有一百多張照片呢。你想不想看？我明天把這些照片都帶過來給你看看。

高飛：太好了！我們一言為定！

Useful words and expressions:

旅行日記(旅行日记) [lǚxíng rìjì]: travel diary
校報(校报) [xiàobào]: school newspaper
登(登) [dēng]: to publish
講(讲) [jiǎng]: to tell, narrate
沿(沿) [yán]: along
南京(南京) [Nánjīng]: Nanjing (capital city of Jiangsu Province), located in central coast of China
武漢(武汉) [Wǔhàn]: Wuhan (capital city of Hubei Province), located in the center of China
長江三峽(长江三峡) [Chángjiāng sānxiá]: the Three Gorges on the Yangtze River
重慶(重庆) [Chóngqìng]: Chongqing, located in the southwestern part of China
外灘(外滩) [Wàitān]: the Bund
建築(建筑) [jiànzhù]: architecture
歐洲(欧洲) [Ōuzhōu]: Europe
風格(风格) [fēnggé]: style
難怪(难怪) [nánguài]: no wonder
巴黎(巴黎) [Bālí]: Paris
國際化(国际化) [guójìhuà]: internationalized
浦東新區(浦东新区) [Pǔdōng xīnqū]: Pudong New Economic Zone (in Shanghai)
分公司(分公司) [fēn gōngsī]: branch company
設(设) [shè]: to establish
活力(活力) [huólì]: vigorous
太極拳(太极拳) [Tàijíquán]: Tai-chi
山水畫(山水画) [shānshuǐhuà]: traditional Chinese painting of mountains and water, landscape painting
王府井(王府井) [Wángfǔjǐng]: Wang Fu Jing (a shopping street in Beijing)
窄(窄) [zhǎi]: narrow
寬敞(宽敞) [kuānchǎng]: spacious
商業(商业) [shāngyè]: business
數碼相機(数码相机) [shùmǎ xiàngjī]: digital camera. 數位相機(数位相机) [shùwèi xiàngjī] is used in Taiwan

旅行日记 Travel Diary —— 接第一百四十五页

关明远: 是的。长江三峡美丽极了，我们的船走在水上，就好像走在山水画里一样。对了，这张照片是我在北京的王府井大街前面照的。去过王府井大街的人都说那儿曾经是一条很窄的老街，现在已经是一条宽敞的商业街了。

高飞: 嗯，听起来很有意思，有机会我也要去中国看看。

关明远: 我的数码相机里还有一百多张照片呢。你想不想看? 我明天把这些照片都带过来给你看看。

高飞: 太好了! 我们一言为定!

練習 (练习) Exercises

1. 關明遠在中國玩了哪些地方?
   关明远在中国玩了哪些地方?

2. 為什麼上海外灘叫做 “東方巴黎”?
   为什么上海外滩叫做 “东方巴黎”?

3. 關明遠看到了中國有哪些變化?
   关明远看到了中国有哪些变化?

成語故事 (成语故事) IDIOM STORY

守株待兔 (守株待兔) [shōuzhū dàitù]

Meaning: Waiting for hares by the tree

Usage: Indicates that someone is stupid and unimaginative about doing things or that someone puts their faith in chance and windfalls

Example: 明天就要考試了，你不努力，只想“守株待兔”，以為考試會很簡單。
明天就要考试了，你不努力，只想“守株待兔”，以为考试会很简单。

Pay attention to the usages of 著; 過; 把……; 往(向) + Direction/location 拐(轉)

(繁體字 **Traditional Character Version**)

從前，宋國有一個農夫，他的農田裡長著很好的莊稼。從他的農田走出來向左拐，有一棵大樹。有一天，他在田裡工作的時候，有一隻兔子往農田這邊跑了過來，可是那隻兔子跑得太快，撞到大樹，死了。農夫從來沒有見過這樣的事，心想：“太好了，天上掉下來了兔子肉!”他想著想著，就把兔子撿起來、帶回去煮了，高高興興地吃了一頓。

農夫沒有花什麼力氣就有兔子肉吃，就想：要是每天有兔子跑過來撞到大樹，那該多好呀，這樣他就不用每天辛苦地到田裡工作了。

這麼想著，他再也不去田裡工作了。他每天都在大樹旁邊坐著，等著有兔子向大樹撞過來。可是一天一天過去了，莊稼枯萎了，還是沒有兔子跑過來。

鄰居覺得他想不勞而獲，就把他的故事編成一個笑話教育年輕人。

(简体字 **Simplified Character Version**)

从前，宋国有一个农夫，他的农田里长着很好的庄稼。从他的农田走出来向左拐，有一棵大树。有一天，他在田里工作的时候，有一只兔子往农田这边跑了过来，可是那只兔子跑得太快，撞到大树，死了。农夫从来没有见过这样的事，心想："太好了，天上掉下来了兔子肉！"他想着想着，就把兔子捡起来、带回去煮了，高高兴兴地吃了一顿。

农夫没有花什么力气就有兔子肉吃，就想：要是每天有兔子跑过来撞到大树，那该多好呀，这样他就不用每天辛苦地到田里工作了。

这么想着，他再也不去田里工作了。他每天都在大树旁边坐着，等着有兔子向大树撞过来。可是一天一天过去了，庄稼枯萎了，还是没有兔子跑过来。

邻居觉得他想不劳而获，就把他的故事编成一个笑话教育年轻人。

Useful words and expressions:
從前(从前) [cóngqián]: once upon a time
宋國(宋国) [Sòngguó]: the State of Song
農夫(农夫) [nóngfū]: peasant, farmer
農田(农田) [nóngtián]: crop field
莊稼(庄稼) [zhuāngjia]: crop
兔子(兔子) [tùzi]: rabbit
掉(掉) [diào]: to drop, fall
肉(肉) [ròu]: meat
撿(捡) [jiǎn]: to pick up
煮(煮) [zhǔ]: to cook
頓(顿) [dùn]: (measure word for meal)
花(花) [huā]: to spend (time, energy, or money)
力氣(力气) [lìqi]: effort
辛苦(辛苦) [xīnkǔ]: toilsome
枯萎(枯萎) [kūwěi]: to wither
鄰居(邻居) [línjū]: neighbor
不勞而獲(不劳而获) [bùláo'érhuò]: reap without sowing; profit by other people's toil
編(编) [biān]: to design
教育(教育) [jiàoyù]: to educate, education

練習 (练习) Exercises

1. 找出有下面語法的句子：著；過；把……；往(向) + Direction/location 拐(轉)
   找出有下面语法的句子：着；过；把……；往(向) + Direction/location 拐(转)
2. 用你自己的話說說"守株待兔"的故事。
   用你自己的话说说"守株待兔"的故事。
3. 請用"守株待兔"造一個句子或者說一個守株待兔的例子。
   请用"守株待兔"造一个句子或者说一个守株待兔的例子。
4. "守株待兔"的故事，告訴了我們什麼?
   "守株待兔"的故事，告诉了我们什么?

練習 (练习) ACTIVITIES

I. 聽力練習 (听力练习)

5-1 In the blanks provided, write the Pinyin for the words you hear:

1. _____ 忘了要在媽媽回來以前 _____ 作業 _____ _____， _____ 衣服 _____ _____， _____ 門窗 _____ _____ 。
   _____ 忘了要在妈妈回来以前 _____ 作业 _____ _____， _____ 衣服 _____ _____， _____ 门窗 _____ _____ 。
2. 你有沒有去 _____ 中國店 _____ _____ _____?
   你有没有去 _____ 中国店 _____ _____ _____?
3. 他等公共汽車 _____ _____ _____ _____ _____?
   他等公共汽车 _____ _____ _____ _____ _____?
4. 沿 [yán](along) _____ 這條街道 _____ _____ _____ _____ 走，過三個 _____ _____ _____ 右 _____，你就能到圖書館了。
   沿 [yán](along) _____ 这条街道 _____ _____ _____ _____ 走，过三个 _____ _____ _____ 右 _____，你就能到图书馆了。

5. 這輛車 _____ 那輛車 _____ _____ 貴，開 _____ _____ _____ 那輛車 _____，可是看 _____ _____ 沒有那輛車 _____。

这辆车 _____ 那辆车 _____ _____ 贵，开 _____ _____ _____ 那辆车 _____，可是看 _____ _____ 没有那辆车 _____。

5-2 Listen to the following passage then answer the questions orally:

Useful words and expressions:

猜(猜) [cāi]: to guess

字謎(字谜) [zìmí]: riddle of a Chinese character

提醒(提醒) [tíxǐng]: to remind

聰明(聪明) [cōngming]: smart, clever

剩下來(剩下来) [shèngxiàlái]: remaining

答案(答案) [dá'àn]: answer

(繁體字 **Traditional Character Version**)

昨天中文課下課以後，小美問大中有沒有猜過字謎，大中說沒有。小美就給大中一個字謎讓他猜猜。小美的字謎是："水池的中間沒有水，土地的上面沒有土。"大中看著字謎想了很久，可是還是猜不出來是什麼字。小美提醒大中，"水池的中間沒有水"就是把"池"這個字的三點水拿走，"土地的上面沒有土"就是把"地"這個字裡面的土拿走。大中說他知道了，把池字裡面的水拿走，把地字裡面的土拿走，剩下來的字就一樣了。這個字謎的答案是"也"字。大中說，原來字謎不難，他想了想，也給小美一個字謎："我沒有，他有；天沒有，地有"。小美說大中很聰明，這個字謎的答案跟第一個字謎的答案一樣。你知道為什麼嗎?

(简体字 **Simplified Character Version**)

昨天中文课下课以后，小美问大中有没有猜过字谜，大中说没有。小美就给大中一个字谜让他猜猜。小美的字谜是：“水池的中间没有水，土地的上面没有土。”大中看着字谜想了很久，可是还是猜不出来是什么字。小美提醒大中，“水池的中间没有水”就是把“池”这个字的三点水拿走，“土地的上面没有土”就是把“地”这个字里面的土拿走。大中说他知道了，把池字里面的水拿走，把地字里面的土拿走，剩下来的字就一样了。这个字谜的答案是“也”字。大中说，原来字谜不难，他想了想，也给小美一个字谜：“我没有，他有；天没有，地有”。小美说大中很聪明，这个字谜的答案跟第一个字谜的答案一样。你知道为什么吗？

問題(问题)：

1. 中文課下課以後，小美跟大中一起做什麼了？
   中文课下课以后，小美跟大中一起做什么了？
2. 小美的字謎是什麼？為什麼是這個答案？
   小美的字谜是什么？为什么是这个答案？
3. 大中的字謎是什麼？答案是什麼？應該怎麼猜大中的字謎？
   大中的字谜是什么？答案是什么？应该怎么猜大中的字谜？

5-3 Read the following lyric, paying special attention to the tones and the rhythm:

Cǎi Sāng Zǐ	采桑子 采桑子
(Xīn Qìjí)	(辛棄疾) (辛弃疾)
Shàonián bù shí chóu zīwèi,	少年不識愁滋味， 少年不识愁滋味，
Ài shàng céng lóu,	愛上層樓， 爱上层楼，
Ài shàng céng lóu,	愛上層樓， 爱上层楼，
Wèi fù xīn cí qiǎng shuō chóu.	為賦新詞強說愁。 为赋新词强说愁。
Rújīn shí jìn chóu zīwèi,	如今識盡愁滋味， 如今识尽愁滋味，
Yù shuō huán xiū,	欲說還休， 欲说还休，
Yù shuō huán xiū,	欲說還休， 欲说还休，
Què dào tiān liáng hǎo gè qiū.	卻道天涼好個秋。 却道天凉好个秋。

To the tune of **Cai Sang Zi**
(Xin, Qiji)

When I was young, I did not know the taste of melancholy,
I liked climbing up the storied tower,
I liked climbing up the storied tower,
In my new lyrics, I am obliged to imbue them with the taste of sadness.

But now I have tasted all the bitterness,
About to speak of them, I stop,
About to speak of them, I stop,
Instead, I say, "Days so cool – What a wonderful autumn."

Practice: What are the rhyming words in this lyric? Write them out in Pinyin:

押 __________ 韻，押韻的字有： ______________________________ 。
押 __________ 韵，押韵的字有： ______________________________ 。

II. 漢字練習 (汉字练习)

5-4 Read the following words, phrases, and sentences:

趕 赶	鬧 闹
趕上 赶上	鬧笑話 闹笑话
終於趕上了 终于赶上了	鬧了笑話 闹了笑话
他們終於趕上飛機了 他们终于赶上飞机了	鬧了不少笑話 闹了不少笑话
他們終於趕上飛往北京的飛機了 他们终于赶上飞往北京的飞机了	他們在中國鬧了不少笑話 他们在中国闹了不少笑话

Now try to use the following characters to create words, phrases, and then sentences:

1. 陰 阴	2. 終 终	3. 誤 误	4. 情 情	5. 津 津	6. 界 界
7. 團 团	8. 笑 笑	9. 繁 繁	10. 榮 荣	11. 挺 挺	12. 值 值

5-5 Form groups of three and create phrases with the following words (pay attention to the various usages of each word):

Example: 樣： 怎麼樣 幾樣菜 跟以前一樣
樣：怎么样 几样菜 跟以前一样

1. 點：
   点：

2. 上：
   上：

3. 本：
   本：
4. 班：
   班：
5. 再：
   再：
6. 熱：
   热：
7. 好：
   好：
8. 味：
   味：
9. 開：
   开：
10. 眼：
    眼：

III. 語法練習 (语法练习)

Read aloud the passage with your instructor and fill in the blanks, then answer the questions orally:

Useful words and expressions:

王府井大街(王府井大街) [Wángfǔjǐng dàjiē]: (name of a renowned commercial street in Beijing)
秀水街(秀水街) [Xiùshuǐjiē]: (name of a famous commercial street in Beijing)
禮物(礼物) [lǐwù]: gift
有名(有名) [yǒumíng]: renowned, famous
商業街(商业街) [shāngyèjiē]: commercial street
天安門廣場(天安门广场) [Tiān'ānmén guǎngchǎng]: Tiananmen Square
寬敞(宽敞) [kuānchǎng]: spacious, wide
各種各樣(各种各样) [gèzhǒng gèyàng]: various
步行街(步行街) [bùxíngjiē]: pedestrian street
自由(自由) [zìyóu]: freedom
快餐(快餐) [kuàicān]: fast food

老字號(老字号) [lǎozìhào]: brand-name
茶葉(茶叶) [cháyè]: tea
文物(文物) [wénwù]: antique; artifacts
繼續(继续) [jìxù]: to continue
逛(逛) [guàng]: to wander around
總是(总是) [zǒngshì]: always
小商品(小商品) [xiǎo shāngpǐn]: small commodity
南北雜貨(南北杂货) [nánběi záhuò]: sundry goods from everywhere
飾品(饰品) [shìpǐn]: accessory
仿古(仿古) [fǎnggǔ]: imitation antique
工藝品(工艺品) [gōngyìpǐn]: craft art
紀念品(纪念品) [jìniànpǐn]: souvenir
應有盡有(应有尽有) [yīngyǒu jìnyǒu]: to have everything that one expects to find
討價還價(讨价还价) [tǎojià huánjià]: to bargain
滿載而歸(满载而归) [mǎnzài'érguī]: to return with fruitful results, to return satisfied

1. 我這次去北京旅遊，給美國的朋友們買了一些中國的禮物帶回去。聽北京的朋友們說，王府井大街和秀水街都是買東西的好地方，所以我去這兩個地方走了走，______ ______ 眼界，也 ______ ______ (to buy) 不少東西。

   我这次去北京旅游，给美国的朋友们买了一些中国的礼物带回去。听北京的朋友们说，王府井大街和秀水街都是买东西的好地方，所以我去这两个地方走了走，______ ______ 眼界，也 ______ ______ (to buy) 不少东西。

2. 聽說王府井大街是北京 ______ (the most) 有名的商業街。大街 ______ 天安門廣場很近。從天安門廣場前面 ______ 東走，經過兩條大街 ______ 北 ______ 就是王府井大街了。王府井大街很長也很寬敞。大街的兩邊有很多各種各樣的商店。

   听说王府井大街是北京 ______ (the most) 有名的商业街。大街 ______ 天安门广场很近。从天安门广场前面 ______ 东走，经过两条大街 ______ 北 ______ 就是王府井大街了。王府井大街很长也很宽敞。大街的两边有很多各种各样的商店。

3. 這裡有全國 ______ 大的 (the biggest) 書店和照相館，有中國的餐館和外國的快餐店，還有不少老字號商店，比如藥店、帽店、茶葉店和文物店等等。王府井是步行街，沒有車能開 ______ ______ (to enter)，人們可以在路上自由地走。我逛了逛，還 ______ 我的照相機拿 ______ ______ (use 把) (to take out)，______ 漂亮的王府井大街照了下來 (use 把)。

   这里有全国 ______ 大的 (the biggest) 书店和照相馆，有中国的餐馆和外国的快餐店，还有不少老字号商店，比如药店、帽店、茶叶店和文物店等等。王府井是步行街，没有车能开 ______ ______ (to enter)，人们可以在路上自由地走。我逛了逛，还 ______ 我的照相机拿 ______ ______ (use 把) (to take out)，______ 漂亮的王府井大街照了下来 (use 把)。

4. 從王府井大街走出來繼續 ______ 東走，經過三條大街再 ______ 北 ______ (to turn north) 就到秀水街了。秀水街 ______ 王府井大街短 (shorter)，也 ______ ______ 王府井大街那麼寬敞 (not so . . . as . . .)，但是街上的人跟王府井大街 ______ ______ 多(the same as)。

   从王府井大街走出来继续 ______ 东走，经过三条大街再 ______ 北 ______ (to turn north) 就到秀水街了。秀水街 ______ 王府井大街短 (shorter)，也 ______ ______ 王府井大街那么宽敞 (not so . . . as . . .)，但是街上的人跟王府井大街 ______ ______ 多 (the same as)。

5. 因為逛街的人太多，總是有人從鏡頭前走 ______ ______ (to walk by)，我拿著照相機拿了五分鐘，才能照到一張相片。不 ______ (like) 王府井大街，秀水街上賣的主要是小商品，南北雜貨從穿的衣服，用的飾品到仿古的工藝品、小紀念品應有盡有。會討價還價的人總是能在這兒買到很便宜的小東西。

   因为逛街的人太多，总是有人从镜头前走 ______ ______ (to walk by)，我拿着照相机拿了五分钟，才能照到一张相片。不 ______ (like) 王府井大街，秀水街上卖的主要是小商品，南北杂货从穿的衣服，用的饰品到仿古的工艺品、小纪念品应有尽有。会讨价还价的人总是能在这儿买到很便宜的小东西。

6. 我在王府井大街和秀水街，給爸爸、媽媽、還有朋友們買了很多禮物，滿載而歸。下次來北京我一定還要到這兒來。

   我在王府井大街和秀水街，给爸爸、妈妈、还有朋友们买了很多礼物，满载而归。下次来北京我一定还要到这儿来。

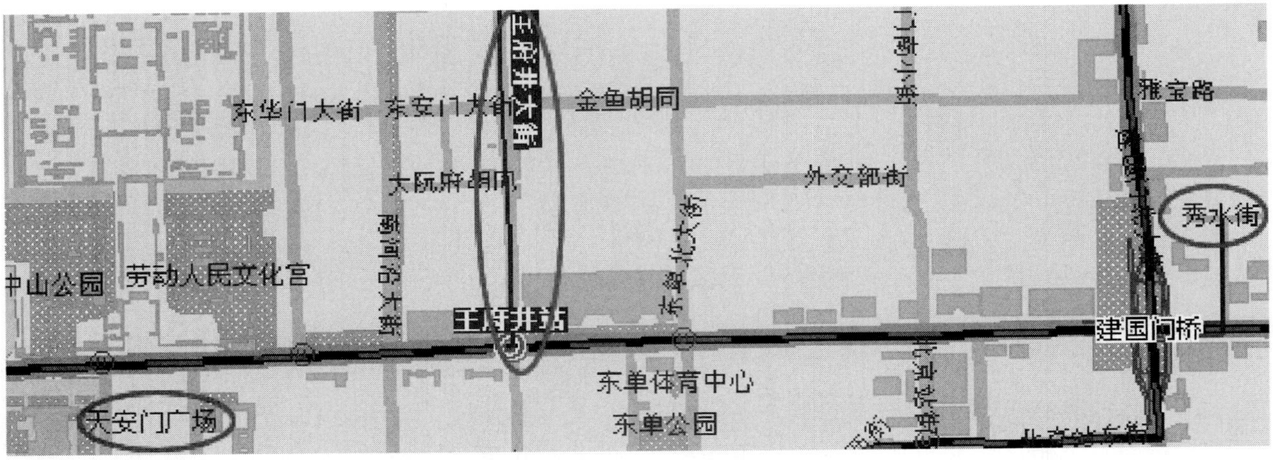

問題(问题)：

1. 王府井大街和秀水街為什麼這麼有名？
   王府井大街和秀水街为什么这么有名？
2. 從天安門廣場到王府井應該怎麼走？
   从天安门广场到王府井应该怎么走？
3. 王府井大街上有些什麼？
   王府井大街上有些什么？
4. 從王府井大街到秀水街應該怎麼走？
   从王府井大街到秀水街应该怎么走？
5. 秀水街跟王府井大街有什麼不一樣的嗎？
   秀水街跟王府井大街有什么不一样的吗？
6. 從上面的故事中找出這一課的主要語法 (e.g. 結果補語 resultative complement; 把 sentences; the aspects 了，著，and 過；有(多) + adj; ask and give directions; 比較 comparison: 比較，最，更)。

   从上面的故事中找出这一课的主要语法 (e.g. 结果补语 resultative complement; 把 sentences; the aspects 了，着，and 过；有(多) + adj; ask and give directions; 比较 comparison: 比较，最，更)。

IV. 交際活動 (交际活动)

Read aloud the passage with the instructor, then answer the questions orally:

Useful words and expressions:

有錢人(有钱人) [yǒuqiánrén]: rich man
瞧不起(瞧不起) [qiáobuqǐ]: to look down on
行禮(行礼) [xínglǐ]: to salute
片(片) [piàn]: (measure word/classifier for field)
生氣(生气) [shēngqì]: to get angry
灰溜溜(灰溜溜) [huīliūliū]: dejected, crestfallen
勢利(势利) [shìlì]: snobbish
窮人(穷人) [qióngrén]: poor people
經過(经过) [jīngguò]: to pass
農夫(农夫) [nóngfū]: farmer, peasant

1. 從前有一個有錢人，非常勢利。他瞧不起窮人，還要窮人在見到他的時候向他行禮。有一天這個有錢人騎著馬經過一片農田，他見到有一個農夫正坐在農田的旁邊休息。農夫看到有錢人的時候沒有走開，也沒有站起來向有錢人行禮。

   从前有一个有钱人，非常势利。他瞧不起穷人，还要穷人在见到他的时候向他行礼。有一天这个有钱人骑着马经过一片农田，他见到有一个农夫正坐在农田的旁边休息。农夫看到有钱人的时候没有走开，也没有站起来向有钱人行礼。

2. 這個有錢人很生氣，叫人把農夫帶過來，問農夫為什麼不行禮。農夫問："我為什麼要向你行禮呢?" 有錢人說："因為我比你有錢。" 農夫又說："那是你的錢，又不是我的錢。我不用向你行禮。" 有錢人說："那我把我的錢給你一半，你會向我行禮嗎?" 農夫說："那麼我的錢就跟你的錢一樣多了，我為什麼還要向你行禮呢?"

   这个有钱人很生气，叫人把农夫带过来，问农夫为什么不行礼。农夫问："我为什么要向你行礼呢?" 有钱人说："因为我比你有钱。" 农夫又说："那是你的钱，又不是我的钱。我不用向你行礼。" 有钱人说："那我把我的钱给你一半，你会向我行礼吗?" 农夫说："那么我的钱就跟你的钱一样多了，我为什么还要向你行礼呢?"

3. 有錢人又説："好吧。我把我的錢全都給你，現在你應該向我行禮了吧。"農夫最後説："那麼我的錢就比你的錢多了，我是有錢人，你是窮人，我就更不用向你行禮了!"有錢人不知道説什麼好，只好騎著馬灰溜溜地走了。

   有钱人又说："好吧。我把我的钱全都给你，现在你应该向我行礼了吧。"农夫最后说："那么我的钱就比你的钱多了，我是有钱人，你是穷人，我就更不用向你行礼了!"有钱人不知道说什么好，只好骑着马灰溜溜地走了。

問題(问题)：

1. 有錢人要窮人見到他的時候做什麼?
   有钱人要穷人见到他的时候做什么?
2. 有錢人是在哪兒見到農夫的?
   有钱人是在哪儿见到农夫的?
3. 有錢人第一次要把多少錢給農夫? 農夫會向有錢人行禮嗎? 為什麼?
   有钱人第一次要把多少钱给农夫? 农夫会向有钱人行礼吗? 为什么?
4. 有錢人又要把多少錢給農夫? 農夫有沒有向有錢人行禮? 為什麼?
   有钱人又要把多少钱给农夫? 农夫有没有向有钱人行礼? 为什么?
5. 最後有錢人怎麼樣了?
   最后有钱人怎么样了?
6. 從上面的故事中找出這一課的主要語法。
   从上面的故事中找出这一课的主要语法。

文化知識 (文化知识) Culture Link

文化點滴 (文化点滴) CULTURE NOTES

中國的交通 (中国的交通) [Zhōngguó de jiāotōng] Transportation in China

Since the 1950s, China has formed a comprehensive transportation system, including traditional transportation options such as railways, air travel, and waterways, as well as relatively new transportation options such highways and subways.

Railways: With over 100,000 kilometers of track in total, China has the most extensive railway network in the world. In China, there is a north-south trunk line with Beijing as its hub, and an east-west trunk line with 鄭州(郑州) [Zhèngzhōu] as its hub. The latter extends westward reaching to the railways in Kazakhstan. Thus Asia and Europe are connected by railways from 連雲港(连云港) [Liányúngǎng] in China to Rotterdam in the Netherlands. Furthermore, new railway lines have been built in mountainous areas. Among them, the 青藏鐵路(青藏铁路) [Qīngzàng tiělù] (Qinghai-Tibet railway) is the first railway to connect inland China with Tibet, which due to its altitude and terrain is the last region in China to be accessible by rail. The 青藏鐵路(青藏铁路) is the world's highest railway.

Air Travel: Between 1949 and 1978, China invested several billion RMB in building or expanding a number of airports, which has established a foundation for air travel. In 2005 China had an estimated 250 airports. Radiating from Beijing, China has more than 1,000 domestic airlines connecting hundreds of major cites. There are also about 130 international airlines reaching more than 40 countries.

Waterways: China's mainland coast is over 18,000 kilometers long, and has over 220,000 kilometers of rivers. Its excellent natural conditions make it convenient for developing inland river transportation systems and ocean shipping. Among the main inland rivers, the 長江(长江) [Chángjiāng] (Yangtze River) is regarded as the 黃金水道 [huángjīn shuǐdào] (golden waterway), being used for both freight and passenger

Taxis line up to pick up passengers in front of the Shenzhen Railway Station. In order to keep traffic flowing in the busy railway station, taxis are restricted to particular routes when they enter and exit. Generally speaking, taxis are plentiful, and it's very convenient to use a taxi to travel within or between cities in China.

Subways in China are generally very new and clean. Because the ticket prices are relatively higher, subways are not as crowded as buses.

transportation. Ocean shipping offshore of China is divided into the northern zone and the southern zone. 上海 [Shànghǎi] and 大連(大连) [Dàlián] are the main shipping hubs in the northern zone, while the southern hubs are 廣州(广州) [Guǎngzhōu] (Guangzhou) and 香港 [Xiānggǎng] (Hong Kong).

Highways: In 2005, mainland China had 1.21 million kilometers of highways, the second largest total of all countries. These are linked by an increasing network of highways and expressways. Nationwide highways often begin with the letter **G**, which stands for 國(国) (country), followed by three numerals, e.g.: G107. National Highways stretch to all four corners of mainland China, 新疆 [Xīnjiāng], 西藏 [Xīzàng] (Tibet),

黑龍江(黑龙江) [Hēilóngjiāng], and the south and southeastern Chinese coast. Nowadays most counties and townships are within reach via highway.

Subways: There are a growing number of metropolitan areas in China that have subways, most of which have been constructed in recent years. Beijing's subway system was the first such system in mainland China. Construction began in 1965, and the system became operational in 1969. In Hong Kong, the subway system, which was opened in 1979, is called the MTR (Mass Transit Railway). In Taiwan, it is the 捷運(捷运) [Jiéyùn] (Mass Rapid Transit, MRT), and began to operate in 1996. 上海 [Shànghǎi], 廣州(广州) [Guǎngzhōu], 天津 [Tiānjīn], 深圳 [Shēnzhèn], and 南京 [Nánjīng] are other cities with subway systems. Many other cities are currently constructing or planning to construct their own subway systems.

問題討論 (问题讨论) Discussion Questions

1. 除了文章中提到的交通運輸方式以外，你還知道別的什麼交通方式嗎？請跟同學們談談。

   除了文章中提到的交通运输方式以外，你还知道别的什么交通方式吗？请跟同学们谈谈。

   Besides the transportation means mentioned in the article, what others do you know of? Please share what you know with your classmates.

2. 在你的國家，主要的交通方式是什麼？請與中國的交通方式做一個比較。

   在你的国家，主要的交通方式是什么？请与中国的交通方式做一个比较。

   What are the major means of transportation in your country? Please compare them with transportation in China.

3. 你聽過中國的公共汽車或者自行車嗎？請說說你的經驗或者有關的故事。

   你听过中国的公共汽车或者自行车吗？请说说你的经验或者有关的故事。

   Have you heard about the use of buses and bicycles in China? Please share with your classmates any interesting stories you have personally experienced or have heard about buses or bicycles in China.

趣味中文 (趣味中文) FUN WITH CHINESE

趕鴨子上架
赶鸭子上架
To hurry the ducks onto the racks. It usually indicates somebody is pushed by force to get things done fast.

gǎn	yāzi	shàng	jià
趕	鴨子	上	架
赶	鸭子	上	架
hurry	duck	up	racks

問題討論 (问题讨论) Discussion Questions

1. Have you ever encountered any situations like 趕鴨子上架 (赶鸭子上架)? Please describe it to your classmates.
2. Please make a sentence by using 趕鴨子上架(赶鸭子上架).

行動吧! (行动吧!) LET'S GO!

北京酒店賓客滿意程度調查表 (北京酒店宾客满意程度调查表) Hotel Guest Satisfaction Survey

When 方小文 traveled to China during the summer vacation, he stayed at a hotel in Beijing. On the hotel desk, there was a note asking the guest to comment about the hotel's service. Let's read the note and help 方小文 figure out how to provide feedback to the hotel.

北京酒店宾客满意程度调查表

		满意	一般	不满意
1. 我们的酒店与您预期的相比如何?				
2. 您在以下各方面如何评价我们的员工?				
A. 微笑和迎接				
B. 友善和乐于助人				
C. 辨认客人				
3. 酒店员工的服务与效率如何?				
A. 经理				
B. 服务员				
C. 接线生				
D. 客房部				
E. 洗衣服务				
F. 商务中心				
G. 外币兑换服务				
4. 请告诉我们您对以下服务项目的评价:				
A. 入住服务				
B. 离店服务				
C. 清洁				
D. 维修				
E. 照明				
F. 餐饮				

您对酒店的意见或建议:

您的姓名: 联系方式:

Useful words and expressions:

賓客(宾客) [bīnkè]: guests
滿意(满意) [mǎnyì]: satisfaction
程度(程度) [chéngdù]: degree
調查表(调查表) [diàochábiǎo]: survey sheet
一般(一般) [yìbān]: neutral
不滿(不满) [bùmǎn]: unsatisfied
酒店(酒店) [jiǔdiàn]: hotel
預期(预期) [yùqī]: to expect
相比(相比) [xiāngbǐ]: to compare
如何(如何) [rúhé]: how
以下(以下) [yǐxià]: below; the following
方面(方面) [fāngmiàn]: aspect
評價(评价) [píngjià]: to evaluate
員工(员工) [yuángōng]: staff
微笑(微笑) [wēixiào]: smile
迎接(迎接) [yíngjiē]: to welcome
友善(友善) [yǒushàn]: friendly
樂於助人(乐于助人) [lèyúzhùrén]: to be happy to help others
辨認(辨认) [biànrèn]: to identify; recognize
客人(客人) [kèrén]: guest
效率(效率) [xiàolǜ]: efficiency
經理(经理) [jīnglǐ]: manager
接線生(接线生) [jiēxiànshēng]: telephone operator
客房(客房) [kèfáng]: guest room
洗衣(洗衣) [xǐyī]: laundry
商務(商务) [shāngwù]: business affairs
中心(中心) [zhōngxīn]: center
外幣(外币) [wàibì]: foreign currency
兌換(兑换) [duìhuàn]: to exchange
告訴(告诉) [gàosu]: to tell

項目(项目) [xiàngmù]: item; project
清潔(清洁) [qīngjié]: to clean
維修(维修) [wéixiū]: to maintain
照明(照明) [zhàomíng]: lighting
餐飲(餐饮) [cānyǐn]: food and beverages
意見(意见) [yìjiàn]: opinion; suggestion
建議(建议) [jiànyì]: recommendation
聯繫(联系) [liánxì]: contact
方式(方式) [fāngshì]: method

練習 (练习) Exercises

1. Translate the form into English.
2. Fill in the following blanks: If you are satisfied with the hotel's services but are not content with the lighting and food facilities, what would you like to write on the form?

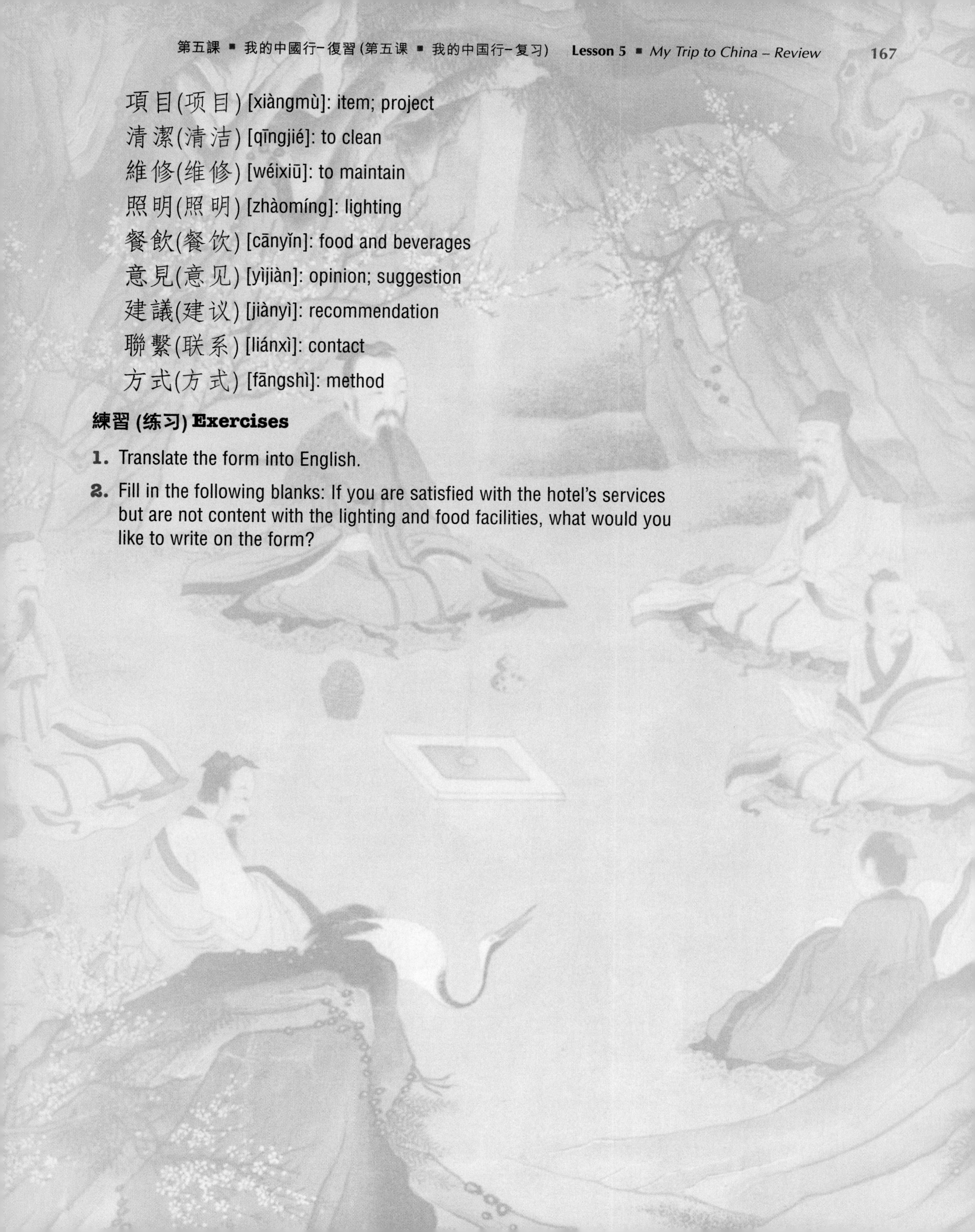

第六課
LESSON

6

我要去銀行開一個帳戶 (我要去银行开一个账户) I Am Going to the Bank to Open an Account

教學目標 (教学目标) OBJECTIVES

- Open a bank account
- Talk about interest rates and exchange rates

Banks in China play an important role in the country's economic development, as well as in daily life.

生詞 (生词) VOCABULARY

核心詞 (核心词) Core Vocabulary

TRADITIONAL	SIMPLIFIED	PINYIN		
1. 銀行	银行	yínháng	N.	bank
2. 開	开	kāi	V.	to open
3. 帳戶	账户	zhànghù	N.	account
4. 存	存	cún	V.	to deposit
5. 款	款	kuǎn	N.	money
6. 取	取	qǔ	V.	to withdraw
7. 方便	方便	fāngbiàn	Adj.	convenient
8. 利率	利率	lìlǜ	N.	interest rate
9. 高	高	gāo	Adj.	high
10. 儲蓄	储蓄	chǔxù	N. V.	savings to save (money)
11. 百分之……	百分之……	bǎifēnzhī . . .	Num.	. . . percent (%)
12. 利息	利息	lìxī	N.	interest
13. 支票	支票	zhīpiào	N.	check
14. 職員	职员	zhíyuán	N.	staff, employee
15. 低	低	dī	Adj.	low
16. 種	种	zhǒng	M.W.	kind
17. 差不多	差不多	chàbuduō		not very different, similar, about the same
18. 夠	够	gòu	Adj.	enough

TRADITIONAL	SIMPLIFIED	PINYIN		
19. 單子	单子	dānzi	N.	form
20. 填	填	tián	V.	to fill in/up
21. 千	千	qiān	Num.	thousand
22. 元	元	yuán	M.W.	dollar
23. 美金	美金	měijīn	N.	US Dollar
24. 寄	寄	jì	V.	to mail
25. 簿	簿	bù	N.	(check) book
26. 拿	拿	ná	V.	to take, fetch; to use
27. 取款卡	取款卡	qǔkuǎnkǎ	N.	ATM card
28. 自動	自动	zìdòng	Adj.	automatic
29. 取款機	取款机	qǔkuǎnjī	N.	banking machine, ATM
30. 現金	现金	xiànjīn	N.	cash
31. 申請	申请	shēnqǐng	N. V.	application to apply
32. 信用卡	信用卡	xìnyòngkǎ	N.	credit card
33. 當然	当然	dāngrán	Adv.	of course
34. 表	表	biǎo	N.	form
35. 換	换	huàn	V.	to change
36. 匯率	汇率	huìlǜ	N.	exchange rate
37. 兌換	兑换	duìhuàn	N. V.	exchange to exchange
38. 外幣	外币	wàibì	N.	foreign currency
39. 櫃台	柜台	guìtái	N.	counter

專名 (专名) Proper Nouns

TRADITIONAL	SIMPLIFIED	PINYIN		
1. 關京華	关京华	Guān Jīnghuá	N.	(name) Jinghua Guan
2. 方小琴	方小琴	Fāng Xiǎoqín	N.	(name) Xiaoqin Fang

補充詞 (补充词) Supplementary Vocabulary

TRADITIONAL	SIMPLIFIED	PINYIN		
1. 新台幣	新台币	Xīntáibì	N.	Taiwan Dollar
2. 港幣	港币	Gǎngbì	N.	Hong Kong Dollar
3. 美元	美元	Měiyuán	N.	US Dollar
4. 歐元	欧元	Ōuyuán	N.	Euro, currency used in the European Union
5. 英磅	英磅	Yīngbàng	N.	British Pound
6. 法郎	法郎	Fǎláng	N.	French Franc
7. 馬克	马克	Mǎkè	N.	Deutsch Mark
8. 盧布	卢布	Lúbù	N.	Russian Ruble
9. 日元	日元	Rìyuán	N.	Japanese Yen
10. 信用卡	信用卡	xìnyòngkǎ	N.	credit card
11. 簽證卡	签证卡	qiānzhèngkǎ	N.	Visa card
12. 萬事達卡	万事达卡	wànshìdákǎ	N.	Master card
13. 美國運通卡	美国运通卡	Měiguó yùntōngkǎ	N.	American Express card
14. 定期存款	定期存款	dìngqī cúnkuǎn	N.	certificate of deposit; fixed deposit
15. 活期存款	活期存款	huóqī cúnkuǎn	N.	current deposit

語文知識 (语文知识) LANGUAGE LINK

The Sentence Patterns provide models that will help you with the Language in Use section. In both sections, pay attention to the grammar points, vocabulary, and expressions.

句型 (句型) Sentence Patterns

A: 我要開一個支票帳戶。
我要开一个支票账户。
Wǒ yào kāi yíge zhīpiào zhànghù.

B: 好，這是開帳戶的單子，請你填一下。
好，这是开账户的单子，请你填一下。
Hǎo, zhè shì kāi zhànghù de dānzi, qǐng nǐ tián yíxià.

A: 今天的利率是多少?
今天的利率是多少?
Jīntiān de lìlǜ shì duōshao?

B: 百分之二點五。
百分之二点五。
Bǎi fēn zhī èr diǎn wǔ.

A: 美元換人民幣的匯率呢?
美元换人民币的汇率呢?
Měiyuán huàn Rénmínbì de huìlǜ ne?

B: 一比七點九八。
一比七点九八。
Yī bǐ qī diǎn jiǔ bā.

A: 兑換外幣的地方在哪兒?
兑换外币的地方在哪儿?
Duìhuàn wàibì de dìfang zài nǎr?

B: 在左邊的櫃台那兒。
在左边的柜台那儿。
Zài zuǒbiān de guìtái nàr.

課文: 我要去銀行開一個帳戶 (繁體字)
Language in Use: Traditional Character Version

SCENE 1: (在路上)

關京華: 小琴，我要去銀行開一個帳戶，這樣我存款、取款就方便多了。你知道哪家銀行比較好嗎?

方小琴: 我常常去大華銀行存款、取款。那兒的服務不錯，利率也比較高，現在儲蓄帳戶的利率是百分之三點二。

關京華: 那我就去大華銀行吧。

SCENE 2: (在銀行)

關京華: 先生，我想開一個有利息的支票帳戶。請問，有利息的支票帳戶利率是多少?

職員: 最近利率都比較低，今天是百分之二點六。

關京華: 怎麼這麼低呀? 我聽說是百分之三點二呢。

職員: 那是儲蓄帳戶，儲蓄帳戶的利率高一點兒，是百分之三點二。這種帳戶每個月可以開三張支票。您想開哪一種?

關京華: 我想一個月開三張支票差不多夠了。我就開一個儲蓄帳戶吧。

職員: 好，請把這張開帳戶的單子填一下，謝謝。請問您今天想存多少錢?

關京華: 我這兒是三千元美金。

職員: 好 …… 一個星期以後，您會收到我們給您寄去的支票簿和取款卡。您可以拿取款卡在自動取款機那兒取現金。

關京華: 我可以在你們這兒申請一張信用卡嗎?

職員: 當然可以。請把這張申請信用卡的表填一下。

關京華: 下個月我要去中國，要換一些人民幣。請問美金換人民幣的匯率是多少?

職員: 今天的匯率是一比七點九八。

關京華: 兌換外幣的地方在哪兒?

職員: 就在左邊的櫃台那兒。

關京華: 謝謝。再見。

课文: 我要去银行开一个账户 (简体字)
Language in Use: Simplified Character Version

SCENE 1: (在路上)

关京华：小琴，我要去银行开一个账户，这样我存款、取款就方便多了。你知道哪家银行比较好吗?

方小琴：我常常去大华银行存款、取款。那儿的服务不错，利率也比较高，现在储蓄账户的利率是百分之三点二。

关京华：那我就去大华银行吧。

SCENE 2: (在银行)

关京华：先生，我想开一个有利息的支票账户。请问，有利息的支票账户利率是多少?

职员：最近利率都比较低，今天是百分之二点六。

关京华：怎么这么低呀? 我听说是百分之三点二呢。

职员：那是储蓄账户，储蓄账户的利率高一点儿，是百分之三点二。这种账户每个月可以开三张支票。您想开哪一种?

关京华：我想一个月开三张支票差不多够了。我就开一个储蓄账户吧。

职员：好，请把这张开账户的单子填一下，谢谢。请问您今天想存多少钱?

关京华：我这儿是三千元美金。

职员：好 …… 一个星期以后，您会收到我们给您寄去的支票簿和取款卡。您可以拿取款卡在自动取款机那儿取现金。

关京华：我可以在你们这儿申请一张信用卡吗?

职员：当然可以。请把这张申请信用卡的表填一下。

关京华：下个月我要去中国，要换一些人民币。请问美金换人民币的汇率是多少?

职员：今天的汇率是一比七点九八。

关京华：兑换外币的地方在哪儿?

职员：就在左边的柜台那儿。

关京华：谢谢。再见。

注釋 (注释) LANGUAGE NOTES

1. 開 (开)

開(开) means "to open." It is used when opening a bank account 開銀行帳戶(开银行账户), writing a check 開支票(开支票), and writing an invoice 開發票(开发票) [kāi fāpiào].

2. 行 (行)

When used in "銀行(银行)," 行(行) is pronounced [háng]. When used as a noun in 旅行(旅行), and an adjective to mean "OK" or "Good," it is pronounced [xíng].

3. 帳 (賬) [帳 (账)]

Referring to "account," both 帳 and 賬 can be used in traditional character texts, i.e. 帳戶 or 賬戶. However, only 账 is used in simplified character text, i.e. 账户.

4. 那 (那)

那(那) means "then" or "in that case." It is often used in conversations to connect sentences.

5. 匯率/兌換率 (汇率/兑换率)

Both 匯率(汇率) and 兌換率(兑换率) are used in mainland China to mean "exchange rate." In Taiwan, 匯率(汇率) is more commonly used.

6. 取款機/提款機 (取款机/提款机)

Both 取款機(取款机) and 提款機(提款机) mean banking machine. 取款機(取款机) is used in mainland China while 提款機(提款机) is commonly used in Taiwan. Another term is 櫃員機(柜员机).

7. 取款卡/提款卡/借記卡 (取款卡/提款卡/借记卡)

取款卡(取款卡), 提款卡(提款卡), and 借記卡(借记卡) all refer to bank cards. 取款卡(取款卡) and 提款卡(提款卡) are ATM cards, and 借記卡(借记卡) is a debit card. Note that 提款卡(提款卡) is more commonly used in Taiwan.

語法 (语法) GRAMMAR

1. Various kinds of phrases

A phrase is a combination of words that are grammatically related. There are more than 10 kinds of phrases in Chinese which can be used as different parts of a sentence. The major types are juxtaposed phrases, endocentric phrases, Subj. + V. phrases, and V. + Obj. phrases.

A. Juxtaposed phrase:

This construction is formed by two or more words that are of the same quality and that may be connected by a conjunction (such as 和, 又……又) or a Chinese comma "、," or neither. Look at the following examples:

爸爸、媽媽 — 爸爸媽媽
爸爸、妈妈 — 爸爸妈妈

存款、取款 — 存款取款
存款、取款 — 存款取款

洗好、掛好 — 洗好掛好
洗好、挂好 — 洗好挂好

健康、年輕 — 健康年輕
健康、年轻 — 健康年轻

又拉又吹，又唱又跳，又睏又累
又拉又吹，又唱又跳，又困又累

認真地、努力地 — 認真(地)努力地
认真地、努力地 — 认真(地)努力地

Note:

- A juxtaposed construction can be used basically as any part of a sentence, depending on the category of the words.
- The order of the words can be reversed without affecting the meaning. However, some constructions have a fixed order, e.g. 父親母親(父亲母亲) (Chinese seldom use 母親父親(母亲父亲)).

B. Endocentric 偏正(偏正) [piānzhèng] phrase:

An endocentric construction is composed of a modifier 偏(偏) and the modified 正(正) (focus). For example,

Modifier	*the Modified*
支票 支票	帳戶 账户
今天的 今天的	匯率 汇率
自動 自动	取款機 取款机
認真地 认真地	學習 学习

Note:

- The order of words in an endocentric construction cannot be reversed because it indicates a fixed modifying relationship between the words.
- Similar to a compound phrase, an endocentric phrase can be used as any part of a sentence.

C. Subj. + V. phrase:

This kind of phrase is one in which the relationship between the components is like that between a subject and a verbal predicate. For example,

	Subj.	+	V.	
	我們		寄去	的支票簿
	我们		寄去	的支票簿
	你		會做飯	太好了
	你		会做饭	太好了
這件衣服	顏色		太深	
这件衣服	颜色		太深	
我覺得	這兒的服務		又快又好	
我觉得	这儿的服务		又快又好	

Note:

- The order of a Subj. + V. construction is fixed. The subject always precedes the verbal predicate.
- A Subj. + V. phrase can function as any part of a sentence.

D. V. + Obj. phrase:

A V. + Obj. phrase is formed by a transitive verb and a noun that serves as its object. Here are some examples:

V.	+	Obj.	
有		利息	的支票帳戶
有		利息	的支票账户
開		帳戶	的單子
开		账户	的单子
申請		信用卡	的表
申请		信用卡	的表
兌換		外幣	的地方
兑换		外币	的地方

Note:
- The order of a V. + Obj. phrase is fixed and cannot be changed.
- No conjunction should be used between the verb and its object.
- A particle 的 must be used after V. + Obj.

2. Ways to express percentage and proportion

The way to express percentage in Chinese is to use 百分之 plus the number of percentage. For example:

1% = 百分之一 (百分之一)
15% = 百分之十五 (百分之十五)
80% = 百分之八十 (百分之八十)
100% = 百分之百/百分之一百 (百分之百/百分之一百)

…… 分之 …… also applies to other fractions, such as one-third and three-fourths. The number before it is the denominator and the one after it is the numerator. Here are some examples:

$\frac{1}{3}$ = 三分之一 (三分之一)　　$\frac{3}{4}$ = 四分之三 (四分之三)

3. Decimals

A decimal number in Chinese is expressed by "A + 點 + B." Here A indicates the integer and B the decimal. For example:

2.5 = 二點五 (二点五)　　1.8 = 一點八 (一点八)
17.9 = 十七點九 (十七点九)　　26.9 = 二十六點九 (二十六点九)

4. Noun/Pronoun + 這兒/那兒(这儿/那儿)

When a noun or a pronoun is used to indicate a location, it is often followed by 這兒(这儿) or 那兒(那儿), depending on where the speaker is. If it is with or close to the speaker, 這兒(这儿) is used; otherwise, 那兒(那儿) should be used. Here are some examples:

我們這兒 (here with us)
我们这儿

他們那兒 (there with them)
他们那儿

櫃台這兒 (here at the counter)
柜台这儿

自動取款機那兒 (there at the ATM)
自动取款机那儿

Examples:

你的支票在我這兒。
你的支票在我这儿。
Your checks are here with me.

兑換外幣在櫃台那兒。
兑换外币在柜台那儿。
Go to the counter there to convert foreign exchange.

補充課文 (补充课文) SUPPLEMENTARY PRACTICE

This section will help you test your comprehension of the grammar and vocabulary you have learned in this lesson. Be prepared to answer questions about the meaning of the passage.

在美國交稅 Paying Tax in the U.S. (繁體字 Traditional Character Version)

小華:

你好!

時間過得真快，我來美國已經一年了。我在這兒除了學習以外，還辦了很多別的事兒，比如說開了銀行帳戶，申請了信用卡，買了健康保險等等。美國的一切對我來說都很新鮮，其中我最感興趣的是這兒的稅收制度。

美國的稅收制度跟中國的很不一樣。在日常生活中，無論是吃飯、買東西，還是銀行的存款利息、打工的收入等等都得交稅。怪不得人們把美國叫做"萬稅之國"呢。

在美國生活一定要了解美國的稅法，尤其是個人所得稅的稅收制度。美國的個人所得稅包括聯邦稅、州稅和市稅。聯邦稅的稅率全國都一樣，可是各個地方的州稅和市稅卻很不同：比如二零零四年加州的個人所得稅稅率高達百分之九點三，比賓州的百分之三點零七貴得多，有的州甚至沒有州稅；每個城市的市稅差別就更大了。至於個人的所得稅，有些要佔收入的三分之一甚至二分之一，非常高。

每年的四月十五號以前，這兒的人們都會忙著報稅或者申請退稅。人們可以把報稅或者退稅的申請表寄給稅務局，或者用電腦和報稅軟件通過網絡把申請表發送給稅務局。報稅的人可以用信用卡或者銀行帳戶付稅，稅務局也會用支票把退回來的稅寄給退稅申請人，方便極了。

我覺得我在這兒要學習的東西還很多，所以我得多看、多聽、多問、多想，這樣才能進步。好，下次再聊。

祝

好

小明

二零零七年十一月三日

補充課文 (补充课文) SUPPLEMENTARY PRACTICE

This section will help you test your comprehension of the grammar and vocabulary you have learned in this lesson. Be prepared to answer questions about the meaning of the passage.

在美国交税 Paying Tax in the U.S. (简体字 Simplified Character Version)

小华：

你好！

时间过得真快，我来美国已经一年了。我在这儿除了学习以外，还办了很多别的事儿，比如说开了银行账户，申请了信用卡，买了健康保险等等。美国的一切对我来说都很新鲜，其中我最感兴趣的是这儿的税收制度。

美国的税收制度跟中国的很不一样。在日常生活中，无论是吃饭、买东西，还是银行的存款利息、打工的收入等等都得交税。怪不得人们把美国叫做"万税之国"呢。

在美国生活一定要了解美国的税法，尤其是个人所得税的税收制度。美国的个人所得税包括联邦税、州税和市税。联邦税的税率全国都一样，可是各个地方的州税和市税却很不同：比如二零零四年加州的个人所得税税率高达百分之九点三，比宾州的百分之三点零七贵得多，有的州甚至没有州税；每个城市的市税差别就更大了。至于个人的所得税，有些要占收入的三分之一甚至二分之一，非常高。

每年的四月十五号以前，这儿的人们都会忙着报税或者申请退税。人们可以把报税或者退税的申请表寄给税务局，或者用电脑和报税软件通过网络把申请表发送给税务局。报税的人可以用信用卡或者银行账户付税，税务局也会用支票把退回来的税寄给退税申请人，方便极了。

我觉得我在这儿要学习的东西还很多，所以我得多看、多听、多问、多想，这样才能进步。好，下次再聊。

祝

好

小明

二零零七年十一月三日

Useful words and expressions:
辦(办) [bàn]: to handle, prepare
健康保險(健康保险) [jiànkāng bǎoxiǎn]: health insurance
一切(一切) [yíqiè]: whole, entire, all
對……來說(对……来说) [duì . . . láishuō]: as to . . . ; as for . . .
新鮮(新鲜) [xīnxiān]: novel, fresh
稅收制度(税收制度) [shuìshōu zhìdù]: tax system
無論(无论) [wúlùn]: no matter what
收入(收入) [shōurù]: income
交稅(交税) [jiāoshuì]: to pay tax
怪不得(怪不得) [guàibudé]: no wonder
萬(万) [wàn]: ten thousand
聯邦稅(联邦税) [liánbāngshuì]: federal tax
州稅(州税) [zhōushuì]: state tax
市稅(市税) [shìshuì]: city tax
稅率(税率) [shuìlǜ]: tax rate
卻(却) [què]: but
達(达) [dá]: to reach, go to
賓州(宾州) [Bīnzhōu]: State of Pennsylvania
差別(差别) [chābié]: difference
交(交) [jiāo]: to submit, pay
至於(至于) [zhìyú]: as to, as for
佔(占) [zhàn]: account for, occupy
甚至(甚至) [shènzhì]: even
報稅(报税) [bàoshuì]: to declare tax
退稅(退税) [tuìshuì]: to refund tax
申請表(申请表) [shēnqǐng biǎo]: application form
稅務局(税务局) [shuìwùjú]: tax bureau
軟件(软件) [ruǎnjiàn]: software
通過(通过) [tōngguò]: via, through
網絡(网络) [wǎngluò]: internet
發送(发送) [fāsòng]: to send out

練習 (练习) Exercises

1. 到美國以後，除了學習以外，小明還做了什麼別的事?
   到美国以后，除了学习以外，小明还做了什么别的事?

2. 為什麼人們把美國叫做“萬稅之國”?
   为什么人们把美国叫做“万税之国”?

3. 在美國，稅率怎麼樣? 人們怎麼報稅?
   在美国，税率怎么样? 人们怎么报税?

成語故事(成语故事) IDIOM STORY

井底之蛙 [井底之蛙] [jǐng dǐ zhī wā]

Meaning: A frog in a well

Usage: A person with a very limited outlook

Example: 你真是一個“井底之蛙”，不知道現在中國那兒已經有很多人使用信用卡了。

你真是一个“井底之蛙”，不知道现在中国那儿已经有很多人使用信用卡了。

Pay attention to the usages of various phrases, expression of percentages, portions, decimals, and 這兒(这儿)，那兒(那儿):

(繁體字 **Traditional Character Version**)

從前，一個井裡住著一隻青蛙。有一天，青蛙在井邊碰到了一隻從海裡來的大海龜。青蛙就對海龜說：

“你看，我住在這裡多快樂！高興的時候，就在井邊玩兒；累了的時候，就在井裡睡覺。看看那些小魚小蝦，誰也比不上我。我是這兒的主人，在這個井裡舒服極了。你要不要下來到我這兒玩兒呢?”

海龜聽了青蛙的話，很想進去看看。可是它才把左腳伸進井裡，右腳就已經絆住了。它退出水井，問青蛙：“你見過大海嗎?”青蛙說：“我沒見過大海，不過我這兒一定比大海那兒舒服。”海龜笑了笑，把大海的情形告訴青蛙說：

“這個井的大小還不及大海的百萬分之一。大海可以大到幾千里，可以深到幾千丈。下大雨的時候，大海的水漲不到零點一米；天旱的時候，大海的水也下降不到零點二米。所以大海是不受旱澇影響的。住在那樣的大海裡，才是真的快樂呢!”

井蛙聽了海龜的話以後，吃驚地說不出話來了。

(简体字 **Simplified Character Version**)

从前，一个井里住着一只青蛙。有一天，青蛙在井边碰到了一只从海里来的大海龟。青蛙就对海龟说：

"你看，我住在这里多快乐！高兴的时候，就在井边玩儿；累了的时候，就在井里睡觉。看看那些小鱼小虾，谁也比不上我。我是这儿的主人，在这个井里舒服极了。你要不要下来到我这儿玩儿呢？"

海龟听了青蛙的话，很想进去看看。可是它才把左脚伸进井里，右脚就已经绊住了。它退出水井，问青蛙："你见过大海吗？"青蛙说："我没见过大海，不过我这儿一定比大海那儿舒服。"海龟笑了笑，把大海的情形告诉青蛙说：

"这个井的大小还不及大海的百万分之一。大海可以大到几千里，可以深到几千丈。下大雨的时候，大海的水涨不到零点一米；天旱的时候，大海的水也下降不到零点二米。所以大海是不受旱涝影响的。住在那样的大海里，才是真的快乐呢！"

井蛙听了海龟的话以后，吃惊地说不出话来了。

Useful words and expressions:
井(井) [jǐng]: well
青蛙(青蛙) [qīngwā]: frog
海龜(海龟) [hǎiguī]: turtle
魚(鱼) [yú]: fish
蝦(虾) [xiā]: shrimp
主人(主人) [zhǔrén]: master
腳(脚) [jiǎo]: foot
絆(绊) [bàn]: to stumble
退出(退出) [tuìchū]: to step back, retreat
情形(情形) [qíngxíng]: situation
百萬(百万) [bǎiwàn]: million
廣大(广大) [guǎngdà]: broad
深度(深度) [shēndù]: depth
丈(丈) [zhàng]: unit of length (=3.3 meters)
漲(涨) [zhǎng]: to rise
米(米) [mǐ]: meter
旱(旱) [hàn]: drought
降(降) [jiàng]: to drop
受……影響(受……影响) [shòu . . . yǐngxiǎng]: to be affected by . . .
澇(涝) [lào]: flood
吃驚(吃惊) [chījīng]: to startle

練習 (练习) Exercises

1. 找出有下面語法的句子: various phrases, expression of percentage, portions, decimals, and 這兒, 那兒

   找出有下面语法的句子: various phrases, expression of percentage, portions, decimals, and 这儿, 那儿

2. 用你自己的話說說"井底之蛙"的故事。
   用你自己的话说说"井底之蛙"的故事。

3. 請用"井底之蛙"造一個句子或者說一個井底之蛙的例子。
   请用"井底之蛙"造一个句子或者说一个井底之蛙的例子。

4. "井底之蛙"的故事, 告訴了我們什麼?
   "井底之蛙"的故事, 告诉了我们什么?

練習 (练习) ACTIVITIES

I. 聽力練習 (听力练习)

6-1 關京華(关京华) went to the bank yesterday. Today in class, he is sharing his experience. Listen, then mark the correct statements with a "✔" and the incorrect statements with a "✗".

1. ____ 關京華去銀行開了一個支票帳戶和一個儲蓄帳戶。
   ____ 关京华去银行开了一个支票账户和一个储蓄账户。
2. ____ 美華銀行的服務不太好。
   ____ 美华银行的服务不太好。
3. ____ 儲蓄帳戶沒有利息。
   ____ 储蓄账户没有利息。
4. ____ 現在支票帳戶的利率是百分之二點八。
   ____ 现在支票账户的利率是百分之二点八。
5. ____ 下個星期關京華就能收到取款卡了。
   ____ 下个星期关京华就能收到取款卡了。
6. ____ 美華銀行可以換人民幣。
   ____ 美华银行可以换人民币。

6-2 Listen and complete the following sentences in Pinyin:

1. 因為關京華要 ____ ____、____ ____，所以他去銀行開了帳戶。
   因为关京华要 ____ ____、____ ____，所以他去银行开了账户。
2. 小琴覺得美華銀行的 ____ ____ 很好。
   小琴觉得美华银行的 ____ ____ 很好。
3. 最近的 ____ ____ 很低。
   最近的 ____ ____ 很低。
4. 關京華還在銀行 ____ ____ 了信用卡。
   关京华还在银行 ____ ____ 了信用卡。
5. 有了取款卡，他就可以在 ____ ____ ____ ____ ____ 那兒存款、取款了。
   有了取款卡，他就可以在 ____ ____ ____ ____ ____ 那儿存款、取款了。

6-3 Read the following lyric, paying special attention to the tones and the rhythm:

Yú Zhī Zǐ	漁枝子 渔枝子
(Zhāng Zhìhé)	(張志和) (张志和)
Xīsài shān qián báilù fēi,	西塞山前白鷺飛， 西塞山前白鹭飞，
Táohuā liúshuǐ guìyú féi,	桃花流水鱖魚肥。 桃花流水鳜鱼肥。
Qīng ruò lì.	青箬笠， 青箬笠，
Lǜ suō yī,	綠蓑衣， 绿蓑衣，
Xiéfēng xìyǔ bù xū guī.	斜風細雨不須歸。 斜风细雨不须归。

To the tune of **Yu Zhizi**
(Zhang, Zhihe)

White egret is flying in front of Mount Xisai,
Peach flowers are blossoming, water is running and the mandarin fish is fat.
With dark green bamboo hat and green straw rain cape on,
I do not need to return home even when there is wind and drizzling rain.

Practice: What are the rhyming words in this lyric? Write them out in Pinyin:

押 ________ 韻，押韻的字有：______________________________。

押 ________ 韵，押韵的字有：______________________________。

II. 漢字練習 (汉字练习)

6-4 Read the following words, phrases, and sentences:

開 开	換 换
開支票 开支票	換人民幣 换人民币
開支票帳戶 开支票账户	美元換人民幣 美元换人民币
開一個支票帳戶 开一个支票账户	美元換人民幣的匯率 美元换人民币的汇率
開一個有利息的支票帳戶 开一个有利息的支票账户	美元換人民幣的匯率是多少 美元换人民币的汇率是多少
開一個有利息的支票帳戶很方便 开一个有利息的支票账户很方便	美元換人民幣的匯率是一比七點九八 美元换人民币的汇率是一比七点九八

Now try to use the following characters to make words, phrases, and then sentences:

1. 存 存	2. 取 取	3. 利 利	4. 儲 储	5. 之 之	6. 低 低
7. 種 种	8. 填 填	9. 金 金	10. 簿 簿	11. 動 动	12. 兑 兑

6-5 Form groups of two. Complete the following sentences with the help of the pictures provided:

Useful words and expressions:

百分之……，帳戶，支票，取款機，開，取款卡，填
百分之……，账户，支票，取款机，开，取款卡，填

1. **A:** 我可以去哪兒取款?
   B: 你可以拿____ ____ ____在自動____ ____ ____那兒取款。

   A: 我可以去哪儿取款?
   B: 你可以拿____ ____ ____在自动____ ____ ____那儿取款。

2. **A:** 這個帳戶怎麼用?
   B: 這個帳戶每個月可以____三張____ ____。

   A: 这个账户怎么用?
   B: 这个账户每个月可以____三张____ ____。

3. **A:** 請問，現在利率是多少?
   B: 這種帳戶的____ ____是____ ____ ____二點九 (2.9%)。

   A: 请问，现在利率是多少?
   B: 这种账户的____ ____是____ ____ ____二点九 (2.9%)。

4. A：我想申請信用卡。
   B：好，你把這張表____一下。

   A：我想申请信用卡。
   B：好，你把这张表____一下。

6-6 京華 wrote a note to 小琴 about his bank account. He cannot write traditional characters so he wrote the note in simplified form. 小琴 has not studied simplified characters. Can you help her? Circle all the simplified characters in this note and then write out the traditional forms:

学校旁边有一个大华银行。我在那儿开了一个储蓄账户、一个支票账户。大华银行离学校很近，我去存款、取款比较方便。我还有一张取款卡，可以在自动取款机那儿取款。我还申请了信用卡，下个星期就可以拿到了。因为我可能要去中国，所以今天我还在外币柜台那儿换了人民币。

1. ______ 2. ______ 3. ______ 4. ______ 5. ______
6. ______ 7. ______ 8. ______ 9. ______ 10. ______
11. ______ 12. ______ 13. ______ 14. ______ 15. ______
16. ______ 17. ______ 18. ______ 19. ______ 20. ______
21. ______

III. 語法練習 (语法练习)

6-7 The following underlined parts are different kinds of phrases. Please write the number of each phrase in the group to which it belongs:

1. 我搬來了床、書桌和電腦
   我搬来了床、书桌和电脑
2. 他有很多電子用品
   他有很多电子用品

3. 姐姐寄給我的照片
   姐姐寄给我的照片
4. 轉飛機的時候
   转飞机的时候
5. 我去拜訪以前的老師
   我去拜访以前的老师
6. 上海的小吃真棒!
   上海的小吃真棒!
7. 這是出租汽車站
   这是出租汽车站
8. 你喜歡的文學書
   你喜欢的文学书
9. 别忘了吃菜
   别忘了吃菜
10. 我沒有去過北京和長城
    我没有去过北京和长城

Juxtaposed phrase: ______________________________

Endocentric phrase: ______________________________

Subj. + V. phrase: ______________________________

V. + Obj. phrase: ______________________________

6-8 Please say the following in Chinese:

1. 15% ____________________
2. 1 : 2.5 ____________________
3. 28.3% ____________________
4. 9 : 47 ____________________
5. 34.6% ____________________
6. 1 : 3 : 8 ____________________

6-9 Fill in the table below with data describing the students in your class:

		人數 人数	全班學生數的 % 全班学生数的 %
全班學生人數 (全班学生人数) [quánbān xuésheng rénshù] *Number of students in the class*	男生人數 (男生人数)		
	女生人數 (女生人数)		
	男生：女生 (男生：女生)		
	華裔 (华裔) [Huáyì] (Chinese origin)		
	其他亞裔 (其他亚裔) [qítā Yàyì] (other Asians)		
	歐洲裔 (欧洲裔) [Ōuzhōuyì] (European origin)		
	非洲裔 (非洲裔) [Fēizhōuyì] (African origin)		
	華裔：其他亞裔：歐洲裔：非洲裔 (华裔：其他亚裔：欧洲裔：非洲裔)		
	一年級學生(一年级学生)		
	二年級學生(二年级学生)		
	三年級學生(三年级学生)		
	四年級學生(四年级学生)		
	一年級學生：二年級學生： 三年級學生：四年級學生 (一年级学生：二年级学生： 三年级学生：四年级学生)		

6-10 Look at the diagram below and form groups of three to answer the questions:

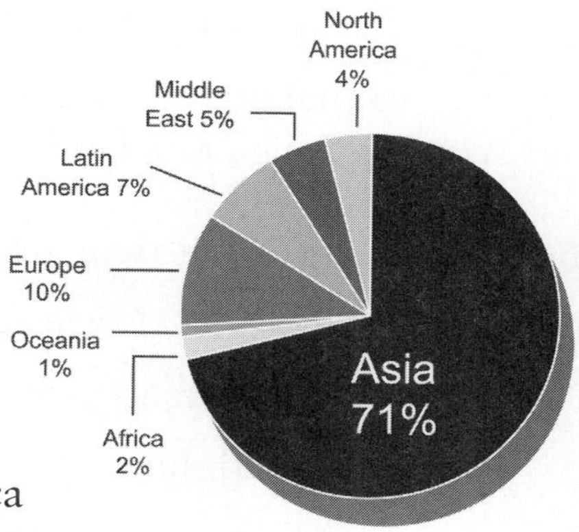

Useful words and expressions:

亞洲(亚洲) [Yàzhōu]: Asia
非洲(非洲) [Fēizhōu]: Africa
大洋洲(大洋洲) [Dàyángzhōu]: Oceania
北美洲(北美洲) [Běiměizhōu]: North America
中東(中东) [Zhōngdōng]: Middle East
拉丁美洲(拉丁美洲) [Lādīngměizhōu]: Latin America
歐洲(欧洲) [Ōuzhōu]: Europe

問題(问题):

1. 這個學校有百分之幾的非洲學生?
   这个学校有百分之几的非洲学生?
2. 學校有百分之幾的中東學生? 大洋洲學生呢?
   学校有百分之几的中东学生? 大洋洲学生呢?
3. 歐洲學生和亞洲學生的比例 ([bǐlì]: ratio) 是多少?
   欧洲学生和亚洲学生的比例 ([bǐlì]: ratio) 是多少?
4. 拉丁美洲學生和亞洲學生的比例是多少?
   拉丁美洲学生和亚洲学生的比例是多少?

IV. 交際活動 (交际活动)

6-11 Role play:

Work in pairs. Make up a dialogue between a customer and a bank clerk. The following may serve as clues:

1. Various kinds of bank accounts (e.g.: 儲蓄帳戶，支票帳戶)
   Various kinds of bank accounts (e.g.: 储蓄账户，支票账户)
2. Different interest rates (percentage) (e.g.: 利率，利息)
   Different interest rates (percentage) (e.g.: 利率，利息)
3. Depositing and withdrawing money (amount) (e.g.: 存款，取款)
   Depositing and withdrawing money (amount) (e.g.: 存款，取款)

4. Credit card, service (e.g.: 信用卡，服務)
   Credit card, service (e.g.: 信用卡，服务)

5. Exchange rate between US$ and another currency (ratio) (e.g.: 換，美金，匯率)
   Exchange rate between US$ and another currency (ratio) (e.g.: 换，美金，汇率)

6-12 Form groups of two, and describe the information shown in the chart below.

Useful words and expressions:

十(十) [shí]: ten
百(百) [bǎi]: hundred
千(千) [qiān]: thousand
萬(万) [wàn]: ten thousand
億(亿) [yì]: hundred million
兆(兆) [zhào]: ten billion

國家(国家) [guójiā]: country
面積(面积) [miànjī]: area
平方公里(平方公里) [píngfāng gōnglǐ]: square kilometer
水(水) [shuǐ]: water
人口(人口) [rénkǒu]: population
貨幣(货币) [huòbì]: currency

首都(首都) [shǒudū]: capital
華盛頓特區(华盛顿特区) [Huáshèngdùn tèqū]: Washington D.C.
渥太華(渥太华) [Wòtàihuá]: Ottawa
多倫多(多伦多) [Duōlúnduō]: Toronto
倫敦(伦敦) [Lúndūn]: London
巴黎(巴黎) [Bālí]: Paris
柏林(柏林) [Bólín]: Berlin
東京(东京) [Dōngjīng]: Tokyo

加元(加元) [Jiāyuán]: Canadian Dollar
英鎊(英镑) [Yīngbàng]: British Pound
歐元(欧元) [Ōuyuán]: Euro
日元(日元) [Rìyuán]: Japanese Yen

Useful grammar patterns:

左右，百分之……，比，最，第……位，M 換 N 的匯率是
左右，百分之……，比，最，第……位，M 换 N 的汇率是

國家 (国家)	中國 (中国)	美國 (美国)	加拿大 (加拿大)	英國 (英国)	法國 (法国)	德國 (德国)	日本 (日本)

首都 (首都)	北京 (北京)	華盛頓特區 (华盛顿特区)	渥太華 (渥太华)	倫敦 (伦敦)	巴黎 (巴黎)	柏林 (柏林)	東京 (东京)
最大的城市 (最大的城市)	上海 (上海)	紐約 (纽约)	多倫多 (多伦多)	倫敦 (伦敦)	巴黎 (巴黎)	柏林 (柏林)	東京 (东京)
面積 (面积) 平方公里 (平方公里)	九百六十萬 (九百六十万) (4th)	九百六十三萬 (九百六十三万) (3rd)	九百九十八萬 (九百九十八万) (2nd)	二十四萬 (二十四万) (77th)	六十七萬 (六十七万) (40th)	三十五萬 (三十五万) (61st)	三十七萬 (三十七万) (4th)
水面積 (水面积)	2.8%	4.87%	8.62%	1.34%		2.416 %	0.8%
人口 (人口)	十三億 (十三亿) (1st)	三億 (三亿) (3rd)	三千三百萬 (三千三百万) (35th)	六千萬 (六千万) (22nd)	六千萬 (六千万) (20th)	八千万 (八千萬) (14th)	一億三千萬 (一亿三千万) (10th)
貨幣 (货币)	人民幣 (人民币)	美元 (美元)	加元 (加元)	英鎊 (英镑)	歐元 (欧元)	歐元 (欧元)	日元 (日元)
兑美元的匯率 (兑美元的汇率)	1:7.98		1: 1.17	1:0.56	1:5.43	1:1.62	1:115.82

Useful words and expressions:

憑條(凭条) [píngtiáo]: evidence slip
借(借) [jiè]: debit
貸(贷) [dài]: credit
幣別(币别) [bìbié]: type of currency
金額(金额) [jīn'é]: amount of money
小寫(小写) [xiǎoxiě]: the ordinary form of a Chinese numeral; small letter
存期(存期) [cúnqī]: period of deposit
入賬(入账) [rùzhàng]: amount of money to deposit in the account
帳號(账号) [zhànghào]: account number
客戶(客户) [kèhù]: client, customer
證件(证件) [zhèngjiàn]: identity card
本人(本人) [běnrén]: oneself, in person
確認(确认) [quèrèn]: confirmation
所辦業務(所办业务) [suǒbàn yèwù]: the business (being) handled
與(与) [yǔ]: with
記錄(记录) [jìlù]: record
相符(相符) [xiāngfú]: to conform with, agree with
代辦(代办) [dàibàn]: to act on somebody's behalf
簽字(签字) [qiānzì]: to sign one's signature
回單(回单) [huídān]: bank statement
卡號(卡号) [kǎhào]: card number
戶名(户名) [hùmíng]: account name
附件(附件) [fùjiàn]: appendix, attachment
事後監督(事后监督) [shìhòujiāndū]: post-event supervision
復核(复核) [fùhé]: double check
授權(授权) [shòuquán]: authorization
經辦(经办) [jīngbàn]: to be handled by (somebody)

填空 Fill in the blanks:

What should 小京 write into the blanks:

币别 ______ 金额(小写) ____________________

復習 (复习) Review

LESSON 5 TO LESSON 6

1. Read the following passage with the instructor, then briefly retell the story in Chinese

Useful words and expressions:

南轅北轍(南辕北辙) [nányuán běizhé]: going south by driving the carriage north
從前(从前) [cóngqián]: long long ago
駕(驾) [jià]: to drive
楚國(楚国) [Chǔguó]: the State of Chu
條件(条件) [tiáojiàn]: condition
魏國(魏国) [Wèiguó]: the State of Wei
馬車(马车) [mǎchē]: carriage
雖然(虽然) [suīrán]: although

南轅北轍 (繁體字 Traditional Character Version)

從前，魏國有一個駕著馬車要到楚國去。楚國明明在魏國的南邊，可是他卻往北邊走。有人問他："楚國在南邊，你為什麼向北邊走呢?"魏國人說："我的馬很好，每天能跑一千里。"那個人又說："馬跑得雖然快，但是走的不是去楚國的路啊。"魏國人說："我帶的錢很多。"那人又說："錢多也沒有用啊!"魏國人很不高興地說："我很會駕車。"雖然那個魏國人去楚國的條件都很好，但是他卻越走離楚國越遠了。

南辕北辙 (简体字 Simplified Character Version)

从前，魏国有一个驾着马车要到楚国去。楚国明明在魏国的南边，可是他却往北边走。有人问他："楚国在南边，你为什么向北边走呢?"魏国人说："我的马很好，每天能跑一千里。"那个人又说："马跑得虽然快，但是走的不是去楚国的路啊。"魏国人说："我带的钱很多。"那人又说："钱多也没有用啊!"魏国人很不高兴地说："我很会驾车。"虽然那个魏国人去楚国的条件都很好，但是他却越走离楚国越远了。

2. Fill in the blanks

Useful words and expressions:
汽車保險(汽车保险) [qìchē bǎoxiǎn]: car insurance
健康保險(健康保险) [jiànkāng bǎoxiǎn]: health insurance
大概(大概) [dàgài]: about

(繁體字: **Traditional Character Version**)

小文:

你好！我從匹兹堡搬來波士頓已經一個星期了。這個星期我做了很多事兒：我把房子整理 ___ ___ 了(clean up the house)，___ (open) 了銀行賬户，___ ___ (apply) 了信用卡，還買了汽車保險和健康保險。波士頓的很多東西都 ___ 匹兹堡 ___ (more expensive than)，比如房租，在匹兹堡一房一廳的房子每個月的房租只要大概六百美金，在波士頓 ___ ___ ___ (the same) 房子要一千一百美金，差不多是匹兹堡的 ___ 倍 (two times)。還有買東西，在匹兹堡買衣服不用交稅，可是在波士頓要交 ___ ___ ___ ___ (7%) 的稅。還有汽車保險，我以前覺得匹兹堡的汽車保險很貴，每年要八百美金，可是即使這樣，匹兹堡的汽車保險也只有波士頓的 ___ 分 ___ 一 (one third)。但是波士頓的中國菜卻 ___ 匹兹堡的 ___ ___ (cheaper than)。波士頓的中國飯館 ___ 匹兹堡的 ___ (more than)，中國菜也 ___ 匹兹堡的飯館 ___ ___ (more authentic than)。所以在波士頓我要多吃一點兒中國菜。

好了，就説到這兒。下次再聊。

小明

2007 年 10 月 31 日

(简体字：**Simplified Character Version**)

小文：

你好！我从匹兹堡搬来波士顿已经一个星期了。这个星期我做了很多事儿：我把房子整理 ___ ___ 了 (clean up the house)，___ (open) 了银行账户，___ ___ (apply) 了信用卡，还买了汽车保险和健康保险。波士顿的很多东西都 ___ 匹兹堡 ___ (more expensive than)，比如房租，在匹兹堡一房一厅的房子每个月的房租只要大概六百美金，在波士顿 ___ ___ ___ (the same) 房子要一千一百美金，差不多是匹兹堡的 ___ 倍 (two times)。还有买东西，在匹兹堡买衣服不用交税，可是在波士顿要交 ___ ___ ___ ___ (7%) 的税。还有汽车保险，我以前觉得匹兹堡的汽车保险很贵，每年要八百美金，可是即使这样，匹兹堡的汽车保险也只有波士顿的 ___ 分 ___ 一 (one third)。但是波士顿的中国菜却 ___ 匹兹堡的 ___ ___ (cheaper than)。波士顿的中国饭馆 ___ 匹兹堡的 ___ (more than)，中国菜也 ___ 匹兹堡的饭馆 ___ ___ (more authentic than)。所以在波士顿我要多吃一点儿中国菜。

好了，就说到这儿。下次再聊。

小明

2007 年 10 月 31 日

3. Furniture Moving

There was a big soccer match in Europe recently. As a soccer fan, in order to watch the games at midnight, 小文 moved his TV from the living room to his bedroom. He also adjusted the other furniture's position in both the living room and bedroom. Please look at the pictures below and use "把" sentence to describe how the furniture was moved.

(before)

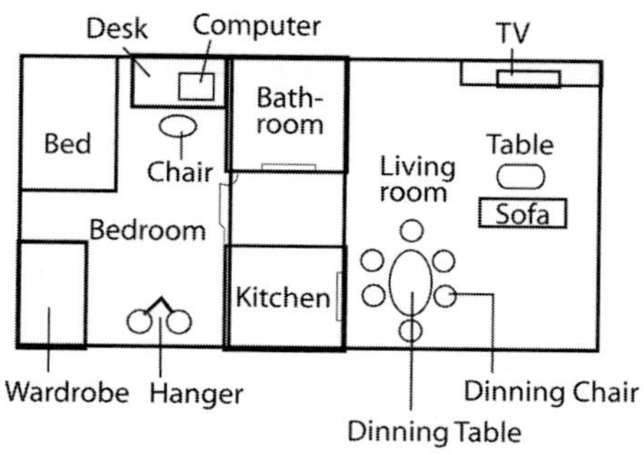

(after)

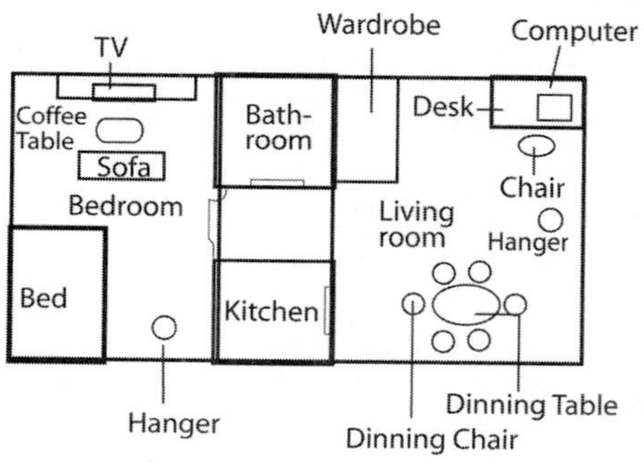

4. Picture description

Look at the pictures below and tell a story. Try to apply 把，了，著，過，往，… 起來，比… when creating the story.

Useful words and expressions:

踢球(踢球) [tīqiú]: to play (kick) the ball
滾(滚) [gǔn]: to roll
井(井) [jǐng]: the well
倒(倒) [dào]: to pour
追(追) [zhuī]: to chase
樹洞(树洞) [shùdòng]: hole in a tree
桶(桶) [tǒng]: bucket
浮(浮) [fú]: to float

(1)

(2)

(3)

(4)

(5)

(6)

5. Traditional and Simplified Characters

Read each character aloud. Write its traditional form. Then create a phrase and a sentence using the character.

For example: 学 → 學 → 學生 → 我是學生

阴 (　) 飞 (　) 团 (　) 闹 (　)
种 (　) 单 (　) 储 (　) 柜 (　)

第七課
LESSON

7

我的電話簿找不到了
(我的电话簿找不到了)
I Can't Find My Phone Book

教學目標 (教学目标) OBJECTIVES

- Talk about possibility and feasibility
- Book plane tickets

Traveling has become one of the most popular activities for Chinese and travel agencies are everywhere in China. This poster is located outside a travel agency in Guangzhou, China.

生詞 (生词) VOCABULARY

核心詞 (核心词) Core Vocabulary

TRADITIONAL	SIMPLIFIED	PINYIN		
1. 寒假	寒假	hánjià	N.	winter vacation
2. 旅遊	旅游	lǚyóu	N.	tour
3. 旅行社	旅行社	lǚxíngshè	N.	travel agency
4. 訂	订	dìng	V.	to book, make reservations
5. 機票	机票	jīpiào	N.	plane ticket
6. 羨慕	羡慕	xiànmù	V.	to envy
7. 打算	打算	dǎsuàn	V. N.	to plan plan
8. 親戚	亲戚	qīnqi	N.	relative
9. 原來	原来	yuánlái	Adv.	originally
10. 抽空	抽空	chōukòng	V.O.	to manage to find time
11. 拜訪	拜访	bàifǎng	V. N.	to visit visit
12. 一直	一直	yìzhí	Adv.	always
13. 查	查	chá	V.	to check
14. 網站	网站	wǎngzhàn	N.	website
15. 買不起	买不起	mǎibuqǐ		cannot afford to buy
16. 買到	买到	mǎidào	V.C.	to succeed in buying
17. 找得到	找得到	zhǎodedào		to be able to find
18. 便宜	便宜	piányi (piányí)	Adj.	inexpensive

TRADITIONAL	SIMPLIFIED	PINYIN		
19. 其實	其实	qíshí	Adv.	as a matter of fact, actually
20. 要是	要是	yàoshi	Conj.	if
21. 南方	南方	nánfāng	N.	southern part
22. 四季如春	四季如春	sìjìrúchūn		to be like spring all year round
23. 風景如畫	风景如画	fēngjǐngrúhuà		with picturesque scenic beauty
24. 少數民族	少数民族	shǎoshùmínzú	N.	minority nationalities
25. 如果	如果	rúguǒ	Conj.	if
26. 簽證	签证	qiānzhèng	N.	visa
27. 辦	办	bàn	V.	to apply, process
28. 大概	大概	dàgài	Adv.	probably
29. 來得及	来得及	láidejí		to have enough time to

專名 (专名) Proper Nouns

TRADITIONAL	SIMPLIFIED	PINYIN		
1. 香港	香港	Xiānggǎng	N.	Hong Kong
2. 雲南	云南	Yúnnán	N.	Yunnan, a province in the southwestern part of China
3. 昆明	昆明	Kūnmíng	N.	Kunming, the capital city of Yunnan province

補充詞 (补充词) Supplementary Vocabulary

TRADITIONAL	SIMPLIFIED	PINYIN		
1. 單程	单程	dānchéng	N.	one-way trip
2. 回程	回程	huíchéng	N.	trip back
3. 往返票	往返票	wǎngfǎnpiào	N.	round-trip ticket
4. 訂房間	订房间	dìng fángjiān	V.O.	to reserve a room
5. 導遊	导游	dǎoyóu	N.	guide
6. 領事館	领事馆	lǐngshìguǎn	N.	consulate
7. 大使館	大使馆	dàshǐguǎn	N.	embassy
8. 辦事處	办事处	bànshìchù	N.	office, agency

語文知識 (语文知识) LANGUAGE LINK

The Sentence Patterns provide models that will help you with the Language in Use section. In both sections, pay attention to the grammar points, vocabulary, and expressions.

句型 (句型) Sentence Patterns

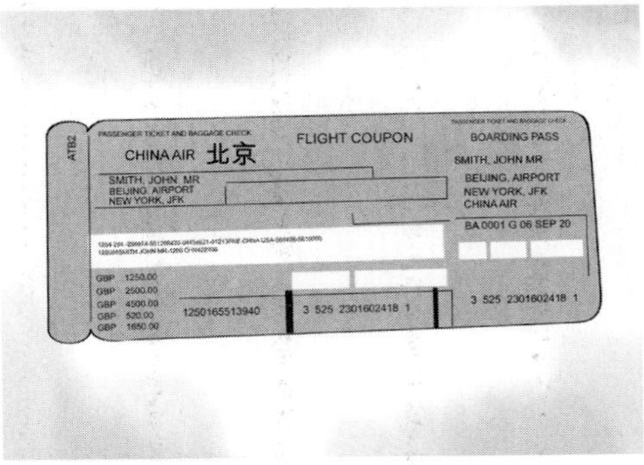

A: 你買得到去北京的機票嗎?
你买得到去北京的机票吗?
Nǐ mǎidedào qù Běijīng de jīpiào ma?

B: 現在機票很難買，我買不到。
现在机票很难买，我买不到。
Xiànzài jīpiào hěnnán mǎi, wǒ mǎibudào.

A: 坐飛機到得了到不了昆明?
坐飞机到得了到不了昆明?
Zuò fēijī dàodeliǎo dàobuliǎo Kūnmíng?

B: 到得了。
到得了。
Dàodeliǎo.

A: 今年寒假你有什麼打算嗎?
今年寒假你有什么打算吗?
Jīnnián hánjià nǐ yǒu shénme dǎsuàn ma?

B: 我打算去北京旅遊。
我打算去北京旅游。
Wǒ dǎsuàn qù Běijīng lǚyóu.

課文: 我的電話簿找不到了(繁體字)
Language in Use: Traditional Character Version

方小琴: 文華, 你在找什麼?

金文華: 我在找一本電話簿, 我的電話簿找不到了。

方小琴: 你看看電話旁邊有沒有?

金文華: 好像沒有…… 啊, 我看到了, 在桌子下面。今年寒假我和方明要去中國旅遊, 我要找一家旅行社的電話號碼, 我想訂去中國的機票。

方小琴: 真的嗎? 太棒了! 我真羨慕你們。你們打算去哪兒玩呢?

金文華: 方明在北京有很多親戚, 我們原來想先去北京玩幾天, 跟他的親戚聚一聚, 然後抽空去拜訪他以前的老師, 再去別的地方看看, 可是我一直買不到去北京的機票。

方小琴: 你們上網查了嗎?

金文華: 查了, 我們查了好幾家航空公司的網站, 可是都訂不到機票。有的機票太貴了, 我們買不起。我想問問這家旅行社, 看看他們那兒訂得到訂不到比較便宜的機票。

方小琴: 其實, 要是真的買不到去北京的機票, 你們可以先去南方的城市, 比如上海或者香港, 然後去雲南的昆明, 再從昆明坐飛機去北京。

金文華: 這個主意真不錯。我也聽說昆明是一個四季如春、風景如畫的城市, 雲南那兒還有很多少數民族, 去那兒看看一定會很有意思。可是我在地圖上怎麼找不到昆明呢?

方小琴: 我來幫你看看 …… 啊, 在這兒。你看, 就在中國的西南邊。

金文華: 是啊! 如果我真的想去, 坐飛機到得了到不了昆明?

方小琴: 當然到得了! 你還可以吃得到少數民族的小吃呢!

金文華: 那我一定要去。

方小琴: 對了, 你們的簽證辦好了嗎?

金文華: 方明的簽證已經辦好了。我也已經申請了, 可是不知道下個星期拿得到拿不到。不過還有一個多月, 大概來得及。

课文: 我的电话簿找不到了(简体字)
Language in Use: Simplified Character Version

方小琴：文华，你在找什么？

金文华：我在找一本电话簿，我的电话簿找不到了。

方小琴：你看看电话旁边有没有？

金文华：好像没有……啊，我看到了，在桌子下面。今年寒假我和方明要去中国旅游，我要找一家旅行社的电话号码，我想订去中国的机票。

方小琴：真的吗？太棒了！我真羡慕你们。你们打算去哪儿玩呢？

金文华：方明在北京有很多亲戚，我们原来想先去北京玩几天，跟他的亲戚聚一聚，然后抽空去拜访他以前的老师，再去别的地方看看，可是我一直买不到去北京的机票。

方小琴：你们上网查了吗？

金文华：查了，我们查了好几家航空公司的网站，可是都订不到机票。有的机票太贵了，我们买不起。我想问问这家旅行社，看看他们那儿订得到订不到比较便宜的机票。

方小琴：其实，要是真的买不到去北京的机票，你们可以先去南方的城市，比如上海或者香港，然后去云南的昆明，再从昆明坐飞机去北京。

金文华：这个主意真不错。我也听说昆明是一个四季如春、风景如画的城市，云南那儿还有很多少数民族，去那儿看看一定会很有意思。可是我在地图上怎么找不到昆明呢？

方小琴：我来帮你看看……啊，在这儿。你看，就在中国的西南边。

金文华：是啊！如果我真的想去，坐飞机到得了到不了昆明？

方小琴：当然到得了！你还可以吃得到少数民族的小吃呢！

金文华：那我一定要去。

方小琴：对了，你们的签证办好了吗？

金文华：方明的签证已经办好了。我也已经申请了，可是不知道下个星期拿得到拿不到。不过还有一个多月，大概来得及。

注釋 (注释) LANGUAGE NOTES

1. 網站/網址/網頁 (网站/网址/网页)

網站(网站) [wǎngzhàn]: website 網址(网址) [wǎngzhǐ]: URL
網頁(网页) [wǎngyè]: web page

2. 南方/南部 (南方/南部)

南方(南方) is generally used to indicate both a direction and an area while 南部(南部) generally refers to an area or territory.

3. 去得了 [liǎo] (去得了)

去得了(去得了) means to be accessible or able to be reached.

4. 便 (便) [pián, biàn]

Note that the word 便(便) has two different pronunciations. It is pronounced as [pián] in 便宜(便宜) (cheap), but is pronounced as [biàn] in 方便(方便) (convenient).

5. 要是/如果 (要是/如果)

Both 要是(要是) and 如果(如果) are used as conjunctions to mean "if," but 要是(要是) is more colloquial and used more in conversations, while 如果(如果) is relatively more formal.

語法 (语法) GRAMMAR

1. 可能補語 (可能补语) Potential complement

Sometimes, a verb, an adjective, or a phrase can be used after a verb to indicate the possibility or impossibility of achieving a desired result through an action. Such constructions are called **potential complements.** A potential complement usually follows the pattern:

Major V. + 得 with the directional complement phrase
Major V. + 得 with the resultative complement phrase

Examples:

Directional complement:	上去 →	我爬得上去。	I am able to climb up there.
		我爬不上去。	I am not able to climb up there.
Resultative complement:	找到 →	我找得到他。	I am able to find him.
		我找不到他。	I am not able to find him.

Note:

1. The difference between a potential complement and a resultative or directional complement is mainly in the use of the structural particle 得. When 得 is added, the complement becomes a potential complement. Compare the following:

Resultative Complement (RC)	**Potential Complement (PC)**
看見(看见) 聽清楚(听清楚) 買到(买到)	看得見/看不見 (看得见/看不见) 聽得清楚/聽不清楚 (听得清楚/听不清楚) 買得到/買不到 (买得到/买不到)
Directional Complement (DC)	
搬上來(搬上来) 走進去(走进去)	搬得上來/搬不上來 (搬得上来/搬不上来) 走得進去/走不進去 (走得进去/走不进去)

2. The A 不 A pattern used in a potential complement is as follows:

   (V. + 得 + C) + (V. + 不 + C)

   走得到(走得到) + 走不到(走不到)

3. To make a question, either place the 嗎(吗) or use the "A 不 A" pattern of the potential complement.

Examples:

i) **A:** 去北京的飛機票買得到嗎？ / 去北京的飞机票买得到吗？ — Are plane tickets to Beijing available now?

   B: 買不到。 / 买不到。 — No, they are not available.

ii) **A:** 飛機票很貴，你買得起嗎？ / 飞机票很贵，你买得起吗？ — The plane tickets are very expensive, can you afford it?

   B: 太貴了，我買不起。 / 太贵了，我买不起。 — They are too expensive, and I can't afford it.

iii) **A:** 飛機到得了到不了昆明？ / 飞机到得了到不了昆明？ — Is Kunming accessible by plane?

   B: 到得了。 / 到得了。 — Yes, it is.

iv) **A:** 這輛車坐得下坐不下六個人？ / 这辆车坐得下坐不下六个人？ — Can this car seat six people?

   B: 坐不下。 / 坐不下。 — No, it can't.

4. 能 or 可以 are sometimes used with a potential complement to emphasize possibility or ability.

   Example: 我能搬得動那塊 [kuài] (measure word for stones) 大石頭 [shítou] (rock).
   我能搬得动那块大石头。
   I am able to move that big rock.

5. When the verb has an object, the object may be placed after the potential complement, or at the beginning of the sentence.

   Examples: 我拿得到簽證。 I am able to get the visa.
   我拿得到签证。

   簽證我拿得到。 As for the visa, I am able to get it.
   签证我拿得到。

6. The following are some adjectives or verbs commonly used as potential complements:

   到 – indicating the potential of achieving a purpose
   e.g.: 找得到/找不到 (to be able/not able to find)
   看得到/看不到 (to be able/not able to see)

   動 – indicating the potential of moving
   e.g.: 拿得動/拿不动 (to be able/not able to carry)

   下 – indicating potential space capacity
   e.g.: 吃得下/吃不下 (to be able/not able to finish eating/eat up)

   了 [liǎo] – indicating the potential ability to do something
   e.g.: 做得了/做不了 (to be able/not able to handle)

   及 – indicating the potential of having enough time to do something
   e.g.: 來得及/来不及 (to have/not to have enough time to do)

2. Questions with structural particles 嗎/呢 (吗/呢)

Usually a question in Chinese is formed by using a question word in a sentence, such as,

你什麼時候去北京?
你什么时候去北京?

她想去哪兒?
她想去哪儿?

But sometimes these kinds of questions may also have the particle 嗎(吗) or 呢(呢) added at the end. When 嗎(吗) is added, the answer to this kind of questions is often either positive or negative, with details optional. When 呢(呢) is added at the end, the emphasis of the question does not change very much but the tone of the question is much softer. Compare the following questions:

1. **A:** 寒假你有什麼打算?
   寒假你有什么打算?
   (The emphasis is on the specific plan.)

   B: 我想先去南方，再去北京。
   我想先去南方，再去北京。

   A: 寒假你有什麼打算呢?
   寒假你有什么打算呢?
   (The emphasis is still on the specific plan, but the tone is softer.)

   B: 我想先去南方，再去北京。
   我想先去南方，再去北京。

   A: 寒假你有什麼打算嗎?
   寒假你有什么打算吗?
   (The emphasis is on whether you have a plan or not, and the tone is softer.)

   B: 有，我想先去南方，再去北京。
   有，我想先去南方，再去北京。

2. **A:** 我怎麼沒有想到?
   我怎么没有想到?
   (Emphasizing 怎麼/how)

   B: 我怎麼沒有想到呢?
   我怎么没有想到呢?
   (The question is the same but the tone is much softer.)

補充課文 (补充课文) SUPPLEMENTARY PRACTICE

This section will help you test your comprehension of the grammar and vocabulary you have learned in this lesson. Be prepared to answer questions about the meaning of the passage.

寒假在中國 Winter Break in China (繁體字 Traditional Character Version)

小琴:

你好嗎? 今天是十二月二十八日。我正在昆明給你寫這封信，希望你在元旦以後馬上就能收得到。

我和方明到中國已經有一個多星期了。因為到上海的飛機票比較容易買得到，所以我們是先到上海的。

在上海我們參觀了很多地方，比如浦東新區、上海博物館等等。上海的變化太大了，簡直是日新月異。方明來過上海，可是很多地方他都已經認不出來了。我們還去了上海附近的蘇州和南京，看了很多中國江南的園林，也去了南京的中山陵和夫子廟。

這些地方都各有特色，非常有意思。我們還吃到了很多各種小吃，在上海過了聖誕節，真的很開心。本來如果時間來得及，我們還打算去杭州。"上有天堂，下有蘇杭"嘛，應該去看看。可是很遺憾，時間來不及了，只好下次再去了。

我們是昨天到昆明的。昆明真是一個好地方，山青水秀、風景如畫，漂亮極了。這兒的天氣也很好，四季如春，很舒服。這兒有很多少數民族，他們的風俗習慣跟我們的不太一樣，有意思極了。

我們打算在這兒玩三天，然後坐飛機去北京，方明的很多親戚都在北京等著我們呢。今天上午我們要去航空公司問問，看我們買得到買不到去北京的機票，希望能在元旦以前到得了北京。

你的寒假過得怎麼樣? 你一定很羨慕我們吧! 希望你以後也有機會到中國來玩玩，真的非常值得。

祝你

寒假愉快!

文華

二〇〇七年十二月二十八日

補充課文 (补充课文) SUPPLEMENTARY PRACTICE

This section will help you test your comprehension of the grammar and vocabulary you have learned in this lesson. Be prepared to answer questions about the meaning of the passage.

寒假在中国 Winter Break in China (简体字 Simplified Character Version)

小琴：

你好吗？今天是十二月二十八日。我正在昆明给你写这封信，希望你在元旦以后马上就能收得到。

我和方明到中国已经有一个多星期了。因为到上海的飞机票比较容易买得到，所以我们是先到上海的。

在上海我们参观了很多地方，比如浦东新区、上海博物馆等等。上海的变化太大了，简直是日新月异。方明来过上海，可是很多地方他都已经认不出来了。我们还去了上海附近的苏州和南京，看了很多中国江南的园林，也去了南京的中山陵和夫子庙。

这些地方都各有特色，非常有意思。我们还吃到了很多各种小吃，在上海过了圣诞节，真的很开心。本来如果时间来得及，我们还打算去杭州。“上有天堂，下有苏杭”嘛，应该去看看。可是很遗憾，时间来不及了，只好下次再去了。

我们是昨天到昆明的。昆明真是一个好地方，山青水秀、风景如画，漂亮极了。这儿的天气也很好，四季如春，很舒服。这儿有很多少数民族，他们的风俗习惯跟我们的不太一样，有意思极了。

我们打算在这儿玩三天，然后坐飞机去北京，方明的很多亲戚都在北京等着我们呢。今天上午我们要去航空公司问问，看我们买得到买不到去北京的机票，希望能在元旦以前到得了北京。

你的寒假过得怎么样？你一定很羡慕我们吧！希望你以后也有机会到中国来玩玩，真的非常值得。

祝你

寒假愉快！

文华

二〇〇七年十二月二十八日

Useful words and expressions:
元旦(元旦) [Yuándàn]: New Year's Day
博物館(博物馆) [bówùguǎn]: museum
簡直(简直) [jiǎnzhí]: simply; at all
日新月異(日新月异) [rìxīnyuèyì]: to change with each passing day
江南(江南) [jiāngnán]: south of the Yangtze River
園林(园林) [yuánlín]: gardens
各有特色(各有特色) [gèyǒutèsè]: each has its own special features
聖誕節(圣诞节) [Shèngdànjié]: Christmas
天堂(天堂) [tiāntáng]: paradise; heaven
遺憾(遗憾) [yíhàn]: to regret; pity
山青水秀(山青水秀) [shānqīng shuǐxiù]: green mountains and clear waters
風俗(风俗) [fēngsú]: custom
習慣(习惯) [xíguàn]: habit
值得(值得) [zhídé]: worthwhile

Proper Nouns:
浦東新區(浦东新区) [Pùdōng xīnqū]: Pudong New Development Zone (in Shanghai)
蘇州(苏州) [Sūzhōu]: Suzhou, a city in the southeastern part of China
南京(南京) [Nánjīng]: Nanjing, a city in the southeastern part of China
中山陵(中山陵) [Zhōngshānlín]: Dr. Sun Yat-san's Mausleum (in Nanjing)
夫子廟(夫子庙) [Fūzǐmiào]: Temple of Confucius, an old traditional shopping center in Nanjing
杭州(杭州) [Hángzhōu]: Hangzhou, a city in the southeastern part of China

練習 (练习) Exercises

1. 文華寒假去了中國的哪些地方，他還打算去哪兒?
   文华寒假去了中国的哪些地方，他还打算去哪儿?

2. "上有天堂，下有蘇杭"是什麼意思?
   "上有天堂，下有苏杭"是什么意思?

3. 方明的很多親戚都在哪兒? 文華和方明打算怎麼去那兒?
   方明的很多亲戚都在哪儿? 文华和方明打算怎么去那儿?

成語故事 (成语故事) IDIOM STORY

掩耳盜鈴 (掩耳盗铃) [yǎn'ěr dàolíng]

Meaning: Covering one's ears while stealing a bell

Usage: This implies that someone deceives himself/herself

Example: 我們到現在還買不到去北京的機票，簽證也還沒開始申請 。你還說我們下星期一定去得了中國，那不是"掩耳盜鈴"嗎?

我们到现在还买不到去北京的机票，签证也还没开始申请 。你还说我们下星期一定去得了中国，那不是"掩耳盗铃"吗?

Pay attention to the usages of potential complements and questions with 嗎/呢:

(繁體字 **Traditional Character Version**)

從前，有一個小偷在一座廟裡看到了一口特別大的鐘。他想：這口鐘這麼大，要是能賣得了，我就可以得到很多錢。於是，他就想把這口鐘偷走。可是這口鐘太大、太重，他拿不動，偷不走。他試了好幾次，都拿不動。後來，他想：如果我把它砸成碎片，我就能偷得走了。於是，他就用一個錘子砸這口鐘。可是砸鐘的聲音非常響，很遠很遠的地方都能聽得到。他趕快用手把他的耳朵捂起來，這樣他就聽不到了。他覺得這是一個好辦法，所以他就一邊捂著自己的耳朵，一邊砸這口鐘。

可是他沒有想到，雖然他自己聽不見砸鐘的聲音，但是別人都聽得見。結果很多人都跑過來把他抓住了。

"掩耳盜鈴"是一種非常愚蠢的行為，實際上是自己騙自己。

(简体字 **Simplified Character Version**)

从前，有一个小偷在一座庙里看到了一口特别大的钟。他想：这口钟这么大，要是能卖得了，我就可以得到很多钱。于是，他就想把这口钟偷走。可是这口钟太大、太重，他拿不动，偷不走。他试了好几次，都拿不动。后来，他想：如果我把它砸成碎片，我就能偷得走了。于是，他就用一个锤子砸这口钟。可是砸钟的声音非常响，很远很远的地方都能听得到。他赶快用手把他的耳朵捂起来，这样他就听不到了。他觉得这是一个好办法，所以他就一边捂着自己的耳朵，一边砸这口钟。

可是他没有想到，虽然他自己听不见砸钟的声音，但是别人都听得见。结果很多人都跑过来把他抓住了。

"掩耳盗铃"是一种非常愚蠢的行为，实际上是自己骗自己。

Useful words and expressions:
小偷(小偷) [xiǎotōu]: thief
廟(庙) [miào]: temple
口(口) [kǒu]: measure word for bells
鐘(钟) [zhōng]: bell
偷(偷) [tōu]: to steal
砸(砸) [zá]: to hammer
碎片(碎片) [suìpiàn]: bits and pieces
錘子(锤子) [chuízi]: hammer
響(响) [xiǎng]: to ring
聲音(声音) [shēngyīn]: sound, voice
趕快(赶快) [gǎnkuài]: hurriedly
耳朵(耳朵) [ěrduo]: ear
捂(捂) [wǔ]: to cover
辦法(办法) [bànfǎ]: way, solution
結果(结果) [jiéguǒ]: as a result
抓住(抓住) [zhuāzhù]: to grab, to arrest
愚蠢(愚蠢) [yúchǔn]: stupid
行為(行为) [xíngwéi]: behavior
騙(骗) [piàn]: to deceive, fool

練習 (练习) Exercises

1. 找出有下面語法的句子。potential complements and questions with 嗎/呢。
   找出有下面语法的句子。potential complements and questions with 吗/呢。
2. 用你自己的話說說"掩耳盜鈴"的故事。
   用你自己的话说说"掩耳盗铃"的故事。
3. 請用"掩耳盜鈴"造一個句子或者說一個掩耳盜鈴的例子。
   请用"掩耳盗铃"造一个句子或者说一个掩耳盗铃的例子。
4. "掩耳盜鈴"的故事，告訴了我們什麼?
   "掩耳盗铃"的故事，告诉了我们什么?

練習 (练习) ACTIVITIES

I. 聽力練習 (听力练习)

7-1 Listen to the passage, then select the right answer to complete the statements:

1. 昨天我給 __________ 打了電話。
   昨天我给 __________ 打了电话。

   A: 北京的朋友
   北京的朋友

   B: 我的室友
   我的室友

   C: 旅行社
   旅行社

2. 旅行社的工作人員說 ____________________。
   旅行社的工作人员说 ____________________。

   A: 可以買得到去北京的機票
   可以买得到去北京的机票

   B: 去上海的機票很難買
   去上海的机票很难买

C: 訂不到去北京的機票
订不到去北京的机票

3. 申請簽證只要 ________ 就可以收到。
申请签证只要 ________ 就可以收到。

A: 一個星期
一个星期

B: 兩個月
两个月

C: 兩個星期
两个星期

7-2 Read the following lyric, paying special attention to the tones and the rhythm:

Zhúzhī	竹枝 竹枝
(Liú Yǔxí)	(劉禹錫) (刘禹锡)
Yángliǔ qīngqīng jiāngshuǐ píng,	楊柳青青江水平， 杨柳青青江水平，
Wén láng jiāngshàng tà gēshēng.	聞郎江上踏歌聲。 闻郎江上踏歌声。
Dōngbiān rìchū xībiān yǔ,	東邊日出西邊雨， 东边日出西边雨，
Dào shì wú qíng què yǒu qíng.	道是無晴卻有晴。 道是无晴却有晴。

Bamboo branches
(Liu, Yuxi)

The willow trees are green and the river water calm,
I hear my love singing on the river.
The sun comes out in the east and rain in the west,
Would you say they are feelingless but actually they are full of feeling.

In this lyric, the word 晴(晴) is used as a pun. Find from the dictionary the pronunciation of the words 青(青), 晴(晴), 情(情), 請(请), and then see what each word means. Answer the following questions:

1. What do you think is the function of the part 青(青) in 晴(晴), 情(情) and 請(请)?
2. Why is the word 晴(晴) a pun? What does the poet want to tell us by using this word?

II. 漢字練習 (汉字练习)

7-3 Read the following words, phrases, and sentences:

算 算	戚 戚
打算 打算	親戚 亲戚
什麼打算 什么打算	我的親戚 我的亲戚
你有什麼打算 你有什么打算	我的台北親戚 我的台北亲戚
寒假你有什麼打算 寒假你有什么打算	看我的台北親戚 看我的台北亲戚
今年寒假你有什麼打算呢 今年寒假你有什么打算呢	我去看我的台北親戚 我去看我的台北亲戚

Now try to use the following characters to make words, phrases, and then sentences:

1. 查 查	2. 訂 订	3. 方 方	4. 辦 办	5. 便 便	6. 原 原
7. 證 证	8. 及 及	9. 族 族	10. 宜 宜	11. 羨 羡	12. 實 实

7-4 Write out the radical of each of the following characters, then give some examples from the text of characters having the same radical:

Example: [亻] 你 他 俱

1. [ ] 社 ________　　2. [ ] 寒 ________
3. [ ] 戚 ________　　4. [ ] 旅 ________

7-5 Character recognition:

1. The following pairs of characters seem very much alike in appearance. Look carefully at their differences, then for each character write out two expressions.

A: 北(北) ______ ______　　B: 我(我) ______ ______
　 比(比) ______ ______　　　 找(找) ______ ______

C: 訂(订) ______ ______　　D: 其(其) ______ ______
　 計(计) ______ ______　　　 共(共) ______ ______

E: 別(别) ______ ______　　F: 季(季) ______ ______
　 到(到) ______ ______　　　 李(李) ______ ______

2. Each of the following pairs of words contains a character which has two different pronunciations. Write down the Pinyin for each word:

A: 便宜(便宜) ____________　　B: 旅行(旅行) ____________
　 方便(方便) ____________　　　 銀行(银行) ____________

III. 語法練習 (语法练习)

7-6 Use a potential complement to complete the following sentences with positive answers:

1. A: 昆明很偏遠 [piānyuǎn](remote)，飛機到得 ______ 到不 ______？
   昆明很偏远，飞机到得 ______ 到不 ______？

   B: ______ ______ ______。
   ______ ______ ______。

2. A: 你在網上查得 ______ 飛機票的價錢嗎？
   你在网上查得 ______ 飞机票的价钱吗？

   B: 當然 ______ ______ ______。
   当然 ______ ______ ______。

3. A: 這輛車太小，坐得 ______ 坐不 ______ 五個人?
这辆车太小，坐得 ______ 坐不 ______ 五个人?

B: 我看 ______ ______ ______ 。
我看 ______ ______ ______ 。

4. A: 你的簽證明天收得 ______ 收不 ______?
你的签证明天收得 ______ 收不 ______?

B: 我不知道。可能 ______ ______ ______，我是一個星期以前寄去的。
我不知道。可能 ______ ______ ______，我是一个星期以前寄去的。

5. 去中國的機票不太貴，我想我能 ______ ______ ______ 。
去中国的机票不太贵，我想我能 ______ ______ ______ 。

7-7 Rewrite each question using 嗎(吗) or 呢(呢) to switch the emphasis and soften the tone, then answer them accordingly:

Examples: 寒假我有計畫。
寒假我有计划。

嗎(吗)

A: 寒假你有什麼計畫嗎?
寒假你有什么计划吗?

B: 有，我想先去南方，再去北京。
有，我想先去南方，再去北京。

呢(呢)

A: 寒假你有什麼計畫呢?
寒假你有什么计划呢?

B: 我想去台灣玩兒。
我想去台湾玩儿。

– 計畫(计划) [jìhuà]: plan – 台灣(台湾) [Táiwān]: Taiwan

1. 你什麼時候去中國?
你什么时候去中国?

____

____

2. 我打算在北京住幾天。
我打算在北京住几天。

____

____

3. 哪兒可以買得到去上海的機票?
哪儿可以买得到去上海的机票?

____

____

4. 有誰認識旅行社的人?
有谁认识旅行社的人?

____

____

IV. 交際活動 (交际活动)

Discuss what they found.

小琴(小琴) and 文華(文华) are planning a trip to China this winter break. They checked online or made phone calls to various airlines listed in the table below to find out the price for a plane ticket to either Beijing or Shanghai, or both. Below is the information they gathered. Remember to include the following:

1. Use potential complements where necessary.
2. Try to work out some alternatives for the best deal.

Useful words and expressions:

價格(价格) [jiàgé]: price　比較(比较) [bǐjiào]: comparison　日期(日期) [rìqī]: date
票價(票价) [piàojià]: ticket price　往返票(往返票) [wǎngfǎnpiào]: a round trip ticket

飛機票價格比較(飞机票价格比较)

航空公司 (航空公司)	旅行日期 (旅行日期) 去 (去)	回 (回)	去上海的票價 (去上海的票价)	去北京的票價 (去北京的票价)
西北(西北)	12/3	12/12	Yes $850	Yes $830
聯合(联合) [liánhé] (United)	12/28	01/10	Yes $900	Yes $900
中國(中国)	12/11	12/28	Yes $780	Yes $775
新加坡(新加坡) [Xīnjiāpō]: Singapore	12/28	01/28	Yes $910	No
美利堅(美利坚) [Měilìjiān] (American)	12/09	1/03	Yes $880	No

文化知識 (文化知识) Culture Link

文化點滴 (文化点滴) CULTURE NOTES

中國: 一個多民族的國家 (中国: 一个多民族的国家) [Zhōngguó: yíge duō mínzú de guójiā] China: A Multi-ethnic Country

China is a multi-ethnic country with a population of 1.3 billion. 中華民族 [Zhōnghuá mínzú], the term the Chinese use to refer to themselves, is composed of 56 different ethnic groups, all living on the vast expanse of land known as China.

Among the 56 ethnic groups, the Han is the largest, making up 91.59% of China's total population. The remaining 8.41% comprises the other 55 ethnic groups. Among the various minority ethnic groups there is a great difference in population size. 少數民族(少数民族) (the minority ethnic groups) such as Zhuang, Hui, Uygur, Yi, Miao, Manchu, Tibetan, Mongolian, Tujia, Bouyei, Korean, Dong, Yao, Bai and Hani all have a population of over a million. The remaining minority groups all have a population of less than one million, some less than 50,000. The smallest ethnic groups are Hezhen, Gaoshan and Lhoba with populations of less than 5,000.

China has been a multi-ethnic land for several hundred years, becoming even more so during the Qing Dynasty (1644–1911), when China's territory extended to cover a vast piece of land across east and central Asia and eastern Europe. The Han people mostly live in the eastern part of China, including the northeast, 黄河(黄河) [Huánghé] (the Yellow River), 長江(长江) [Chángjiāng] (Yangtze River) and 珠江(珠江) [Zhūjiāng] (Pearl River) valleys, as well as along the coast. They also live in those areas mostly inhabited by the minority ethnic groups. The Han people speak Chinese, also called 漢語(汉语) [Hànyǔ] (literally meaning "Han language").

The minorities, although small in population size, live across a very wide area, mainly in the central and the western parts of China, which constitutes 50–60% of the country's area. Except for the Hui and the Manchu, who also speak 漢語(汉语), the minority ethnic groups have their own languages. A few only have spoken languages, and no written languages. They are encouraged to maintain their own languages, although they also need to learn 漢語(汉语) to function well in economic and political life.

The Chinese government has adopted various measures to encourage the minority groups to preserve their own cultures and traditions. Minority people enjoy privileges in various aspects of social and political life. For example, there are 415 representatives from the 55 minorities at the Tenth National People's Congress, accounting for 13.91% of the total number of representatives, 5.5% higher than their population ratio. Major areas that are mostly inhabited by minority groups have autonomy in running their own affairs. In China today, there are a total of five autonomous regions, plus 30 autonomous prefectures and 120 autonomous counties.

China is a country of all Chinese people. In the long course of historical development of China, all ethnic groups have joined together into one nation and have made tremendous contributions to the nation's economic and cultural development.

問題討論 (问题讨论) Discussion Questions

1. 你知道哪些中國的少數民族? 請說出幾個。
   你知道哪些中国的少数民族? 请说出几个。
   Do you know any of the minority nationalities in China? Please name some of them.

At mountains and rivers that are as beautiful as paintings, a tourist dresses in 壯(壮) [Zhuàng] minority's costume takes a picture. (陽朔(阳朔) [Yángshuò], 廣西(广西) [Guǎngxī] Province, China)

2. 美國有少數民族嗎? 有哪幾個?
美国有少数民族吗? 有哪几个?
Are there any minority ethnic groups in the United States? Provide some examples.

趣味中文 (趣味中文) FUN WITH CHINESE

四海之內皆兄弟
四海之内皆兄弟
All people within the four seas can become (as close as) your older brother and younger brother.

sì	hǎi	zhī	nèi	jiē	xiōngdì
四	海	之	內	皆	兄弟
四	海	之	内	皆	兄弟
four	sea	(particle)	inside	all	brothers

問題討論 (问题讨论) Discussion Questions

1. Can you name some country names in Chinese?
2. What does 四海 refer to? Can you name the 四海 in Chinese?

行動吧!(行动吧!) LET'S GO!

(1) 機票價格表 (机票价格表)
Airline Ticket Price List

全国电脑联网民航特价 以下为上海出港标准票价，如有调整以电脑为准

敬请保留 以备急用

城市	价格	城市	价格	城市	价格	城市	价格	城市	价格
北京	1130	黄山	580	深圳	1400	烟台	790	香港	
郑州	800	吉林	1460	沈阳	1300	宜宾	1500	台北	
成都	1610	济南	760	三亚	1890	宜昌	1040	东京	国际航班来电咨询
重庆	1490	晋江	910	汕头	990	海口	1660	悉尼	
长春	1600	锦州	1060	太原	1200	合肥	490	柏林	
长沙	890	昆明	1900	天津	1030	珠海	1400	巴黎	
大连	1060	兰州	1750	武汉	810	哈尔滨	1760	伦敦	
丹东	1090	洛阳	890	温州	700	景德镇	500	洛杉机	
福州	780	丽江	2430	威海	700	牡丹江	1830	旧金山	
广州	1280	南宁	1660	厦门	960	石家庄	990	慕尼黑	
贵阳	1600	南昌	710	西宁	1850	齐齐哈尔	1850	新加坡	
桂林	1300	宁波	420	西安	1260	乌鲁木齐	2800	吉隆坡	
张家界	1330	青岛	740	柳州	1460	呼和浩特	1350	温哥华	

特价机票挑战火车票! 环线内免费送票

(2) 大巴指南 (大巴指南)
Bus Guide

最 新 机 场 大 巴 专 线 指 南

1号线: 虹桥机场→浦东机场 68346912

2号线: 上海航站楼→浦东机场 62690022

3号线: 银河宾馆→徐家汇上无四厂→张江→浦东机场 68346645

4号线: 东江湾路(虹口公园)→大柏树→五角场→浦东机场 68346830

5号线: 上海火车站→浦东东方医院→浦东机场 68346830

6号线: 桃浦路→浦东机场 68346645

夜间订票:**62274356**

长期有效 敬请保留 以备急用

Useful words and expressions:

For (1) Airline Ticket Price List

聯網(联网) [liánwǎng]: networked
民航(民航) [mínháng]: abbreviation of 中國民用航空公司 (中国民用航空公司) [Zhōngguó mínyòng hángkōng gōngsī]: the Civil Aviation Association of China
特價(特价) [tèjià]: special (discounted) price
以下(以下) [yǐxià]: below
出港(出港) [chūgǎng]: to leave (the port)
標準(标准) [biāozhǔn]: standard
調整(调整) [tiáozhěng]: to adjust
以……為準(以……为准) [yǐ......wéizhǔn]: to take . . . as the official standard
敬請(敬请) [jìngqǐng]: please (a very polite formal way)
保留(保留) [bǎoliú]: to keep, reserve
以備(以备) [yǐbèi]: to be ready for
急用(急用) [jíyòng]: urgent need, for use in an emergency
挑戰(挑战) [tiǎozhàn]: to challenge
環線(环线) [huánxiàn]: circular route around the city
免費(免费) [miǎnfèi]: free of charge

For (2) Bus Guide

大巴(大巴) [dàbā]: big bus
專線(专线) [zhuānxiàn]: special route
指南(指南) [zhǐnán]: guide
浦東(浦东) [Pǔdōng]: Pudong, an area east of the Huangpu River in Shanghai
夜間(夜间) [yèjiān]: night time
訂票(订票) [dìngpiào]: to book tickets

問題討論 (问题讨论) Discussion Questions:

For (1) Airline Ticket Price List

1. Are these regular airline prices? What kind of prices are they?
2. What is the ticket price to fly from Shanghai to Beijing?
3. Are these airline prices much more expensive than train tickets?
4. Do they have a delivery service? How much do they charge?
5. How do you find out the prices for international travel?

For (2) Bus Guide

6. How many bus routes are there that lead to the Pudong Airport in Shanghai?
7. Can you book a ticket at night? And how?
8. What do the following expressions mean in English?

長期有效(长期有效)

敬請保留(敬请保留)

以備急用(以备急用)

第八課
LESSON

8

你比以前忙得多
(你比以前忙得多)
You Are Much Busier Than Before

教學目標 (教学目标) OBJECTIVES

- Describe contrast
- Express personal opinion

China's movie industry has made rapid progress over the past decade. Films from all over the world as well as from China are available to Chinese viewers.

GALAXY CINEMA
放映时间
10:00-24:00
订票/查询电话
8757 6722
8757 6723

To attract more movie-goers, many movie theaters in China show films from morning till midnight.

What is 查詢電話(查询电话) *[cháxún diànhuà] used for?*

生詞 (生词) VOCABULARY

核心詞 (核心词) Core Vocabulary

TRADITIONAL	SIMPLIFIED	PINYIN		
1. 連	连	lián	Prep.	even
2. 影子	影子	yǐngzi	N.	shadow
3. 研究報告	研究报告	yánjiū bàogào	N.	research report
4. 輕鬆	轻松	qīngsōng	Adj.	relieved, relaxed
5. 表妹	表妹	biǎomèi	N.	cousin
6. 強	强	qiáng	Adj.	better than, well off
7. 完	完	wán	V.	to finish
8. 導演	导演	dǎoyǎn	N. V.	director to direct (a film)
9. 部	部	bù	M.W.	(measure word for films, machines, or cars)
10. 功夫片	功夫片	gōngfūpiān	N.	action movie, kongfu movie
11. 主要	主要	zhǔyào	Adj.	major, main
12. 特別	特别	tèbié	Adv.	very, especially
13. 它	它	tā	Pron.	it
14. 場面	场面	chǎngmiàn	N.	scene
15. 情節	情节	qíngjié	N.	story, plot
16. 吸引人	吸引人	xīyǐnrén	Adj.	appealing, attractive
17. 關於	关于	guānyú	Prep.	about, with regard to
18. 古代	古代	gǔdài	Adj.	ancient
19. 故事	故事	gùshi	N.	story
20. 不如	不如	bùrú	V.	to be inferior to, to be not as good as

TRADITIONAL	SIMPLIFIED	PINYIN		
21. 精彩	精彩	jīngcǎi	Adj.	brilliant, wonderful
22. 對	对	duì	Prep.	toward, to
23. 描寫	描写	miáoxiě	N. V.	description, exposition to describe
24. 歷史	历史	lìshǐ	N.	history
25. 同意	同意	tóngyì	V.	to agree
26. 客觀	客观	kèguān	Adj.	factual, objective
27. 感	感	gǎn	V.	to feel, sense
28. 興趣	兴趣	xìngqù	N.	interest
29. 感情	感情	gǎnqíng	N.	emotion
30. 方面	方面	fāngmiàn	N.	aspect
31. 而且	而且	érqiě	Conj.	and also, furthermore
32. 特技	特技	tèjì	N.	special technique
33. 效果	效果	xiàoguǒ	N.	effect
34. 顏色	颜色	yánsè	N.	color
35. 週末	周末	zhōumò	N.	weekend
36. 放	放	fàng	V.	to show (movies), to place
37. 票價	票价	piàojià	N.	ticket price

專名 (专名) Proper Nouns

TRADITIONAL	SIMPLIFIED	PINYIN		
1. 季如春	季如春	Jì Rúchūn	N.	(name) Ruchun Ji
2. 方慕華	方慕华	Fāng Mùhuá	N.	(name) Muhua Fang
3. 張藝謀	张艺谋	Zhāng Yìmóu	N.	Yimou Zhang (Chinese film director)

TRADITIONAL	SIMPLIFIED	PINYIN		
4. 陳道明	陈道明	Chén Dàomíng	N.	Daoming Chen (Chinese movie star)
5. 李連杰	李连杰	Lǐ Liánjié	N.	Jet Li (Chinese kongfu movie star)
6. 張曼玉	张曼玉	Zhāng Mànyù	N.	Maggie Cheung (Chinese movie star)
7. 英雄	英雄	Yīngxióng	N.	Hero (name of a Chinese martial arts film directed by Yimou Zhang)
8. 臥虎藏龍	卧虎藏龙	Wòhǔcánglóng	N.	Crouching Tiger, Hidden Dragon (name of a Chinese martial arts movie directed by Ang Lee 李安)
9. 秦始皇	秦始皇	Qín Shǐhuáng	N.	the First Emperor of the Qin Dynasty (221–206 B.C.)

補充詞 (补充词) Supplementary Vocabulary

TRADITIONAL	SIMPLIFIED	PINYIN		
1. 意見	意见	yìjiàn	N.	opinion
2. 看法	看法	kànfǎ	N.	view, way of looking at things
3. 感想	感想	gǎnxiǎng	N.	reflections, thoughts
4. 心得	心得	xīndé	N.	what one has learned from work or study
5. 瞭解	了解	liǎojiě	V. N.	to understand understanding
6. 倍	倍	bèi	M.W.	times; -fold
7. 製作	制作	zhìzuò	V.	to produce
8. 配樂	配乐	pèiyuè	V.O.	to dub in background music
9. 剪輯	剪辑	jiǎnjí	N.	film editing
10. 服裝	服装	fúzhuāng	N.	costume

語文知識 (语文知识) LANGUAGE LINK

The Sentence Patterns provide models that will help you with the Language in Use section. In both sections, pay attention to the grammar points, vocabulary, and expressions.

句型 (句型) Sentence Patterns

A: 最近為什麼連你的影子都看不見?
最近为什么连你的影子都看不见?
Zuìjìn wèishénme lián nǐ de yǐngzi dōu kànbújiàn?

B: 我最近比以前忙得多，我在寫研究報告。
我最近比以前忙得多，我在写研究报告。
Wǒ zuìjìn bǐ yǐqián máng de duō, wǒ zài xiě yánjiū bàogào.

A: 《英雄》這部電影好看嗎?
《英雄》这部电影好看吗?
Yīngxióng zhèbù diànyǐng hǎokàn ma?

B: 我覺得小說比電影好一些。
我觉得小说比电影好一些。
Wǒ juéde xiǎoshuō bǐ diànyǐng hǎo yìxiē.

A: 《英雄》對秦始皇的描寫跟別的電影不一樣。
《英雄》对秦始皇的描写跟别的电影不一样。
Yīngxióng duì Qínshǐhuáng de miáoxiě gēn biéde diànyǐng bù yíyàng.

B: 我同意，但是我覺得它的描寫很客觀。
我同意，但是我觉得它的描写很客观。
Wǒ tóngyì, dànshì wǒ juéde tā de miáoxiě hěn kèguān.

課文: 你比以前忙得多 (繁體字)
Language in Use: Traditional Character Version

季如春: 慕華，你好像最近比以前忙得多，是嗎?
方慕華: 沒有啊! 你為什麼覺得我比以前忙得多呢?
季如春: 最近連你的影子都看不見。昨天晚上我給你打電話也找不到你。
方慕華: 昨天上午我把一個大的研究報告交出去了，覺得輕鬆多了，所以我就跟我的表妹去看電影了。
季如春: 你比我強得多，我的報告還沒有寫完呢! 對了，你們看了什麼電影? 好看嗎?

方慕華: 我們看的是《英雄》。
季如春: 是不是張藝謀導演的那部功夫片?
方慕華: 是的。主要演員是陳道明、李連杰和張曼玉。其中我特別喜歡李連杰。
季如春: 有人說它沒有《臥虎藏龍》好看，你覺得怎麼樣?
方慕華: 我覺得這兩部電影差不多。你呢? 你看過了沒有?
季如春: 我看過《臥虎藏龍》，沒有看過《英雄》，可是聽說《英雄》的場面比《臥虎藏龍》大得多。是真的嗎?
方慕華: 沒錯。《英雄》的場面比《臥虎藏龍》大一些，可是我覺得它的情節不像《臥虎藏龍》那麼吸引人。
季如春: 聽說《英雄》說的是關於中國古代秦始皇的故事，那麼，比較起來電影和小說哪個好?
方慕華: 我覺得電影不如小說精彩。
季如春: 有人說它對秦始皇的描寫跟歷史上的秦始皇不一樣。
方慕華: 我同意，但是我覺得這部電影描寫得比較客觀。
季如春: 我一直對歷史故事很感興趣，所以我很想去看一看這部電影。
方慕華: 你應該去看看。我覺得《英雄》這部電影對感情方面的描寫比《臥虎藏龍》多一些，而且它的特技效果和顏色都比別的電影好得多。
季如春: 你知道在哪兒可以看得到《英雄》嗎?
方慕華: 這個週末學校會放這部電影，票價只要一元，比電影院的要便宜五元。
季如春: 好，這個週末我就去看。

课文: 你比以前忙得多 (简体字)
Language in Use: Simplified Character Version

季如春：慕华，你好像最近比以前忙得多，是吗？
方慕华：没有啊！你为什么觉得我比以前忙得多呢？
季如春：最近连你的影子都看不见。昨天晚上我给你打电话也找不到你。
方慕华：昨天上午我把一个大的研究报告交出去了，觉得轻松多了，所以我就跟我的表妹去看电影了。
季如春：你比我强得多，我的报告还没有写完呢！对了，你们看了什么电影？好看吗？
方慕华：我们看的是《英雄》。
季如春：是不是张艺谋导演的那部功夫片？
方慕华：是的。主要演员是陈道明、李连杰和张曼玉。其中我特别喜欢李连杰。
季如春：有人说它没有《卧虎藏龙》好看，你觉得怎么样？
方慕华：我觉得这两部电影差不多。你呢？你看过了没有？
季如春：我看过《卧虎藏龙》，没有看过《英雄》，可是听说它的场面比《卧虎藏龙》大得多。是真的吗？
方慕华：没错。《英雄》的场面比《卧虎藏龙》大一些，可是我觉得情节不像《卧虎藏龙》那么吸引人。
季如春：听说《英雄》说的是关于中国古代秦始皇的故事，那么，比较起来电影和小说哪个好？
方慕华：我觉得电影不如小说精彩。
季如春：有人说它对秦始皇的描写跟历史上的秦始皇不一样。
方慕华：我同意，但是我觉得这部电影描写得比较客观。
季如春：我一直对历史故事很感兴趣，所以我很想去看一看这部电影。
方慕华：你应该去看看。我觉得《英雄》这部电影对感情方面的描写比《卧虎藏龙》多一些，而且它的特技效果和颜色都比别的电影好得多。
季如春：你知道在哪儿可以看得到《英雄》吗？
方慕华：这个周末学校会放这部电影，票价只要一元，比电影院的要便宜五元。
季如春：好，这个周末我就去看。

注釋 (注释) LANGUAGE NOTES

1. 影子 (影子)

The literal meaning is "shadow," but here it is used in a very idiomatic expression to mean "I haven't seen you at all, not even your shadow."

2. 表妹 (表妹)

表妹(表妹) is a younger female cousin on your mother's side. Chinese make very clear distinction between relatives on the father's side and the mother's side, and also between older and younger ones. (c.f.: Lesson 6 of *Chinese Link: Elementary Chinese* for detailed list.)

3. 功夫片 (功夫片)

功夫片(功夫片) means martial arts films. Other kinds of films include:

文藝片(文艺片) [wényìpiān]	drama films
喜劇片(喜剧片) [xǐjùpiān]	comedy films
動作片(动作片) [dòngzuòpiān]	action films
恐怖片(恐怖片) [kǒngbùpiān]	horror films
紀錄片(纪录片) [jìlùpiān]	documentary films

4. 差 (差) [chà, chā]

差(差) has two different pronunciations: [chà] and [chā]. In 差不多(差不多) (similar), it is pronounced [chà] and in 時差(时差) (time difference, jetlag), it is pronounced [chā].

5. 秦始皇 (秦始皇)

秦始皇(秦始皇) was the First Emperor of the Qin Dynasty (221–206 B.C.). He unified the country, standardized the writing system, measurements, etc. and also ordered the Great Wall built (at the cost of thousands of lives). His anti-Confucian attitude also led him to persecute several hundred Confucian scholars and to burn books on Confucianism and history. For this he has been historically regarded as a tyrant.

6. 放 (電影) [放 (电影)]

The word 放(放) in 放電影(放电影) means "to show," and in 放下(放下) it means "to place."

語法 (语法) GRAMMAR

1. Comparison (2)

I. A 比 B + V. + degree of complement

- Review Degree of Complement

We learned in Lesson Sixteen of *Chinese Link: Elementary Chinese* that a sentence with a degree of complement is used to describe how an action is performed (such as how fast, how well, how soon, etc.). The pattern is summarized as follows:

Single Verb:	Subj. + V. + 得 + Adv. + Adj.

e.g.: 他跑得很快。 He runs very fast.

Verb-Object (VO):	Subj. + VO. + V. 得 + Adv. + Adj.

e.g.: 他打籃球打得很好。 He plays basketball very well.
他打篮球打得很好。

The object can also be placed at the beginning of a sentence for emphasis:

e.g.: 籃球他打得很好。
篮球他打得很好。

- The degree of complement is commonly used with 比 sentences to indicate the comparison of how an action is performed between A and B. For example:

Pattern:

A 比 B + V. + degree of complement

他比我跑得快。 He runs faster than I do.
他比我跑得快。

我比他寫漢字寫得好。 I write Chinese characters better than he does.
我比他写汉字写得好。

漢字我比他寫得好。 (漢字(汉字) is placed in the beginning of the sentence for emphasis)
汉字我比他写得好。

我比他吃甜食吃得多。 I eat more sweets than he does.
我比他吃甜食吃得多。

II. 比(比) + quantifier

Pattern: A 比 B + Adj. + Quantifier

Quantifier can be:

1. Definite quantifiers: e.g. a number and a measure word

   Examples:

   我比他大三歲。
   我比他大三岁。
   I am three years older than him.

   這張電影票比那張電影票便宜三塊錢。
   这张电影票比那张电影票便宜三块钱。
   This movie ticket is three dollars cheaper than that one.

2. Indefinite quantifiers: e.g. 一些(一些), 一點兒(一点儿), 的多(的多)

   Examples:

   我比他大一點兒。
   我比他大一点儿。
   I am a bit older than him.

   這張電影票比那張電影票便宜一些。
   这张电影票比那张电影票便宜一些。
   This movie ticket is bit cheaper than that one.

   我女朋友的錢比我的多的多。
   我女朋友的钱比我的多的多。
   My girlfriend has much more money than me.

3. Fractions and times: e.g. 一半, 三分之一, 五倍

   Examples:

   我們的學費比你們的少一半。
   我们的学费比你们的少一半。
   Our tuition fee is half of yours.

   這兒的中國人比那兒的多兩倍。
   这儿的中国人比那儿的多两倍。
   There are twice as many Chinese people here than there.

   今年的學生比去年的多三分之一。
   今年的学生比去年的多三分之一。
   There are one–third more students this year than last year.

2. Emphatic Pattern: 連(连) ...... 都/也(都/也) ......

This is a pattern used for emphasis. The part that is emphasized is usually the subject, the object or the verb of a sentence. Look at the following examples,

這部電影真好看。連我都看了兩次了。
这部电影真好看。连我都看了两次了。
This film is really good. Even I have seen it twice.
(This emphasizes the subject 我 and implies that I don't watch films very often.)

她是在中國出生的，可是她連自己的中文名字都不會寫。
她是在中国出生的，可是她连自己的中文名字都不会写。
She was born in China, but she was not even able to write her own name in Chinese.
(This emphasizes the object 自己的中文名字 and implies that her ability to write Chinese is very poor.)

她男朋友送給她一張音樂光碟，她連聽也沒聽，就把它放在旁邊了。
她男朋友送给她一张音乐光碟，她连听也没听，就把它放在旁边了。
– 音樂(音乐) [yīnyuè]: music – 光碟(光碟) [guāngdié]: disc
Her boyfriend gave her a music disc. She did not even spend any time listening to it before she put it aside.
(This emphasizes the action 聽(听) and implies that she had no interest in it at all.)

Note:

- The emphasized part is usually placed between 連(连) and 都/也(都/也).
- Sometimes, 連(连) can be omitted, but 都/也(都/也) can never be omitted.

3. Preposition 對(对)

對(对) can be used as a preposition. Together with its object, the 對- phrase (对- phrase) can be used as an adverbial to modify a verb or verb phrase, or as an attributive to modify a noun or a noun phrase. Here are some examples,

A. 對- phrase (对- phrase) as an adverbial modifying a verb or verb phrase:

對……有興趣 对……有兴趣	to be interested in . . .
對……有幫助 [bāngzhù] 对……有帮助	to be helpful to . . .
對……有用處 [yòngchù] 对……有用处	to be useful to . . .
對……有利 [yǒulì] 对……有利	to be beneficial to . . .

Examples:

他對中國文學有興趣。
他对中国文学有兴趣。
He is interested in Chinese literature.

鍛煉對身體有幫助。
锻炼对身体有帮助。
Exercise is good for your health.

游泳對身體有用處。
游泳对身体有用处。
Swimming is good for your health.

學中文對找工作有利。
学中文对找工作有利。
Studying Chinese is beneficial for finding a job.

B. 對- phrase (对- phrase) as an attributive to be followed by 的 + a noun or a noun phrase:

對……的描寫 对……的描写	the description of . . .
對……的幫助 对……的帮助	the help to . . .
對……的介紹 对……的介绍	the introduction to . . .

Examples:

這部電影對感情方面的描寫很細膩 [xìnì] (delicate, detailed) 。
这部电影对感情方面的描写很细腻 。
The portrayal of emotion in this movie is very delicate.

他對我們的幫助，我們永遠都忘不了。
他对我们的帮助，我们永远都忘不了。
We will never forget his help to us.

他對中國歷史的介紹，講 [jiǎng] (to speak) 得很清楚 。
他对中国历史的介绍，讲得很清楚 。
His introduction to Chinese history was very clearly spoken.

補充課文 (补充课文) SUPPLEMENTARY PRACTICE

This section will help you test your comprehension of the grammar and vocabulary you have learned in this lesson. Be prepared to answer questions about the meaning of the passage.

看電影 Watching Movies (繁體字 Traditional Character Version)

十一月十五日　　天氣：晴到多雲

今天上午我總算把一個大的研究報告交出去了，覺得輕鬆多了。下午沒有課，我就跟如春一起去看了一場電影。

我們是去大光明電影院看的電影。大光明電影院在市中心，那兒放的電影總是比別的電影院好。我們看了一場中國電影《十面埋伏》，是張藝謀導演的一部功夫片。影片的色彩和特技效果都比別的電影好，場面也比《英雄》和《臥虎藏龍》大得多。如春說《十面埋伏》的情節不如《英雄》和《臥虎藏龍》精彩，可是我不同意，我覺得《十面埋伏》比那兩部電影有意思得多。它還是威尼斯電影節上的開幕片呢。

有人說功夫片不像動作片那麼緊張、好看，可是我覺得好的功夫片比動作片精彩多了。我非常喜歡成龍和李連杰這兩個演員，尤其是李連杰，演得很不錯。

我對張藝謀導演的片子特別有興趣。他導演的很多片子我都看過，連他自己以前演的片子我也看了。我覺得他對電影情有獨鍾，思想很開放，風格也很獨特。他跟陳凱歌、李安這些導演差不多，都很有創新精神。

很多功夫片說的都是歷史故事。我對中國歷史非常感興趣，也有一些了解。中國的歷史那麼悠久，有五千多年了，比美國歷史要長四千多年。中國的傳統文化也特別豐富多彩。今後有機會，我一定要去中國學習中國歷史、傳統和文化。

補充課文 (补充课文) SUPPLEMENTARY PRACTICE

This section will help you test your comprehension of the grammar and vocabulary you have learned in this lesson. Be prepared to answer questions about the meaning of the passage.

看电影 Watching Movies (简体字 Simplified Character Version)

十一月十五日　　　天气：晴到多云

今天上午我总算把一个大的研究报告交出去了，觉得轻松多了。下午没有课，我就跟如春一起去看了一场电影。

我们是去大光明电影院看的电影。大光明电影院在市中心，那儿放的电影总是比别的电影院好。我们看了一场中国电影《十面埋伏》，是张艺谋导演的一部功夫片。影片的色彩和特技效果都比别的电影好，场面也比《英雄》和《卧虎藏龙》大得多。如春说《十面埋伏》的情节不如《英雄》和《卧虎藏龙》精彩，可是我不同意，我觉得《十面埋伏》比那两部电影有意思得多。它还是威尼斯电影节上的开幕片呢。

有人说功夫片不像动作片那么紧张、好看，可是我觉得好的功夫片比动作片精彩多了。我非常喜欢成龙和李连杰这两个演员，尤其是李连杰，演得很不错。

我对张艺谋导演的片子特别有兴趣。他导演的很多片子我都看过，连他自己以前演的片子我也看了。我觉得他对电影情有独钟，思想很开放，风格也很独特。他跟陈凯歌、李安这些导演差不多，都很有创新精神。

很多功夫片说的都是历史故事。我对中国历史非常感兴趣，也有一些了解。中国的历史那么悠久，有五千多年了，比美国历史要长四千多年。中国的传统文化也特别丰富多彩。今后有机会，我一定要去中国学习中国历史、传统和文化。

Notes:
總算(总算) [zǒngsuàn]: finally, eventually
市中心(市中心) [shìzhōngxīn]: downtown
總是(总是) [zǒngshì]: always
同意(同意) [tóngyì]: to agree
開幕片(开幕片) [kāimùpiān]: film shown at the opening ceremony
動作片(动作片) [dòngzuòpiān]: action movie
緊張(紧张) [jǐnzhāng]: breathtaking
尤其(尤其) [yóuqí]: especially
情有獨鍾(情有独钟) [qíngyǒudúzhōng]: to be especially resonant
思想(思想) [sīxiǎng]: way of thinking
開放(开放) [kāifàng]: open-minded
風格(风格) [fēnggé]: style
獨特(独特) [dútè]: unique
創新(创新) [chuàngxīn]: to be creative
精神(精神) [jīngshén]: spirit
悠久(悠久) [yōujiǔ]: long
傳統(传统) [chuántǒng]: tradition
文化(文化) [wénhuà]: culture
豐富多彩(丰富多彩) [fēngfùduōcǎi]: rich and colorful
機會(机会) [jīhuì]: opportunity

Proper Nouns:
威尼斯(威尼斯) [Wēinísī]: Venice
成龍(成龙) [Chéng Lóng]: Jack Cheng (a Chinese kongfu movie star)
陳凱歌(陈凯歌) [Chén Kǎigē]: Kaige Chen (a Chinese film director)
李安(李安) [Lǐ Ān]: Ang Lee (a Chinese film director)

練習 (练习) Exercises

1. 方慕華覺得《十面埋伏》跟《英雄》和《臥虎藏龍》比起來怎麼樣?
   方慕华觉得《十面埋伏》跟《英雄》和《卧虎藏龙》比起来怎么样?
2. 他為什麼對張藝謀導演的片子特別有興趣?
   他为什么对张艺谋导演的片子特别有兴趣?
3. 中國的歷史和美國的歷史比起來怎麼樣?
   中国的历史和美国的历史比起来怎么样?

成語故事 (成语故事) IDIOM STORY

得意揚揚 (得意扬扬) [déyìyángyáng]

Meaning: Feeling complacent or extremely proud

Usage: This is used to describe someone who is immensely proud or looks triumphant

Example: 他在那部電影裡只出現了一下子，就整天一副“得意揚揚”的樣子。
他在那部电影里只出现了一下子，就整天一副“得意扬扬”的样子。

Pay attention to the usages of grammar points: A 比 B + V. + degree of complement, 比(比) + quantifier, 對(对) used as a preposition

(繁體字 **Traditional Character Version**)

兩千多年前的春秋戰國時期，有一個馬夫趕馬車趕得又快又穩，比別的馬夫好得多。那時有一個宰相名字叫晏子，很有學問，懂的比別人多得多，可是他很謙虛，因此大家都很尊敬他。晏子知道那個馬夫趕馬車趕得好，就請他當了自己的馬夫。馬夫非常高興，也非常驕傲。他覺得別人都不如自己那麼了不起，所以每次他趕著馬車出去的時候，都很得意，看上去比晏子神氣得多。

有一次，晏子坐著馬車經過馬夫的家門前，馬夫的妻子正好看見了馬夫得意揚揚的樣子，心裡很不高興。馬夫回家時，妻子就說她想離開他。馬夫對妻子的話很不理解，妻子說：你只是一個給宰相趕馬車的馬夫，可是你卻那麼驕傲。趕車的時候那麼得意揚揚，比別人神氣得多。晏子比你的地位高得多，可是他不像你那麼驕傲、得意揚揚。你自以為比別人了不起，我對你很失望。我不願意跟你在一起生活了。

馬夫覺得妻子說得很對。從那以後，他變得比以前謙虛得多。晏子問他為什麼變了，他說連他的妻子都說他不應該那麼得意揚揚的樣子，他怎麼能再驕傲呢！晏子聽了以後覺得馬夫的妻子是一個非常懂道理的女子。後來他就讓馬夫當了官。

這個故事告訴我們：一個人應該謙虛，而不應該自以為了不起。

(简体字 **Simplified Character Version**)

两千多年前的春秋战国时期，有一个马夫赶马车赶得又快又稳，比别的马夫好得多。那时有一个宰相名字叫晏子，很有学问，懂的比别人多得多，可是他很谦虚，因此大家都很尊敬他。晏子知道那个马夫赶马车赶得好，就请他当了自己的马夫。马夫非常高兴，也非常骄傲。他觉得别人都不如自己那么了不起，所以每次他赶着马车出去的时候，都很得意，看上去比晏子神气得多。

有一次，晏子坐着马车经过马夫的家门前，马夫的妻子正好看见了马夫得意扬扬的样子，心里很不高兴。马夫回家时，妻子就说她想离开他。马夫对妻子的话很不理解，妻子说：你只是一个给宰相赶马车的马夫，可是你却那么骄傲。赶车的时候那么得意扬扬，比别人神气得多。晏子比你的地位高得多，可是他不像你那么骄傲、得意扬扬。你自以为比别人了不起，我对你很失望。我不愿意跟你在一起生活了。

马夫觉得妻子说得很对。从那以后，他变得比以前谦虚得多。晏子问他为什么变了，他说连他的妻子都说他不应该那么得意扬扬的样子，他怎么能再骄傲呢！晏子听了以后觉得马夫的妻子是一个非常懂道理的女子。后来他就让马夫当了官。

这个故事告诉我们：一个人应该谦虚，而不应该自以为了不起。

Useful words and expressions:

得意揚揚(得意扬扬) [déyìyángyáng]: to feel complacent or extremely proud
春秋(春秋) [Chūnqiū]: Spring & Autumn (770–476 B.C.), a historical period in China
戰國(战国) [Zhànguó]: Warring States (475–221 B.C.), a historical period in China
時期(时期) [shíqī]: period
馬夫(马夫) [mǎfū]: horse carriage driver
趕馬(赶马) [gǎnmǎ]: to drive a horse
穩(稳) [wěn]: steady, stable
宰相(宰相) [zǎixiàng]: prime minister
晏子(晏子) [Yànzǐ]: (name of the prime minister of State of Qi)
學問(学问) [xuéwèn]: knowledge
謙虛(谦虚) [qiānxū]: to be modest
尊敬(尊敬) [zūnjìng]: respect; to respect
驕傲(骄傲) [jiāo'ào]: arrogant
神氣(神气) [shénqì]: to look cocky
妻子(妻子) [qīzi]: wife
理解(理解) [lǐjiě]: understanding; to understand
卻(却) [què]: on the contrary
地位(地位) [dìwèi]: (social) status
自以為(自以为) [zìyǐwéi]: to consider oneself . . .
對……失望(对……失望) [duì . . . shīwàng]: to be disappointed at . . .
懂道理(懂道理) [dǒngdàolǐ]: to be sensible and intelligent, to know the hows and whys
當官(当官) [dāngguān]: to take the position of an official

練習 (练习) Exercises

1. 找出有下面語法的句子: A 比 B + V. + degree of complement, 比 + quantifier, 對 used as a preposition

   找出有下面语法的句子: A 比 B + V. + degree of complement, 比 + quantifier, 对 used as a preposition

2. 用你自己的話說說“得意揚揚”的故事。
   用你自己的话说说“得意扬扬”的故事。

3. 請用“得意揚揚”造一個句子或者說一個得意揚揚的例子。
   请用“得意扬扬”造一个句子或者说一个得意扬扬的例子。

4. “得意揚揚”的故事，告訴了我們什麼?
   “得意扬扬”的故事，告诉了我们什么?

練習 (练习) ACTIVITIES

I. 聽力練習 (听力练习)

8-1 In the blanks provided, write the Pinyin for the words you hear:

1. 他們倆 ____ ____ 大，不過哥哥 ____ 弟弟 ____ ____ ____ ____。
   他们俩 ____ ____ 大，不过哥哥 ____ 弟弟 ____ ____ ____ ____。

2. 這一幢大樓 ____ 那一幢 ____ ____ ____。
   这一幢大楼 ____ 那一幢 ____ ____ ____。

3. 同學們 ____ 我的 ____ ____ 很大。
   同学们 ____ 我的 ____ ____ 很大。

4. 紐約的房租 ____ 這兒的 ____ ____ ____。
   纽约的房租 ____ 这儿的 ____ ____ ____。

5. 小說 ____ 電影 ____ ____ ____ ____。
   小说 ____ 电影 ____ ____ ____ ____。

6. 吃維生素 ____ 健康 ____ ____ ____。
   吃维生素 ____ 健康 ____ ____ ____。

7. 小琴 ____ 中國書法 ____ ____ ____ ____ 。
   小琴 ____ 中国书法 ____ ____ ____ ____ 。

8. 這部電影太短了， ____ 一個小時 ____ ____ ____ 。
   这部电影太短了， ____ 一个小时 ____ ____ ____ 。

8-2 Listen to the following stories and then answer the questions:

第一個故事(第一个故事) [dìyī ge gùshi] (Story 1):

Useful words and expressions:

古時候(古时候) [gùshíhòu]: ancient times
孔融(孔融) [Kǒng Róng]: name of a person
梨子(梨子) [lízi]: pear
笑(笑) [xiào]: to smile, laugh

第一段問題(第一段问题):

1. 孔融有幾個哥哥? 他是最小的孩子嗎?
   孔融有几个哥哥? 他是最小的孩子吗?
2. 孔融拿的梨子是什麼樣 [shénmeyàng] (what kind) 的?
   孔融拿的梨子是什么样 [shénmeyàng] (what kind) 的?
3. 孔融為什麼拿那個梨子?
   孔融为什么拿那个梨子?

第二個故事(第二个故事) (Story 2):

Useful words and expressions:

二手車(二手车) [èrshǒuchē]: used car
決定(决定) [juédìng]: to decide; decision
油(油) [yóu]: gasoline, oil
傷腦筋(伤脑筋) [shāngnǎojīn]: knotty, bothersome
優點(优点) [yōudiǎn]: merit, strong point
缺點(缺点) [quēdiǎn]: weakness

List the traits of the two types of cars in the table below. Then use 比 sentences to make comparisons

	日本車(日本车)	德國車(德国车)
優點 (优点)		
缺點 (缺点)		

8-3 Read the following lyric, paying special attention to the tones and the rhythm:

Rú Mèng Lìng	如夢令 如梦令
(Lǐ Qīngzhào)	(李清照) (李清照)
Cháng jì xītíng rì mù,	常記溪亭日暮, 常记溪亭日暮,
Chénzuì bù zhī guīlù.	沉醉不知歸路。 沉醉不知归路。
Xìng jìn wǎn huí zhōu,	興盡晚回舟, 兴尽晚回舟,
Wù rù ǒuhuā shēnchù.	誤入藕花深處。 误入藕花深处。
Zhēng dù, zhēng dù,	爭渡,爭渡, 争渡,争渡,
Jīngqǐ yìtān ōu lù.	驚起一灘鷗鷺。 惊起一滩鸥鹭。

To the tune of **Ru Meng Ling**
(Li, Qingzhao)

My memory always lingers on sunset over the riverside pavilion,
Intoxicated, not knowing our way home.
Getting tired, we tried to row our boats homeward,
We entered deep into the lotus pond by mistake.
We rowed the boats chasing one another,
A flock of herons were startled and fluttered up to the sky.

Practice: What are the rhyming words in this lyric? Write them out in Pinyin.

押 __________ 韻，押韻的字有：______；______；______；______；______；______。
押 __________ 韵，押韵的字有：______；______；______；______；______；______。

II. 漢字練習 (汉字练习)

8-4 Read the following words, phrases, and sentences:

關 关	對 对
關於 关于	對風景的描寫 对风景的描写
關於歷史 关于历史	對風景的描寫感興趣 对风景的描写感兴趣
關於中國歷史 关于中国历史	導演對風景的描寫很感興趣 导演对风景的描写很感兴趣
他喜歡關於中國歷史的小說 他喜欢关于中国历史的小说	看起來導演對風景的描寫很感興趣 看起来导演对风景的描写很感兴趣

Now try to use the following characters to make words, phrases, and then sentences:

1. 連 连	2. 影 影	3. 強 强	4. 告 告	5. 吸 吸	6. 節 节
7. 代 代	8. 它 它	9. 而 而	10. 顏 颜	11. 末 末	12. 價 价

8-5 Form groups of three to create phrases with the following words (pay attention to the various usages of each word):

Example: 影：影子，電影
影：影子，电影

1. 報：
   报：
2. 輕：
   轻：
3. 別：
   别：
4. 差：
   差：
5. 場：
   场：
6. 趣：
   趣：
7. 情：
   情：
8. 票：
   票：
9. 客：
   客：
10. 精：
    精：

III. 語法練習 (语法练习)

8-6 The following table lists the collections of several categories of books in a library. Please form pairs to make comparisons about the book collections. Make at least four comparison sentences for each category.

Useful comparison patterns:

A 比 B

A 比 B + V. + Degree of Complement

A 比 B + Adj. + Quantifier

Useful words and expressions:

商業 [shāngyè]: business

	文學(文学)	工程(工程)	商業(商业)
中文書 (中文书)	501 本	135 本	356 本
英文書 (英文书)	5250 本	557 本	1587 本
法文書 (法文书)	2138 本	223 本	625 本
德文書 (德文书)	1253 本	454 本	489 本
西班牙文書 (西班牙文书)	2517 本	743 本	652 本
日文書 (日文书)	489 本	264 本	422 本

8-7 Fill in the blanks with appropriate words:

1. 她的頭髮 ____ 他男朋友的頭髮要 ____ ____ ____ 。
   她的头发 ____ 他男朋友的头发要 ____ ____ ____ (much shorter) 。
2. 這門課很輕鬆, ____ 期末考試 ____ ____ ____ 。
   这门课很轻松, ____ 期末考试 ____ ____ ____ (even has no final exam) 。
3. 她用電腦打中文字 ____ 打英文字 ____ ____ ____ 。
   她用电脑打中文字 ____ 打英文字 ____ ____ ____ (much slower than) 。
4. 老師和師母 ____ 學生們都很 ____ ____ 。
   老师和师母 ____ 学生们都很 ____ ____ (warm-hearted towards students) 。

5. 早睡早起 [zǎoshuì zǎoqǐ] (go to bed early, get up early) _____ 身體 _____ _____ _____ 。

   早睡早起 _____ 身体 _____ _____ _____ (is beneficial to health) 。

6. 我的手錶 _____ 你的 _____ 五分鐘。
   我的手表 _____ 你的 _____ 五分钟 (five minutes faster) 。

7. 老闆常常忙得連喝水的時間 _____ _____ _____ 。
   老板常常忙得连喝水的时间 _____ _____ _____ (even has no time to drink water) 。

8. 在秀水街 [Xiùshuǐjiē] (Xiushui Street) 買東西的外國人 _____ 中國人 _____ _____ _____ 。

   在秀水街买东西的外国人 _____ 中国人 _____ _____ _____ (twice as many) 。

8-8 Translate the following Chinese into English orally:

Useful words and expressions:

飲料(饮料) [yǐnliào]: beverage
有效率(有效率) [yǒuxiàolǜ]: efficient
巴西(巴西) [Bāxī]: Brazil
生產(生产) [shēngchǎn]: to produce
國家(国家) [guójiā]: country
茶葉(茶叶) [cháyè]: tea leaves
品種(品种) [pǐnzhǒng]: variety, assortment
加糖(加糖) [jiātáng]: to add sugar
容易(容易) [róngyì]: easy
發胖(发胖) [fāpàng]: to gain weight

咖啡和茶(咖啡和茶)

(繁體字：**Traditional Character Version**)

咖啡和茶都是人們愛喝的飲料。累的時候喝一點兒咖啡或者茶，都會覺得很有精神，工作起來比沒喝以前要有效率得多。人們每年喝的咖啡比茶多三倍，可是喝茶的人比喝咖啡的人多得多。巴西是生產咖啡最多的國家。中國是茶葉品種最多的國家。咖啡和茶都很好喝，可是因為很多人喝咖啡的時候都喜歡加糖，所以咖啡喝多了容易發胖。茶葉裡面有很多維生素，所以喝茶對健康很有好處。

(简体字：**Simplified Character Version**)

咖啡和茶都是人们爱喝的饮料。累的时候喝一点儿咖啡或者茶，都会觉得很有精神，工作起来比没喝以前要有效率得多。人们每年喝的咖啡比茶多三倍，可是喝茶的人比喝咖啡的人多得多。巴西是生产咖啡最多的国家。中国是茶叶品种最多的国家。咖啡和茶都很好喝，可是因为很多人喝咖啡的时候都喜欢加糖，所以咖啡喝多了容易发胖。茶叶里面有很多维生素，所以喝茶对健康很有好处。

IV. 交際活動 (交际活动)

Role play:

Below are a list of items held at the Lost and Found service counter. 小明 lost a bag in the airport. Form pairs, one taking the role of 小明 and the other the role of an employee in the Lost and Found Office. Make comparisons to see whether the claiming item is 小明's.

時間(时间)		地點(地点)	物品(物品)
2004/7/9	下午 02:00	美國航空公司服務台 (美国航空公司服务台)	柯達數碼相機 (柯达数码相机)
2004/7/1	上午 11:15	一樓女洗手間 (一楼女洗手间)	外套 (外套)
2004/6/28	上午 07:30	西北航空公司候機廳 (西北航空公司候机厅)	鑰匙 (钥匙)
2004/6/23	晚上 09:40	安全檢查通道 (安全检查通道)	手錶 (手表)
2004/6/10	下午 03:25	咖啡廳 (咖啡厅)	皮包 (皮包)

Useful words and expressions:

失物(失物) [shīwù]: lost item
地點(地点) [dìdiǎn]: place
服務台(服务台) [fúwùtái]: service desk
數碼相機(数码相机) [shùmǎ xiàngjī]: digital camera
外套(外套) [wàitào]: overcoat
鑰匙(钥匙) [yàoshi]: key
安全檢查(安全检查) [ānquán jiǎnchá]: security check
咖啡廳(咖啡厅) [kāfēitīng]: cafe
招領(招领) [zhāolǐng]: to be claimed
物品(物品) [wùpǐn]: items, things
柯達(柯达) [kēdá]: Kodak
洗手間(洗手间) [xǐshǒujiān]: restroom
候機廳(候机厅) [hòujītīng]: waiting room
手錶(手表) [shǒubiǎo]: watch
通道(通道) [tōngdào]: passage
皮包(皮包) [píbāo]: purse, bag

Useful expressions:

Comparison: 1. A 比 B + V. + degree of complement
2. A 比 B + Adj. + quantifier (三倍，一些，一點兒，的多)
(三倍，一些，一点儿，的多)

連……都，對……有幫助(有利)
连……都，对……有帮助(有利)

文化知識 (文化知识) Culture Link

文化點滴 (文化点滴) CULTURE NOTES

中國的電影事業 (中国的电影事业) [Zhōngguó de diànyǐng shìyè] The Movie Industry in China

The first film shot in China, about a Peking Opera performance, was produced in 1905. Then, in the 1930s China's film industry experienced its first peak. The second peak came during the 1950s to the mid-1960s. However, during the Cultural Revolution, the film industry suffered from 1966 to 1976, during which few feature films were made. Chinese films started to flourish again in the early 1980s. Since then, a good number of films produced by the new generation of directors, actors and actresses have won awards at international film festivals and gained worldwide reputation. Most prominent among them are film directors 張藝謀 (张艺谋) [Zhāng Yìmóu] and 陳凱歌(陈凯歌) [Chén Kǎigē], and actresses 鞏俐(巩俐) [Gǒng Lì] and 章子怡 [Zhāng Zǐyí]. In 2005, China celebrated the 100th year of its movie industry, which is now capable of producing more than 100 films, 7,000 TV series, and importing more than 1,000 movies and TV programs from overseas each year.

Films in China today fall into four categories: 1) "mainstream films" which are generally government-funded and mainly depict political figures and historic events of the Chinese Communist Party; 2) artistic films which portray the life and thoughts of people in contemporary China; 3) entertainment and commercial films which began to be made in the late 1980s and roughly are of two types: the comic-style "New Year celebration films" and martial arts films; and 4) new-generation films shot by young artists who have received professional education in arts and theatrical institutes and who emphasize rebellion and advocate an avant-garde style.

Along with the globalization of China's economy and its entry into the WTO, China has begun reforms in film distribution, release and marketing. Five group companies and three film production centers have been established in China with the aim of making full and better use of the capital and human resources available to promote China's film industry to meet international standards.

Today many movie theaters in China offer digital movies. Here is the entrance of one of them in Guangzhou.

Foreign investors are now welcomed and encouraged to participate in the construction and renovation of movie theaters as long as they own no more than 49% of the shares. The government also encourages film directors, actors and actresses to "step out of the door of the country" to "face the world" (面向世界 [miàn xiàng shìjiè]). As a result, more and more Chinese films have entered the international community and more and more Chinese actors and actresses have been invited to participate in foreign films.

In addition, new laws have been formulated to guard against copyright infringement, protect the lawful rights of all parties concerned and establish a rating system to protect young viewers.

As the new laws clearly delineate what can and cannot be done, it is easier now for movie-makers to focus on movie-making instead of dealing with bureaucracy. The implementation of a new law governing movie advertising and distribution has laid the legal foundation for smoother international exchanges. China has entered the world movie industry and will play a more and more important role in it.

問題討論 (问题讨论) Discussion Questions

1. 你看過什麼中國電影? 你最喜歡的中國電影是什麼?

你看过什么中国电影? 你最喜欢的中国电影是什么?

What Chinese movies have you seen? Which Chinese movie do you like the best?

2. 你知道哪些有名的中國演員？請說說他們為什麼有名？

你知道哪些有名的中国演员？请说说他们为什么有名？

Do you know any famous Chinese actors or actresses? Why are they famous?

趣味中文 (趣味中文) FUN WITH CHINESE

比上不足，比下有餘
比上不足，比下有余
Not as much as those above, but more than those below.

bǐ	shàng	bùzú,	bǐ	xià	yǒu	yú
比	上	不足，	比	下	有	餘
比	上	不足，	比	下	有	余
to compare	up	not enough	to compare	down	to have	surplus

This phrase is usually used to tell someone to "be satisfied."

問題討論 (问题讨论) Discussion Questions

1. Do you like somebody who always compares his/her strengths/weaknesses with others? Why?
2. Are there any expressions in your language which tell you to be satisfied?
3. Try to use your own words to explain 比上不足，比下有餘 (比上不足，比下有余) in Chinese.

行動吧! (行动吧!) LET'S GO!

電影票和戲票 (电影票和戏票)
Movie and opera tickets

When they studied Chinese in China last summer, 文美 and 慕華 (慕华) went to the movie and the Beijing Opera. Following are the movie and the opera tickets. Please read them carefully and answer the questions below:

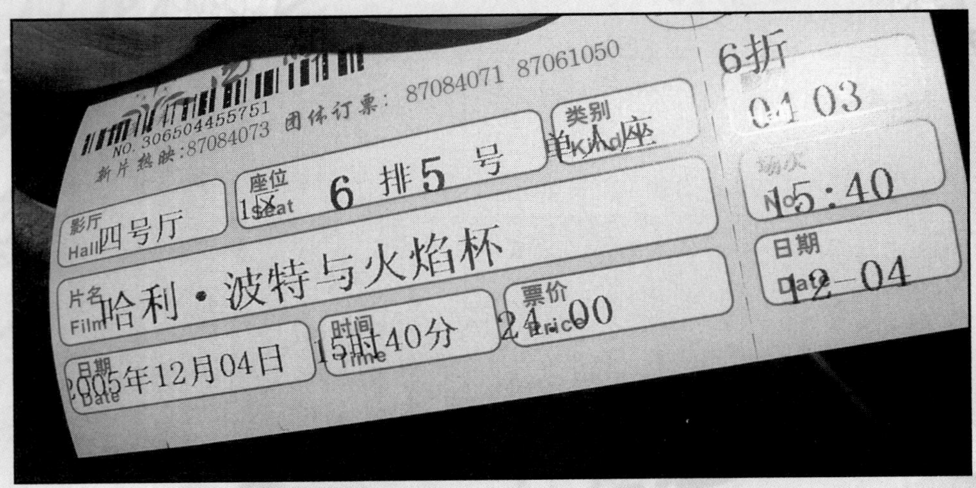

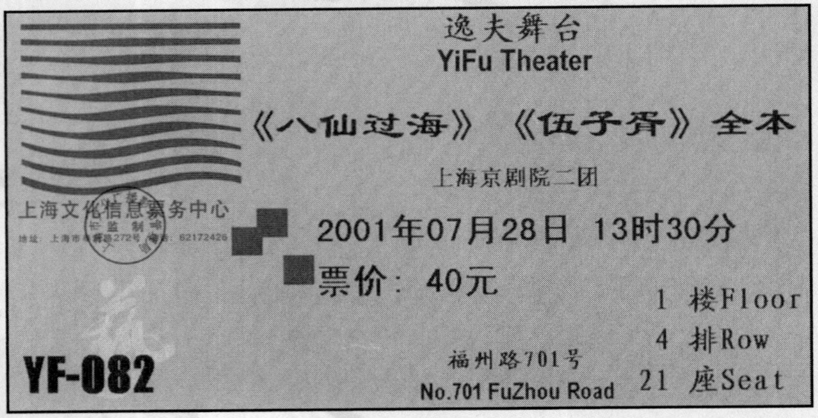

Useful words and expressions:

新片(新片) [xīnpiān]: new film
熱映(热映) [rèyìng]: to be a hot/popular show
團體(团体) [tuántǐ]: group
訂(订) [dìng]: to book
折(折) [zhé]: discount
日期(日期) [rìqī]: date
影廳(影厅) [yǐngtīng]: showing hall, movie theatre
座位(座位) [zuòwèi]: seat

類別(类别) [lèibié]: category

哈利波特與火焰杯(哈利波特与火焰杯) [Hālì Bōtè yǔ huǒyànbēi]: Harry Potter and the Goblet of Fire

逸夫(逸夫) [Yìfū]: Yifu Shao, name of a philanthropist who has made many donations to libraries, museums, theaters, etc. in China and Hong Kong. These places were all later named after him.

舞台(舞台) [wǔtái]: platform

仙(仙) [xiān]: celestial being

伍子胥(伍子胥) [Wǔzǐxū]: a famous loyal official in the historical period of Three Kingdoms (220–286?) whose hair turned white overnight because of his worry about his country

團(团) [tuán]: troupe

文化(文化) [wénhuà]: culture

信息(信息) [xìnxī]: information

票務(票务) [piàowù]: ticket affairs

中心(中心) [zhōngxīn]: center

問題討論 (问题讨论) Discussion Questions

1. What movie did 文美 and 慕華(慕华) watch?
2. What date did they watch it? At what time?
3. How much was the ticket? How much of a discount did they get?
4. Where did they watch Beijing Opera?
5. What opera did they watch?
6. How much is a Beijing Opera ticket?
7. What is 上海文化信息票務中心(上海文化信息票务中心)?

復習 (复习) Review

LESSON 7 TO LESSON 8

I. Activities

A. You are making a phone call to a travel agency to book two plane tickets to your home in Seattle during the Thanksgiving holiday. You need to use *Verb + potential complement structure* and *the patterns for comparison* to cover the following topics in your phone conversation:

1. 你想買什麼時候的飛機票?
   你想买什么时候的飞机票?
2. 飛機票的價格是多少? 網上的票價便宜還是旅行社的票價便宜?
   飞机票的价格是多少? 网上的票价便宜还是旅行社的票价便宜?
3. 如果旅行社的人告訴你機票訂不到，你願意換時間和航空公司嗎?
   如果旅行社的人告诉你机票订不到，你愿意换时间和航空公司吗?

B. You are deciding between 昆明(昆明) and 北京(北京) for your winter trip. Your roommate has been to those places. Carry on a conversation with your roommate and ask him/her to find out as much information about the two cities as possible. You need to use the following grammatical patterns:

1. Various patterns of comparison
2. Degree of complement
3. Potential complement

The following words and expressions should also be used:

差不多(差不多)，棒(棒)，打算(打算)，原來(原来)，其實(其实)，
南方(南方)，比如(比如)，風景如畫(风景如画)，
連(连) …… 都(都) ……，網站(网站)，先(先)……，
然後(然后) ……，再(再) ……

C. You have just watched a Chinese movie. It was a martial arts movie about Chinese history. You enjoyed it very much. Now you are talking to your roommate about this movie and trying to encourage him/her to go and watch it because you know he/she is very interested in Chinese history. You should include the following topics:

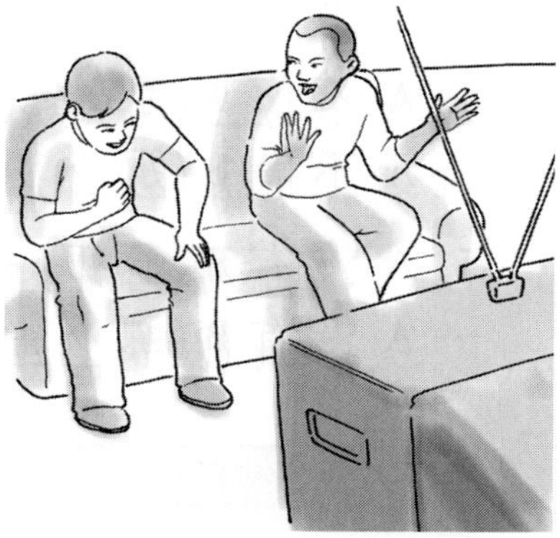

1. 電影的名字是什麼?
   电影的名字是什么?
2. 你為什麼會去看這部電影?
   你为什么会去看这部电影?
3. 你覺得這部電影怎麼樣? 為什麼?
   你觉得这部电影怎么样? 为什么?

II. Review of grammar

A. Fill in the blanks of each sentence with a word as potential complement and then provide a positive answer:

1. 老師上課的時候你聽得 ______ 嗎?
   老师上课的时候你听得 ______ 吗?
   ________________________________ 。
2. 文華找得 ______ 找不 ______ 他的電話簿?
   文华找得 ______ 找不 ______ 他的电话簿?
   ________________________________ 。
3. 文華現在訂不 ______ 去中國的飛機票。你覺得她今年寒假能去得 ______ 中國嗎?
   文华现在订不 ______ 去中国的飞机票。你觉得她今年寒假能去得 ______ 中国吗?
   ________________________________ 。
4. 中國的飛機到得 ______ 到不 ______ 昆明?
   中国的飞机到得 ______ 到不 ______ 昆明?
   ________________________________ 。

B. Compare China and the US. Find their similarities and differences. You must use the following patterns for comparison:

1. A 跟 B 一樣 + stative V. / adj
   A 跟 B 一样 + stative V. / adj

B. Match the traditional/simplified form of the following characters:

1. 觀 ______	2. 關 ______	3. 導 ______	4. 興 ______
5. 輕 ______	6. 鬆 ______	7. 歷 ______	8. 場 ______

A. 历 B. 场 C. 松 D. 兴 E. 关 F. 轻 G. 导 H. 观

IV. Review: Useful words and expressions

For 旅遊(旅游):

旅行社(旅行社), 訂(订), 飛機票(飞机票), 聚(聚), 貴(贵), 查(查), 網站(网站), 地圖(地图), 四季如春(四季如春), 風景如畫(风景如画), 西南(西南), 買到(买到), 城市(城市), 地方(地方), 辦(办), 簽證(签证)

For 電影(电影):

導演(导演), 演員(演员), 功夫片(功夫片), 好看(好看), 情節(情节), 場面(场面), 特技(特技), 效果(效果), 顏色(颜色), 票價(票价), 電影院(电影院), 歷史故事(历史故事), 吸引人(吸引人), 精彩(精彩), 部(部)

第九課
LESSON
9

你越來越精神了 (你越来越精神了) You Are Getting More and More Energetic

教學目標 (教学目标) OBJECTIVES

- Talk about fitness
- Make comparisons

Many internationally renowned beauty parlor chains have expanded into mainland China. Chlitina is just one of them.

Do you know what 专业美容护肤中心 *is?*

Products for weight loss and skin protection have become very popular. Ads for weight loss and skin protection products are everywhere.

What is 好身材*? How can one get a* 好身材 *according to this ad?*

生詞 (生词) VOCABULARY

核心詞 (核心词) Core Vocabulary

TRADITIONAL	SIMPLIFIED	PINYIN		
1. 越來越……	越来越……	yuèláiyuè		more and more . . .
2. 需要	需要	xūyào	V.	to require
3. 鐘頭	钟头	zhōngtóu	N.	hour
4. 瘦	瘦	shòu	Adj.	thin, slim, skinny
5. 減肥	减肥	jiǎnféi	V.O.	to lose weight
6. 堅持	坚持	jiānchí	V.	to persist, persevere
7. 體重	体重	tǐzhòng	N.	body weight
8. 輕	轻	qīng	Adj	light
9. 磅	磅	bàng	M.W.	pound (weight measurement)
10. 怪不得	怪不得	guàibude		no wonder
11. 苗條	苗条	miáotiao	Adj.	slim
12. 女孩子	女孩子	nǚháizi	N.	girl
13. 控制	控制	kòngzhì	V.	to control
14. 飲食	饮食	yǐnshí	N.	food and drink, eating
15. 注意	注意	zhùyì	N. V.	attention to pay attention to

TRADITIONAL	SIMPLIFIED	PINYIN		
16. 甜食	甜食	tiánshí	N.	sweet food
17. 早	早	zǎo	Adv. Adj.	(to emphasize long ago) early
18. 個子	个子	gèzi	N.	height, stature
19. 矮	矮	ǎi	Adj.	short
20. 呎	呎	chǐ	N.	foot (British measurement)
21. 吋	吋	cùn	N.	inch (British measurement)
22. 超過	超过	chāoguò	V.	to surpass
23. 靈活	灵活	línghuó	Adj.	dexterous, agile, flexible
24. 總是	总是	zǒngshì	Adv.	always
25. 重要	重要	zhòngyào	Adj.	important
26. 更	更	gèng	Adv.	more

專名 (专名) Proper Nouns

TRADITIONAL	SIMPLIFIED	PINYIN		
1. 白思琴	白思琴	Bái Sīqín	N.	(name) Siqin Bai
2. 胡欣明	胡欣明	Hú Xīnmíng	N.	(name) Xinming Hu

補充詞 (补充词) Supplementary Vocabulary

TRADITIONAL	SIMPLIFIED	PINYIN		
1. 盎司	盎司	àngsī	N.	ounce
2. 公斤	公斤	gōngjīn	N.	kilogram
3. 公尺	公尺	gōngchǐ	N.	meter
4. 公分	公分	gōngfēn	N.	centimeter

語文知識 (语文知识) LANGUAGE LINK

The Sentence Patterns provide models that will help you with the Language in Use section. In both sections, pay attention to the grammar points, vocabulary, and expressions.

句型 (句型) Sentence Patterns

A: 最近我很少游泳，每星期都要比以前少游兩、三次。
最近我很少游泳，每星期都要比以前少游两、三次。
Zuìjìn wǒ hěnshǎo yóuyǒng, měi xīngqī dōu yào bǐ yǐqián shǎo yóu liǎng, sān cì.

B: 其實你越忙越需要鍛煉。
其实你越忙越需要锻炼。
Qíshí nǐ yuè máng yuè xūyào duànliàn.

A: 你控制飲食嗎?
你控制饮食吗?
Nǐ kòngzhì yǐnshí ma?

B: 是的。我現在甜食吃得越來越少了。
是的。我现在甜食吃得越来越少了。
Shìde. Wǒ xiànzài tiánshí chī de yuèláiyuè shǎo le.

A: 你比前幾個月還瘦了不少!
你比前几个月还瘦了不少!
Nǐ bǐ qián jǐge yuè hái shòu le bù shǎo!

B: 如果你多運動，身體就會比以前更好。
如果你多运动，身体就会比以前更好。
Rúguǒ nǐ duō yùndòng, shēntǐ jiù huì bǐ yǐqián gèng hǎo.

課文: 你越來越精神了 (繁體字)
Language in Use: Traditional Character Version

白思琴: 欣明，你最近常去健身房鍛煉嗎?

胡欣明: 這兩個星期是我最忙的時候，鍛煉得比以前少得多。以前我差不多天天游泳，最近差不多每星期都要比以前少游兩、三次，這個星期一次也沒去過。

白思琴: 那可不好。其實越忙越需要鍛煉。我每天都要去運動一個鐘頭，現在我的精神越來越好了。你看，我比前幾個月還瘦了不少吧!

胡欣明: 真的，你看上去比上學期瘦了很多。你最近在減肥嗎?

白思琴: 是呀! 我已經堅持了三個月了。效果不錯吧! 體重比以前輕了十幾磅。

胡欣明: 怪不得你越來越苗條了，差不多是我們女孩子中最苗條的了。你是怎麼減肥的? 控制飲食嗎?

白思琴: 主要是鍛煉，當然在吃的方面我也比較注意。我以前最喜歡吃甜食，可是現在我吃得越來越少了。

胡欣明: 你怎麼會想到要減肥呢?

白思琴: 我早就想減肥了。我的個子有點兒矮，只有五呎一吋，可是三個月以前我的體重超過了一百三十磅。

胡欣明: 那你最重的時候比我還要重呢!

白思琴: 是呀! 我要是太重了就會覺得不太靈活，也很不舒服。

胡欣明: 我真應該向你學習，可是我總是覺得功課太多、太忙，沒有時間鍛煉。現在我每天都比別人還要少睡兩、三個鐘頭呢。

白思琴: 其實，最重要的是要多鍛煉、多運動。運動了以後你的身體會比以前更好，你會更有精神，學習的效果可能就會更好了。

课文：你越来越精神了 (简体字)
Language in Use: Simplified Character Version

白思琴：欣明，你最近常去健身房锻炼吗？

胡欣明：这两个星期是我最忙的时候，锻炼得比以前少得多。以前我差不多天天游泳，最近差不多每星期都要比以前少游两、三次，这个星期一次也没去过。

白思琴：那可不好。其实越忙越需要锻炼。我每天都要去运动一个钟头，现在我的精神越来越好了。你看，我比前几个月还瘦了不少吧！

胡欣明：真的，你看上去比上学期瘦了很多。你最近在减肥吗？

白思琴：是呀！我已经坚持了三个月了。效果不错吧！体重比以前轻了十几磅。

胡欣明：怪不得你越来越苗条了，差不多是我们女孩子中最苗条的了。你是怎么减肥的？控制饮食吗？

白思琴：主要是锻炼，当然在吃的方面我也比较注意。我以前最喜欢吃甜食，可是现在我吃得越来越少了。

胡欣明：你怎么会想到要减肥呢？

白思琴：我早就想减肥了。我的个子有点儿矮，只有五呎一吋，可是三个月以前我的体重超过了一百三十磅。

胡欣明：那你最重的时候比我还要重呢！

白思琴：是呀！我要是太重了就会觉得不太灵活，也很不舒服。

胡欣明：我真应该向你学习，可是我总是觉得功课太多、太忙，没有时间锻炼。现在我每天都比别人还要少睡两、三个钟头呢。

白思琴：其实，最重要的是要多锻炼、多运动。运动了以后你的身体会比以前更好，你会更有精神，学习的效果可能就会更好了。

注釋 (注释) LANGUAGE NOTES

1. 那可不好 (那可不好)

那可不好(那可不好) means "That is not very good." This is a colloquial expression often used in conversations to express dissatisfaction, disagreement, disappointment, etc. in a mild way.

2. 怪不得 (怪不得)

怪不得(怪不得) means "no wonder," "so that's why." This is also a colloquial expression often used in conversations to indicate that the speaker has understood the reason for something.

3. 個子 (身高)，重量 (體重) [个子 (身高)，重量 (体重)]

個子(个子)/身高(身高) and 重量(重量)/體重(体重) are expressions used to mean "body height" and "body weight." 個子(个子) and 重量(重量) are more informal and usually used in conversations, while 身高(身高) and 體重(体重) are more formal and used more in written Chinese.

4. 鐘頭/小時 (钟头/小时)

Both 鐘頭(钟头) and 小時(小时) mean "hour" but 鐘頭(钟头) is generally used in speaking whereas 小時(小时) is a more formal expression used in both conversation and writing.

語法 (语法) GRAMMAR

1. Comparison (3): 比 (比) and the Emphatic Degree 更 (要) [更 (要)], 還 (要) [还 (要)]

Pattern:

A	(compare with) 比(比)	B	(even more) 更 / 更要 (更 / 更要) 還 / 還要 (还 / 还要)	Adj.

Example:

她很瘦，可是你比她還(要)瘦。
她很瘦，可是你比她还(要)瘦。 — She is quite thin but you are even thinner than her.

她很瘦，可是你比她更(要)瘦。
她很瘦，可是你比她更(要)瘦。

昨天很熱，今天比昨天還(要)熱。
昨天很热，今天比昨天还(要)热。

昨天很熱，今天比昨天更(要)熱。
昨天很热，今天比昨天更(要)热。
It was hot yesterday. Today is even hotter than yesterday.

2. Progressive change 越來越 (越来越) ……

When we need to express progressive changes in degree, the pattern "越來越(越来越) + Verb" is used. Look at the following examples:

你越來越苗條了。
你越来越苗条了。
You are getting slimmer and slimmer.

我越來越喜歡功夫片了。
我越来越喜欢功夫片了。
I like kongfu movies more and more.

她看上去越來越年輕了。
她看上去越来越年轻了。
She looks younger and younger.

Note:
- 越來越(越来越) …… can only be placed before a verb to function as an adverb. It is never placed before the subject of a sentence.
- The 越來越(越来越) …… phrase is often followed by 了 at the end of the sentence to emphasize the change.

3. 越 (越) …… 越 (越) …… pattern

The "越(越)……越(越)……" sentence is equivalent to "The more . . . , the more . . ." in English. Look at the following examples,

我們越忙越需要鍛煉。
我们越忙越需要锻炼。
The busier we are, the more we need to exercise.

我覺得中文越學越有意思。
我觉得中文越学越有意思。
The more I study Chinese, the more interesting I find it to be.

他越說我越不懂。
他越说我越不懂。
The more he talks, the more I don't understand.

補充課文 (补充课文) SUPPLEMENTARY PRACTICE

This section will help you test your comprehension of the grammar and vocabulary you have learned in this lesson. Be prepared to answer questions about the meaning of the passage.

我的健身計畫 (繁體字 Traditional Character Version)

三年前我得了一場病，雖然吃了藥以後病好了，可是感覺身體越來越不好。看上去人很胖，實際上體質越來越弱，還常常會感到頭暈。醫生說我需要多運動，鍛煉鍛煉。

我早就想訂一個健身計畫，好好地鍛煉鍛煉，可是總是覺得功課太多，沒有時間。前天，我的高中同學白思琴來看我，她的變化使我大吃一驚。以前她是班上有名的"小胖子"，是所有女生中最矮、最胖的。可是昨天看到她那麼苗條，那麼有精神，我簡直不相信自己的眼睛。她告訴我，她堅持鍛煉健身已經三個多月了，效果非常好，不但體重減輕了十多磅，而且精神越來越好，學習的時候精力比以前集中得多，學習成績也就越來越好。

我說我也很想鍛煉，可是功課太多，時間不夠。思琴說其實越忙越需要鍛煉，因為越鍛煉會越有精神，精力越能集中，學習的效果就會越好。我覺得她說得很對，決定聽她的話，訂一個計畫，好好地執行。

我的計畫是這樣的：

從下個星期開始，星期一、三、五我去健身房游泳游一個小時，星期二、四、六去打球或者跑步，星期日休息一天。因為我每天都有課，所以我可以在早上上課以前或者下午下課以後去鍛煉。如果有特殊情況，我可以靈活安排。

思琴說鍛煉身體"重在堅持"，我相信我一定能堅持下去。"有志者，事竟成。"只要我下決心，就一定能成功。

補充課文 (补充课文) SUPPLEMENTARY PRACTICE

This section will help you test your comprehension of the grammar and vocabulary you have learned in this lesson. Be prepared to answer questions about the meaning of the passage.

我的健身计划 (简体字 Simplified Character Version)

三年前我得了一场病，虽然吃了药以后病好了，可是感觉身体越来越不好。看上去人很胖，实际上体质越来越弱，还常常会感到头晕。医生说我需要多运动，锻炼锻炼。

我早就想订一个健身计划，好好地锻炼锻炼，可是总是觉得功课太多，没有时间。前天，我的高中同学白思琴来看我，她的变化使我大吃一惊。以前她是班上有名的“小胖子”，是所有女生中最矮、最胖的。可是昨天看到她那么苗条，那么有精神，我简直不相信自己的眼睛。她告诉我，她坚持锻炼健身已经三个多月了，效果非常好，不但体重减轻了十多磅，而且精神越来越好，学习的时候精力比以前集中得多，学习成绩也就越来越好。

我说我也很想锻炼，可是功课太多，时间不够。思琴说其实越忙越需要锻炼，因为越锻炼会越有精神，精力越能集中，学习的效果就会越好。我觉得她说得很对，决定听她的话，订一个计划，好好地执行。

我的计划是这样的：

从下个星期开始，星期一、三、五我去健身房游泳游一个小时，星期二、四、六去打球或者跑步，星期日休息一天。因为我每天都有课，所以我可以在早上上课以前或者下午下课以后去锻炼。如果有特殊情况，我可以灵活安排。

思琴说锻炼身体“重在坚持”，我相信我一定能坚持下去。“有志者，事竟成。”只要我下决心，就一定能成功。

Useful words and expressions:
場(场) [chǎng]: measure word for illness, games, films, etc.
實際上(实际上) [shíjìshàng]: in fact, as a matter of fact
弱(弱) [ruò]: weak
頭暈(头晕) [tóuyūn]: to feel dizzy
使(使) [shǐ]: to make
大吃一驚(大吃一惊) [dàchīyìjīng]: to be greatly surprised, amazed, astonished
有名(有名) [yǒumíng]: famous, well-known
簡直(简直) [jiǎnzhí]: simply
相信(相信) [xiāngxìn]: to believe, to be sure
精力(精力) [jīnglì]: energy
集中(集中) [jízhōng]: to concentrate, focus
執行(执行) [zhíxíng]: to execute, to put into action
開始(开始) [kāishǐ]: to begin, beginning
特殊(特殊) [tèshū]: special
安排(安排) [ānpái]: to arrange, arrangement
重在堅持(重在坚持) [zhòng zài jiānchí]: the key lies in persistence
有志者，事竟成(有志者，事竟成) [yǒuzhìzhě, shì jìng chéng]: where there is a will, there is a way.
決心(决心) [juéxīn]: to be determined, determination
成功(成功) [chénggōng]: to succeed, success

練習 (练习) Exercises

1. 她為什麼想要訂一個健身計畫呢?
   她为什么想要订一个健身计划呢?
2. 她的同學白思琴有什麼變化? 以前怎麼樣? 現在又怎麼樣?
   她的同学白思琴有什么变化? 以前怎么样? 现在又怎么样?
3. 她的健身計畫是怎麼安排的? 她覺得自己能堅持下去嗎?
   她的健身计划是怎么安排的? 她觉得自己能坚持下去吗?

成語故事 (成语故事) IDIOM STORY

畫蛇添足 (画蛇添足) [huàshé tiānzú]

Meaning: To add feet to a snake while drawing it

Usage: This is used to describe someone who tries to make undesirable or superfluous additions

Example: 你已經很苗條了，還控制飲食，不吃甜食，常鍛煉，你就不要再"畫蛇添足"，買減肥藥了。

你已经很苗条了，还控制饮食，不吃甜食，常锻炼，你就不要再"画蛇添足"，买减肥药了。

Pay attention to the usages of 比 and the emphatic degree 更(要)[更(要)], 還(要)[还(要)], progressive change 越來越(越来越)……, and the "越(越)…… 越(越)……" pattern.

(繁體字 **Traditional Character Version**)

有一天，一些人得到了一壺酒，他們都想喝。可是一壺酒不夠，想喝酒的人越多，每個人能喝的就越少。怎麼辦呢？有人說："我們大家想想辦法吧！"結果你也想，我也想，想出來的辦法越來越多。可是這些辦法都不如其中一個人的辦法好。這個人說："我們來比賽畫蛇。誰畫得最快就給誰喝，你們覺得怎麼樣？"大家聽了，都說這個辦法比別的辦法簡單，所以都同意了。

畫蛇比賽開始了。大家都比平時更專心地畫著。有一個人平時做事都比別人快得多，這次畫蛇他畫得更快。很快地，他就把蛇畫好了，而且他畫的蛇也比別人的好得多。他看到別人都比他畫得慢，就越來越覺得自己比別人能幹得多。他越想越高興，就說："你們畫得都比我慢，我再給蛇加上兩隻腳吧！"於是，他就給蛇加了兩隻腳。可是他在畫腳的時候，有一個人的蛇畫好了。他拿起酒壺，一下子就把酒都喝完了。畫蛇腳的人趕快把酒壺搶過去，可是連一滴酒也沒有了。他非常不高興，可是喝酒的人說，"蛇是沒有腳的。你給蛇加了腳，那就不是蛇了。"他聽了以後，連一句話也說不出來。雖然他越想越生氣，可是因為蛇是沒有腳的，他也沒有辦法。

這個故事告訴我們：花時間做不必要的事是沒有用的。

(简体字 **Simplified Character Version**)

有一天，一些人得到了一壶酒，他们都想喝。可是一壶酒不够，想喝酒的人越多，每个人能喝的就越少。怎么办呢？有人说："我们大家想想办法吧！"结果你也想，我也想，想出来的办法越来越多。可是这些办法都不如其中一个人的办法好。这个人说："我们来比赛画蛇。谁画得最快就给谁喝，你们觉得怎么样？"大家听了，都说这个办法比别的办法简单，所以都同意了。

画蛇比赛开始了。大家都比平时更专心地画着。有一个人平时做事都比别人快得多，这次画蛇他画得更快。很快地，他就把蛇画好了，而且他画的蛇也比别人的好得多。他看到别人都比他画得慢，就越来越觉得自己比别人能干得多。他越想越高兴，就说："你们画得都比我慢，我再给蛇加上两只脚吧！"于是，他就给蛇加了两只脚。可是他在画脚的时候，有一个人的蛇画好了。他拿起酒壶，一下子就把酒都喝完了。画蛇脚的人赶快把酒壶抢过去，可是连一滴酒也没有了。他非常不高兴，可是喝酒的人说，"蛇是没有脚的。你给蛇加了脚，那就不是蛇了。"他听了以后，连一句话也说不出来。虽然他越想越生气，可是因为蛇是没有脚的，他也没有办法。

这个故事告诉我们：花时间做不必要的事是没有用的。

Useful words and expressions:
蛇(蛇) [shé]: snake
添(添) [tiān]: to add
足(足) [zú]: foot
壺(壶) [hú]: (measure word for pots)
辦法(办法) [bànfǎ]: way, solution
比賽(比赛) [bǐsài]: race, competition, contest
簡單(简单) [jiǎndān]: simple, easy
同意(同意) [tóngyì]: to agree
開始(开始) [kāishǐ]: to begin
平時(平时) [píngshí]: usually
專心(专心) [zhuānxīn]: attentive
能幹(能干) [nénggàn]: capable
高興(高兴) [gāoxìng]: happy
加(加) [jiā]: to add (the same as 添, but 加 is more informal)
腳(脚) [jiǎo]: foot (the same as 足, 腳 is more colloquial)
赶快(赶快) [gǎnkuài]: to hurry
搶(抢) [qiǎng]: to snatch
滴(滴) [dī]: drop (measure word for liquid kind of things)
生氣(生气) [shēngqì]: to be angry
告訴(告诉) [gàosù]: to tell
必要(必要) [bìyào]: necessary

練習 (练习) Exercises

1. 找出有下面語法的句子: 比 and the emphatic degree 更(要), 還(要), progressive change 越來越……, and the 越…… 越…… pattern.
   找出有下面语法的句子: 比 and the emphatic degree 更(要), 还(要), progressive change 越来越……, and the 越…… 越…… pattern.
2. 用你自己的話說說"畫蛇添足"的故事。
   用你自己的话说说"画蛇添足"的故事。
3. 請用"畫蛇添足"造一個句子或者說一個畫蛇添足的例子。
   请用"画蛇添足"造一个句子或者说一个画蛇添足的例子。
4. "畫蛇添足"的故事, 告訴了我們什麼?
   "画蛇添足"的故事, 告诉了我们什么?

練習 (练习) ACTIVITIES

I. 聽力練習 (听力练习)

9-1 Listen to the following dialogue and then select the correct answer to each question:

1. 最近為什麼白健看不到常明在健身房鍛煉呢?
   最近为什么白健看不到常明在健身房锻炼呢?

a. 因為常明要減肥。
因为常明要减肥。

b. 因為常明要參加比賽。
因为常明要参加比赛。

c. 因為常明去看女朋友了。
因为常明去看女朋友了。

2. 為什麼白健說常明應該參加游泳比賽?
为什么白健说常明应该参加游泳比赛?

a. 因為白健是常明的好朋友。
因为白健是常明的好朋友。

b. 因為常明游泳的時候看上去最靈活。
因为常明游泳的时候看上去最灵活。

c. 因為常明游泳游得很快。
因为常明游泳游得很快。

3. 常明為什麼要減肥?
常明为什么要减肥?

a. 因為他的女朋友要他減肥。
因为他的女朋友要他减肥。

b. 因為他覺得他不如王華靈活。
因为他觉得他不如王华灵活。

c. 因為他覺得他要控制吃甜食。
因为他觉得他要控制吃甜食。

4. 常明的女朋友為什麼學習成績越來越好?
常明的女朋友为什么学习成绩越来越好?

a. 因為她每天睡得很少,學習得很用功。
因为她每天睡得很少,学习得很用功。

b. 因為她也在減肥,所以精神很好。
因为她也在减肥,所以精神很好。

c. 因為她每天鍛煉,精神很好。
因为她每天锻炼,精神很好。

9-2 Based on the short passage you have just heard, complete the following sentences:

1. 常明 ________ 是系裡游泳游得 ________ 。
   常明 ________ 是系里游泳游得 ________ 。
2. ________ 王華比常明游泳游得 ________ 。
   ________ 王华比常明游泳游得 ________ 。
3. 白健知道常明喜歡吃 ________，他覺得常明應該 ________ 。
   白健知道常明喜欢吃 ________，他觉得常明应该 ________ 。
4. 常明的女朋友最近比以前 ________ 多了，因為她也在 ________ 。
   常明的女朋友最近比以前 ________ 多了，因为她也在 ________ 。

9-3 Read the following lyric, paying special attention to the tones and the rhythm:

Shēngcházǐ	生查子 生查子
(Ōuyáng Xiū)	(歐陽修) (欧阳修)
Qùnián yuányè shí,	去年元夜時， 去年元夜时，
Huāshì dēng rú zhòu.	花市燈如晝。 花市灯如昼。
Yuè shàng liǔ shāotóu,	月上柳梢頭， 月上柳梢头，
Rén yuē huánghūn hòu.	人約黃昏後。 人约黄昏后。
Jīnnián yuányè shí,	今年元夜時， 今年元夜时，
Yuè yǔ dēng yījiù.	月與燈依舊。 月与灯依旧。
Bú jiàn qùnián rén,	不見去年人， 不见去年人，
Lèi shī chūnshān xiù.	淚濕春衫袖。 泪湿春衫袖。

To the tune of **Sheng Cha Zi**
(Ouyang, Xiu)

On the night of last year's Yuanxiao Festival,
The lanterns at the flower market were as bright as daytime.
When the moon climbed onto the top of the tree,
We dated after the dusk.

At this year's Yuanxiao night,
The moon and the lanterns remain unchanged.
But no more is the love I dated last year,
I can only weep and wet my sleeves.

Practice: What are the rhyming words in this lyric? Write them out in Pinyin:

押 ________ 韻，押韻的字有：________________________________。
押 ________ 韵，押韵的字有：________________________________。

II. 漢字練習 (汉字练习)

9-4 Read the following words, phrases, and sentences:

煉 炼	靈 灵
鍛煉 锻炼	靈活 灵活
要鍛煉 要锻炼	更靈活 更灵活
需要鍛煉 需要锻炼	會更靈活 会更灵活
越需要鍛煉 越需要锻炼	比以前會更靈活 比以前会更灵活
越忙越需要鍛煉 越忙越需要锻炼	運動以後會比以前更靈活 运动以后会比以前更灵活
其實越忙越需要鍛煉 其实越忙越需要锻炼	你運動以後會比以前更靈活 你运动以后会比以前更灵活

Now try to use the following characters to make words, phrases, and then sentences:

1. 健 健	2. 光 光	3. 控 控	4. 甜 甜	5. 靈 灵	6. 堅 坚
7. 瘦 瘦	8. 減 减	9. 矮 矮	10. 超 超	11. 怪 怪	12. 膚 肤

9-5 Each of the following pairs of characters look very similar in appearance, but they are actually two very different words. Write out the Pinyin for each character and then create a word or phrase by using the characters:

Example: 苗(苗) miáo 苗條(苗条)

1. 輕(轻) ______ ______
   經(经) ______ ______
2. 瘦(瘦) ______ ______
   病(病) ______ ______
3. 效(效) ______ ______
   放(放) ______ ______
4. 飲(饮) ______ ______
   飯(饭) ______ ______
5. 住(住) ______ ______
   注(注) ______ ______
6. 害(害) ______ ______
   宜(宜) ______ ______

9-6 Match the traditional characters with their simplified forms:

靈	輕	鐘	總	膚	體	頭
肤	头	体	总	灵	轻	钟

III. 語法練習 (语法练习)

9-7 Use A 比 B + 更(更)/更要(更要) + Adj. pattern to describe the following situations:
還(还)/還要(还要)

1. 印度(印度) ([Yìndù]: India) has a big 人口(人口) ([rénkǒu]: population); China has the largest population in the world.
2. Britain is a 發達國家(发达国家) ([fādá guójiā]: developed country); the U.S. is an even more developed country.
3. 黃河(黄河) ([Huánghé]: the Yellow River) is very long; 長江(长江) ([Chángjiāng]: the Yangtze River) is even longer.
4. He has been more energetic than before.

9-8 Sentence–making competition:

Form groups of three. The instructor will provide stative verbs/adjectives. Each group tries to make sentences with the pattern "越來越(越来越)......" as quickly as possible. The group that makes the most sentences within the time allowed wins the game.

Note: The subjects and the verbs used have to be varied from sentence to sentence. No repetition is allowed.

Example: 好：我的中文越來越好。
好：我的中文越来越好。

高：我弟弟越來越高。
高：我弟弟越来越高。

Some suggested adjectives:

好(好)，高(高)，低(低)，靈活(灵活)，矮(矮)，輕(轻)，光滑(光滑)，重(重)，苗條(苗条)，甜(甜)，精神(精神)，方便(方便)，不錯(不错)，棒(棒)，多(多)，貴(贵)，有意思(有意思)，忙(忙)，輕鬆(轻松)，舒服(舒服)，精彩(精彩)，吸引人(吸引人)，有興趣(有兴趣)，大(大)，客觀(客观)，便宜(便宜)，健康(健康)，年輕(年轻)，老(老)，花(花)，熱(热)，地道(地道)，高興(高兴)，好吃(好吃)，快(快)，熱情(热情)，好客(好客)，不好意思(不好意思)

9-9 Combine the following pairs of sentences using the "越(越)...... 越(越)......" pattern:

1. 她現在經常鍛煉；她比以前苗條了很多。
   她现在经常锻炼；她比以前苗条了很多。
2. 她每次運動以後；學習的效果很好。
   她每次运动以后；学习的效果很好。
3. 她的體重輕了；她覺得輕鬆多了。
   她的体重轻了；她觉得轻松多了。
4. 老師、師母總是非常熱情；我總是覺得不好意思。
   老师、师母总是非常热情；我总是觉得不好意思。

IV. 交際活動 (交际活动)

Your friend is a bit overweight and he has been trying various ways to lose weight with no avail. He is also becoming less and less focused when studying. You think his major problem is too little exercise. So you are now giving him some suggestions on how to lose weight and keep fit. Remember to use the following patterns in your sentences:

1. A 比 B + 更(更)/更要(更要) + Adj.
+ 還(还)/還要(还要) +
2. 越來越(越来越)……
3. 越(越)…… 越(越)……
4. 怪不得(怪不得)
5. 那可不好(那可不好)
6. 不如(不如)

文化知識 (文化知识) Culture Link

文化點滴 (文化点滴) CULTURE NOTES

中國的瘦身美容業 (中国的瘦身美容业) [Zhōngguó de shòushēn měiróngyè] The Culture of Slimness and Beauty in China

Because of the rapid growth of the Chinese economy, Chinese people now have more money to spend. Finding enough food to eat, a goal for many families in the past, has given way to becoming slim and "beautiful". This does not only apply to the young, but also to middle-aged and even older people.

As Chinese society becomes more and more open, people's concepts about life have also been very much liberated. To love beauty is human nature. With the availability of higher income and a relaxed atmosphere in society, more and more people are now spending a great amount of time and money on their appearance. In addition, personal appearance has become a factor that may sway the decision of employers in the ever more competitive job market. Therefore, a wide variety of 美容護膚品 (美容护肤品) [měiróng hùfūpǐn] (beauty and skin-protection products) are becoming very popular.

Following the rise in the standard of living, Chinese people are now facing the problem of overweight and even obesity. By 2004 there were approximately 70,000,000 overweight Chinese. As a result, 減肥產品 (减肥产品) [jiǎnféi chǎnpǐn] (weight-loss products) and programs have flourished in China. Recent years have also witnessed a surge in 美容手術(美容手术) [měiróng shǒushù] (cosmetic surgery).

A great number of middle-aged and older people are taking positive steps to keep fit. They join fitness clubs or do daily exercises, such as walking, jogging, swimming, and dancing. However, there are also growing numbers of people, especially young ladies, who rely on diet pills, weight reducing products or even cosmetic surgery to become slimmer. The culture of slimness – a relatively new phenomenon in China – has begun to affect and control women's attitudes about themselves.

A survey conducted in Beijing, Shanghai and Guangzhou in 2004 shows that not only overweight people are trying to reduce their weight, but so are those whose weight is normal or even below normal, especially some young women and girls. Among all women engaging in various ways to lose weight, those who are actually overweight account for 43.8%, and 3.8% are young females whose weight is actually below normal.

Why, then, are so many women dissatisfied with their weight, even when their weight is normal? It is likely that commercial advertisements have played a large role. Modern ads create cultural ideals of beauty and slimness. Weight-loss companies are chasing profits and preying on women's self-doubts. Their ads promote products to women, claiming they will help them look better.

Today, the Chinese people are becoming very concerned with health and beauty, but a better understanding of the true sense of the word "beauty" would help them take a big step towards becoming even more healthy and beautiful.

Beauty parlors like this are everywhere in the urban areas of China.

Chlitina, a beauty parlor owned by people outside Mainland China, mainly serves white-collar workers in urban areas.

問題討論 (问题讨论) Discussion Questions

1. 你想過要瘦身美容嗎? 你用過什麼方法?
   你想过要瘦身美容吗? 你用过什么方法?
   Have you thought about losing weight and becoming more beautiful? What kinds of methods have you used?

2. 你聽說過中國的針灸 [zhēnjiǔ] (acupuncture) 美容嗎? 你會想試試看嗎? 為什麼?
   你听说过中国的针灸 [zhēnjiǔ] (acupuncture) 美容吗? 你会想试试看吗? 为什么?
   Have you heard about Chinese acupuncture for slimness and beauty? Would you like to try it out? Why?

趣味中文 (趣味中文) FUN WITH CHINESE

人不可貌相
人不可貌相
A man's worth cannot be measured by his looks.

rén	bù	kě	mào	xiàng
人	不	可	貌	相
人	不	可	貌	相
person	not	can	appearance	to judge

問題討論 (问题讨论) Discussion Questions

1. Do you know anyone whose talent surprises you so much that you would describe him/her as 人不可貌相?
2. Are there any expressions in your language which are similar to 人不可貌相?

行動吧! (行动吧!) LET'S GO!

瘦身廣告 (瘦身广告)
Weight Loss Advertisement

For some time 思琴 has not been happy about her weight so she's been interested in weight loss products. Below is a weight loss advertisement. Based on what you see in the advertisements, answer the questions below:

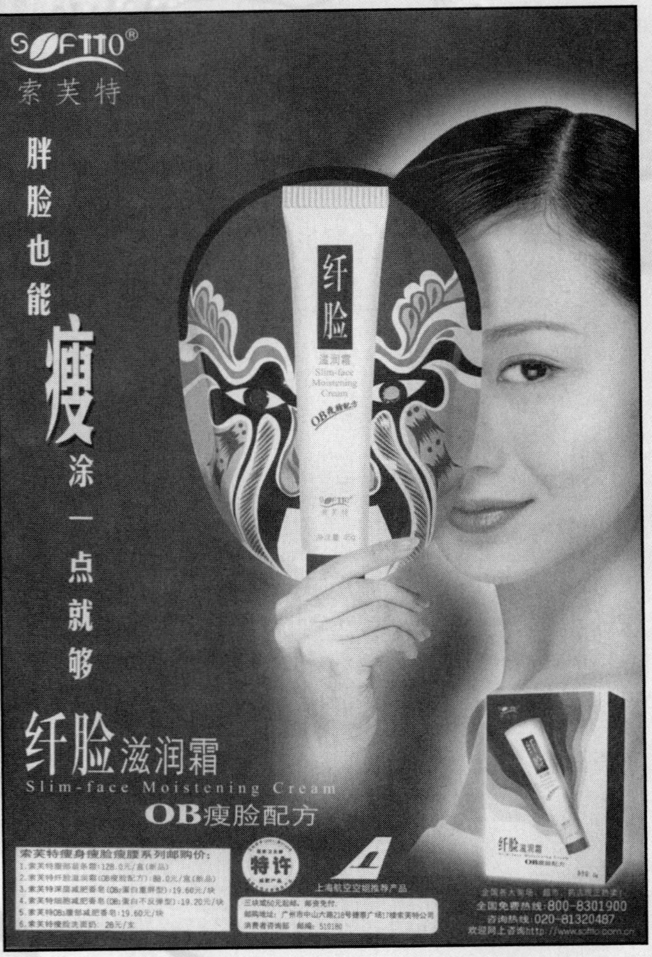

Useful words and expressions:

塗(涂) [tú]: to coat with, spread on
纖(纤) [xiān]: slim and delicate
滋潤(滋润) [zīrùn]: to moisturize
霜(霜) [shuāng]: cream
配方(配方) [pèifāng]: formula chemicals or metallurgical products
免費熱線(免费热线) [miǎnfèi rèxiàn]: free hotline
特許(特许) [tèxǔ]: with special permission

問題討論 (问题讨论) Discussion Questions

1. What is the product? What is its function?
2. What is the name of the manufacturer?
3. What are the English translations for the following?

    纖臉(纤脸)
    滋潤霜(滋润霜)

第十課
LESSON
10

我的寒假計畫–復習
(我的寒假计划–复习)
My Plan for the Winter Vacation – Review

教學目標 (教学目标) OBJECTIVES

- Make an oral report
- Discuss plans

Airlines in China often give out discounts to attract passengers, especially when students are on vacation. Sometimes the airline tickets are even less expensive than train tickets.

What does "最新打折卡" mean?

A very typical southern-style garden in China

Do you know why Chinese like round-shaped doors or entrances?

生詞 (生词) VOCABULARY

核心詞 (核心词) Core Vocabulary

TRADITIONAL	SIMPLIFIED	PINYIN		
1. 計畫	计划	jìhuà	V. N.	to plan plan
2. 最後	最后	zuìhòu	Adv.	finally
3. 說好了	说好了	shuōhǎo le		to have agreement on, agree
4. 希望	希望	xīwàng	V. N.	to hope hope
5. 旬	旬	xún	N.	a period of 10 days in a month
6. 付款	付款	fùkuǎn	V.O.	to make payment
7. 接受	接受	jiēshòu	V.	to accept
8. 商店	商店	shāngdiàn	N.	store
9. 根據	根据	gēnjù	Prep.	according to, based on
10. 當天	当天	dāngtiān	Adv.	on that day
11. 安全	安全	ānquán	Adj.	safe
12. 零	零	líng	Num.	zero
13. 爬	爬	pá	V.	to climb
14. 頂	顶	dǐng	N.	top
15. 幫助	帮助	bāngzhù	N.	help
16. 非	非	fēi	Adv.	not (used in Classical Chinese)
17. 好漢	好汉	hǎohàn	N.	hero
18. 告訴	告诉	gàosu	V.	to tell
19. 壯觀	壮观	zhuàngguān	Adj.	magnificent
20. 曲折	曲折	qūzhé	Adj.	with twists and turns, complicated
21. 滿載而歸	满载而归	mǎnzài'érguī		to return with tremendous accomplishments

專名 (专名) Proper Nouns

TRADITIONAL	SIMPLIFIED	PINYIN		
1. 黄山	黄山	Huángshān	N.	Mount Huang (the Yellow Mountain, a famous tourist attraction in Anhui Province, central China)
2. 十面埋伏	十面埋伏	Shímiàn máifu	N.	House of Flying Daggers (name of a Chinese martial art film)

語文知識 (语文知识) LANGUAGE LINK

The Sentence Patterns provide models that will help you with the Language in Use section. In both sections, pay attention to the grammar points, vocabulary, and expressions.

句型 (句型) Sentence Patterns

現在美元換人民幣的匯率
现在美元换人民币的汇率
Xiànzài Měiyuán huàn Rénmínbì de huìlǜ
是一比七點九八。
是一比七点九八。
shì yī bǐ qī diǎn jiǔ bā.

這班飛機到得了到不了北京?
这班飞机到得了到不了北京?
Zhè bān fēijī dàodeliǎo dàobùliǎo Běijīng?

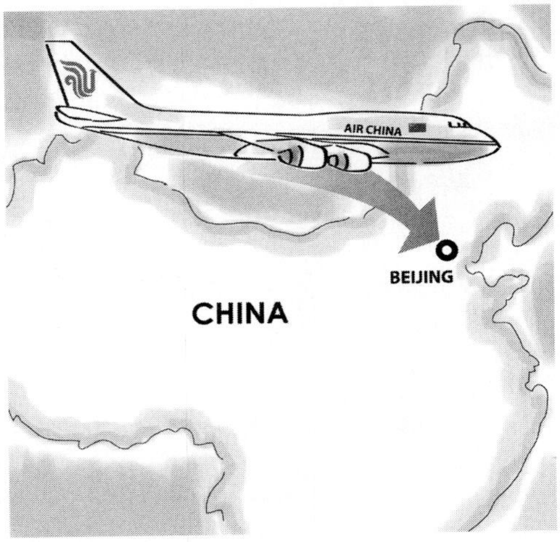

小說比電影好一些。
小说比电影好一些。
Xiǎoshuō bǐ diànyǐng hǎo yìxiē.

你看上去越來越苗條了。
你看上去越来越苗条了。
Nǐ kàn shàngqù yuèlái yuè miáotiao le.

我希望這次中國行會比上次更好，
我希望这次中国行会比上次更好，
Wǒ xīwàng zhècì Zhōngguó xíng huì bǐ shàngcì gèng hǎo,

能滿載而歸，然後可以跟大家報告一下。
能满载而归，然后可以跟大家报告一下。
néng mǎnzàiérguī, ránhòu kěyǐ gēn dàjiā bàogào yíxià.

課文: 我的寒假計畫 (繁體字)
Language in Use: Traditional Character Version

同學們好!

今天, 我想把我的寒假計畫跟大家報告一下。

今年是我在大學的最後一個寒假。我已經跟我的男朋友說好了, 一起去中國旅遊。我們在北京有很多親戚朋友, 我希望這次去北京能見得到他們每個人。

這兩年去中國的人比以前多了很多, 所以飛機票也比前兩年難買多了。特別是去北京的機票, 更難買得到, 我們到現在還沒有訂到票呢。我們打算十二月中旬出發, 一月上旬回來。現在已經給好幾家旅行社打了電話, 還不知道買得到買不到。我們上個星期已經申請了去中國的簽證, 不知道這個星期收得到收不到。不過我們還有不少時間, 大概來得及。

我還要去銀行取一些現金, 買幾張旅行支票。在中國用信用卡付款不像在美國這麼方便。不過, 聽說現在接受信用卡的商店越來越多了, 而且在中國銀行還可以取美金, 也可以根據當天的匯率換成人民幣, 這比帶很多現金要安全得多。最近人民幣換美金的匯率差不多是一比七點九七, 比上個月低了零點一個百分點。

這次去中國我最想去的地方是長城。聽說爬長城很累, 只有百分之五十的人能爬得到長城的頂上。我覺得那是一個很好的鍛煉, 還能幫助我減肥呢! 而且, 中國人不是說"不到長城非好漢"嗎? 所以我一定要試一試。我還想去黃山, 我的朋友告訴我黃山那兒風景如畫, 美極了!

我還想去看看張藝謀導演的功夫片《十面埋伏》。看過這部電影的人都說它的場面比《英雄》還要壯觀, 情節也很曲折。

你們看, 我今年寒假要做的事多不多? 我希望我從中國回來的時候, 能滿載而歸。

這就是我今天的報告。謝謝大家!

课文: 我的寒假计划 (简体字)
Language in Use: Simplified Character Version

同学们好!

今天，我想把我的寒假计划跟大家报告一下。

今年是我在大学的最后一个寒假。我已经跟我的男朋友说好了，一起去中国旅游。我们在北京有很多亲戚朋友，我希望这次去北京能见得到他们每个人。

这两年去中国的人比以前多了很多，所以飞机票也比前两年难买多了。特别是去北京的机票，更难买得到，我们到现在还没有订到票呢。我们打算十二月中旬出发，一月上旬回来。现在已经给好几家旅行社打了电话，还不知道买得到买不到。我们上个星期已经申请了去中国的签证，不知道这个星期收得到收不到。不过我们还有不少时间，大概来得及。

我还要去银行取一些现金，买几张旅行支票。在中国用信用卡付款不像在美国这么方便。不过，听说现在接受信用卡的商店越来越多了，而且在中国银行还可以取美金，也可以根据当天的汇率换成人民币，这比带很多现金要安全得多。最近人民币换美金的汇率差不多是一比七点九七，比上个月低了零点一个百分点。

这次去中国我最想去的地方是长城。听说爬长城很累，只有百分之五十的人能爬得到长城的顶上。我觉得那是一个很好的锻炼，还能帮助我减肥呢! 而且，中国人不是说“不到长城非好汉”吗? 所以我一定要试一试。我还想去黄山，我的朋友告诉我黄山那儿风景如画，美极了!

我还想去看看张艺谋导演的功夫片《十面埋伏》。看过这部电影的人都说它的场面比《英雄》还要壮观，情节也很曲折。

你们看，我今年寒假要做的事多不多? 我希望我从中国回来的时候，能满载而归。

这就是我今天的报告。谢谢大家!

注釋 (注释) LANGUAGE NOTES

1. 計畫 (计划)

計畫(计划) means plan, can be written as 計劃 in traditional form.

2. 旬 (旬)

旬(旬) is a period of ten days. In Chinese a month can be divided into three ten-day periods that are labeled by 上(上), 中(中), and 下(下). Therefore, the 1st to the 10th of a month is called 上旬(上旬), the 11th to the 20th 中旬(中旬) and the 21st to the end of the month 下旬(下旬). When using 旬(旬), the speaker's emphasis is on the ten-day period, not on any specific day in it.

3. 說好了 (说好了)

Here 好(好) is used to indicate a result meaning "being settled successfully."

4. 零點一個百分點 (零点一个百分点)

零點一個百分點(零点一个百分点) means 0.1%. . . . 百分點(百分点) is an alternative way of expressing percentage, hence, 10% can be either "百分之十(百分之十)" or "十個百分點(十个百分点)."

5. 黃山 (黄山)

黃山(黄山) is the Yellow Mountain, a mountain in Anhui Province in China. It is about 350 miles northwest of Shanghai. It is one of the most famous tourist attractions in China and has been acknowledged by the United Nations as one of the geographical heritages of the world.

語法 (语法) GRAMMAR

Review: The main grammar points from Lesson 6 to Lesson 9

1. Phrases

The following is a list of different types of phrases in Chinese:

Name	Definition	Examples
Juxtaposed Phrases	formed by two or more words that are of the same feature	存款、取款(存款、取款) 學習和工作(学习和工作) 又唱又跳(又唱又跳)
Endocentric Phrases	composed of a modifier (偏[piān]) and the modified (正[zhèng])	儲蓄帳戶(储蓄账户) 努力學習(努力学习)
Subj. + V. Phrases	a phrase in which the relationship between the components is like that between a subject and a verb predicate	我游泳的地方(我游泳的地方) 你們寄來的支票簿 (你们寄来的支票簿) 我覺得這兒的服務又快又好。 (我觉得这儿的服务又快又好。)
V. + Obj. Phrases	formed by a transitive verb and a noun that serves as its object	換外幣的柜台(换外币的柜台) 申請信用卡的表(申请信用卡的表)

2. Percentage and proportion

Percentage	百分之…… 百分之……	百分之三十五 百分之三十五	35% (35 percent)
Proportion	N_1 比 N_2 N_1 比 N_2	五比一 五比一	5 to 1 (5:1)

3. Complements

Potential complement:

Name	Definition	Examples
Potential complement	a verb, an adjective, or a phrase used after a verb to indicate the potential result of the main verb	我的電話簿找不到了。 (我的电话簿找不到了。) 今年寒假你去得了北京嗎? (今年寒假你去得了北京吗?) 這輛車坐得下五個人嗎? (这辆车坐得下五个人吗?)

4. Comparison

The following is a list of the common different ways used to make comparisons:

Types of Comparison	Pattern	Examples
Simple comparison	A 比(比) B + Adjective	你比我高。 (你比我高。)
Comparison with quantifier	A 比(比) B + Adj. + Quantifier	你比我高五公分。 (你比我高五公分。)
Comparison with degree of complement	A 比(比) B + Adj. + degree of complement	中文字比英文字難得多。 (中文字比英文字难得多。) 他比我游泳游得快。 (他比我游泳游得快。)
Negative forms	1. A 沒有(没有) B + Adj. 2. A 不如(不如) B + Adj. 3. A 不像(不像) B + 那麼(那么) + Adj.	電影沒有小說精彩。 (电影没有小说精彩。) 電影不如小說精彩。 (电影不如小说精彩。) 電影不像小說那麼精彩。 (电影不像小说那么精彩。)
Comparative and the emphatic degree	A 比(比) B + 更(更)/更要(更要) + Adj. 還(还)/還要(还要)	電影比小說更精彩。 (电影比小说更精彩。)
Relative and superlative degree	比較(比较) + Adj./Adv. 最(最)	這部電影比較精彩。 (这部电影比较精彩。) 這部電影最精彩。 (这部电影最精彩。)

5. Progressive change 越來越 (越来越)……

她越來越胖了。
她越来越胖了。
She is getting fatter and fatter.

6. 越 (越)……越 (越)……pattern

她越胖，我就越喜歡她。
她越胖，我就越喜欢她。
The fatter she is, the more I like her.

補充課文 (补充课文) SUPPLEMENTARY PRACTICE

This section will help you test your comprehension of the grammar and vocabulary you have learned in this lesson. Be prepared to answer questions about the meaning of the passage.

寒假計畫 Plan for the Winter Vacation (繁體字 Traditional Character Version)

謝進學: 李訪，你今天做報告了嗎?

李訪: 還沒有呢。今天時間來不及了，所以我明天才做報告。今天我們聽了五個同學的報告。

謝進學: 他們的報告做得怎麼樣?

李訪: 都很不錯，不過我更喜歡方文華的報告，我覺得她的報告最有意思，她的中文也說得最好。

謝進學: 她的報告是關於什麼的?

李訪: 是關於她的寒假計畫的。她告訴我們今年寒假她打算去中國旅遊，同時也去看看她的親戚朋友。

謝進學: 她是美籍華人嗎?

李訪: 她不是美籍華人，不過他的男朋友是，他在北京有很多親戚。

謝進學: 聽說現在去中國的人越來越多，所以飛機票越來越難買。恐怕她要早一點訂票。票訂得越晚，票價越貴，也就越難買得到。

李訪: 一點兒也不錯。文華也說了，去北京的飛機票比去上海和廣州的更難買，現在已經買不到了，所以他們打算先去南方玩玩，再到北京。

謝進學: 他們可以先去昆明，那是一個四季如春、風景如畫的城市，聽說那兒百分之六十的人是少數民族，很值得去看看。

Continued on page 314

補充課文（补充课文） SUPPLEMENTARY PRACTICE

This section will help you test your comprehension of the grammar and vocabulary you have learned in this lesson. Be prepared to answer questions about the meaning of the passage.

寒假计划 Plan for the Winter Vacation (简体字 Simplified Character Version)

谢进学：李访，你今天做报告了吗？

李访：还没有呢。今天时间来不及了，所以我明天才做报告。今天我们听了五个同学的报告。

谢进学：他们的报告做得怎么样？

李访：都很不错，不过我更喜欢方文华的报告，我觉得她的报告最有意思，她的中文也说得最好。

谢进学：她的报告是关于什么的？

李访：是关于她的寒假计划的。她告诉我们今年寒假她打算去中国旅游，同时也去看看她的亲戚朋友。

谢进学：她是美籍华人吗？

李访：她不是美籍华人，不过他的男朋友是，他在北京有很多亲戚。

谢进学：听说现在去中国的人越来越多，所以飞机票越来越难买。恐怕她要早一点订票。票订得越晚，票价越贵，也就越难买得到。

李访：一点儿也不错。文华也说了，去北京的飞机票比去上海和广州的更难买，现在已经买不到了，所以他们打算先去南方玩玩，再到北京。

谢进学：他们可以先去昆明，那是一个四季如春、风景如画的城市，听说那儿百分之六十的人是少数民族，很值得去看看。

Continued on page 315

寒假計畫 Plan for the Winter Vacation — **接第三百一十二頁**

李訪： 正是。文華打算先去廣州，再去昆明，然後到上海，最後從上海再去北京。

謝進學： 哇噻！寒假這麼短的時間，她能去得了這麼多的地方嗎？

李訪： 她打算十二月中旬出發，一月上旬回來。她的計畫安排得特別好，內容特別豐富多彩。

謝進學： 她還想做些什麼呢？

李訪： 她還想去看一場京劇，再去爬一爬長城，做一個真正的“好漢”呢。

謝進學： 太棒了！真希望我也能有這樣的機會！

李訪： 我也希望我的報告能像她的報告那麼精彩，可是我的寒假計畫比她的簡單得多，也不如她的那麼有趣。不過我想我的寒假也會過得很愉快，會很有收穫的。

Useful words and expressions:

關於(关于) [guānyú]: about
美籍華人(美籍华人) [Měijí huárén]: Chinese American
恐怕(恐怕) [kǒngpà]: to be afraid that
值得(值得) [zhídé]: to be worthwhile
正是(正是) [zhèngshì]: exactly
哇噻(哇噻) [wàsài]: Wow (an expression to show amazement)
內容(内容) [nèiróng]: content
豐富多彩(丰富多彩) [fēngfùduōcǎi]: rich and colorful
希望(希望) [xīwàng]: to hope
愉快(愉快) [yúkuài]: to be happy
收穫(收获) [shōuhuò]: harvest, achievement

寒假计划 Plan for the Winter Vacation — **接第三百一十三页**

李访：　正是。文华打算先去广州，再去昆明，然后到上海，最后从上海再去北京。

谢进学：哇噻！寒假这么短的时间，她能去得了这么多的地方吗？

李访：　她打算十二月中旬出发，一月上旬回来。她的计划安排得特别好，内容特别丰富多彩。

谢进学：她还想做些什么呢？

李访：　她还想去看一场京剧，再去爬一爬长城，做一个真正的"好汉"呢。

谢进学：太棒了！真希望我也能有这样的机会！

李访：　我也希望我的报告能像她的报告那么精彩，可是我的寒假计划比她的简单得多，也不如她的那么有趣。不过我想我的寒假也会过得很愉快，会很有收获的。

練習 (练习) Exercises

1. 李訪為什麼喜歡方文華的報告？
   李访为什么喜欢方文华的报告？

2. 李訪說文華應該先買機票到哪兒？然後再怎麼計畫？
   李访说文华应该先买机票到哪儿？然后再怎么计划？

3. 文華旅行的時候還要做什麼？
   文华旅行的时候还要做什么？

成語故事 (成语故事) IDIOM STORY

夜郎自大 (夜郎自大) [Yèláng zìdà]

Meaning: The arrogance of Yelang

Usage: This is used to describe someone who is ignorant and boastful

Example: 小王沒有看過小李的報告，不知道小李的報告好極了，可是小王卻很“夜郎自大”，覺得他的報告是最好的。

小王没有看过小李的报告，不知道小李的报告好极了，可是小王却很“夜郎自大”，觉得他的报告是最好的。

Pay attention to the usages of A 比 B….. ; A (不)像/(沒)有 B…..

(繁體字 **Traditional Character Version**)

古時候，在中國的西南邊，有個夜郎國，它的周圍都是山，交通很不方便，所以夜郎國的人很少到別的地方去。它的周圍有十幾個部落，都沒有它大。夜郎國的國王叫多同，他也從來沒有到過別的地方。他覺得夜郎國比別的國家都大。

有一天，多同帶著一些人出去玩。看到一座高山就說：“這座山多麼高呀！天底下沒有一座山像這座山這麼高。你們說對嗎？”他周圍的人都一邊點頭、一邊說：“您說得很對，這座山比別的山都高。”他們上了山，看到下邊的夜郎國，覺得夜郎國特別大。多同驕傲地對周圍的人說：“我的夜郎國多麼大呀，你們知道還有哪一個國家像夜郎國這麼大呢？”周圍的人一邊搖頭、一邊說：“沒有，沒有，夜郎國是最大的。”後來，他們又走到了一條小河的旁邊。多同又說：“看，這條大河多麼寬、多麼長，哪個國家有這麼長的大河呢？”他周圍的人也說：“這是天底下最長最大的河！”

多同聽了以後高興極了，他變得一天比一天驕傲，對周圍的國家一點兒也看不起。

有一次，一些漢人經過夜郎國，跟多同介紹了他們的情況，多同聽了以後很不相信地問：“你們比我們夜郎國大嗎？”那些漢人笑了，說：“我們比你的夜郎國大幾十倍呢！”

“夜郎自大”這個成語常常用來諷刺那些知道得很少，但是總是覺得自己特別了不起的人。

(简体字 **Simplified Character Version**)

古时候，在中国的西南边，有个夜郎国，它的周围都是山，交通很不方便，所以夜郎国的人很少到别的地方去。它的周围有十几个部落，都没有它大。夜郎国的国王叫多同，他也从来没有到过别的地方。他觉得夜郎国比别的国家都大。

有一天，多同带着一些人出去玩。看到一座高山就说："这座山多么高呀！天底下没有一座山像这座山这么高。你们说对吗？"他周围的人都一边点头、一边说："您说得很对，这座山比别的山都高。"他们上了山，看到下边的夜郎国，觉得夜郎国特别大。多同骄傲地对周围的人说："我的夜郎国多么大呀，你们知道还有哪一个国家像夜郎国这么大呢？"周围的人一边摇头、一边说："没有，没有，夜郎国是最大的。"后来，他们又走到了一条小河的旁边。多同又说："看，这条大河多么宽、多么长，哪个国家有这么长的大河呢？"他周围的人也说："这是天底下最长最大的河！"

多同听了以后高兴极了，他变得一天比一天骄傲，对周围的国家一点儿也看不起。

有一次，一些汉人经过夜郎国，跟多同介绍了他们的情况，多同听了以后很不相信地问："你们比我们夜郎国大吗？"那些汉人笑了，说："我们比你的夜郎国大几十倍呢！"

"夜郎自大"这个成语常常用来讽刺那些知道得很少，但是总是觉得自己特别了不起的人。

Useful words and expressions:
周圍(周围) [zhōuwéi]: in the surrounding area
交通(交通) [jiāotōng]: traffic, transportation
部落(部落) [bùluò]: tribes
從來(从来) [cónglái]: from the beginning (used only in a negative expression)
座(座) [zuò]: (measure word for mountains)
天底下(天底下) [tiāndǐxià]: (a spoken expression) in the world; on earth
點頭(点头) [diǎntóu]: to nod
驕傲(骄傲) [jiāo'ào]: arrogant; conceited
搖頭(摇头) [yáotóu]: to shake one's head
河(河) [hé]: river
寬(宽) [kuān]: wide
看不起(看不起) [kànbuqǐ]: to look down upon
漢人(汉人) [Hànrén]: here refers to Han people in the Han Dynasty (202 B.C.–220 A.D.)
經過(经过) [jīngguò]: to pass
相信(相信) [xiāngxìn]: to believe
倍(倍) [bèi]: times
用來(用来) [yònglái]: to be used for
諷刺(讽刺) [fěngcì]: to satirize
了不起(了不起) [liǎobuqǐ]: terrific; extraordinary

練習 (练习) Exercises

1. 夜郎國的人常常到別的地方去嗎? 為什麼?
   夜郎国的人常常到别的地方去吗? 为什么?
2. 夜郎國的國王覺得他的國家怎麼樣?
   夜郎国的国王觉得他的国家怎么样?
3. 這個成語告訴了我們什麼? 你能用它造一個句子嗎?
   这个成语告诉了我们什么? 你能用它造一个句子吗?

練習 (练习) ACTIVITIES

I. 聽力練習 (听力练习)

10-1 高友華(高友华) has big plans for her winter vacation. Listen to what she tells us and then do the following:

Useful words and expressions:

秦始皇墓(秦始皇墓) [Qínshǐhuáng mù]: Tomb of the first emperor of the Qin Dynasty (221–206 B.C.)
兵馬俑(兵马俑) [bīngmǎyǒng]: terracotta worriers and horses
商店(商店) [shāngdiàn]: shopping store
個人支票(个人支票) [gèrén zhīpiào]: personal check

1. Ask and answer the following questions in pairs. When you finish the questions and answers with your partner, the instructor will ask the questions and each pair will answer the questions accordingly:

   a) 她的寒假大計畫是什麼? 為什麼她去年沒有去成?
   她的寒假大计划是什么? 为什么她去年没有去成?

   ____

   b) 哪個城市是她最想去的? 為什麼?
   哪个城市是她最想去的? 为什么?

   ____

   c) 她想在北京做什麼?
   她想在北京做什么?

   ____

   d) 西安那兒有什麼? 她還想去哪兒?
   西安那儿有什么? 她还想去哪儿?

   ____

   e) 中國的銀行現在有什麼服務?
   中国的银行现在有什么服务?

   ____

2. Use your own words to retell the passage.

10-2 Read the following lyric, paying special attention to the tones and the rhythm:

Yì Jiāngnán	憶江南 忆江南
(Bái Jūyì)	(白居易) (白居易)
Jiāngnán hǎo,	江南好， 江南好，
Fēngjǐng jiù céng ān.	風景舊曾諳。 风景旧曾谙。
Rì chū jiāng huā hóng shèng huǒ,	日出江花紅勝火， 日出江花红胜火，
Chūn lái jiāng shuǐ lǜ rú lán,	春來江水綠如蘭， 春来江水绿如兰，
Néng bú yì jiāngnán?	能不憶江南？ 能不忆江南？

To the tune of **Yi Jiangnan**
(Bai, Juyi)

My hometown in the south of the Yangtze River is a place so nice
Its beauty I know so well
When arising on top of the waves the sun is redder than the fire
And the water in the river in spring is as green as orchid flowers
How can I not miss my hometown down in the south of the Yangtze

Practice:

1. What are the rhyming words in this lyric? Write them out in Pinyin:

押 ________ 韻，押韻的字有：______________________________。
押 ________ 韵，押韵的字有：______________________________。

2. With the help of a dictionary, find the meaning of the following two words.

似 ______________；　如 ______________
似 ______________；　如 ______________

II. 漢字練習 (汉字练习)

10-3 Read the following words, phrases, and sentences:

發 发	觀 观
出發 出发	壯觀 壮观
從紐約出發 从纽约出发	景色很壯觀 景色很壮观
十二月從紐約出發 十二月从纽约出发	長城的景色很壯觀 长城的景色很壮观
十二月上旬從紐約出發 十二月上旬从纽约出发	中國的長城景色很壯觀 中国的长城景色很壮观
十二月上旬從紐約出發去台北 十二月上旬从纽约出发去台北	我覺得中國的長城景色很壯觀 我觉得中国的长城景色很壮观

Now try to use the following characters to make words, phrases, and then sentences:

1. 旬 旬
2. 畫 划
3. 私 私
4. 爬 爬
5. 折 折
6. 據 据
7. 零 零
8. 頂 顶
9. 漢 汉
10. 載 载
11. 私 私
12. 歸 归

10-4 Write the radical for each group of characters:

1. _____ 打，接，據，換，折
   _____ 打，接，据，换，折
2. _____ 寒，安，它
   _____ 寒，安，它
3. _____ 計，訂，證，試，訴
   _____ 计，订，证，试，诉
4. _____ 這，還，道，過，近
   _____ 这，还，道，过，近

III. 語法練習 (语法练习)

10-5 Use "Verb + resultative complement 好(好)" in the following sentences:

1. 我的研究報告已經 ________ 了，現在我輕鬆多了。
   我的研究报告已经 ________ 了，现在我轻松多了。
2. 方明的電話 ________ 了沒有？我想找他去鍛煉。
   方明的电话 ________ 了没有？我想找他去锻炼。
3. 你的簽證 ________ 了沒有？沒有多少時間了。
   你的签证 ________ 了没有？没有多少时间了。

10-6 Group the underlined phrases based on their structure:

Juxtaposed phrases (JP) Endocentric phrases (EP)
"Subj. + Verb" phrases (SVP) "Verb + Obj" phrases (VOP)

1. 去北京的機票 ______
   去北京的机票 ______
2. 爬長城很累 ______
   爬长城很累 ______
3. 現金和支票 ______
   现金和支票 ______
4. 張藝謀導演的功夫片 ______
   张艺谋导演的功夫片 ______
5. 看過這部電影的人 ______
   看过这部电影的人 ______
6. 支票帳戶 ______
   支票账户 ______
7. 我最想做的事 ______
   我最想做的事 ______
8. 親戚朋友 ______
   亲戚朋友 ______

10-7 The following is a list of exchange rates between US dollars and other currencies. Write out the Chinese for the ratio between US$ and each of the following currencies, then practice saying the whole sentence aloud.

US$	RMB ¥	HK$	NTD	Euro	Japanese ¥
1	7.98	7.76	32.57	0.82	107.82

Example: 美元：人民幣 ____一比七點九八____
美元：人民币 ____一比七点九八____

美元匯率：現在美元兑人民幣的匯率是一比七點九八
美元汇率：现在美元兑人民币的汇率是一比七点九八

美元：港幣 ____________________
美元：港币 ____________________

美元：新台幣 ____________________
美元：新台币 ____________________

美元：歐元 ____________________
美元：欧元 ____________________

美元：日元 ____________________
美元：日元 ____________________

10-8 You are going to open a bank account. There are three banks near your school. Compare their interest rates and complete the following paragraph:

大華銀行 (大华银行)		民生銀行 (民生银行)		美華銀行 (美华银行)	
支票帳戶 (支票账户)	儲蓄帳戶 (储蓄账户)	支票帳戶 (支票账户)	儲蓄帳戶 (储蓄账户)	支票帳戶 (支票账户)	儲蓄帳戶 (储蓄账户)
2.8%	3.5%	2.9%	3.6%	2.8%	3.7%

在三家銀行裡，民生銀行的利息 ________ (to be the highest)，支票帳戶
在三家银行里，民生银行的利息 ________ (to be the highest)，支票账户

和儲蓄帳戶的利率都比大華銀行高 ________ (0.1%)。美華銀行也
和储蓄账户的利率都比大华银行高 ________ (0.1%)。美华银行也

不錯，可是它的支票帳戶的利息 _____ 大華銀行的 ________ (same)，
不错，可是它的支票账户的利息 _____ 大华银行的 ________ (same)，

只有 ____________ (2.8%)。不過它的
只有 ____________ (2.8%)。不过它的

儲蓄帳戶的利息比較高，比大華銀行
储蓄账户的利息比较高，比大华银行

____________ (0.2% higher)。我決定去
____________ (0.2% higher)。我决定去

美華銀行開帳戶。
美华银行开账户。

IV. 交際活動 (交际活动)

10-9 Your classmate 高信華(高信华) shared her plans for the winter vacation. You and your girl/boyfriend are now working on your own plans. Take what 高信華(高信华) said as a reference and discuss what you are going to do.

10-10 Work in pairs and find out whether your friend is able to do the following (use the Verb + potential complement structure in the questions and answers):

1. to be able to afford to buy a plane ticket to Hong Kong
2. to be able to understand the movie "Crouching Tiger and Hidden Dragon" in Chinese
3. to be able to find the movie theater nearby
4. to be able to finish all the homework today
5. whether their classroom can seat more than 30 people
6. to be able to finish 40 dumplings in one meal

Example:

A: 你找得到找不到那家銀行?
你找得到找不到那家银行?

B: 我一定能找得到。
我一定能找得到。

You may ask more questions by using the same structure. Try to find out as much as you can about your friend.

文化知識 (文化知识) Culture Link

文化點滴 (文化点滴) CULTURE NOTES

中國的長城 (中国的长城) [Zhōngguó de Chángchéng] The Great Wall of China

The Great Wall in China, one of the greatest wonders of the world, is probably the most widely acknowledged symbol of China. Wherever you go in the world, you will see pictures of the Great Wall in any place related to China. Like a gigantic dragon, it crawls through 11 provinces in the northern part of the country, stretching nearly 6,700 kilometers (4,163 miles) from the east to the west of China. In 1987 it was listed by UNESCO as one of the greatest pieces of World Heritage. With its unique architectural and historic significance, the Great Wall is now one of the most appealing attractions to people all over the world. As a Chinese saying goes: "不到長城非好漢(不到长城非好汉)" ([bú dào Chángchéng fēi hǎohàn]: You will not be regarded as a hero unless you have been to the Great Wall.)

The Great Wall was originally several independent walls built separately as defensive fortifications during 周朝(周朝) ([Zhōu Cháo]: the Zhou Dynasty), 春秋戰國時代(春秋战国时代) ([Chūnqiū Zhànguó shídài]: the Spring and Autumn and Warring States Periods) more than 2,500 years ago. After constant extensions and repairs, 秦始皇帝(秦始皇帝) ([Qín shǐ huángdì]: the first emperor of the Qin Dynasty), after he unified China in 221 B.C., decided to have the walls joined together to fend off invasions from the Huns in the north. Since then, the Great Wall has served as a monument and symbol of the Chinese nation throughout history.

The Chinese call it 萬里長城(万里长城) ([wànlǐ chángchéng]: the Great Wall) which literally means "ten thousand li long wall." It took more than ten years and over a million laborers to complete the construction. As the construction traversed mountain ridges and plateaus, the unimaginable difficulty and hardships of the construction cost the lives of hundreds and thousands of laborers, some of whom were later buried under the wall. The construction materials, primarily stones, earth and bricks, were mainly drawn from local resources. The result is considered a manifestation of the wisdom and tenacity of the Chinese people.

What we see today as the Great Wall was not built during the Qin Dynasty, but in 明朝(明朝) ([Míngcháo]: the Ming Dynasty) more than 1,500 years later. It took nearly 200 years during the Ming Dynasty to repair and rebuild the Great Wall. The result is what we see today, a wall which has a thickness of 4.5–8 meters and numerous signal towers, and stretches 6,700 kilometers from the Shanhaiguan Pass in Hebei Province in the east to Jiayuguan Pass of Gansu Province in the west.

To protect and preserve this wonder, the China Great Wall Academy conducted a 45-day survey of 101 sections of the Great Wall in 2002 and found that 70% of the Wall had been damaged by Mother Nature and human negligence. The Academy called for more effective protection of this important world relic. A voluntary campaign started to collect donations of funds to repair and preserve the Great Wall. With the support of UNESCO, the Chinese government has also taken measures to preserve and recover this great treasure.

The Great Wall viewed from different angles

問題討論(问题讨论) Discussion Questions

1. 你去過長城嗎? 你去中國的時候想去爬長城嗎? 為什麼?

   你去过长城吗? 你去中国的时候想去爬长城吗? 为什么?

   Have you been to the Great Wall? When you go to China, would you like to climb the Great Wall? Why?

2. 你知道中國還有什麼有名的地方嗎? 請說出幾個。
你知道中国还有什么有名的地方吗? 请说出几个。
Do you know any other famous spots in China? Provide some examples.

趣味中文 (趣味中文) FUN WITH CHINESE

滿載而歸
满载而归
to return home fully laden with riches, gifts, etc.

mǎn	zài	ér	guī
滿	載	而	歸
满	载	而	归
full	to carry	and then	to return

問題討論 (问题讨论) Discussion Questions

1. In what kinds of situation can you use 滿載而歸(满载而归)? Please describe these situations in Chinese by using 滿載而歸 (满载而归).
2. Do you know some other Chinese phrases containing the word "而(而)"? What are these phrases and what does "而(而)" mean in these phrases?

行動吧！(行动吧！) LET'S GO!

簽證申請表(签证申请表) Visa Application Form

小琴 is going to China so she needs to apply for visa. Here is the visa application form. Please take a look at it and then answer the questions:

Useful words and expressions:

共和國(共和国) [gònghéguó]: republic
曾用名(曾用名) [céngyòngmíng]: name once used
性別(性别) [xìngbié]: gender
護照(护照) [hùzhào]: passport
國籍(国籍) [guójí]: citizenship, nationality
單位(单位) [dānwèi]: (work) unit
種類(种类) [zhǒnglèi]: kind, type
普通(普通) [pǔtōng]: ordinary
外交(外交) [wàijiāo]: diplomatic
公務(公务) [gōngwù]: public service
官員(官员) [guānyuán]: official
其他(其他) [qítā]: other
有效期(有效期) [yǒuxiàoqī]: valid period
赴(赴) [fù]: to go to
事由(事由) [shìyóu]: purpose
地點(地点) [dìdiǎn]: spot, place
入境(入境) [rùjìng]: to enter; entrance
次數(次数) [cìshù]: times
領事(领事) [lǐngshì]: consul
預計(预计) [yùjì]: pre-planned
建議(建议) [jiànyì]: to suggest
提前(提前) [tíqián]: ahead of time, in advance
不得(不得) [bùdé]: not allowed
停留(停留) [tíngliú]: to stay
取件(取件) [qǔjiàn]: to pick up (letters or packages)
加急(加急) [jiājí]: express (service)
特急(特急) [tèjí]: rush (service)
加收(加收) [jiāshōu]: to receive extra (fee)
服務費(服务费) [fúwùfèi]: service fee
快遞(快递) [kuàidì]: express delivery
辦理(办理) [bànlǐ]: to process
邀請(邀请) [yāoqǐng]: to invite
否(否) [fǒu]: (Classical Chinese) not
拒絕(拒绝) [jùjué]: to refuse

中华人民共和国签证申请表 (Q-1)

Visa Application Form of the People's Republic of China

(此表不适用于香港特区/Not for Hong Kong SAR Visa)

1. 中文姓名 / Chinese Name (if any)	2. 曾用名 / Former Name (if any)	3. 性别 / Sex: ☐男 / M ☐女 / F	请将2寸护照照片粘贴于此 Please affix One passport photo
4. 外文姓名 / Full Name Last Name:	First Name:		
5. 出生日期: 年 月 日 Date of Birth: Y M D	7. 国籍 / Nationality		
6. 出生地点 (省 / 市) Place (Province/State) of Birth:	8. 曾有何国籍 / Former Nationality (if any)		

9. 职业 ______________________
Occupation:　　　　工作单位电话 / Office Tel. (　　　　) -
工作单位:
Company Name:

10. 家庭住址 / Home Address:　　　　家庭电话 / Home Tel. (　　　　) -

11. 护照种类: Passport Type:	普通 ☐ Regular	外交 ☐ Diplomat	公务/官员 ☐ Service / Official	其它证件 (名称) ☐ Other (Please specify)
护照有效期: 年 月 日 Passport Expiration date: Y M D	护照号码: Passport No.		电子信箱: Email: @	

12. 申请赴中国事由 / Purpose of your visit to China:

13. 前往中国地点 (省、区、市、县) / Cities or Counties, Provinces to visit in China:

14. 计划入境的次数 (何种签证及签证次数将由领事决定) / Intended Number of Entries (Type of Visa and number of entries will be decided by consuls.)	☐ 一次 (三个月内入出境有效) / Single entry valid within 3 months ☐ 二次 (六个月内入出境有效) / Two-entry valid within 6 months ☐ 半年内有效多次入出境有效 / Multiple entry valid within 6 months ☐ 一年内有效多次入出境有效 / Multiple entry valid within 12 months ☐ 两年内有效多次入出境有效 / Multiple entry valid within 24 months
15. 预计入境的日期 (建议提前1–2 个月申请签证，但不得早于3 个月申请签证) / Intended Date of Each Entry into China (Suggested to apply for the visa 1–2 months ahead of the tentative date of your first entry into China, but no earlier than 3 months.)	☐ 年 / Y 月 / M 日 / D ☐ 年 / Y 月 / M 日 / D
16. 预计每次在中国停留天数 / Utmost Duration of (Each) Stay in China	☐ 天 / days; ☐ 天 / days
17. 计划取证件日期 (加急和特急需加收服务费。签证不能邮寄或快递办理) / Pickup Date Requested (Extra fee should be paid for express or rush service. Visa can not be done by mail or any delivery services.)	☐ 正常 (4个工作日) Regular (4 workdays) ☐ 加急 (2–3 个工作日) Express (2–3 workdays) ☐ 特急 (当天) Rush (Same day)

18. 邀请单位 / 个人姓名、地址、电话 / Name, Address and Phone No. of the Organization or Person to be visited in China:

19. 你是否申请过赴华签证 / Have you ever applied for a Chinese visa before?　☐ 是 / Yes ☐ 否 / No

20. 你是否被拒绝过赴华签证 / Have you ever been declined for your Chinese visa application?　☐ 是 / Yes ☐ 否 / No
被拒绝时间、地点 / If ever declined, when and where?

問題討論 (问题讨论) Discussion Questions

1. May this form also be used to apply for a visa to Hong Kong?
2. What is the size of the photo required?
3. How many types of passports are there? What are they?
4. Please translate the following into Chinese:

粘贴于此 ____________________

申请赴中国事由 ____________________

三个月内出入境有效 ____________________

加收服务费 ____________________

邀请单位 ____________________

復習(复习) Review

LESSON 9 TO LESSON 10

I. Activities

A. Are you satisfied with your weight? Do you have a weight control/loss plan? If you do, tell us something about your plan. The following questions are for your reference:

1. 你原來身體怎麼樣? 體重怎麼樣?
   你原来身体怎么样? 体重怎么样?
2. 你是怎樣控制你的體重的?
   你是怎样控制你的体重的?
3. 你控制體重的方法效果好嗎? 為什麼?
   你控制体重的方法效果好吗? 为什么?

Please also use the following sentence patterns plus any other sentence patterns for comparison:

1. 越來越(越来越)...... for progressive comparison
2. 越(越)......越(越)...... pattern

B. You have not seen your high school classmate for about two years. He/she used to be very chubby. You went to visit him/her during the Thanksgiving Holiday. He/she seemed to have lost quite a bit of weight and looked very healthy. You were amazed by the change and began to ask him/her questions. Carry on a conversation of about ten sentences each between you and him/her and chat about his/her change. Use the following words, expressions and sentences patterns:

1. Any sentences patterns for comparison
2. 最(最) and 更(更)
3. Words and expressions such as

   羨慕(羡慕), 差不多(差不多), 次(次), 瘦/苗條(瘦/苗条), 減肥(减肥), 堅持(坚持), 效果(效果), 輕(轻), 精神(精神), 控制(控制), 鍛煉(锻炼), 注意(注意), 比(比), 靈活(灵活), 磅/公斤(磅/公斤)

C. Make a report on your plan for the winter vacation. Exchange your thoughts with your friend. The following words and expressions must be used:

計畫(计划)，旅遊(旅游)，中文班(中文班)，旬(旬)，航空公司(航空公司)，旅行社(旅行社)，飛機票(飞机票)，買(买)，支票(支票)，信用卡(信用卡)，付款(付款)，外幣(外币)，匯率(汇率)，滿載而歸(满载而归)

II. Review of grammar

A. Use 越來越(越来越)...... to complete the following sentences:

1. 去中國的機票 ________________。我還沒有買到。
   去中国的机票 ________________。我还没有买到。
2. 因為效果很好，我現在 ________________ 鍛煉了。
   因为效果很好，我现在 ________________ 锻炼了。
3. 你知道為什麼他的精神 ________________ 了嗎?
   你知道为什么他的精神 ________________ 了吗?
4. 現在 ____________ 的中國人喜歡看美國好萊塢 ([hǎoláiwū]: Hollywood) 的電影。

   现在 ____________ 的中国人喜欢看美国好莱坞 ([hǎoláiwū]: Hollywood) 的电影。

B. Use 越(越)......越(越)...... to combine the following pairs of sentences:

1. 他鍛煉得很多，他很靈活。
   他锻炼得很多，他很灵活。
2. 去中國的人非常多，機票很難買。
   去中国的人非常多，机票很难买。
3. 他買了很多飛機票，票價很便宜。
   他买了很多飞机票，票价很便宜。
4. 電影的情節很曲折，我非常喜歡。
   电影的情节很曲折，我非常喜欢。

III. Review of characters

A. Compare the following pairs of characters to see whether they are the same and what differences there are between them. Write out their Pinyin and create a word or phrase:

Example: 很(很) hěn 很好

1. 旬(旬) ______ ________
   句(句) ______ ________
2. 雪(雪) ______ ________
   零(零) ______ ________
3. 超(超) ______ ________
   起(起) ______ ________
4. 精(精) ______ ________
   情(情) ______ ________
5. 跟(跟) ______ ________
   根(根) ______ ________
6. 受(受) ______ ________
   收(收) ______ ________
7. 劇(剧) ______ ________
   據(据) ______ ________
8. 付(付) ______ ________
   什(什) ______ ________

B. Fill in the blanks in the following dialogues with appropriate words from the following words and expressions:

根據，說好了，希望，怪不得，不但……而且……，其實，總是，當然
根据，说好了，希望，怪不得，不但……而且……，其实，总是，当然

1. **A:** 我要兌換一百元美金。
   我要兑换一百元美金。

   B: ______ 今天的匯率，一百元美金可以換八百二十六元人民幣。
   ______ 今天的汇率，一百元美金可以换八百二十六元人民币。

2. **A:** 方明，你說什麼是減肥的最好方法?
   方明，你说什么是减肥的最好方法?

   B: ______ 運動是最好的減肥方法。
   ______ 运动是最好的减肥方法。

3. **A:** 你為什麼 ______ 想去中國?
   你为什么 ______ 想去中国?

   B: 因為中國是一個非常有意思的國家。
   因为中国是一个非常有意思的国家。

4. A: 我在北京有很多親戚。
我在北京有很多亲戚。

B: ________ 你今年冬天想去北京。
________ 你今年冬天想去北京。

5. 我已經跟我的爸爸媽媽 ________，明年夏天去上海參加暑期中文班學習。
我已经跟我的爸爸妈妈 ________，明年夏天去上海参加暑期中文班学习。

6. A: 這是我認識的一個朋友的電話號碼。他在旅行社工作。
这是我认识的一个朋友的电话号码。他在旅行社工作。

B: ________ 他能幫助我訂到去中國的飛機票。
________ 他能帮助我订到去中国的飞机票。

7. A: 你喜歡看中國的功夫片嗎?
你喜欢看中国的功夫片吗?

B: ________。我最喜歡看李連杰的電影。
________。我最喜欢看李连杰的电影。

8. A: 你看過張藝謀 [Zhāng Yìmóu] 導演的電影嗎?
你看过张艺谋 [Zhāng Yìmóu] 导演的电影吗?

B: 我 ______ 看過他最近導演的電影，______ 還看過他以前自己演的電影。
我 ______ 看过他最近导演的电影，______ 还看过他以前自己演的电影。

IV. Report

Last summer, you joined 20 other students in a Chinese study abroad program in Beijing. It was a wonderful experience for you and you had a very good time there. You did a lot of things and took part in many activities including taking classes, traveling, watching movies and other shows, getting together with Chinese students, learning taichi, etc. Now write a brief report of your summer experience and share it with your good friend. Encourage him/her to go too. Use as many words and expressions from the lessons as you can. (at least 12 sentences)

附錄：生詞表 (附录：生词表)
APPENDIX: VOCABULARY LIST

Lesson 1

倒	別	房東	樹	撞	壞
倒	别	房东	树	撞	坏
呀	小心	鏡子	破	分工合作	
呀	小心	镜子	破	分工合作	
主意	負責	行李	放	裝	掃
主意	负责	行李	放	装	扫
整理	箱子	衣服	掛	累	請客
整理	箱子	衣服	挂	累	请客
死	附近	忘	門	窗	關上
死	附近	忘	门	窗	关上
外套	咱們				
外套	咱们				

補充詞(补充词):

鑰匙	地下室	樓梯	層	地毯	地板
钥匙	地下室	楼梯	层	地毯	地板
整齊	方便	乾淨	亂	髒	亮
整齐	方便	干净	乱	脏	亮

Lesson 2

牆	著	照片	服裝	舞台	擺
墙	着	照片	服装	舞台	摆
各種	樂器	演員	表演	樂師	打
各种	乐器	演员	表演	乐师	打
鼓	拉	胡琴	彈奏	自己	齣
鼓	拉	胡琴	弹奏	自己	出

戲	畫	臉	拿	把	刀
戏	画	脸	拿	把	刀
神氣	座位	滿	觀眾	站	一言為定
神气	座位	满	观众	站	一言为定

專名(专名):

李訪	關明遠	關公	北京	長城
李访	关明远	关公	北京	长城

補充詞(补充词):

敲鑼	吹笛子	鋼琴	小提琴	吉他	專心
敲锣	吹笛子	钢琴	小提琴	吉他	专心
欣賞	關於				
欣赏	关于				

Lesson 3

往	各位	旅客	降落	安全帶	繫上
往	各位	旅客	降落	安全带	系上
計算機	電子	用品	搭乘	航空	出租
计算机	电子	用品	搭乘	航空	出租
旅館	路人	棟	交叉口	左	拐
旅馆	路人	栋	交叉口	左	拐
一直	路口	司機	假日	公里	後車箱
一直	路口	司机	假日	公里	后车箱
發展	變化	本來	農田	變成	馬路
发展	变化	本来	农田	变成	马路
喔	公尺	紅綠燈	向	右	轉
喔	公尺	红绿灯	向	右	转
小吃店	彎兒	車費	人民幣	找	
小吃店	弯儿	车费	人民币	找	

專名(专名):

浦東 浦东	中山路 中山路

補充詞(补充词):

載 载	方向 方向	雙行道 双行道	單行道 单行道	超車 超车	出差 出差	橋 桥

Lesson 4

師母 师母	些 些	維生素 维生素	永遠 永远	健康 健康	年輕 年轻
破費 破费	小意思 小意思	難得 难得	特地 特地	拿手菜 拿手菜	涼 凉
精神 精神	白頭髮 白头发	眼睛 眼睛	花 花	適應 适应	時差 时差
白天 白天	睏 困	睡不著 睡不着	街道 街道	習慣 习惯	長 长
年糕 年糕	味道 味道	地道 地道	香 香	俱全 俱全	飽 饱
只是 只是	家常便飯 家常便饭	相聚 相聚	乾杯 干杯		

有朋自遠方來，不亦樂乎?
有朋自远方来，不亦乐乎?

專名(专名):

匹茲堡
匹兹堡

補充詞(补充词):

藥草 药草	失眠 失眠	燙 烫

Lesson 5

陰	終於	本來	飛行	轉機	誤點
阴	终于	本来	飞行	转机	误点
趕上	班機	熱情	好客	津津有味	大開眼界
赶上	班机	热情	好客	津津有味	大开眼界
團	方向	鬧	笑話	繁榮	大廈
团	方向	闹	笑话	繁荣	大厦
雖然	別人	小吃	挺	值得	
虽然	别人	小吃	挺	值得	

Lesson 6

銀行	開	帳戶	存	款	取
银行	开	账户	存	款	取
方便	利率	高	儲蓄	百分之……	
方便	利率	高	储蓄	百分之……	
利息	支票	職員	低	種	差不多
利息	支票	职员	低	种	差不多
夠	單子	填	千	元	美金
够	单子	填	千	元	美金
寄	簿	拿	取款卡	自動	取款機
寄	簿	拿	取款卡	自动	取款机
現金	申請	信用卡	當然	表	換
现金	申请	信用卡	当然	表	换
匯率	兌換	外幣	櫃台		
汇率	兑换	外币	柜台		

專名(专名):

關京華	方小琴
关京华	方小琴

補充詞(补充词):

新台幣 新台币	港幣 港币	美元 美元	歐元 欧元	英磅 英磅	法郎 法郎
馬克 马克	盧布 卢布	日元 日元	信用卡 信用卡	簽證卡 签证卡	萬事達卡 万事达卡
美國運通卡 美国运通卡		定期存款 定期存款	活期存款 活期存款		

Lesson 7

寒假 寒假	旅遊 旅游	旅行社 旅行社	訂 订	機票 机票	羨慕 羡慕
打算 打算	親戚 亲戚	原來 原来	抽空 抽空	拜訪 拜访	一直 一直
查 查	網站 网站	買不起 买不起	買到 买到	找得到 找得到	便宜 便宜
其實 其实	要是 要是	南方 南方	四季如春 四季如春	風景如畫 风景如画	少數民族 少数民族
如果 如果	簽證 签证	辦 办	大概 大概	來得及 来得及	

專名(专名):

香港 香港	雲南 云南	昆明 昆明

補充詞(补充词):

單程 单程	回程 回程	往返票 往返票	訂房間 订房间	導遊 导游	領事館 领事馆
大使館 大使馆	辦事處 办事处				

Lesson 8

連	影子	研究報告	輕鬆	表妹	強
连	影子	研究报告	轻松	表妹	强
完	導演	部	功夫片	主要	演員
完	导演	部	功夫片	主要	演员
特别	它	場面	情節	吸引人	關於
特别	它	场面	情节	吸引人	关于
古代	故事	不如	精彩	對	描寫
古代	故事	不如	精彩	对	描写
歷史	同意	客觀	感	興趣	感情
历史	同意	客观	感	兴趣	感情
方面	而且	特技	效果	顏色	週末
方面	而且	特技	效果	颜色	周末
放	票價				
放	票价				

專名(专名):

季如春	方慕華	張藝謀	陳道明	李連杰	張曼玉
季如春	方慕华	张艺谋	陈道明	李连杰	张曼玉
英雄	臥虎藏龍	秦始皇			
英雄	卧虎藏龙	秦始皇			

補充詞(补充词):

意見	看法	感想	心得	瞭解	倍
意见	看法	感想	心得	了解	倍
製作	配樂	剪輯	服裝		
制作	配乐	剪辑	服装		

Lesson 9

越來越…	需要	鐘頭	瘦	減肥	堅持
越来越…	需要	钟头	瘦	减肥	坚持

體重 体重	輕 轻	磅 磅	怪不得 怪不得	苗條 苗条	女孩子 女孩子
控制 控制	飲食 饮食	注意 注意	甜食 甜食	早 早	個子 个子
矮 矮	呎 呎	吋 吋	超過 超过	靈活 灵活	總是 总是
重要 重要	更 更				

專名(专名):

白思琴 白思琴	胡欣明 胡欣明

補充詞(补充词):

盎司 盎司	公斤 公斤	公尺 公尺	公分 公分

Lesson 10

計畫 计划	最後 最后	說好了 说好了	希望 希望	旬 旬	付款 付款
接受 接受	商店 商店	根據 根据	當天 当天	安全 安全	零 零
爬 爬	頂 顶	幫助 帮助	非 非	好漢 好汉	告訴 告诉
壯觀 壮观	曲折 曲折	滿載而歸 满载而归			

專名(专名):

黃山 黄山	十面埋伏 十面埋伏

附錄：繁/簡體字對照表
附录：繁/简体字对照表
APPENDIX: TRADITIONAL/SIMPLIFIED CHINESE CHARACTER TABLE

繁體字(繁体字)：[fán tǐ zì] traditional character (or complex character)
簡體字(简体字)：[jiǎn tǐ zì] simplified character

第一课 Lesson 1

繁：	樹	壞	鏡	負	責	裝	掃	掛
简：	树	坏	镜	负	责	装	扫	挂

第二课 Lesson 2

繁：	牆	著	擺	種	彈	齣	戲	畫	臉	滿	眾
简：	墙	着	摆	种	弹	出	戏	画	脸	满	众
繁：	長										
简：	长										

第三课 Lesson 3

繁：	全	繫	計	棟	變	農	燈	費	幣
简：	全	系	计	栋	变	农	灯	费	币

第四课 Lesson 4

繁：	維	輕	涼	髮	適	睏	慣	飽	乾
简：	维	轻	凉	发	适	困	惯	饱	干

第五课 Lesson 5

繁：	陰	終	於	誤	趕	團	鬧	榮	廈	雖
简：	阴	终	于	误	赶	团	闹	荣	厦	虽

第六课 Lesson 6

繁:	銀	帳	戶	儲	職	夠	單	當	換	匯	櫃
简:	银	账	户	储	职	够	单	当	换	汇	柜

第七课 Lesson 7

繁:	遊	訂	羨	親	訪	數	簽	證	辦
简:	游	订	羡	亲	访	数	签	证	办

第八课 Lesson 8

繁:	連	報	鬆	強	導	節	歷	顏	週	價
简:	连	报	松	强	导	节	历	颜	周	价

第九课 Lesson 9

繁:	減	堅	飲	靈	總
简:	减	坚	饮	灵	总

第十课 Lesson 10

繁:	據	頂	漢	訴	壯	載	歸
简:	据	顶	汉	诉	壮	载	归

附錄 (附录)：課文 (课文)
APPENDIX: LANGUAGE IN USE (TRADITIONAL/SIMPLIFIED CHARACTER)

第一課　我把車停在旁邊

謝進學：我們到了，讓我把車停在旁邊。
常　天：等一會兒，我先把我的車開走，你再把車開過來。
夏中明：你在倒車的時候，我幫你看看，別把房東的樹撞壞了。
常　天：對呀！上次我們搬進來的時候，不小心把房東的鏡子打破了，真不好意思。
謝進學：我們先把床和書桌搬到樓上去，然後再分工合作，怎麼樣？
夏中明：好主意，我負責把行李搬下來、放好，我也會把電腦裝好。
謝進學：好，我來掃地、整理客廳，再把書放好。
常　天：我來洗碗，把箱子打開，再把衣服掛好。
謝進學：謝謝你們幫我的忙，這次搬家把你們累壞了。今天晚上想吃什麼？我請客！
常　天：好極了！我快餓死了。
夏中明：這附近有一家很不錯的中國飯館，可是我把地址忘了。
常　天：沒關係，我有。你們看，我找到了。
謝進學：太好了，讓我先把門窗關上。
夏中明：別忘了把外套穿上，咱們走吧！

第一课　我把车停在旁边

谢进学：我们到了，让我把车停在旁边。
常　天：等一会儿，我先把我的车开走，你再把车开过来。
夏中明：你在倒车的时候，我帮你看看，别把房东的树撞坏了。
常　天：对呀！上次我们搬进来的时候，不小心把房东的镜子打破了，真不好意思。
谢进学：我们先把床和书桌搬到楼上去，然后再分工合作，怎么样？
夏中明：好主意，我负责把行李搬下来、放好，我也会把电脑装好。
谢进学：好，我来扫地、整理客厅，再把书放好。
常　天：我来洗碗，把箱子打开，再把衣服挂好。

谢进学：谢谢你们帮我的忙，这次搬家把你们累坏了。今天晚上想吃什么？我请客！
常　天：好极了！我快饿死了。
夏中明：这附近有一家很不错的中国饭馆，可是我把地址忘了。
常　天：没关系，我有。你们看，我找到了。
谢进学：太好了，让我先把门窗关上。
夏中明：别忘了把外套穿上，咱们走吧！

第二課　牆上掛著一張照片

李　訪：那邊牆上掛著一張照片。那是誰？我好像沒見過。
關明遠：那是我姐姐照的照片。
李　訪：她現在在哪兒？
關明遠：她現在正在北京留學，她在那兒學中文，已經在那兒住了一年多了。
李　訪：她學中文學了多久了？
關明遠：她學了三年了。
李　訪：那是京劇的服裝吧！
關明遠：是的。這是她上個月去看京劇的時候照的照片。以前她沒看過京劇，現在看到了，她很高興。
李　訪：舞台上面擺著什麼？好像是中國的各種樂器。
關明遠：沒錯！你看台上京劇演員，正忙著表演呢。旁邊還坐著幾個樂師，有的在打鼓，有的在拉胡琴，他們都忙著彈奏自己的樂器。
李　訪：這齣戲說的是什麼？好像很不錯。
關明遠：這齣戲說的是關公。你看關公他畫著紅臉，手上拿著一把大刀，真神氣！
李　訪：人真不少啊！你看，座位都坐滿了，有的觀眾還得站著。對了，你看過京劇嗎？
關明遠：我看過兩次，都是在上海看的。
李　訪：你在中國的時候去過上海，還去過哪兒？
關明遠：我只去過上海。那時候，我每天都忙著上課，所以沒有機會去北京和長城。
李　訪：我聽說上海的小籠包很好吃，你吃過嗎？
關明遠：吃過，我還學過做小籠包呢！
李　訪：真有意思！我也想去中國看看。

關明遠：我下個月要去中國，你跟我去吧！我們可以一起去看京劇，怎麼樣？

李　訪：好，一言為定！

第二课　墙上挂着一张照片

李　访：那边墙上挂着一张照片。那是谁？我好像没见过。

关明远：那是我姐姐照的照片。

李　访：她现在在哪儿？

关明远：她现在正在北京留学，她在那儿学中文，已经在那儿住了一年多了。

李　访：她学中文学了多久了？

关明远：她学了三年了。

李　访：那是京剧的服装吧！

关明远：是的。这是她上个月去看京剧的时候照的照片。以前她没看过京剧，现在看到了，她很高兴。

李　访：舞台上面摆着什么？好像是中国的各种乐器。

关明远：没错！你看台上京剧演员，正忙着表演呢。旁边还坐着几个乐师，有的在打鼓，有的在拉胡琴，他们都忙着弹奏自己的乐器。

李　访：这出戏说的是什么？好像很不错。

关明远：这出戏说的是关公。你看关公他画着红脸，手上拿着一把大刀，真神气！

李　访：人真不少啊！你看，座位都坐满了，有的观众还得站着。对了，你看过京剧吗？

关明远：我看过两次，都是在上海看的。

李　访：你在中国的时候去过上海，还去过哪儿？

关明远：我只去过上海。那时候，我每天都忙着上课，所以没有机会去北京和长城。

李　访：我听说上海的小笼包很好吃，你吃过吗？

关明远：吃过，我还学过做小笼包呢！

李　访：真有意思！我也想去中国看看。

关明远：我下个月要去中国，你跟我去吧！我们可以一起去看京剧，怎么样？

李　访：好，一言为定！

关明远：李访说这儿的天气比匹兹堡热。还有，这儿的人也比匹兹堡多，街道上到处都是人，他还不太习惯。
李　访：我长这么大，第一次看到这么多人。
师　母：你们俩谁比较大？
关明远：我跟李访一样大，都是二十四岁。
师　母：对了，不要只说话，忘了吃菜。来，来，来，多吃一点儿。
老　师：这是师母做的年糕，味道很地道，你们尝尝。
……
关明远：师母您做的饭真好吃。
李　访：是啊！色香味俱全，我吃了很多，现在已经很饱了。
师　母：哪里，哪里！只是家常便饭。
老　师：难得我们相聚，来，一起来干一杯。今天真高兴，"有朋自远方来，不亦乐乎！"
老师，师母，关明远，李访：干杯！

第五課　我的中國行
(復習)

十月二十日 星期三 天氣：陰

我們坐了三十多個小時的飛機，終於回到美國來了。從中國到美國本來十幾個小時就到了，但是在日本轉機的時候，因為我們的飛機誤點了，所以沒趕上我們的班機。我們在機場等了五個小時以後，才坐上了飛機。這次飛機誤點把我跟李訪累壞了。在飛機上，我們一把行李放好，就一直睡覺，睡到飛機降落以後才起來。

不過這次很高興能在上海和老師再次相聚。老師和師母看起來都很精神，他們還是跟以前一樣非常熱情、好客。師母還特地做了幾樣很地道的上海菜，讓我們嚐嚐，其中我最喜歡的是上海年糕。真好吃！

我還帶李訪去看了京劇，我們看得津津有味，他也覺得大開眼界。不過，我聽說現在的京劇劇團比以前少了，所以票也比以前貴了。

上海真的變得很快，有些路都很難找到了。我們手裡拿著地圖，忙著問路、找方向。常常應該向左拐的時候，我們轉錯了，往右拐了，鬧了不少笑話。

中國真的是一天比一天繁榮、進步了。在大城市裡，高樓大廈跟美國的一樣高，到處都能看到外國人。

這次在中國的時間雖然很短，可是我們都玩得很高興。李訪說他現在可以跟別人說他去過中國、看過京劇了。還有，他也嚐了很多中國的小吃，都很棒!

我們倆都覺得這次去中國旅行，挺不錯的，也非常值得。下次有機會，我們還要再去。

第五课 我的中国行
(复习)

十月二十日 星期三 天气：阴

我们坐了三十多个小时的飞机，终于回到美国来了。从中国到美国本来十几个小时就到了，但是在日本转机的时候，因为我们的飞机误点了，所以没赶上我们的班机。我们在机场等了五个小时以后，才坐上了飞机。这次飞机误点把我跟李访累坏了。在飞机上,我们一把行李放好，就一直睡觉，睡到飞机降落以后才起来。

不过这次很高兴能在上海和老师再次相聚。老师和师母看起来都很精神，他们还是跟以前一样非常热情、好客。师母还特地做了几样很地道的上海菜，让我们尝尝，其中我最喜欢的是上海年糕。真好吃!

我还带李访去看了京剧，我们看得津津有味，他也觉得大开眼界。不过，我听说现在的京剧剧团比以前少了，所以票也比以前贵了。

上海真的变得很快，有些路都很难找到了。我们手里拿着地图，忙着问路、找方向。常常应该向左拐的时候，我们转错了，往右拐了，闹了不少笑话。

中国真的是一天比一天繁荣、进步了。在大城市里，高楼大厦跟美国的一样高，到处都能看到外国人。

这次在中国的时间虽然很短，可是我们都玩得很高兴。李访说他现在可以跟别人说他去过中国、看过京剧了。还有，他也尝了很多中国的小吃，都很棒!

我们俩都觉得这次去中国旅行，挺不错的，也非常值得。下次有机会，我们还要再去。

第六課　我要去銀行開一個帳戶

(在路上)

關京華：小琴，我要去銀行開一個帳戶，這樣我存款、取款就方便多了。你知道哪家銀行比較好嗎?

方小琴：我常常去大華銀行存款、取款。那兒的服務不錯，利率也比較高，現在儲蓄帳戶的利率是百分之三點二。

關京華：那我就去大華銀行吧。

(在銀行)

關京華：先生，我想開一個有利息的支票帳戶。請問，有利息的支票帳戶利率是多少?

職　員：最近利率都比較低，今天是百分之二點六。

關京華：怎麼這麼低呀? 我聽說是百分之三點二呢。

職　員：那是儲蓄帳戶，儲蓄帳戶的利率高一點兒，是百分之三點二。這種帳戶每個月可以開三張支票。您想開哪一種?

關京華：我想一個月開三張支票差不多夠了。我就開一個儲蓄帳戶吧。

職　員：好，請把這張開帳戶的單子填一下，謝謝。請問您今天想存多少錢?

關京華：我這兒是三千元美金。

職　員：好……一個星期以後，您會收到我們給您寄去的支票簿和取款卡。您可以拿取款卡在自動取款機那兒取現金。

關京華：我可以在你們這兒申請一張信用卡嗎?

職　員：當然可以。請把這張申請信用卡的表填一下。

關京華：下個月我要去中國，要換一些人民幣。請問美金換人民幣的匯率是多少?

職　員：今天的匯率是一比七點九八。

關京華：兑換外幣的地方在哪兒?

職　員：就在左邊的櫃台那兒。

關京華：謝謝。再見。

第六课　我要去银行开一个账户

(在路上)

关京华：小琴，我要去银行开一个账户，这样我存款、取款就方便多了。你知道哪家银行比较好吗？

方小琴：我常常去大华银行存款、取款。那儿的服务不错，利率也比较高，现在储蓄账户的利率是百分之三点二。

关京华：那我就去大华银行吧。

(在银行)

关京华：先生，我想开一个有利息的支票账户。请问，有利息的支票账户利率是多少？

职　员：最近利率都比较低，今天是百分之二点六。

关京华：怎么这么低呀？我听说是百分之三点二呢。

职　员：那是储蓄账户，储蓄账户的利率高一点儿，是百分之三点二。这种账户每个月可以开三张支票。您想开哪一种？

关京华：我想一个月开三张支票差不多够了。我就开一个储蓄账户吧。

职　员：好，请把这张开账户的单子填一下，谢谢。请问您今天想存多少钱？

关京华：我这儿是三千元美金。

职　员：好……一个星期以后，您会收到我们给您寄去的支票簿和取款卡。您可以拿取款卡在自动取款机那儿取现金。

关京华：我可以在你们这儿申请一张信用卡吗？

职　员：当然可以。请把这张申请信用卡的表填一下。

关京华：下个月我要去中国，要换一些人民币。请问美金换人民币的汇率是多少？

职　员：今天的汇率是一比七点九八。

关京华：兑换外币的地方在哪儿？

职　员：就在左边的柜台那儿。

关京华：谢谢。再见。

第七課 我的電話簿找不到了

方小琴：文華，你在找什麼？
金文華：我在找一本電話簿，我的電話簿找不到了。
方小琴：你看看電話旁邊有沒有？
金文華：好像沒有…… 啊，我看到了，在桌子下面。今年寒假我和方明要去中國旅遊，我要找一家旅行社的電話號碼，我想訂去中國的機票。
方小琴：真的嗎？太棒了！我真羡慕你們。你們打算去哪兒玩呢？
金文華：方明在北京有很多親戚，我們原來想先去北京玩幾天，跟他的親戚聚一聚，然後抽空去拜訪他以前的老師，再去別的地方看看，可是我一直買不到去北京的機票。
方小琴：你們上網查了嗎？
金文華：查了，我們查了好幾家航空公司的網站，可是都訂不到機票。有的機票太貴了，我們買不起。我想問問這家旅行社，看看他們那兒訂得到訂不到比較便宜的機票。
方小琴：其實，要是真的買不到去北京的機票，你們可以先去南方的城市，比如上海或者香港，然後去雲南的昆明，再從昆明坐飛機去北京。
金文華：這個主意真不錯。我也聽說昆明是一個四季如春、風景如畫的城市，雲南那兒還有很多少數民族，去那兒看看一定會很有意思。可是我在地圖上怎麼找不到昆明呢？
方小琴：我來幫你看看…… 啊，在這兒。你看，就在中國的西南邊。
金文華：是啊！如果我真的想去，坐飛機到得了到不了昆明？
方小琴：當然到得了！你還可以吃得到少數民族的小吃呢！
金文華：那我一定要去。
方小琴：對了，你們的簽證辦好了嗎？
金文華：方明的簽證已經辦好了。我也已經申請了，可是不知道下個星期拿得到拿不到。不過還有一個多月，大概來得及。

第七课 我的电话簿找不到了

方小琴：文华，你在找什么？
金文华：我在找一本电话簿，我的电话簿找不到了。
方小琴：你看看电话旁边有没有？

金文华：好像没有……啊，我看到了，在桌子下面。今年寒假我和方明要去中国旅游，我要找一家旅行社的电话号码，我想订去中国的机票。
方小琴：真的吗？太棒了！我真羡慕你们。你们打算去哪儿玩呢？
金文华：方明在北京有很多亲戚，我们原来想先去北京玩几天，跟他的亲戚聚一聚，然后抽空去拜访他以前的老师，再去别的地方看看，可是我一直买不到去北京的机票。
方小琴：你们上网查了吗？
金文华：查了，我们查了好几家航空公司的网站，可是都订不到机票。有的机票太贵了，我们买不起。我想问问这家旅行社，看看他们那儿订得到订不到比较便宜的机票。
方小琴：其实，要是真的买不到去北京的机票，你们可以先去南方的城市，比如上海或者香港，然后去云南的昆明，再从昆明坐飞机去北京。
金文华：这个主意真不错。我也听说昆明是一个四季如春、风景如画的城市，云南那儿还有很多少数民族，去那儿看看一定会很有意思。可是我在地图上怎么找不到昆明呢？
方小琴：我来帮你看看……啊，在这儿。你看，就在中国的西南边。
金文华：是啊！如果我真的想去，坐飞机到得了到不了昆明？
方小琴：当然到得了！你还可以吃得到少数民族的小吃呢！
金文华：那我一定要去。
方小琴：对了，你们的签证办好了吗？
金文华：方明的签证已经办好了。我也已经申请了，可是不知道下个星期拿得到拿不到。不过还有一个多月，大概来得及。

第八課　你比以前忙得多

季如春：慕華，你好像最近比以前忙得多，是嗎？
方慕華：沒有啊！你為什麼覺得我比以前忙得多呢？
季如春：最近連你的影子都看不見。昨天晚上我給你打電話也找不到你。
方慕華：昨天上午我把一個大的研究報告交出去了，覺得輕鬆多了，所以我就跟我的表妹去看電影了。
季如春：你比我強多，我的報告還沒有寫完呢！對了，你們看了什麼電影？好看嗎？

方慕華：我們看的是《英雄》。
季如春：是不是張藝謀導演的那部功夫片？
方慕華：是的。主要演員是陳道明、李連杰和張曼玉。其中我特別喜歡李連杰。
季如春：有人說它沒有《臥虎藏龍》好看，你覺得怎麼樣？
方慕華：我覺得這兩部電影差不多。你呢？你看過沒有？
季如春：我看過《臥虎藏龍》，沒有看過《英雄》，可是聽說《英雄》的場面比《臥虎藏龍》大得多。是真的嗎？
方慕華：沒錯。《英雄》的場面比《臥虎藏龍》大一些，可是我覺得它的情節不像《臥虎藏龍》那麼吸引人。
季如春：聽說《英雄》說的是關於中國古代秦始皇的故事，那麼，比較起來電影和小說哪個好？
方慕華：我覺得電影不如小說精彩。
季如春：有人說它對秦始皇的描寫跟歷史上的秦始皇不一樣。
方慕華：我同意，但是我覺得這部電影描寫得比較客觀。
季如春：我一直對歷史故事很感興趣，所以我很想去看一看這部電影。
方慕華：你應該去看看。我覺得《英雄》這部電影對感情方面的描寫比《臥虎藏龍》多一些，而且它的特技效果和顏色都比別的電影好得多。
季如春：你知道在哪兒可以看得到《英雄》嗎？
方慕華：這個週末學校會放這部電影，票價只要一元，比電影院的票要便宜五元。
季如春：好，這個週末我就去看。

第八课　你比以前忙得多

季如春：慕华，你好像最近比以前忙得多，是吗？
方慕华：没有啊！你为什么觉得我比以前忙得多呢？
季如春：最近连你的影子都看不见。昨天晚上我给你打电话也找不到你。
方慕华：昨天上午我把一个大的研究报告交出去了，觉得轻松多了，所以我就跟我的表妹去看电影了。
季如春：你比我强多了，我的报告还没有写完呢！对了，你们看了什么电影？好看吗？
方慕华：我们看的是《英雄》。

季如春：是不是张艺谋导演的那部功夫片？
方慕华：是的。主要演员是陈道明、李连杰和张曼玉。其中我特别喜欢李连杰。
季如春：有人说它没有《卧虎藏龙》好看，你觉得怎么样？
方慕华：我觉得这两部电影差不多。你呢？你看过没有？
季如春：我看过《卧虎藏龙》，没有看过《英雄》，可是听说《英雄》的场面比《卧虎藏龙》大得多。是真的吗？
方慕华：没错。《英雄》的场面比《卧虎藏龙》大一些，可是我觉得它的情节不像《卧虎藏龙》那么吸引人。
季如春：听说《英雄》说的是关于中国古代秦始皇的故事，那么，比较起来电影和小说哪个好？
方慕华：我觉得电影不如小说精彩。
季如春：有人说它对秦始皇的描写跟历史上的秦始皇不一样。
方慕华：我同意，但是我觉得这部电影描写得比较客观。
季如春：我一直对历史故事很感兴趣，所以我很想去看一看这部电影。
方慕华：你应该去看看。我觉得《英雄》这部电影对感情方面的描写比《卧虎藏龙》多一些，而且它的特技效果和颜色都比别的电影好得多。
季如春：你知道在哪儿可以看得到《英雄》吗？
方慕华：这个周末学校会放这部电影，票价只要一元，比电影院的票要便宜五元。
季如春：好，这个周末我就去看。

第九課　你越來越精神了

白思琴：欣明，你最近常去健身房鍛煉嗎？
胡欣明：這兩個星期是我最忙的時候，鍛煉得比以前少得多。以前我差不多天天游泳，最近差不多每星期都要比以前少游兩、三次，這個星期一次也沒去過。
白思琴：那可不好。其實越忙越需要鍛煉。我每天都要去運動一個鐘頭，現在我的精神越來越好了。你看，我比前幾個月還瘦了不少吧！
胡欣明：真的，你看上去比上學期瘦了很多。你最近在減肥嗎？
白思琴：是呀！我已經堅持了三個月了。效果不錯吧！體重比以前輕了十幾磅。

胡欣明：怪不得你越來越苗條了，差不多是我們女孩子中最苗條的了。你是怎麼減肥的？控制飲食嗎？

白思琴：主要是鍛煉，當然在吃的方面我也比較注意。我以前最喜歡吃甜食，可是現在我吃得越來越少了。

胡欣明：你怎麼會想到要減肥呢？

白思琴：我早就想減肥了。我的個子有點兒矮，只有五呎一吋，可是三個月以前我的體重超過了一百三十磅。

胡欣明：那你最重的時候比我還要重呢！

白思琴：是呀！我要是太重了就會覺得不太靈活，也很不舒服。

胡欣明：我真應該向你學習，可是我總是覺得功課太多、太忙，沒有時間鍛煉。現在我每天都比別人還要少睡兩、三個鐘頭呢。

白思琴：其實，最重要的是要多鍛煉、多運動。運動了以後你的身體會比以前更好，你會更有精神，學習的效果可能就會更好了。

第九课　你越来越精神了

白思琴：欣明，你最近常去健身房锻炼吗？

胡欣明：这两个星期是我最忙的时候，锻炼得比以前少得多。以前我差不多天天游泳，最近差不多每星期都要比以前少游两、三次，这个星期一次也没去过。

白思琴：那可不好。其实越忙越需要锻炼。我每天都要去运动一个钟头，现在我的精神越来越好了。你看，我比前几个月还瘦了不少吧！

胡欣明：真的，你看上去比上学期瘦了很多。你最近在减肥吗？

白思琴：是呀！我已经坚持了三个月了。效果不错吧！体重比以前轻了十几磅。

胡欣明：怪不得你越来越苗条了，差不多是我们女孩子中最苗条的了。你是怎么减肥的？控制饮食吗？

白思琴：主要是锻炼，当然在吃的方面我也比较注意。我以前最喜欢吃甜食，可是现在我吃得越来越少了。

胡欣明：你怎么会想到要减肥呢？

白思琴：我早就想减肥了。我的个子有点儿矮，只有五呎一吋，可是三个月以前我的体重超过了一百三十磅。

胡欣明：那你最重的时候比我还要重呢！

白思琴：是呀！我要是太重了就会觉得不太灵活，也很不舒服。

胡欣明：我真应该向你学习，可是我总是觉得功课太多、太忙，没有时间锻炼。现在我每天都比别人还要少睡两、三个钟头呢。

白思琴：其实，最重要的是要多锻炼、多运动。运动了以后你的身体会比以前更好，你就会更有精神，学习的效果可能就会更好了。

第十課 我的寒假計畫 (復習)

同學們好！

今天，我想把我的寒假計畫跟大家報告一下。

今年是我在大學的最後一個寒假。我已經跟我的男朋友說好了，一起去中國旅遊。我們在北京有很多親戚朋友，我希望這次去北京能見得到他們每個人。

這兩年去中國的人比以前多了很多，所以飛機票也比前兩年難買多了。特別是去北京的機票，更難買得到。我們到現在還沒有訂到票呢。我們打算十二月中旬出發，一月上旬回來。現在已經給好幾家旅行社打了電話，還不知道買得到買不到。我們上個星期已經申請了去中國的簽證，不知道這個星期收得到收不到。不過我們還有不少時間，大概來得及。

我還要去銀行取一些現金，買幾張旅行支票。在中國用信用卡付款不像在美國這麼方便。不過，聽說現在接受信用卡的商店越來越多了，而且在中國銀行還可以取美金，也可以根據當天的匯率換成人民幣，這比帶很多現金要安全得多。最近人民幣換美金的匯率差不多是一比七點九七，比上個月低了零點一個百分點。

這次去中國我最想去的地方是長城。聽說爬長城很累，只有百分之五十的人能爬得到長城的頂上。我覺得那是一個很好的鍛煉，還能幫助我減肥呢！而且，中國人不是說"不到長城非好漢"嗎？所以我一定要試一試。我還想去黃山，我的朋友告訴我黃山那兒風景如畫，美極了！

我還想去看看張藝謀導演的功夫片《十面埋伏》。看過這部電影的人都說它的場面比《英雄》的還要壯觀，情節也很曲折。

你們看，我今年寒假要做的事多不多？我希望我從中國回來的時候，能滿載而歸。

這就是我今天的報告。謝謝大家！

第十课 我的寒假计划
(复习)

同学们好!

今天,我想把我的寒假计划跟大家报告一下。

今年是我在大学的最后一个寒假。我已经跟我的男朋友说好了,一起去中国旅游。我们在北京有很多亲戚朋友,我希望这次去北京能见得到他们每个人。

这两年去中国的人比以前多了很多,所以飞机票也比前两年难买多了。特别是去北京的机票,更难买得到。我们到现在还没有订到票呢。我们打算十二月中旬出发,一月上旬回来。现在已经给好几家旅行社打了电话,还不知道买得到买不到。我们上个星期已经申请了去中国的签证,不知道这个星期收得到收不到。不过我们还有不少时间,大概来得及。

我还要去银行取一些现金,买几张旅行支票。在中国用信用卡付款不像在美国这么方便。不过,听说现在接受信用卡的商店越来越多了,而且在中国银行还可以取美金,也可以根据当天的汇率换成人民币,这比带很多现金要安全得多。最近人民币换美金的汇率差不多是一比七点九七,比上个月低了零点一个百分点。

这次去中国我最想去的地方是长城。听说爬长城很累,只有百分之五十的人能爬得到长城的顶上。我觉得那是一个很好的锻炼,还能帮助我减肥呢!而且,中国人不是说"不到长城非好汉"吗?所以我一定要试一试。我还想去黄山,我的朋友告诉我黄山那儿风景如画,美极了!

我还想去看看张艺谋导演的功夫片《十面埋伏》。看过这部电影的人都说它的场面比《英雄》的还要壮观,情节也很曲折。

你们看,我今年寒假要做的事多不多?我希望我从中国回来的时候,能满载而归。

这就是我今天的报告。谢谢大家!

附錄：課文英文翻譯
附录：课文英文翻译
APPENDIX: LANGUAGE IN USE – ENGLISH TRANSLATION

Lesson 1 I Parked the Car on the Side

Xie Jinxue:	Here we are. Let me park my car on the side.
Chang Tian:	Wait a minute. Let me move my car away first, then you drive your car over here.
Xia Zhongming:	When you back up, I will check for you. Don't knock down the landlord's tree.
Chang Tian:	Right! When we moved in last time, we were not careful enough and broke the landlord's mirror. How embarrassing.
Xie Jinxue:	Let's first move the bed and desk upstairs, then we'll divide the tasks. How about that?
Xia Zhongming:	Good idea! I'll be responsible for getting the luggage down and putting it away. I'll also install the computer.
Xie Jinxue:	OK, I'll sweep the floor, tidy the living-room, and then put the books in order.
Chang Tian:	I'll wash the dishes, open the boxes and hang up the clothes.
Xie Jinxue:	Thanks for your help. This move is going to tire you out. What would you like to eat for dinner? My treat!
Chang Tian:	Great! I'm starving.
Xia Zhongming:	There is a pretty good Chinese restaurant nearby, but I've forgotten its address.
Chang Tian:	Don't worry. I've got it. Look, I've found it.
Xie Jinxue:	Great! Let me close the door and windows first.
Xia Zhongming:	Don't forget to put on your jacket. Let's go!

Lesson 2 There Is a Picture Hanging on the Wall

Li Fang:	There's a picture hanging on the wall over there. Who's that? I don't think I've seen her before.
Guan Mingyuan:	That's a picture taken by my older sister.
Li Fang:	Where is she now?
Guan Mingyuan:	Right now she is studying abroad in Beijing. She is there learning Chinese, and has been living there for over a year.
Li Fang:	How long has she been studying Chinese?
Guan Mingyuan:	She has been studying Chinese for three years.
Li Fang:	That's a Peking Opera costume, right?
Guan Mingyuan:	Yes. This is a picture she took when she went to see a Peking Opera last month. She'd never watched Peking Opera before and now she's seen it. She is very happy.

Li Fang:	What are those laid out on the stage? It seems to be various kinds of Chinese musical instruments.
Guan Mingyuan:	You're right. Look, the opera singers are busy performing. And there are some musicians sitting at the side. Some are beating drums, some playing (*Erhu*) two-stringed bowed instruments. They are all busy playing their own musical instruments.
Li Fang:	What's this play about? It seems to be pretty interesting.
Guan Mingyuan:	It's about Guan Gong. Look, Guan Gong is wearing a red face and holding a big knife in his hand. Really dignified!
Li Fang:	What a crowd! You see, all the seats are occupied. Some people even had to stand. Oh! By the way, have you ever seen Peking Opera?
Guan Mingyuan:	I've seen it twice, both times in Shanghai.
Li Fang:	You went to Shanghai when you were in China. Where else did you go in China?
Guan Mingyuan:	I only went to Shanghai. At that time, I was busy with my classes every day. So I didn't have a chance to Beijing and the Great Wall.
Li Fang:	I heard that the mini steamed dumplings in Shanghai are very good. Have you had them?
Guan Mingyuan:	I have. I've even learned how to make them!
Li Fang:	That's really interesting! I also want to go and see China.
Guan Mingyuan:	I'm going to China next month. Why don't you come with me? We can go see Peking Opera together. How does that sound?
Li Fang:	Good. It's a deal!

Lesson 3 Go Straight from Here

(Scene 1: On the airplane)
Hello, passengers. The plane will land in 20 minutes. We will soon arrive at *Pudong* Airport in Shanghai. Please go back to your seats and fasten your seat belts. Please also turn off your computers and other electronic appliances. Thank you for your cooperation. And thank you again for flying with China Airlines.

(Scene 2: At the airport)

Guan Mingyuan:	We're here. Let's take a cab to the hotel. It will be faster by cab.
Li Fang:	How fast is it by cab?
Guan Mingyuan:	I think we'll be able to get there in less than 10 minutes.
Li Fang:	Good. Let's ask for directions.
Guan Mingyuan:	Excuse me, Sir, but could you tell me where the taxi station is?
Pedestrian:	The taxi station is behind that building. Go straight from here, make a left at the crossroad up there, and then walk straight ahead. After you pass two intersections, you will see the taxi station.
Li Fang:	Thank you.
Pedestrian:	You're welcome.

(Scene 3: At the taxi station)

Driver: Excuse me, you two gentlemen are looking for a cab? Right?

Guan Mingyuan: Yes. We're going to the Holiday Hotel. How far is it from here?

Driver: It's three kilometers. Not very far. Please get in. Here, I'll put the luggage in the trunk first.

. . . . . .

Li Fang: China seems to develop pretty fast.

Guan Mingyuan: Yes! But things have changed too fast here!

Driver: It sounds like you've been to Shanghai before.

Guan Mingyuan: Yes, I came here two years ago, but there are quite a few roads that I can't remember.

Driver: You're right. Shanghai has changed very fast. Look, it was originally all farmland here, but now everything has changed into big buildings and major streets.

Li Fang: Look! That building is really tall. Don't know how tall it is?

Driver: Oh! That building is new. I heard that it's ninety meters tall.

Guan Mingyuan: Yes, now I remember. That's *Zhongshan* Road. I used to wait at that traffic light to cross the road. After crossing the road, I turned right, walked for another two or three minutes and there was the Shanghai Snackbar. The food there is really delicious!

Driver: The Holiday Hotel is right ahead. But I can't turn left here. I have to make a few more turns.

Li Fang: OK, no problem.

. . . . . .

Driver: Here we are.

Li Fang: How much is the cab fare?

Driver: Altogether twenty eight *kuai* RMB.

Guan Mingyuan: Here's thirty *kuai*.

Driver: Here's two *kuai* change. Thank you.

Lesson 4 You Are the Same As Before

Professor: Welcome, welcome. Come in, please.

Guan Mingyuan: Come, Li Fang. Let me introduce you. This is Professor Wang, and this is Mrs. Wang.

Li Fang: Hello.

Guan Mingyuan: Professor, here are some books on American literature that you like. Mrs. Wang, these vitamins are for you and Professor. Wishing you everlasting health and youth.

Mrs. Wang: It's good enough that you could come. You didn't have to bring so many things. You'll spend all your money!

Guan Mingyuan: It's nothing. Just a small token.

Professor: You don't come to Shanghai very often. My wife has specially cooked some of her favorite dishes for you. Come, come, be seated. The dishes are getting cold.

Guan Mingyuan:	Professor, Mrs. Wang, you two are still the same as before. You look really energetic!
Mrs. Wang:	Not any more! We're getting older day by day. Got more grey hair than before, the eyes are getting blurry, and we can't do things as quickly anymore.
Professor:	Li Fang, This is your first visit to China. Are you adjusting OK?
Li Fang:	Not too bad. I still have some jetlag. I feel sleepy during the day, but can't get to sleep at night. But I'm much better today than yesterday.
Guan Mingyuan:	Li Fang says that the weather here is warmer than in Pittsburgh, and also, there are more people here. The streets are full of people and he's not quite used to it yet.
Li Fang:	This the first time in my life I've ever seen so many people!
Mrs. Wang:	Who is older between you two?
Guan Mingyuan:	I'm the same age as Li Fang. We're both 24.
Mrs. Wang:	Come, don't just talk and forget to eat. Come on, have some more.
Professor:	This is the rice cake my wife made. It's very authentic. Have a taste.
Guan Mingyuan:	Mrs. Wang, your food is really delicious!
Li Fang:	Absolutely! The color, the flavor and the taste are all perfect. I've had so much and am very full now.
Mrs. Wang:	Not really, not really. Just some simple home-made dishes.
Professor:	It's such a rare chance that we could get together. Come, let's have a toast. I am so happy today. "Friends come from afar, isn't is a happy thing?"

Professor, Mrs. Wang, Guan and Li: Cheers!

Lesson 5 My Trip to China (Review)

Wednesday, Oct. 20 Weather: overcast

After being on the plane for more than 30 hours we're finally back in the US. It should have taken over 10 hours from China to the USA, but when we switched flights in Japan our plane was delayed so we missed our flight. We waited at the airport for five hours before we finally got a flight. This flight delay made Li Fang and me so exhausted that as soon as we put our luggage away on the plane we just kept sleeping until the plane landed.

Nevertheless I was very happy that I could go to visit my professor in Shanghai. Professor and his wife both look very healthy. They were still as warm-hearted and hospitable as before. Mrs. Wang also specially made some very authentic (Chinese) dishes for us to have a taste. Among them I like the Shanghai rice cake the best. Really delicious!

I also took Li Fang to go and watch a Peking Opera. We were fascinated. It really opened our eyes. But I hear there are not as many Peking Opera troupes as before so the tickets are more expensive now.

Shanghai has really changed very fast. Some roads are very hard to find now. We were holding a map in our hand and busy asking directions. Often when we should have made a left turn, we got it wrong and turned right. We made quite a few stupid mistakes.

China is really becoming more prosperous and developed day by day. In large cities, the skyscrapers are as high as those in the US and foreigners can be seen everywhere.

Although our stay in China this time was short, we had a great time. Li Fang says that he can now tell others that he has been to China and watched Peking Opera, and also he tasted many kinds of Chinese snacks!

We both feel that it was really worthwhile for us to make this trip to China. We will go again when we get a chance next time.

Lesson 6 I'm Going to the Bank to Open an Account

(On the road)

Guan Jinghua: Xiaoqin, I'm going to the bank to open an account. Then it will be much more convenient to deposit or withdraw money. Do you know which bank is better?

Fang Xiaoqin: I often go to the Great China Bank to deposit or withdraw money. Their service is good and their interest rate is also relatively high. For a savings account, the current rate is 3.2%.

Guan Jinghua: Then I'll go to the Great China Bank.

(At the bank)

Guan Jinghua: Sir, I'd like to open a checking account with interest. May I ask what the interest rate is for a checking account with interest?

Clerk: The rate has been pretty low recently. It is 2.6% today.

Guan Jinhua: How come it is so low? I heard it was 3.2%.

Clerk: That's for the savings account. The rate for the savings account is a little higher, 3.2%. That kind of account allows you to write three checks a month. Which account would you prefer?

Guan Jinhua: Three checks a month is about enough. I'll just open a savings account then.

Clerk: Good. Please fill in this account opening form. Thank you. How much would you like to deposit into the account today?

Guan Jinghua: I have $3,000 here.

Clerk: OK . . .
In a week you will receive the check book and the ATM card. You may use your ATM card to withdraw cash at the ATM.

Guan Jinghua: May I apply for a credit card here?

Clerk: Of course you may. Please fill in this credit card application form.

Guan Jinhua: I'm going to China next month. I need to exchange for some Renminbi. May I ask what the exchange rate is from US dollars to Renminbi?

Clerk: Today's exchange rate is 1 : 7.98.

Guan Jinghua: Where can I exchange foreign currency?

Clerk: Just at the counter to the left.

Guan Jinghua: Thanks. Bye.

Lesson 7 I Can't Find My Phone Book

Fang Xiaoqin:	Wenhua, what are you looking for?
Jin Wenhua:	I am looking for a phone book. I can't find my phone book.
Fang Xiaoqin:	See if it's by the phone.
Jin Wenhua:	I see nothing . . . Oh, I see it. It's under the table. I'm going on a trip to China with Fang Ming this winter break. I need to look for a travel agency's phone number. I want to book some plane tickets.
Fang Xiaoqin:	Really? That's wonderful! I really envy you. Where exactly are you going then?
Jin Wenhua:	Fang Ming has many relatives in Beijing. Originally we planned to stay in Beijing for a few days, have a get-together with his relatives, take some time to visit his former teachers, and then go to other places to have a look. But I haven't been successful in booking the tickets to Beijing.
Fang Xiaoqin:	Have you checked on the web yet?
Jin Wenhua:	We've checked several airlines' websites, but still haven't been able to book the tickets. Some tickets are too expensive and we cannot afford them. I want to check with this travel agency to see whether I can book some relatively cheaper tickets or not.
Fang Xiaoqin:	Actually, if you really can't get plane tickets to Beijing, you could first go to a city in the south, such as Shanghai or Hong Kong, then go to Kunming in Yunnan. After that you can fly to Beijing from Kunming.
Jin Wenhua:	That's a good idea. I hear Kunming is a city where it's like spring all year round and the scenery is picturesque. There are also many minority nationalities there in Yunnan. It would certainly be very interesting to have a look there. But how come I can't find Kunming on the map?
Fang Xiaoqin:	Let me help you . . . Look, right here, in the southwest of China.
Jin Wenhua:	Oh, yes! If I really want to go, is it accessible by plane to Kunming?
Fang Xiaoqin:	Of course it is! You will also be able to taste snacks made by the minority people.
Jin Wenhua:	Then I'll definitely go.
Fang Xiaoqin:	Oh yeah, have you got your visas yet?
Jin Wenhua:	Ming's visa is done already. I have also applied. I don't know whether I'll receive it next week or not, but there is still a month to go. It should be in time.

Lesson 8 You Are Much Busier than Before

Ji Ruchun:	Muhua, you seem to be much busier than before recently, right?
Fang Muhua:	Not really! Why do you think I'm much busier than before?
Ji Ruchun:	Recently I don't even get to see your shadow. When I called you last night, you were not available, either.
Fang Muhua:	I submitted a major project report yesterday morning and felt much more relaxed, so I went to see a movie with my cousin.

Ji Ruchun: You are much better than I am. I haven't finished my report yet. By the way, what movie did you watch? Was it good?

Fang Muhua: We watched "Hero".

Ji Ruchun: Is it the one directed by Yimou Zhang?

Fang Muhua: Yes. The main actors are Daoming Chen, Jet Li and Maggie Cheung. Among them I especially like Jet Li.

Ji Ruchun: Some people say it is not as good as "Crouching Tiger and Hidden Dragon". What do you think?

Fang Muhua: I think both movies are about the same. Have you seen them?

Ji Ruchun: I've seen "Crouching Tiger and Hidden Dragon", not "Hero", but I hear that "Hero" has a much grander cinematography than "Crouching Tiger and Hidden Dragon". Is that true?

Fang Muhua: Exactly. Its cinematography is grander, but I don't think its plot is as fascinating as "Crouching Tiger and Hidden Dragon".

Ji Ruchun: It's said that "Hero" is about the First Emperor of the *Qin* Dynasty in ancient China. Then, comparatively speaking, which one is better, the movie or the novel?

Fang Muhua: My feeling is that the movie is not as good as the novel.

Ji Ruchen: Some say that its description of the First Emperor of the *Qin* Dynasty is not the same as the one in history.

Fang Muhua: I agree, but I think the description in the movie is more objective.

Ji Ruchun: I have always been very interested in historical stories, so I'd very much like to watch this movie.

Fang Muhua: You should go and watch it. "Hero" has some more scenes about love than "Crouching Tiger and Hidden Dragon", and its special effects and colors are much better than other movies.

Ji Ruchun: Do you know where I can see it?

Fang Muhua: It will be shown on campus this weekend, and the tickets only cost $1 each. That's 5 dollars cheaper than tickets at the cinema.

Ji Ruchun: Good. I'll go and watch it this weekend then.

Lesson 9 You Are Getting More and More Energetic

Bai Siqin: Xinming, have you been regularly going to the gym to exercise recently?

Hu Xinming: These two weeks have been my busiest time, and I have exercised much less than before. I used to go swimming almost every day, but now it's two or three times less than before. And I haven't gone swimming even once this week.

Bai Siqin: That is not very good. Actually, the busier you are, the more you need to exercise. I exercise for an hour every day. Now I feel more and more energetic. You see, I am much thinner than several months ago!

Hu Xinming: That's true. You look much slimmer than last semester. Have you been on a diet recently?

Bai Siqin: Yes. I have kept with it for three months. The result is not bad, huh? I've lost over ten pounds.

Hu Xinming: No wonder you are getting slimmer and slimmer, almost the slimmest girl among us. How have you managed to lose weight? By controlling your diet?

Bai Siqin: Mainly by exercising. And of course I do watch my diet as well. I used to love sweet things, but now I eat less and less sweet food.

Hu Xinming: How did you come to think of losing weight?

Bai Siqin: I wanted to do it a long time ago. I am a bit short, only 5′1″, but my weight was over 130 pounds three months ago.

Hu Xinming: Then you were even heavier than me when you were the heaviest.

Bai Siqin: That's right. If I am too heavy, I am not so agile and I don't feel comfortable.

Hu Xinming: I really should learn from you. But I always feel that I have too much homework, I am too busy, and I don't have time to exercise. Every day I even sleep two or three hours less than everyone else.

Bai Siqin: Actually, the most important thing is to exercise, and do more sports. After you exercise, your health will be better than before, you will feel more spirited, and you will be able to concentrate more, and so you may achieve better result in your studies.

Lesson 10 My Plans For the Winter Vacation (Review)

Hello, everyone!

Today, I would like to report to you my plans for the winter vacation.

This is my last winter vacation at the university. I have talked to my boyfriend and we've decided to go for a trip to China. We have many relatives and friends in Beijing. I hope we will be able to meet every one of them this time.

In the past two years, many more people are going to China. As a result, it is getting much harder to buy plane tickets, especially those to Beijing, which are more difficult to be obtained. We have not been successful in booking our tickets yet. We plan to leave in the middle of December and return in early January. We have called quite a few travel agencies and still don't know whether we will be able to book the tickets. We sent in our visa applications last week and don't know whether we will be able to receive them this week. But we still have plenty of time and we will get them in time.

I also need to withdraw some cash and buy some traveler's checks from the bank. In China, it is not as convenient as in the US to pay with a credit card there. But it is said that credit cards are being accepted at more and more stores. And you may withdraw US dollars at the Bank of China, or exchange for Renminbi according to the exchange rate of that day. This is much safer than carrying a lot of cash. Recently the exchange rate between American dollars and Renminbi is approximately 1:7.97, 0.1% lower than last month.

What I want to go most this time when I am in China is the Great Wall. I hear it is very tiresome to climb the Great Wall, and only 50% of those who tried have succeeded in getting to the top. I think it is a good exercise and will help me lose weight as well. And as the Chinese say: "You will not be a hero unless you have climbed the Great Wall." So, I must give it a try. I also want to go to Mount Huang. My friends told me that the scenery there is picturesque. Very beautiful!

I also want to go and watch the martial arts film "House of the Flying Daggers" directed by Zhang Yimou. Those who have seen it all say that it has even grander cinematography than "Hero", and its plot is also very complicated.

You see, there are many things that I want to do this winter vacation, aren't there? I hope it will be a very rewarding journey.

That is my report today. Thank you all.

附錄：課文拼音
附录：课文拼音
APPENDIX: LANGUAGE IN USE WITH PINYIN

第一課　我把車停在旁邊
第一课　我把车停在旁边
Dì yī kè　Wǒ bǎ chē tíng zài pángbiān

謝進學：我們到了，讓我把車停在旁邊。
谢进学：我们到了，让我把车停在旁边。
Xiè Jìnxué: Wǒmen dào le, ràng wǒ bǎ chē tíng zài pángbiān.

常天：等一會兒，我先把我的車開走，你再把車開過來。
常天：等一会儿，我先把我的车开走，你再把车开过来。
Cháng Tiān: Děng yíhuèr, wǒ xiān bǎ wǒde chē kāi zǒu, nǐ zài bǎ chē kāi guòlái.

夏中明：你在倒車的時候，我幫你看看，別把房東的樹撞壞了。
夏中明：你在倒车的时候，我帮你看看，别把房东的树撞坏了。
Xià Zhōngmíng: Nǐ zài dàochē de shíhou, wǒ bāng nǐ kànkan, bié bǎ fángdōng de shù zhuàng huài le.

常天：對呀！上次我們搬進來的時候，不小心把房東的鏡子打破了，真不好意思。
常天：对呀！上次我们搬进来的时候，不小心把房东的镜子打破了，真不好意思。
Cháng Tiān: Duìya! Shàngcì wǒmen bān jìnlái de shíhou, bù xiǎoxīn bǎ fángdōng de jìngzi dǎpò le, zhēn bùhǎoyìsi.

謝進學：我們先把床和書桌搬到樓上去，然後再分工合作，怎麼樣？
谢进学：我们先把床和书桌搬到楼上去，然后再分工合作，怎么样？
Xiè Jìnxué: Wǒmen xiān bǎ chuáng hé shūzhuō bān dào lóushàng qù, ránhòu zài fēngōnghézuò, zěnmeyàng?

夏中明:	好主意，我負責把行李搬下來、放好，我也會把電腦裝好。	
夏中明:	好主意，我负责把行李搬下来、放好，我也会把电脑装好。	
Xià Zhōngmíng:	Hǎo zhǔyi, wǒ fùzé bǎ xíngli bān xiàlái, fàng hǎo, wǒ yě huì bǎ diànnǎo zhuāng hǎo.	

夏中明: 好主意，我負責把行李搬下來、放好，我也會把電腦裝好。
夏中明: 好主意，我负责把行李搬下来、放好，我也会把电脑装好。
Xià Zhōngmíng: Hǎo zhǔyi, wǒ fùzé bǎ xíngli bān xiàlái, fàng hǎo, wǒ yě huì bǎ diànnǎo zhuāng hǎo.

謝進學: 好，我來掃地、整理客廳，再把書放好。
谢进学: 好，我来扫地、整理客厅，再把书放好。
Xiè Jìnxué: Hǎo, wǒ lái sǎodì, zhěnglǐ kètīng, zài bǎ shū fàng hǎo.

常天: 我來洗碗，把箱子打開，再把衣服掛好。
常天: 我来洗碗，把箱子打开，再把衣服挂好。
Cháng Tiān: Wǒ lái xǐwǎn, bǎ xiāngzi dǎkāi, zài bǎ yīfu guàhǎo.

謝進學: 謝謝你們幫我的忙，這次搬家把你們累壞了。今天晚上想吃什麼？我請客！
谢进学: 谢谢你们帮我的忙，这次搬家把你们累坏了。今天晚上想吃什么？我请客！
Xiè Jìnxué: Xièxie nǐmen bāng wǒde máng, zhècì bānjiā bǎ nǐmen lèihuài le. Jīntiān wǎnshàng xiǎng chī shénme? Wǒ qǐngkè!

常天: 好極了！我快餓死了。
常天: 好极了！我快饿死了。
Cháng Tiān: Hǎo jí le! Wǒ kuài è sǐ le.

夏中明: 這附近有一家很不錯的中國飯館，可是我把地址忘了。
夏中明: 这附近有一家很不错的中国饭馆，可是我把地址忘了。
Xià Zhōngmíng: Zhè fùjìn yǒu yìjiā hěn búcuò de Zhōngguó fànguǎn, kěshì wǒ bǎ dìzhǐ wàng le.

常天: 沒關係，我有。你們看，我找到了。
常天: 没关系，我有。你们看，我找到了。
Cháng Tiān: Méi guānxi, wǒ yǒu. Nǐmen kàn, wǒ zhǎodào le.

謝進學: 太好了，讓我把門窗關上。
谢进学: 太好了，让我把门窗关上。
Xiè Jìnxué: Tài hǎole, ràng wǒ bǎ ménchuāng guānshàng.

夏中明：	别忘了把外套穿上，咱們走吧！
夏中明：	别忘了把外套穿上，咱们走吧！
Xià Zhōngmíng:	Bié wàngle bǎ wàitào chuānshàng, zánmen zǒu ba!

第二課 牆上掛著一張照片
第二课 墙上挂着一张照片
Dì èr kè Qiángshàng guàzhe yìzhāng zhàopiàn

李訪：	那邊牆上掛著一張照片。那是誰？
李访：	那边墙上挂着一张照片。那是谁？
Lǐ Fǎng:	Nàbiān qiángshàng guàzhe yìzhāng zhàopiàn. Nà shì shéi?
	我好像沒見過。
	我好像没见过。
	Wǒ hǎoxiàng méi jiàn guo.
關明遠：	那是我姐姐照的照片。
关明远：	那是我姐姐照的照片。
Guān Míngyuǎn:	Nà shì wǒ jiějie zhàode zhàopiàn.
李訪：	她現在在哪兒？
李访：	她现在在哪儿？
Lǐ Fǎng:	Tā xiànzài zài nǎr?
關明遠：	她現在正在北京留學，她在那兒學中文，
关明远：	她现在正在北京留学，她在那儿学中文，
Guān Míngyuǎn:	Tā xiànzài zhèngzài Běijīng liúxué, tā zài nàr xué Zhōngwén,
	已經在那兒住了一年多了。
	已经在那儿住了一年多了。
	yǐjīng zài nàr zhùle yìnián duō le.
李訪：	她學中文學了多久了？
李访：	她学中文学了多久了？
Lǐ Fǎng:	Tā xué Zhōngwén xué le duō jiǔ le?
關明遠：	她學了三年了。
关明远：	她学了三年了。
Guān Míngyuǎn:	Tā xué le sānnián le.

李訪:	那是京劇的服裝吧!
李访:	那是京剧的服装吧!
Lǐ Fǎng:	Nà shì jīngjù de fúzhuāng ba!
關明遠:	是的。這是她上個月去看京劇的時候照的照片。
关明远:	是的。这是她上个月去看京剧的时候照的照片。
Guān Míngyuǎn:	Shìde. Zhè shì tā shàngge yuè qù kàn jīngjù de shíhou zhào de zhàopiàn.
	以前她沒看過京劇, 現在看到了, 她很高興。
	以前她没看过京剧, 现在看到了, 她很高兴。
	Yǐqián tā méi kàn guo jīngjù, xiànzài kàndào le, tā hěn gāoxìng.
李訪:	舞台上面擺著什麼? 好像是中國的各種樂器。
李访:	舞台上面摆着什么? 好像是中国的各种乐器。
Lǐ Fǎng:	Wǔtái shàngmiàn bǎizhe shénme? Hǎoxiàng shì Zhōngguó de gèzhǒng yuèqì.
關明遠:	沒錯! 你看台上京劇演員, 正忙著表演呢。
关明远:	没错! 你看台上京剧演员, 正忙着表演呢。
Guān Míngyuǎn:	Méicuò! Nǐ kàn táishàng jīngjù yǎnyuán, zhèng máng zhe biǎoyǎn ne.
	旁邊還坐著幾個樂師, 有的在打鼓, 有的在拉胡琴,
	旁边还坐着几个乐师, 有的在打鼓, 有的在拉胡琴,
	Pángbiān hái zuò zhe jǐge yuèshī, yǒude zài dǎgǔ, yǒude zài lā húqín,
	他們都忙著彈奏自己的樂器。
	他们都忙着弹奏自己的乐器。
	tāmen dōu máng zhe tánzòu zìjǐ de yuèqì.
李訪:	這齣戲說的是什麼? 好像很不錯。
李访:	这出戏说的是什么? 好像很不错。
Lǐ Fǎng:	Zhèchū xì shuōde shì shénme? Hǎoxiàng hěn búcuò.
關明遠:	這齣戲說的是關公。你看關公他畫著紅臉,
关明远:	这出戏说的是关公。你看关公他画着红脸,
Guān Míngyuǎn:	Zhèchū xì shuōde shì Guāngōng. Nǐ kàn Guāngōng tā huà zhe hóngliǎn,
	手上拿著一把大刀, 真神氣!
	手上拿着一把大刀, 真神气!
	shǒushàng ná zhe yìbǎ dàdāo, zhēn shénqì!

李訪： 人真不少啊！你看，座位都坐滿了，有的觀眾
李访： 人真不少啊！你看，座位都坐满了，有的观众
Lǐ Fǎng: Rén zhēn bùshǎo a! Nǐ kàn, zuòwèi dōu zuòmǎn le, yǒude guānzhòng

還得站著。對了，你看過京劇嗎？
还得站着。对了，你看过京剧吗？
hái děi zhàn zhe. Duìle, nǐ kàn guo jīngjù ma?

關明遠： 我看過兩次，都是在上海看的。
关明远： 我看过两次，都是在上海看的。
Guān Míngyuǎn: Wǒ kàn guo liǎngcì, dōushì zài Zhànghǎi kàn de.

李訪： 你在中國的時候去過上海，還去過哪兒？
李访： 你在中国的时候去过上海，还去过哪儿？
Lǐ Fǎng: Nǐ zài Zhōngguó de shíhou qù guo Shànghǎi, hái qù guo nǎr?

關明遠： 我只去過上海。那時候，我每天都忙著上課，
关明远： 我只去过上海。那时候，我每天都忙着上课，
Guān Míngyuǎn: Wǒ zhǐ qù guo Shànghǎi. Nà shíhou, wǒ měitiān dōu máng zhe shàngkè,

所以沒有機會去北京和長城。
所以没有机会去北京和长城。
suǒyi méiyou jīhuì qù Běijīng hé Chángchéng.

李訪： 我聽說上海的小籠包很好吃，你吃過嗎？
李访： 我听说上海的小笼包很好吃，你吃过吗？
Lǐ Fǎng: Wǒ tīngshuō Shànghǎi de xiǎolóngbāo hěn hǎochī, nǐ chī guo ma?

關明遠： 吃過，我還學過做小籠包呢！
关明远： 吃过，我还学过做小笼包呢！
Guān Míngyuǎn: Chī guo, wǒ hái xué guo zuò xiǎolóngbāo ne!

李訪： 真有意思！我也想去中國看看。
李访： 真有意思！我也想去中国看看。
Lǐ Fǎng: Zhēn yǒu yìsi! Wǒ yě xiǎng qù Zhōngguó kànkan.

關明遠： 我下個月要去中國，你跟我去吧！我們可以一起去
关明远： 我下个月要去中国，你跟我去吧！我们可以一起去
Guān Míngyuǎn: Wǒ xiàge yuè yào qù Zhōngguó, nǐ gēn wǒ qù ba! Wǒmen kěyi yìqǐ qù

看京劇，怎麼樣？
看京剧，怎么样？
kàn jīngjù, zěnmeyàng?

李訪： 好，一言為定！
李访： 好，一言为定！
Lǐ Fǎng: Hǎo, yì yán wéi dìng!

第三課 從這兒往前走
第三课 从这儿往前走
Dì sān kè Cóng zhèr wǎng qián zǒu

Scene 1: (在飛機上)
(在飞机上)
(Zài fēijī shàng)

各位旅客，飛機再過二十分鐘就要降落了，
各位旅客，飞机再过二十分钟就要降落了，
Gèwèi lǚkè, fēijī zài guò èrshí fēnzhōng jiùyào jiàngluò le,

我們就要到上海的浦東機場了。請您回到您的座位坐好，
我们就要到上海的浦东机场了。请您回到您的座位坐好，
wǒmen jiùyào dào Shànghǎi de Pǔdōng Jīchǎng le. Qǐng nín huídào nín de zuòwèi zuòhǎo,

把安全帶繫上。請您也把計算機等電子用品關上。
把安全带系上。请您也把计算机等电子用品关上。
bǎ ānquándài jìshàng. Qǐng nín yě bǎ jìsuànjī děng diànzǐ yòngpǐn guānshàng.

謝謝您的合作。再次感謝您搭乘中國航空。
谢谢您的合作。再次感谢您搭乘中国航空。
Xièxie nín de hézuò. Zài cì gǎnxiè nín dāchéng Zhōngguó Hángkōng.

Scene 2: (在機場)
(在机场)
(Zài jīchǎng)

關明遠： 我們到了，我們搭出租汽車去旅館吧！搭出租汽車
关明远： 我们到了，我们搭出租汽车去旅馆吧！搭出租汽车
Guān Míngyuǎn: Wǒmen dàole, wǒmen dā chūzū qìchē qù lǚguǎn ba! Dā chūzū qìchē

去快多了。
去快多了。
qù kuàiduō le.

李訪： 搭出租汽車去有多快？
李访： 搭出租汽车去有多快？
Lǐ Fǎng: Dā chūzū qìchē qù yǒu duōkuài?

關明遠:	我想，不到十分鐘就可以到了。
关明远:	我想，不到十分钟就可以到了。
Guān Míngyuǎn:	Wǒ xiǎng, búdào shí fēngzhōng jiù kěyǐ dào le.
李訪:	好的。我們來問路吧!
李访:	好的。我们来问路吧!
Lǐ Fǎng:	Hǎode. Wǒmen lái wènlù ba!
關明遠:	先生，對不起，請問，出租汽車站在哪兒?
关明远:	先生，对不起，请问，出租汽车站在哪儿?
Guān Míngyuǎn:	Xiānsheng, duìbuqǐ, qǐngwèn, chūzūqìchē zhàn zài nǎr?
路人:	出租汽車站在那棟樓的後邊。你從這兒往前走，走到前面的交叉口，往左拐。從那兒再往前一直走，過兩個路口，你就能看到出租汽車站了。
路人:	出租汽车站在那栋楼的后边。你从这儿往前走，走到前面的交叉口，往左拐。从那儿再往前一直走，过两个路口，你就能看到出租汽车站了。
Lùrén:	Chūzūqìchē zhàn zài nà dòng lóu de hòubiān. Nǐ cóng zhèr wǎng qián zǒu, zǒudào qiánmiàn de jiāochākǒu, wǎng zuǒ guǎi. Cóng nàr zài wǎng qián yìzhí zǒu, guò liǎngge lùkǒu, nǐ jiù néng kàndào chūzū qìchē zhàn le.
李訪:	謝謝。
李访:	谢谢。
Lǐ Fǎng:	Xièxie.
路人:	不客氣。
路人:	不客气。
Lùrén:	Búkèqi.

Scene 3: (在出租汽車站)
(在出租汽车站)
(Zài chūzū qìchē zhàn)

司機:	請問，兩位先生要搭車，是嗎?
司机:	请问，两位先生要搭车，是吗?
Sījī:	Qǐngwèn, liǎngwèi xiānsheng yào dāchē, shìma?
關明遠:	是的，我們要去假日旅館，離這兒有多遠?
关明远:	是的，我们要去假日旅馆，离这儿有多远?
Guān Míngyuǎn:	Shìde, wǒmen yào qù jiàrì lǚguǎn, lí zhèr yǒu duō yuǎn?

司機： 司机： Sījī:	有三公里，不太遠，請上車。來，我先把行李 有三公里，不太远，请上车。来，我先把行李 Yǒu sān gōnglǐ, bú tài yuǎn, qǐng shàngchē. Lái, wǒ xiān bǎ xíngli
	放到後車箱去。 放到后车箱去。 fàngdào hòu chēxiāng qù.

……

李訪： 李访： Lǐ Fǎng:	中國看起來發展得很快。 中国看起来发展得很快。 Zhōngguó kàn qǐlái fāzhǎn de hěnkuài.
關明遠： 关明远： Guān Míngyuǎn:	是呀！可是這兒變得太快了！ 是呀！可是这儿变得太快了！ Shì ya! Kěshì zhèr biàn de tài kuài le!
司機： 司机： Sījī:	聽起來你好像來過上海。 听起来你好像来过上海。 Tīng qǐlái nǐ hǎoxiàng lái guo Shànghǎi.
關明遠： 关明远： Guān Míngyuǎn:	是的。我兩年前來過，可是現在有很多路 是的。我两年前来过，可是现在有很多路 Shì de. Wǒ liǎng nián qián lái guo, kěshì xiànzài yǒu hěnduō lù
	我都想不起來了。 我都想不起来了。 wǒ dōu xiǎng bù qǐlái le.
司機： 司机： Sījī:	沒錯！上海變化得非常快，你看，本來這兒 没错！上海变化得非常快，你看，本来这儿 Méicuò! Shànghǎi biànhuà de fēicháng kuài, nǐ kàn, běnlái zhèr
	還都是農田，現在都變成大樓和大馬路了。 还都是农田，现在都变成大楼和大马路了。 hái dōu shì nóngtián, xiànzài dōu biànchéng dàlóu hé dà mǎlù le.
李訪： 李访： Lǐ Fǎng:	你看，那棟樓真高，不知道有多高？ 你看，那栋楼真高，不知道有多高？ Nǐ kàn, nà dòng lóu zhēngāo, bùzhīdào yǒu duō gāo?

司機： 喔！那棟樓是新的，聽說有九十公尺高。
司机： 喔！那栋楼是新的，听说有九十公尺高。
Sījī: Ō! Nàdòng lóu shì xīnde, tīngshuō yǒu jiǔ shí gōngchǐ gāo.

關明遠： 對了，我想起來了，那條是中山路。以前我常
关明远： 对了，我想起来了，那条是中山路。以前我常
Guān Míngyuǎn: Duì le, wǒ xiǎng qǐlái le, nà tiáo shì Zhōngshān lù. Yǐqián wǒ cháng

在那個紅綠燈等著過馬路，過了馬路以後我就向
在那个红绿灯等着过马路，过了马路以后我就向
zài nàge hónglǜdēng děng zhe guò mǎlù, guò le mǎlù yǐhòu wǒ jiù xiàng

右轉，再走兩三分鐘，就到了上海小吃店。
右转，再走两三分钟，就到了上海小吃店。
yòu zhuǎn, zài zǒu liǎng sān fēnzhōng, jiù dào le Shànghǎi xiǎochīdiàn.

那兒的東西好吃極了！
那儿的东西好吃极了！
Nàr de dōngxi hǎochī jí le!

司機： 假日旅館就在前面，可是我不能在這兒往左轉，
司机： 假日旅馆就在前面，可是我不能在这儿往左转，
Sījī: Jiàrì lǚguǎn jiùzài qiánmiàn, kěshì wǒ bùnéng zài zhèr wǎng zuǒzhuǎn,

我得多拐幾個彎兒。
我得多拐几个弯儿。
wǒ děi duō guǎi jǐge wār.

李訪： 行，沒問題。
李访： 行，没问题。
Lǐ Fǎng: Xíng, méiwèntí.

……

司機： 好，我們到了。
司机： 好，我们到了。
Sījī: Hǎo, wǒmen dào le.

李訪： 車費多少錢?
李访： 车费多少钱?
Lǐ Fǎng: Chēfèi duōshǎo qián?

司機：	一共是二十八塊人民幣。
司机：	一共是二十八块人民币。
Sījī:	Yígòng shì èr shí bā kuài Rénmínbì.
關明遠：	給你三十塊。
关明远：	给你三十块。
Guān Míngyuǎn:	Gěi nǐ sān shí kuài.
司機：	找你兩塊，謝謝！
司机：	找你两块，谢谢！
Sījī:	Zhǎo nǐ liǎng kuài, xièxie!

第四課　你們跟以前一樣
第四课　你们跟以前一样
Dì sì kè　Nǐmen gēn yǐqián yíyàng

老師：	歡迎，歡迎，請進！
老师：	欢迎，欢迎，请进！
Lǎoshī:	Huānyíng, huānyíng, qǐngjìn!
關明遠：	李訪，來，我給你們介紹一下，這是王老師，這是師母。
关明远：	李访，来，我给你们介绍一下，这是王老师，这是师母。
Guān Míngyuǎn:	Lǐ Fǎng, lái, wǒ gěi nǐmen jièshào yíxià, zhèshì Wáng Lǎoshī, zhèshì Shīmǔ.
李訪：	你們好。
李访：	你们好。
Lǐ Fǎng:	Nǐmen hǎo.
關明遠：	老師，這是一些您喜歡的美國文學書。師母，這些維生素是給您和老師吃的，祝你們永遠健康年輕。
关明远：	老师，这是一些您喜欢的美国文学书。师母，这些维生素是给您和老师吃的，祝你们永远健康年轻。
Guān Míngyuǎn:	Lǎoshī, zhèshì yìxiē nín xǐhuān de Měiguó wénxué shū. Shīmǔ, zhèxiē wéishēngsù shì gěi nín hé lǎoshī chī de, zhù nǐmen yǒngyuǎn jiànkāng niánqīng.

師母:	來了就好，怎麼還帶東西來呢！讓你破費了。
师母:	来了就好，怎么还带东西来呢！让你破费了。
Shīmǔ:	Láile jiùhǎo, zěnme hái dài dōngxi lái ne! Ràng nǐ pòfèi le.
關明遠:	沒什麼，小意思。
关明远:	没什么，小意思。
Guān Míngyuǎn:	Méi shénme, xiǎoyìsi.
老師:	你們難得來上海，師母特地做了一些拿手菜。來，來，快上座，菜都要涼了！
老师:	你们难得来上海，师母特地做了一些拿手菜。来，来，快上座，菜都要凉了！
Lǎoshī:	Nǐmen nándé lái Shànghǎi, Shīmǔ tèdì zuò le yìxiē náshǒucài. Lái, lái, kuài shàngzuò, cài dōuyào liáng le!
關明遠:	老師，師母，你們倆還是跟以前一樣，看起來真精神。
关明远:	老师，师母，你们俩还是跟以前一样，看起来真精神。
Guān Míngyuǎn:	Lǎoshī, Shīmǔ, nǐmen liǎ háishì gēn yǐqián yíyàng, kàn qǐlái zhēn jīngshen.
師母:	不行了！我們是一天比一天老了，白頭髮比以前多了，眼睛也花了，做事也沒有以前那麼快了。
师母:	不行了！我们是一天比一天老了，白头发比以前多了，眼睛也花了，做事也没有以前那么快了。
Shīmǔ:	Bùxíng le! Wǒmen shì yìtiān bǐ yìtiān lǎo le, bái tóufa bǐ yǐqián duō le, yǎnjīng yě huā le, zuòshì yě méiyou yǐqián nàme kuài le.
老師:	李訪，第一次來中國，適應嗎?
老师:	李访，第一次来中国，适应吗?
Lǎoshī:	Lǐ Fǎng, dìyīcì lái Zhōngguó, shìyìng ma?
李訪:	還可以，現在還有一點兒時差。白天覺得很睏，晚上就睡不著。不過，今天比昨天好多了。
李访:	还可以，现在还有一点儿时差。白天觉得很困，晚上就睡不着。不过，今天比昨天好多了。
Lǐ Fǎng:	Hái kěyǐ, xiànzài háiyǒu yìdiǎr shíchā. Báitiān juéde hěn kùn, wǎnshàng jiù shuìbuzháo. Búguò, jīntiān bǐ zuótiān hǎoduō le.

關明遠: 李訪說這兒的天氣比匹茲堡熱。還有，這兒的人
关明远: 李访说这儿的天气比匹兹堡热。还有，这儿的人
Guān Míngyuǎn: Lǐ Fǎng shuō zhèr de tiānqì bǐ Pǐzībǎo rè. Háiyǒu, zhèr de rén

也比匹茲堡多，街道上到處都是人，他還不太習慣。
也比匹兹堡多，街道上到处都是人，他还不太习惯。
yě bǐ Pǐzībǎo duō, jiēdào shàng dàochù dōushì rén, tā hái bú tài xíguàn.

李訪: 我長這麼大，第一次看到這麼多人。
李访: 我长这么大，第一次看到这么多人。
Lǐ Fǎng: Wǒ zhǎng zhème dà, dìyīcì kàndào zhème duō rén.

師母: 你們倆誰比較大?
师母: 你们俩谁比较大?
Shīmǔ: Nǐmen liǎ shéi bǐjiào dà?

關明遠: 我跟李訪一樣大，都是二十四歲。
关明远: 我跟李访一样大，都是二十四岁。
Guān Míngyuǎn: Wǒ gēn Lǐ Fǎng yíyàng dà, dōushì èrshí sì suì.

師母: 對了，不要只說話，忘了吃菜。來，來，來，多吃一點兒。
师母: 对了，不要只说话，忘了吃菜。来，来，来，多吃一点儿。
Shīmǔ: Duìle, búyào zhǐ shuōhuà, wàng le chīcài. Lái, lái, lái, duō chī yìdiǎr.

老師: 這是師母做的年糕，味道很地道，你們嚐嚐。
老师: 这是师母做的年糕，味道很地道，你们尝尝。
Lǎoshī: Zhèshì shīmǔ zuò de niángāo, wèidao hěn dìdao, nǐmen chángchang.

……

關明遠: 師母您做的飯真好吃。
关明远: 师母您做的饭真好吃。
Guān Míngyuǎn: Shīmǔ nín zuò de fàn zhēn hǎochī.

李訪: 是啊! 色香味俱全，我吃了很多，現在已經很飽了。
李访: 是啊! 色香味俱全，我吃了很多，现在已经很饱了。
Lǐ Fǎng: Shì a! Sè xiāng wèi jù quán, wǒ chī le hěnduō, xiànzài yǐjīng hěnbǎo le.

師母: 哪裡，哪裡! 只是家常便飯。
师母: 哪里，哪里! 只是家常便饭。
Shīmǔ: Nǎlǐ, nǎlǐ! Zhǐshì jiācháng biànfàn.

老師：　難得我們相聚，來，一起來乾一杯。今天真高興，
老师：　难得我们相聚，来，一起来干一杯。今天真高兴，
Lǎoshī:　Nándé wǒmen xiāngjù, lái, yìqǐ lái gān yìbēi. Jīntiān zhēn gāoxìng,

"有朋自遠方來，不亦樂乎！"
"有朋自远方来，不亦乐乎！"
"yǒu péng zì yuǎnfāng lái, bú yì yuè hū!"

老師，師母，關明遠，李訪：乾杯！
老师，师母，关明远，李访：干杯！
Lǎoshī, Shīmǔ, Guān Míngyuǎn, Lǐ Fǎng: Gānbēi!

第五課　我的中國行 (復習)
第五课　我的中国行 (复习)
Dì wǔ kè　Wǒde Zhōngguó xíng (fùxí)

十月二十日　星期三　天氣：陰
十月二十日　星期三　天气：阴
Shíyuè èrshí rì　Xīngqī Sān　Tiānqì: Yīn

我們坐了三十多個小時的飛機，終於回到美國來了。從中國
我们坐了三十多个小时的飞机，终于回到美国来了。从中国
Wǒmen zuòle sānshíduōge xiǎoshí de fēijī, zhōngyú huídào Měiguó láile. Cóng Zhōngguó

到美國本來十幾個小時就到了，但是在日本轉機的時候，因為我們
到美国本来十几个小时就到了，但是在日本转机的时候，因为我们
dào Měiguó běnlái shíjǐge xiǎoshí jiù dào le, dànshì zài Rìběn zhuǎnjīde shíhou, yīnwèi wǒmen

的飛機誤點了，所以沒趕上我們的班機。我們在機場等了五個小時
的飞机误点了，所以没赶上我们的班机。我们在机场等了五个小时
de fēijī wùdiǎn le, suǒyi méi gǎnshàng wǒmen de bānjī. Wǒmen zài jīchǎng děngle wǔge xiǎoshí

以後，才坐上了飛機。這次飛機誤點把我跟李訪累壞了。在飛機上，
以后，才坐上了飞机。这次飞机误点把我跟李访累坏了。在飞机上，
yǐhòu, cái zuòshàngle fēijī. Zhècì fēijī wùdiǎn bǎ wǒ gēn Lǐ Fǎng lèi huài le. Zài fēijī shàng,

我們一把行李放好，就一直睡覺，睡到飛機降落以後才起來。
我们一把行李放好，就一直睡觉，睡到飞机降落以后才起来。
wǒmen yì bǎ xíngli fànghǎo, jiù yìzhí shuìjiào, shuìdào fēijī jiàngluò yǐhòu cái qǐlái.

不過這次很高興能在上海和老師再次相聚。老師和師母
不过这次很高兴能在上海和老师再次相聚。老师和师母
Búguò zhècì hěn gāoxìng néng zài Shànghǎi hé lǎoshī zàicì xiāngjù. Lǎoshī hé shīmǔ

看起來都很精神，他們還是跟以前一樣非常熱情、好客。師母還
看起来都很精神，他们还是跟以前一样非常热情、好客。师母还
kàn qǐlái dōu hěn jīngshen, tāmen háishì gēn yǐqián yíyàng fēicháng rèqíng, hàokè. Shīmǔ hái

特地做了幾樣很地道的上海菜，讓我們嚐嚐，其中我最喜歡
特地做了几样很地道的上海菜，让我们尝尝，其中我最喜欢
tèdì zuòle jǐyàng hěn dìdao de Shànghǎi cài, ràng wǒmen chángchang, qízhōng wǒ zuì xǐhuān

的是上海年糕。真好吃！
的是上海年糕。真好吃！
de shì Shànghǎi niángāo. Zhēn hǎochī!

我還帶李訪去看了京劇，我們看得津津有味，他也覺得大開眼界。
我还带李访去看了京剧，我们看得津津有味，他也觉得大开眼界。
Wǒ hái dài Lǐ Fǎng qù kànle jīngjù, wǒmen kànde jīnjīnyǒuwèi, tā yě juéde dà kāi yǎnjiè.

不過，我聽說現在的京劇劇團比以前少了，所以票也比以前貴了。
不过，我听说现在的京剧剧团比以前少了，所以票也比以前贵了。
Búguò, wǒ tīngshuō xiànzàide jīngjù jùtuán bǐ yǐqián shǎole, suǒyi piào yě bǐ yǐqián guì le.

上海真的變得很快，有些路都很難找到了。我們手裡
上海真的变得很快，有些路都很难找到了。我们手里
Shànghǎi zhēnde biànde hěn kuài, yǒuxiē lù dōu hěn nán zhǎodào le. Wǒmen shǒuli

拿著地圖，忙著問路、找方向。常常應該向左拐的時候，
拿着地图，忙着问路、找方向。常常应该向左拐的时候，
názhe dìtú, mángzhe wènlù, zhǎo fāngxiàng. Chángcháng yīnggāi xiàng zuǒ guǎi de shíhou,

我們轉錯了，往右拐了，鬧了不少笑話。
我们转错了，往右拐了，闹了不少笑话。
wǒmen zhuǎn cuò le, wǎng yòu guǎile, nàole bùshǎo xiàohua.

中國真的是一天比一天繁榮、進步了。在大城市裡，高樓大廈
中国真的是一天比一天繁荣、进步了。在大城市里，高楼大厦
Zhōngguó zhēnde shì yìtiān bǐ yìtiān fánróng, jìnbù le. Zài dà chéngshì lǐ, gāolóu dàshà

跟美國的一樣高，到處都能看到外國人。
跟美国的一样高，到处都能看到外国人。
gēn Měiguó de yíyàng gāo, dàochù dōu néng kàndào wàiguórén.

這次在中國的時間雖然很短，可是我們都玩得很高興。
这次在中国的时间虽然很短，可是我们都玩得很高兴。
Zhècì zài Zhōngguó de shíjīan suīrán hěn duǎn, kěshì wǒmen dōu wánde hěn gāoxìng.

李訪說他現在可以跟別人說他去過中國、看過京劇了。還有，
李访说他现在可以跟别人说他去过中国、看过京剧了。还有，
Lǐ Fǎng shuō tā xiànzài kěyǐ gēn biérén shuō tā qù guo Zhōngguó, kàn guo jīngjù le. Háiyǒu,

他也嚐了很多中國的小吃，都很棒！
他也尝了很多中国的小吃，都很棒！
tā yě cháng le hěnduō Zhōngguó de xiǎochī, dōu hěn bàng!

我們倆都覺得這次去中國旅行，挺不错的，也非常值得。下次
我们俩都觉得这次去中国旅行，挺不错的，也非常值得。下次
Wǒmen liǎ dōu juéde zhècì qù Zhōngguó lǚxíng, tǐng búcuò de, yě fēicháng zhídé. Xiàcì

有機會，我們還要再去。
有机会，我们还要再去。
yǒu jīhuì, wǒmen hái yào zài qù.

第六課　我要去銀行開一個帳戶
第六课　我要去银行开一个账户
Dì liù kè　Wǒ yào qù yínháng kāi yíge zhànghù

Scene 1: (在路上)
(在路上)
(Zài lùshàng)

關京華：小琴，我要去銀行開一個帳戶，這樣我存款、
关京华：小琴，我要去银行开一个账户，这样我存款、
Guān Jīnghuá: Xiǎoqín, wǒ yào qù yínháng kāi yíge zhànghù, zhèyàng wǒ cúnkuǎn,

取款就方便多了。你知道哪家銀行比較好嗎?
取款就方便多了。你知道哪家银行比较好吗?
qǔkuǎn jiù fāngbiàn duō le. Nǐ zhīdào nǎ jiā yínháng bǐjiào hǎo ma?

方小琴：我常常去大華銀行存款、取款。那兒的服務不錯，
方小琴：我常常去大华银行存款、取款。那儿的服务不错，
Fāng Xiǎoqín: Wǒ chángcháng qù Dàhuá Yínháng cúnkuǎn, qǔkuǎn. Nàr de fúwù búcuò,

利率也比較高，現在儲蓄帳戶的利率是百分之三點二。
利率也比较高，现在储蓄账户的利率是百分之三点二。
lìlǜ yě bǐjiào gāo, xiànzài chǔxù zhànghù de lìlǜ shì bǎifēn zhī sān diǎn èr.

關京華: 那我就去大華銀行吧。
关京华: 那我就去大华银行吧。
Guān Jīnghuá: Nà wǒ jiù qù Dàhuá Yínháng ba.

Scene 2: (在銀行)
(在银行)
(Zài yínháng)

關京華: 先生，我想開一個有利息的支票帳戶。請問，
关京华: 先生，我想开一个有利息的支票账户。请问，
Guān Jīnghuá: Xiānsheng, wǒ xiǎng kāi yíge yǒu lìxi de zhīpiào zhànghù. Qǐngwèn,

有利息的支票帳戶利率是多少?
有利息的支票账户利率是多少?
yǒu lìxi de zhīpiào zhànghù lìlǜ shì duōshǎo?

職員: 最近利率都比較低，今天是百分之二點六。
职员: 最近利率都比较低，今天是百分之二点六。
Zhíyuán: Zuìjìn lìlǜ dōu bǐjiào dī, jīntiān shì bǎifēn zhī èr diǎn liù.

關京華: 怎麼這麼低呀? 我聽說是百分之三點二呢。
关京华: 怎么这么低呀? 我听说是百分之三点二呢。
Guān Jīnghuá: Zěnme zhème dī ya? Wǒ tīngshuō shì bǎi fēn zhī sān diǎn èr ne.

職員: 那是儲蓄帳戶，儲蓄帳戶的利率高一點兒，是百分之
职员: 那是储蓄账户，储蓄账户的利率高一点儿，是百分之
Zhíyuán: Nà shì chǔxù zhànghù, chǔxù zhànghù de lìlǜ gāo yìdiǎr, shì bǎifēn zhī

三點二。這種帳戶每個月可以開三張支票。
三点二。这种账户每个月可以开三张支票。
sān diǎn èr. Zhèzhǒng zhànghù měige yuè kěyǐ kāi sānzhāng zhīpiào.

您想開哪一種?
您想开哪一种?
Nín xiǎng kāi nǎyìzhǒng?

關京華: 我想一個月開三張支票差不多夠了。我就開一個
关京华: 我想一个月开三张支票差不多够了。我就开一个
Guān Jīnghuá: Wǒ xiǎng yíge yuè kāi sānzhāng zhīpiào chàbuduō gòu le. Wǒ jiù kāi yíge

儲蓄帳戶吧。
储蓄账户吧。
chǔxù zhànghù ba.

職員：　好，請把這張開帳户的單子填一下，謝謝。請問
职员：　好，请把这张开账户的单子填一下，谢谢。请问
Zhíyuán: Hǎo, qǐng bǎ zhèzhāng kāi zhànghù de dānzi tián yíxià, xièxie. Qǐngwèn

您今天想存多少錢？
您今天想存多少钱？
nín jīntiān xiǎng cún duōshǎo qián?

關京華：　我這兒是三千元美金。
关京华：　我这儿是三千元美金。
Guān Jīnghuá: Wǒ zhèr shì sānqiān yuán Měijīn.

職員：　好……一個星期以後，您會收到我們給您寄去的支票簿
职员：　好……一个星期以后，您会收到我们给您寄去的支票簿
Zhíyuán: Hǎo ...... Yíge xīngqī yǐhòu, nín huì shōudào wǒmen gěi nín jìqù de zhīpiàobù

和取款卡。您可以拿取款卡在自動取款機那兒取現金。
和取款卡。您可以拿取款卡在自动取款机那儿取现金。
hé qǔkuǎnkǎ. Nín kěyǐ ná qǔkuǎnkǎ zài zìdòng qǔkuǎnjī nàr qǔ xiànjīn.

關京華：　我可以在你們這兒申請一張信用卡嗎？
关京华：　我可以在你们这儿申请一张信用卡吗？
Guān Jīnghuá: Wǒ kěyǐ zài nǐmen zhèr shēnqǐng yìzhāng xìnyòngkǎ ma?

職員：　當然可以。請把這張申請信用卡的表填一下。
职员：　当然可以。请把这张申请信用卡的表填一下。
Zhíyuán: Dāngrán kěyi. Qǐng bǎ zhèzhāng shēnqǐng xìnyòngkǎ de biǎo tián yíxià.

關京華：　下個月我要去中國，要換一些人民幣。
关京华：　下个月我要去中国，要换一些人民币。
Guān Jīnghuá: Xiàge yuè wǒ yào qù Zhōngguó, yào huàn yìxiē Rénmínbì.

請問美金換人民幣的匯率是多少？
请问美金换人民币的汇率是多少？
Qǐngwèn Měijīn huàn Rénmínbì de huìlǜ shì duōshǎo?

職員：　今天的匯率是一比七點九八。
职员：　今天的汇率是一比七点九八。
Zhíyuán: Jīntiān de huìlǜ shì yī bǐ qī diǎn jiǔ bā.

關京華：　兑換外幣的地方在哪兒？
关京华：　兑换外币的地方在哪儿？
Guān Jīnghuá: Duìhuàn wàibì de dìfang zài nǎr?

職員： 就在左邊的櫃台那兒。
职员： 就在左边的柜台那儿。
Zhíyuán: Jiù zài zuǒbiān de guìtái nàr.

關京華： 謝謝。再見。
关京华： 谢谢。再见。
Guān Jīnghuá: Xièxie. Zàijiàn.

第七課 我的電話簿找不到了
第七课 我的电话簿找不到了
Dì qī kè Wǒde diànhuàbù zhǎobudào le

方小琴： 文華，你在找什麼？
方小琴： 文华，你在找什么？
Fāng Xiǎoqín: Wénhuá, nǐ zài zhǎo shénme?

金文華： 我在找一本電話簿，我的電話簿找不到了。
金文华： 我在找一本电话簿，我的电话簿找不到了。
Jīn Wénhuá: Wǒ zài zhǎo yìběn diànhuàbù, wǒde diànhuàbù zhǎobudào le.

方小琴： 你看看電話旁邊有沒有？
方小琴： 你看看电话旁边有没有？
Fāng Xiǎoqín: Nǐ kànkan diànhuà pángbiān yǒuméiyǒu?

金文華： 好像沒有……啊，我看到了，在桌子下面。今年寒假
金文华： 好像没有……啊，我看到了，在桌子下面。今年寒假
Jīn Wénhuá: Hǎoxiàng méiyǒu .... À, wǒ kàndào le, zài zhuōzi xiàmiàn. Jīnnián hánjià

我和方明要去中國旅遊，我要找一家
我和方明要去中国旅游，我要找一家
wǒ hé Fāng Míng yào qù Zhōngguó lǚyóu, wǒ yào zhǎo yì jiā

旅行社的電話號碼，我想訂去中國的機票。
旅行社的电话号码，我想订去中国的机票。
lǚxíngshè de diànhuà hàomǎ, wǒ xiǎng dìng qù Zhōngguó de jīpiào.

方小琴： 真的嗎？太棒了！我真羨慕你們。
方小琴： 真的吗？太棒了！我真羡慕你们。
Fāng Xiǎoqín: Zhēnde ma? Tài bàng le! Wǒ zhēn xiànmù nǐmen.

你們打算去哪兒玩呢？
你们打算去哪儿玩呢？
Nǐmen dǎsuàn qù nǎr wár ne?

金文華：方明在北京有很多親戚，我們原來想先去北京玩幾天，跟他的親戚聚一聚，然後抽空去拜訪他以前的老師，再去別的地方看看，可是我一直買不到去北京的機票。
金文华：方明在北京有很多亲戚，我们原来想先去北京玩几天，跟他的亲戚聚一聚，然后抽空去拜访他以前的老师，再去别的地方看看，可是我一直买不到去北京的机票。
Jīn Wénhuá: Fāng Míng zài Běijīng yǒu hěnduō qīnqi. Wǒmen yuánlái xiǎng xiān qù Běijīng wán jǐ tiān, gēn tā de qīnqi jùyijù, ránhòu chōukòng qù bàifǎng tā yǐqián de lǎoshī, zài qù bié de dìfang kànkan, kěshì wǒ yìzhí mǎibudào qù Běijīng de jīpiào.

方小琴：你們上網查了嗎？
方小琴：你们上网查了吗？
Fāng Xiǎoqín: Nǐmen shàngwǎng chá le ma?

金文華：查了，我們查了好幾家航空公司的網站，可是都訂不到機票。有的機票太貴了，我們買不起。我想問問這家旅行社，看看他們那兒訂得到訂不到比較便宜的機票。
金文华：查了，我们查了好几家航空公司的网站，可是都订不到机票。有的机票太贵了，我们买不起。我想问问这家旅行社，看看他们那儿订得到订不到比较便宜的机票。
Jīn Wénhuá: Chá le, wǒmen chá le hǎo jǐjiā hángkōng gōngsī de wǎngzhàn, kěshì dōu dìngbudào jīpiào. Yǒude jīpiào tàiguì le, wǒmen mǎibuqǐ. Wǒ xiǎng wènwen zhè jiā lǚxíngshè, kànkan tāmēn nàr dìngdedào dìngbudào bǐjiào piányi de jīpiào.

方小琴：其實，要是真的買不到去北京的機票，你們可以先去南方的城市，比如上海或者香港，然後去雲南的昆明，再從昆明坐飛機去北京。
方小琴：其实，要是真的买不到去北京的机票，你们可以先去南方的城市，比如上海或者香港，然后去云南的昆明，再从昆明坐飞机去北京。
Fāng Xiǎoqín: Qíshí, yàoshi zhēnde mǎibudào qù Běijīng de jīpiào, nǐmen kěyǐ xiān qù nánfāng de chéngshì, bǐrú Shànghǎi huòzhě Xiānggǎng, ránhòu qù Yúnnán de Kūnmíng, zài cóng Kūnmíng zuò fēijī qù Běijīng.

金文華： 這個主意真不錯。我也聽說昆明是一個四季如春、
金文华： 这个主意真不错。我也听说昆明是一个四季如春、
Jīn Wénhuá: Zhège zhǔyi zhēn búcuò. Wǒ yě tīngshuō Kūnmíng shì yíge sìjì rúchūn,

風景如畫的城市，雲南那兒還有很多少數民族，
风景如画的城市，云南那儿还有很多少数民族，
fēngjǐng rúhuà de chéngshì, Yúnnán nàr háiyǒu hěnduō shǎoshù mínzú,

去那兒看看一定會很有意思。可是我在地圖上怎麼
去那儿看看一定会很有意思。可是我在地图上怎么
qù nàr kànkan yídìng huì hěnyǒuyìsi. Kěshì wǒ zài dìtú shàng zěnme

找不到昆明呢？
找不到昆明呢？
zhǎobudào Kūnmíng ne?

方小琴： 我來幫你看看……啊，在這兒。你看，就在中國的西南邊。
方小琴： 我来帮你看看……啊，在这儿。你看，就在中国的西南边。
Fāng Xiǎoqín: Wǒ lái bāng nǐ kànkan ...... À, zài zhèr. Nǐ kàn, jiù zài Zhōngguó de xīnánbiān.

金文華： 是啊！如果我真的想去，坐飛機到得了到不了昆明？
金文华： 是啊！如果我真的想去，坐飞机到得了到不了昆明？
Jīn Wénhuá: Shì a! Rúguǒ wǒ zhēnde xiǎng qù, zuò fēijī dàodeliǎo dàobuliǎo Kūnmíng?

方小琴： 當然到得了！你還可以吃得到少數民族的小吃呢！
方小琴： 当然到得了！你还可以吃得到少数民族的小吃呢！
Fāng Xiǎoqín: Dāngrán dàodeliǎo! Nǐ hái kěyǐ chīdedào shǎoshù mínzú de xiǎochī ne!

金文華： 那我一定要去。
金文华： 那我一定要去。
Jīn Wénhuá: Nà wǒ yídìng yào qù.

方小琴： 對了，你們的簽證辦好了嗎？
方小琴： 对了，你们的签证办好了吗？
Fāng Xiǎoqín: Duì le, nǐmen de qiānzhèng bàn hǎo le ma?

金文華： 方明的簽證已經辦好了。我也已經申請了，可是
金文华： 方明的签证已经办好了。我也已经申请了，可是
Jīn Wénhuá: Fāng Míng de qiānzhèng yǐjīng bànhǎo le, wǒ yě yǐjīng shēnqǐng le, kěshì

不知道下個星期拿得到拿不到。不過還有一個多月，
不知道下个星期拿得到拿不到。不过还有一个多月，
bù zhīdào xiàge xīngqī nádedào nábudào. Búguò hái yǒu yíge duō yuè,

大概來得及。
大概来得及。
dàgài láidejí.

第八課 你比以前忙得多
第八课 你比以前忙得多
Dì bā kè Nǐ bǐ yǐqián máng de duō

季如春： 慕華，你好像最近比以前忙得多，是嗎？
季如春： 慕华，你好像最近比以前忙得多，是吗？
Jì Rúchūn: Mùhuá, nǐ hǎoxiàng zuìjìn bǐ yǐqián mángdeduō, shì ma?

方慕華： 沒有啊！你為什麼覺得我比以前忙得多呢？
方慕华： 没有啊！你为什么觉得我比以前忙得多呢？
Fāng Mùhuá: Méiyou ā! Nǐ wèishénme juéde wǒ bǐ yǐqián máng de duō ne?

季如春： 最近連你的影子都看不見。昨天晚上我給你打
季如春： 最近连你的影子都看不见。昨天晚上我给你打
Jì Rúchūn: Zuìjìn lián nǐ de yǐngzi dōu kànbujiàn. Zuótiān wǎnshàng wǒ gěi nǐ dǎ

電話也找不到你。
电话也找不到你。
diànhuà yě zhǎobudào nǐ.

方慕華： 昨天上午我把一個大的研究報告交出去了，覺得
方慕华： 昨天上午我把一个大的研究报告交出去了，觉得
Fāng Mùhuá: Zuótiān shàngwǔ wǒ bǎ yíge dàde yánjiū bàogào jiāo chūqù le, juéde

輕鬆多了，所以我就跟我的表妹去看電影了。
轻松多了，所以我就跟我的表妹去看电影了。
qīngsōng duō le, suǒyǐ wǒ jiù gēn wǒde biǎomèi qù kàn diànyǐng le.

季如春：	你比我強得多，我的報告還沒有寫完呢！對了，你們
季如春：	你比我强得多，我的报告还没有写完呢！对了，你们
Jì Rúchūn:	Nǐ bǐ wǒ qiáng de duō, wǒ de bàogào hái méiyou xiě wán ne! Duìle, nǐmen
	看了什麼電影？好看嗎？
	看了什么电影？好看吗？
	kàn le shénme diànyǐng? Hǎo kàn ma?
方慕華：	我們看的是《英雄》。
方慕华：	我们看的是《英雄》。
Fāng Mùhuá:	Wǒmen kàn de shì《Yīngxióng》.
季如春：	是不是張藝謀導演的那部功夫片？
季如春：	是不是张艺谋导演的那部功夫片？
Jì Rúchūn:	Shìbushì Zhāng Yìmóu dǎoyǎn de nà bù gōngfūpiān?
方慕華：	是的。主要演員是陳道明、李連杰和張曼玉。
方慕华：	是的。主要演员是陈道明、李连杰和张曼玉。
Fāng Mùhuá:	Shìde. Zhǔyào yǎnyuán shì Chén Dàomíng, Lǐ Liánjié hé Zhāng Mànyù.
	其中我特別喜歡李連杰。
	其中我特别喜欢李连杰。
	Qízhōng wǒ tèbié xǐhuān Lǐ Liánjié.
季如春：	有人說它沒有《臥虎藏龍》好看，你覺得怎麼樣？
季如春：	有人说它没有《卧虎藏龙》好看，你觉得怎么样？
Jì Rúchūn:	Yǒurén shuō tā méiyou《Wòhǔcánglóng》hǎokàn, nǐ juéde zhěnmeyàng?
方慕華：	我覺得這兩部電影差不多。你看過沒有？
方慕华：	我觉得这两部电影差不多。你看过没有？
Fāng Mùhuá:	Wǒ juéde zhè liǎngbù diànyǐng chàbuduō. Nǐ kàn guo méiyou?
季如春：	我看過《臥虎藏龍》，沒有看過《英雄》，
季如春：	我看过《卧虎藏龙》，没有看过《英雄》，
Jì Rúchūn:	Wǒ kàn guo《Wòhǔcánglóng》, méiyou kàn guo《Yīngxióng》,
	可是聽說《英雄》的場面比《臥虎藏龍》大得多。
	可是听说《英雄》的场面比《卧虎藏龙》大得多。
	kěshì tīngshuō《Yīngxióng》de chǎngmiàn bǐ《Wòhǔcánglóng》dàdeduō.
	是真的嗎？
	是真的吗？
	Shì zhēnde ma?

方慕華： 沒錯。《英雄》的場面比《臥虎藏龍》大一些，可是
方慕华： 没错。《英雄》的场面比《卧虎藏龙》大一些，可是
Fāng Mùhuá: Méi cuò.《Yīngxióng》de chǎngmiàn bǐ《Wòhǔcánglóng》dà yìxiē, kěshì

我覺得它的情節不像《臥虎藏龍》那麼吸引人。
我觉得它的情节不像《卧虎藏龙》那么吸引人。
wǒ juéde tā de qíngjié búxiàng《Wòhǔcánglóng》nàme xīyǐnrén.

季如春： 聽說《英雄》說的是關於中國古代秦始皇
季如春： 听说《英雄》说的是关于中国古代秦始皇
Jì Rúchūn: Tīngshuō《Yīngxióng》shuōde shì guānyú Zhōngguó gǔdài Qínshǐhuáng

的故事，那麼，比較起來電影和小說哪個好?
的故事，那么，比较起来电影和小说哪个好?
de gùshi, nàme, bǐjiào qǐlái diànyǐng hé xiǎoshuō nǎge hǎo?

方慕華： 我覺得電影不如小說精彩。
方慕华： 我觉得电影不如小说精彩。
Fāng Mùhuá: Wǒ juéde diànyǐng bùrú xiǎoshuō jīngcǎi.

季如春： 有人說它對秦始皇的描寫跟歷史上的秦始皇
季如春： 有人说它对秦始皇的描写跟历史上的秦始皇
Jì Rúchūn: Yǒurén shuō tā duì Qínshǐhuáng de miáoxiě gēn lìshǐ shàng de Qíshǐhuáng

不一樣。
不一样。
bù yíyàng.

方慕華： 我同意，但是我覺得這部電影描寫得比較客觀。
方慕华： 我同意，但是我觉得这部电影描写得比较客观。
Fāng Mùhuá: Wǒ tóngyì, dànshì wǒ juéde zhè bù diànyǐng miáoxiě de bǐjiào kèguān.

季如春： 我一直對歷史故事很感興趣，所以我很想去看一看
季如春： 我一直对历史故事很感兴趣，所以我很想去看一看
Jì Rúchūn: Wǒ yìzhí duì lìshǐ gùshi hěn gǎn xìngqu, suǒyǐ wǒ hěn xiǎng qù kànyikàn

這部電影。
这部电影。
zhè bù diànyǐng.

方慕華：你應該去看看。我覺得《英雄》這部電影對感情
方慕华：你应该去看看。我觉得《英雄》这部电影对感情
Fāng Mùhuá: Nǐ yīnggāi qù kànkan. Wǒ juéde《Yīngxióng》zhè bù diànyǐng duì gǎnqíng

方面的描寫比《臥虎藏龍》多一些，而且它的特技效果
方面的描写比《卧虎藏龙》多一些，而且它的特技效果
fāngmiàn de miánxiě bǐ《Wòhǔcánglóng》duō yìxiē, érqiě tā de tèjì xiàoguǒ

和顏色都比別的電影好得多。
和颜色都比别的电影好得多。
hé yánsè dōu bǐ bié de diànyǐng hǎodeduō.

季如春：你知道在哪兒可以看得到《英雄》嗎？
季如春：你知道在哪儿可以看得到《英雄》吗？
Jì Rúchūn: Nǐ zhīdào zài nǎr kěyǐ kàndedào《Yīngxióng》ma?

方慕華：這個週末學校會放這部電影，票價只要一元，
方慕华：这个周末学校会放这部电影，票价只要一元，
Fāng Mùhuá: Zhège zhōumò xuéxiào huì fàng zhè bù diànyǐng, piàojià zhǐyào yì Yuán,

比電影院的要便宜五元。
比电影院的要便宜五元。
bǐ diànyǐngyuàn de yào piányi wǔ Yuán.

季如春：好，這個週末我就去看。
季如春：好，这个周末我就去看。
Jì Rúchūn: Hǎo, zhège zhōumò wǒ jiù qù kàn.

第九課 你越來越精神了
第九课 你越来越精神了
Dì jiǔ kè Nǐ yuè lái yuè jīngshen le

白思琴：欣明，你最近常去健身房鍛煉嗎？
白思琴：欣明，你最近常去健身房锻炼吗？
Bái Sīqín: Xīnmíng, nǐ zuìjìn cháng qù jiànshēnfáng duànliàn ma?

胡欣明: 這兩個星期是我最忙的時候，鍛煉得比以前少得多。以前我差不多天天游泳，最近差不多每星期都要比以前少游兩、三次。這個星期一次也沒去過。
胡欣明: 这两个星期是我最忙的时候，锻炼得比以前少得多。以前我差不多天天游泳，最近差不多每星期都要比以前少游两、三次。这个星期一次也没去过。
Hú Xīnmíng: Zhè liǎngge xīngqī shì wǒ zuì máng de shíhou, duànliàn de bǐ yǐqián shǎo de duō. Yǐqián wǒ chàbuduō tiāntiān yóuyǒng, zuìjìn chàbuduō měi xīngqī dōu yào bǐ yǐqián shǎo yóu liǎng, sān cì. Zhège xīngqī yícì yě méi qù guo.

白思琴: 那可不好。其實越忙越需要鍛煉。我每天都要去運動一個鐘頭，現在我的精神越來越好了。你看，我比前幾個月還瘦了不少吧！
白思琴: 那可不好。其实越忙越需要锻炼。我每天都要去运动一个钟头，现在我的精神越来越好了。你看，我比前几个月还瘦了不少吧！
Bái Sīqín: Nà kě bù hǎo. Qíshí yuè máng yuè xūyào duànliàn. Wǒ měitiān dōu yào qù yùndòng yíge zhōngtóu, xiànzài wǒ de jīngshen yuèlái yuè hǎo le. Nǐ kàn, wǒ bǐ qián jǐge yuè hái shòu le bù shǎo ba!

胡欣明: 真的，你看上去比上學期瘦了很多。你最近在減肥嗎？
胡欣明: 真的，你看上去比上学期瘦了很多。你最近在减肥吗？
Hú Xīnmíng: Zhēn de, nǐ kànshàngqù bǐ shàng xuéqī shòu le hěn duō. Nǐ zuìjìn zài jiǎnféi ma?

白思琴: 是呀！我已經堅持了三個月了。效果不錯吧！體重比以前輕了十幾磅。
白思琴: 是呀！我已经坚持了三个月了。效果不错吧！体重比以前轻了十几磅。
Bái Sīqín: Shì ya! Wǒ yǐjīng jiānchí le sānge yuè le. Xiàoguǒ búcuò ba! Tǐzhòng bǐ yǐqián qīngle shí jǐ bàng.

胡欣明：	怪不得你越來越苗條了，差不多是我們女孩子中
胡欣明：	怪不得你越来越苗条了，差不多是我们女孩子中
Hú Xīnmíng:	Guàibudé nǐ yuèlái yuè miáotiao le, chàbuduō shì wǒmen nǚháizi zhōng
	最苗條的了。你是怎麼減肥的？控制飲食嗎？
	最苗条的了。你是怎么减肥的？控制饮食吗？
	zuì miáotiao de le. Nǐ shì zěnme jiǎnféi de? Kòngzhi yǐnshí ma?
白思琴：	主要是鍛煉，當然在吃的方面我也比較注意。我
白思琴：	主要是锻炼，当然在吃的方面我也比较注意。我
Bái Sīqín:	Zhǔyào shì duànliàn, dāngrán zài chīde fāngmiàn wǒ yě bǐjiào zhùyì. Wǒ
	以前最喜歡吃甜食，可是現在我吃得越來越少了。
	以前最喜欢吃甜食，可是现在我吃得越来越少了。
	yǐqián zuì xǐhuān chī tiánshí, kěshì xiànzài wǒ chī de yuèlái yuè shǎo le.
胡欣明：	你怎麼會想到要減肥呢？
胡欣明：	你怎么会想到要减肥呢？
Hú Xīnmíng:	Nǐ zěnme huì xiǎng dào yào jiǎnféi ne?
白思琴：	我早就想減肥了。我的個子有點兒矮，只有五呎一吋，
白思琴：	我早就想减肥了。我的个子有点儿矮，只有五呎一吋，
Bái Sīqín:	Wǒ zǎo jiù xiǎng jiǎnféi le. Wǒ de gèzi yǒudiǎr ǎi, zhǐyǒu wǔ chǐ yí cùn,
	可是三個月以前我的體重超過了一百三十磅。
	可是三个月以前我的体重超过了一百三十磅。
	kěshì sānge yuè yǐqián wǒ de tǐzhòng chāoguò le yìbǎi sān shí bàng.
胡欣明：	那你最重的時候比我還要重呢！
胡欣明：	那你最重的时候比我还要重呢！
Hú Xīnmíng:	Nà nǐ zuì zhòng de shíhou bǐ wǒ hái yào zhòng ne!
白思琴：	是呀！我要是太重了就會覺得不太靈活，也很不舒服。
白思琴：	是呀！我要是太重了就会觉得不太灵活，也很不舒服。
Bái Sīqín:	Shì ya! Wǒ yàoshì tài zhòng le jiùhuì juéde bù tài línghuó, yě hěn bù shūfu.

胡欣明： 我真應該向你學習，可是我總是覺得功課太多、
胡欣明： 我真应该向你学习，可是我总是觉得功课太多、
Hú Xīnmíng: Wǒ zhēn yīnggāi xiàng nǐ xuéxí, kěshì wǒ zǒngshì juéde gōngkè tài duō,

太忙，沒有時間鍛煉。現在我每天都比別人還要
太忙，没有时间锻炼。现在我每天都比别人还要
tài máng, méiyou shíjiān duànliàn. Xiànzài wǒ měitiān dōu bǐ biérén hái yào

少睡兩、三個鐘頭呢。
少睡两、三个钟头呢。
shǎo shuì liǎng, sān ge zhōngtóu ne.

白思琴： 其實，最重要的是要多鍛煉、多運動。運動了以後
白思琴： 其实，最重要的是要多锻炼、多运动。运动了以后
Bái Sīqín: Qíshí, zuì zhòngyào de shì yào duō duànliàn, duō yùndòng. Yùndòng le yǐhòu

你的身體會比以前更好，你會更有精神，學習的效果
你的身体会比以前更好，你会更有精神，学习的效果
nǐde shēntǐ huì bǐ yǐqián gèng hǎo, nǐ huì gèng yǒu jīngshén, xuéxí de xiàoguǒ

可能就會更好了。
可能就会更好了。
kěnéng jiù huì gèng hǎo le.

第十課 我的寒假計畫 (復習)
第十课 我的寒假计划 (复习)
Dì shí kè Wǒ de hánjià jìhuà (fùxí)

同學們好！
同学们好！
Tóngxuémen hǎo!

今天，我想把我的寒假計畫跟大家報告一下。
今天，我想把我的寒假计划跟大家报告一下。
Jīntiān, wǒ xiǎng bǎ wǒ de hánjià jìhuà gēn dàjiā bàogào yíxià.

今年是我在大學的最後一個寒假。我已經跟我的男朋友
今年是我在大学的最后一个寒假。我已经跟我的男朋友
Jīnnián shì wǒ zài dàxué de zuìhòu yíge hánjià. Wǒ yǐjīng gēn wǒ de nánpéngyou

說好了，一起去中國旅遊。我們在北京有很多親戚朋友，
说好了，一起去中国旅游。我们在北京有很多亲戚朋友，
shuō hǎo le, yìqǐ qù Zhōngguó lǚyóu. Wǒmen zài Běijīng yǒu hěnduō qīnqì péngyou,

我希望這次去北京能見得到他們每個人。
我希望这次去北京能见得到他们每个人。
wǒ xīwàng zhècì qù Běijīng néng jiàndedào tāmen měige rén.

這兩年去中國的人比以前多了很多，所以飛機票也比
这两年去中国的人比以前多了很多，所以飞机票也比
Zhè liǎng nián qù Zhōngguó de rén bǐ yǐqián duō le hěn duō, suǒyǐ fēijīpiào yě bǐ

前兩年難買多了。特別是去北京的機票，更難買得到。我們
前两年难买多了。特别是去北京的机票，更难买得到。我们
qián liǎngnián nán mǎi duō le. Tèbié shì qù Běijīng de jīpiào, gèng nán mǎidedào. Wǒmen

到現在還沒有訂到票呢。我們打算十二月中旬出發，一月
到现在还没有订到票呢。我们打算十二月中旬出发，一月
dào xiànzài hái méiyou dìng dào piào ne. Wǒmen dǎsuàn shí èr yuè zhōngxún chūfā, yīyuè

上旬回來。現在已經給好幾家旅行社打了電話，還不知道
上旬回来。现在已经给好几家旅行社打了电话，还不知道
shàngxún huílai. Xiànzài yǐjīng gěi hǎo jǐ jiā lǚxíngshè dǎ le diànhuà, hái bù zhīdào

買得到買不到。我們上個星期已經申請了去中國的簽證，
买得到买不到。我们上个星期已经申请了去中国的签证，
mǎidedào mǎibudào. Wǒmen shàngge xīngqī yǐjīng shēnqǐng le qù Zhōngguó de qiānzhèng,

不知道這個星期收得到收不到。不過我們還有不少時間，大概
不知道这个星期收得到收不到。不过我们还有不少时间，大概
bù zhīdào zhège xīngqī shōudedào shōubudào. Búguò wǒmen háiyou bù shǎo shíjiān, dàgài

來得及。
来得及。
láidejí.

我還要去銀行取一些現金，買幾張旅行支票。在中國
我还要去银行取一些现金，买几张旅行支票。在中国
Wǒ háiyào qù yínháng qǔ yìxiē xiànjīn, mǎi jǐzhāng lǚxíng zhīpiào. Zài Zhōngguó

用信用卡付款不像在美國這麼方便。不過，聽說現在
用信用卡付款不像在美国这么方便。不过，听说现在
yòng xìnyòngkǎ fùkuǎn búxiàng zài Měiguó zhème fāngbiàn. Búguò, tīngshuō xiànzài

接受信用卡的商店越來越多了，而且在中國銀行還可以取
接受信用卡的商店越来越多了，而且在中国银行还可以取
jiēshòu xìnyòngkǎ de shāngdiàn yuèlái yuè duō le, érqiě zài Zhōngguó Yínháng hái kěyǐ qǔ

美金，也可以根據當天的匯率換成人民幣，這比帶很多現金
美金，也可以根据当天的汇率换成人民币，这比带很多现金
Měijīn, yě kěyǐ gēnjù dāngtiān de huìlǜ huàn chéng Rénmínbì, zhè bǐ dài hěnduō xiànjīn

要安全得多。最近人民幣換美金的匯率差不多是一比
要安全得多。最近人民币换美金的汇率差不多是一比
yào ānquán de duō. Zuìjìn Rénmínbì huàn Měijīn de huìlǜ chàbuduō shì yī bǐ

七點九七，比上個月低了零點一個百分點。
七点九七，比上个月低了零点一个百分点。
qī diǎn jiǔ qī, bǐ shàngge yuè dī le líng diǎn yī ge bǎifēndiǎn.

這次去中國我最想去的地方是長城。聽說爬
这次去中国我最想去的地方是长城。听说爬
Zhècì qù Zhōngguó wǒ zuì xiǎng qù de dìfang shì Chángchéng. Tīngshuō pá

長城很累，只有百分之五十的人爬得到長城的頂上。
长城很累，只有百分之五十的人爬得到长城的顶上。
Chángchéng hěn lèi, zhǐ yǒu bǎi fēn zhī wǔshí de rén pádedào Chángchéng de dǐng shàng.

我覺得那是一個很好的鍛煉，還能幫助我減肥呢！而且，
我觉得那是一个很好的锻炼，还能帮助我减肥呢！而且，
Wǒ juéde nà shì yíge hěnhǎo de duànliàn, hái néng bāngzhù wǒ jiǎnféi ne! Érqiě,

中國人不是說“不到長城非好漢”嗎？所以我一定要
中国人不是说“不到长城非好汉”吗？所以我一定要
Zhōngguórén búshì shuō “bú dào Chángchéng fēi hǎohàn” ma? Suǒyǐ wǒ yídìng yào

試一試。我還想去黃山，我的朋友告訴我黃山那兒
试一试。我还想去黄山，我的朋友告诉我黄山那儿
shìyishì. Wǒ hái xiǎng qù Huángshān, wǒ de péngyou gàosu wǒ Huángshān nàr

風景如畫，美極了！
风景如画，美极了！
fēngjǐngrúhuà, měi jí le!

我還想去看看張藝謀導演的功夫片《十面埋伏》。看
我还想去看看张艺谋导演的功夫片《十面埋伏》。看
Wǒ hái xiǎng qù kànkàn Zhāng Yìmóu dǎoyǎn de gōngfūpiān《Shí Miàn Máifu》. Kàn

過這部電影的人都說它的場面比《英雄》還要
过这部电影的人都说它的场面比《英雄》还要
guo zhè bù diànyǐng de rén dōu shuō tā de chǎngmiàn bǐ《Yīngxióng》hái yào

壯觀，情節也很曲折。
壮观，情节也很曲折。
zhuàngguān, qíngjié yě hěn qūzhé.

你們看，我今年寒假要做的事多不多？我希望我從
你们看，我今年寒假要做的事多不多？我希望我从
Nǐmen kàn, wǒ jīnnián hánjià yào zuò de shì duōbuduō? Wǒ xīwàng wǒ cóng

中國回來的時候，能滿載而歸。
中国回来的时候，能满载而归。
Zhōngguó huílai de shíhou, néng mǎnzài'érguī.

這就是我今天的報告。謝謝大家！
这就是我今天的报告。谢谢大家！
Zhè jiù shì wǒ jīntiān de bàogào. Xièxie dàjiā!

拼音索引 (拼音索引) PINYIN INDEX (LESSONS 1–10)

Each entry lists Pinyin, traditional character, simplified character, part of speech, English meaning, and lesson number.
Note: The letter "s" means that the entry occurs in the supplementary vocabulary to that lesson.

A

ǎi	矮	矮	*Adj.*	short	9
ānquán	安全	安全	*Adj.*	safe	10
ānquándài	安全帶	安全带	*N.*	seat belt, safety belt	3
àngsī	盎司	盎司	*N.*	ounce	9s

B

bǎ	把	把	*M.W.*	measure word (classifier) for an utensil which has a handle	2
báitiān	白天	白天	*N.*	day time	4
báitóufa	白頭髮	白头发	*N.*	gray hair	4
bǎi	擺	摆	*V.*	to place, put	2
bǎifēnzhi	百分之......	百分之......	*Num.*	. . . percent (%)	6
bàifǎng	拜訪	拜访	*V.*	to visit	7
			N.	visit	
bānjī	班機	班机	*N.*	flight	5
bàn	辦	办	*V.*	to apply, process	7
bànshìchù	辦事處	办事处	*N.*	office, agency	7s
bāngzhù	幫助	帮助	*N.*	help	10
bàng	磅	磅	*M.W.*	pound (measure word for weight measurement)	9
bǎo	飽	饱	*Adj.*	full	4
Běijīng	北京	北京	*N.*	Beijing, the capital of China	2
bèi	倍	倍	*M.W.*	times, –fold	8s
běnlái	本來	本来	*Adv.*	originally	3
biànchéng	變成	变成	*V.C.*	to become	3
biànhuà	變化	变化	*V.*	to change	3
			N.	change	
biǎo	表	表	*N.*	form	6
biǎomèi	表妹	表妹	*N.*	cousin	8
biǎoyǎn	表演	表演	*N.*	performance	2
			V.	to perform	
bié	別	别	*Aux.*	don't	1
biérén	別人	别人	*N.*	other people	5
bù	簿	簿	*N.*	(check) book	6

bù	部	部	*M.W.*	(measure word for films, machines, or cars)	8
bùrú	不如	不如	*V.*	to be inferior to, to be not as good as	8

C

céng	層	层	*M.W.*	floor; layer	1s
chá	查	查	*V.*	to check	7
chàbuduō	差不多	差不多	*Adv.*	not very different, similar, about the same	6
Chángchéng	長城	长城	*N.*	the Great Wall	2
chǎngmiàn	場面	场面	*N.*	scene	8
chāochē	超車	超车	*V.O.*	to overtake another car	3s
chāoguò	超過	超过	*V.*	to surpass	9
chēfèi	車費	车费	*N.*	car fare	3
chǐ	呎	呎	*N.*	foot (British measurement)	9
chōukòng	抽空	抽空	*V.O.*	to manage to find time	7
chū	齣	出	*M.W.*	measure word (modifier) for Chinese theatre performance	2
chūchāi	出差	出差	*V.O.*	to go on a business trip	3s
chūzū	出租	出租	*V.*	to rent	3
chǔxù	儲蓄	储蓄	*N.*	savings	6
			V.	to save (money)	
chuāng	窗	窗	*N.*	window	1
chuī dízi	吹笛子	吹笛子	*V.O.*	to play the flute	2s
cún	存	存	*V.*	to deposit	6
cùn	吋	吋	*N.*	inch (British measurment)	9

D

dāchéng	搭乘	搭乘	*V.*	to take (a means of transportation)	3
dǎ	打	打	*V.*	to play (the drum); to hit	2
dǎsuàn	打算	打算	*V.*	to plan	7
			N.	plan	
dàgài	大概	大概	*Adv.*	probably	7
dàkāiyǎnjiè	大開眼界	大开眼界		be exposed to many great new things	5
dàshà	大廈	大厦	*N.*	large and high building	5
dàshǐguǎn	大使館	大使馆	*N.*	embassy	7s
dānchéng	單程	单程	*N.*	one–way trip	7s
dānxíngdào	單行道	单行道	*N.*	one–way road	3s
dānzi	單子	单子	*N.*	form	6
dāngrán	當然	当然	*Adv.*	of course	6
dāngtiān	當天	当天	*Adv.*	on that day	10
dāo	刀	刀	*N.*	knife	2

dǎoyǎn	導演	导演	*N.*	director	8
			V.	to direct (a film)	
dǎoyóu	導遊	导游	*N.*	guide	7s
dào	倒	倒	*V.*	to move backwards	1
dī	低	低	*Adj.*	low	6
dìbǎn	地板	地板	*N.*	(wooden) floor	1s
dìdao	地道	地道	*Adj.*	original, genuine, authentic	4
dìtǎn	地毯	地毯	*N.*	carpet	1s
dìxiàshì	地下室	地下室	*N.*	basement	1s
diànzǐ	電子	电子	*N.*	electronics	3
dǐng	頂	顶	*N.*	top	10
dìng	訂	订	*V.*	to book, make reservations	7
dìng fángjiān	訂房間	订房间	*V.O.*	to reserve a room	7s
dìngqī cúnkuǎn	定期存款	定期存款	*N.*	certificate of deposit; fixed deposit	6s
dòng	棟	栋	*M.W.*	(measure word for buildings)	3
duì	對	对	*Prep.*	toward, to	8
duìhuàn	兌換	兑换	*N.*	exchange	6
			V.	to exchange	

E

érqiě	而且	而且	*Conj.*	and also, furthermore	8

F

fāzhǎn	發展	发展	*V.*	to develop	3
			N.	development	
Fǎláng	法郎	法郎	*N.*	French Franc	6s
fánróng	繁榮	繁荣	*Adj.*	prosperous	5
fāngbiàn	方便	方便	*Adj.*	convenient	6
fāngbiàn	方便	方便	*Adj.*	convenient	1s
fāngmiàn	方面	方面	*N.*	aspect	8
fāngxiàng	方向	方向	*N.*	direction	5
fāngxiàng	方向	方向	*N.*	direction	3s
fángdōng	房東	房东	*N.*	landlord	1
fàng	放	放	*V.*	to place, to put	1
fàng	放	放	*V.*	to show (movies); to place	8
fēi	非	非	*Adv.*	not (used in Classical Chinese)	10
fēixíng	飛行	飞行	*N.*	flight; flying	5
fēngōnghézuò	分工合作	分工合作		to collaborate by dividing up the work	1
fēngjǐngrúhuà	風景如畫	风景如画		with picturesque scenic beauty	7
fúzhuāng	服裝	服装	*N.*	clothes	2
fúzhuāng	服裝	服装	*N.*	costume	8s
fùjìn	附近	附近	*N.*	nearby	1
fùkuǎn	付款	付款	*V.O.*	to make payment	10
fùzé	負責	负责	*V.*	to be responsible for	1

G

gānbēi	乾杯	干杯	*V.O.*	to toast, cheers	4
gānjìng	乾淨	干净	*Adj.*	clean, tidy	1s
gǎn	感	感	*V.*	to feel, sense	8
gǎnqíng	感情	感情	*N.*	emotion	8
gǎnshàng	趕上	赶上	*V.C.*	to catch; catch up with	5
gǎnxiǎng	感想	感想	*N.*	reflections, thoughts	8s
gāngqín	鋼琴	钢琴	*N.*	piano	2s
Gǎngbì	港幣	港币	*N.*	Hong Kong Dollar	6
gāo	高	高	*Adj.*	high	6
gàosu	告訴	告诉	*V.*	to tell	10
gèwèi	各位	各位	*Pron.*	everybody (a term to address people)	3
gèzhǒng	各種	各种	*Adj.*	various, all kinds of	2
gèzi	個子	个子	*N.*	height, stature	9
gēnjù	根據	根据	*Prep.*	according to, based on	10
gèng	更	更	*Adv.*	more	9
gōngchǐ	公尺	公尺	*N.*	meter	3
gōngchǐ	公尺	公尺	*N.*	meter	9s
gōngfēn	公分	公分	*N.*	centimeter	9s
gōngfūpiān	功夫片	功夫片	*N.*	action movie	8
gōngjīn	公斤	公斤	*N.*	kilogram	9s
gōnglǐ	公里	公里	*N.*	kilometer	3
gòu	夠	够	*Adj.*	enough	6
gǔ	鼓	鼓	*N.*	drum	2
gǔdài	古代	古代	*Adj.*	ancient times	8
gùshi	故事	故事	*N.*	story	8
guà	掛	挂	*V.*	to hang	1
guǎi	拐	拐	*V.*	to turn	3
guàibude	怪不得	怪不得		no wonder	9
Guān Gōng	關公	关公	*N.*	Guan Gong (name) a famous general in the Three Kingdoms	2s
guānshàng	關上	关上	*V.*	to close	1
guānyú	關於	关于	*Prep.*	about	2s
guānyú	關於	关于	*Prep.*	about, with regard to	8
guānzhòng	觀眾	观众	*N.*	audience	2
guìtái	櫃台	柜台	*N.*	counter	6

H

hánjià	寒假	寒假	*N.*	winter vacation	7
hángkōng	航空	航空	*N.*	aviation, airline	3
hǎohàn	好漢	好汉	*N.*	hero	10
hàokè	好客	好客	*Adj.*	hospitable	5
hónglǜdēng	紅綠燈	红绿灯	*N.*	traffic light	3

hòuchēxiāng	後車箱	后车箱	*N.*	(car) trunk	3
húqín	胡琴	胡琴	*N.*	two-stringed bowed instruments	2
huā	花	花	*Adj.*	blurred eyesight	4
huà	畫	画	*V.*	to paint, draw	2
			N.	painting	
huài	壞	坏	*Adj.*	bad	
huàn	換	换	*V.*	to change	6
Huángshān	黃山	黄山	*N.*	Mount Huang, (the Yellow Mountain, a famous tourist attraction in Anhui Province of central China)	10
huíchéng	回程	回程	*N.*	return trip	7s
huìlǜ	匯率	汇率	*N.*	exchange rate	6
huóqīcúnkuǎn	活期存款	活期存款	*N.*	demand deposit	6s

J

jīpiào	機票	机票	*N.*	plane ticket	7
jítā	吉他	吉他	*N.*	guitar	2s
jì	寄	寄	*V.*	to mail	6
jìhuà	計畫	计划	*V.*	to plan	10
			N.	plan	
jìshàng	繫上	系上	*V.C.*	to tie, fasten, buckle up	3
jìsuànjī	計算機	计算机	*N.*	computer	3
jiāchángbiànfàn	家常便飯	家常便饭	*N.*	home-made meal	4
jiàrì	假日	假日	*N.*	hoiliday	3
jiānchí	堅持	坚持	*V.*	to persist, persevere	9
jiǎnféi	減肥	减肥	*V.O.*	to lose weight	9
jiǎnjí	剪輯	剪辑	*N.*	film editing	8s
jiànkāng	健康	健康	*Adj.*	healthy	4
jiàngluò	降落	降落	*V.*	to land, descend	3
jiāochākǒu	交叉口	交叉口	*N.*	intersection	3
jiēdào	街道	街道	*N.*	street	4
jiēshòu	接受	接受	*V.*	to accept	10
jīnjīnyǒuwèi	津津有味	津津有味		with relish, with keen pleasure	5
jīngcǎi	精彩	精彩	*Adj.*	brilliant, wonderful	8
jīngshen	精神	精神	*Adj.*	energetic, high-spirited	4
jìngzi	鏡子	镜子	*N.*	mirror	1
jùquán	俱全	俱全		all included, altogether	4

K

kāi	開	开	*V.*	to open	6
kànfǎ	看法	看法	*N.*	view, way of looking at things	8s
kèguān	客觀	客观	*Adj.*	factual, objective	8
kòngzhì	控制	控制	*V.*	to control	9

kuǎn	款	款	*N.*	money	6
Kūnmíng	昆明	昆明	*N.*	Kunming, the capital city of Yunan province	7
kùn	睏	困	*Adj.*	sleepy, dozy	4

L

lā	拉	拉	*V.*	to play (string musical instrument); to pull	2
láidejí	來得及	来得及		to have enough time to	7
lèi	累	累	*Adj.*	tired, get tired of	1
lìlǜ	利率	利率	*N.*	interest rate	6
lìshǐ	歷史	历史	*N.*	history	8
lìxī	利息	利息	*N.*	interest	6
lián	連	连	*Prep.*	even	8
liǎn	臉	脸	*N.*	face	2
liáng	涼	凉	*Adj.*	cool, cold	4
liàng	亮	亮	*Adj.*	bright	1s
liǎojiě	瞭解	了解	*V.* *N.*	to understand understanding	8s
líng	零	零	*Num.*	zero	10
línghuó	靈活	灵活	*Adj.*	dexterous, agile, flexible	9
lǐngshìguǎn	領事館	领事馆	*N.*	consulate	7s
lóutī	樓梯	楼梯	*N.*	stair	1s
Lúbù	盧布	卢布	*N.*	Russian Ruble	6s
lùkǒu	路口	路口	*N.*	blocks, diverging point of a road	3
lùrén	路人	路人	*N.*	passer-by	3
luàn	亂	乱	*Adj.*	messy	1s
lǚguǎn	旅館	旅馆	*N.*	hotel, hostel	3
lǚkè	旅客	旅客	*N.*	traveler, passenger	3
lǚxíngshè	旅行社	旅行社	*N.*	travel agency	7
lǚyóu	旅遊	旅游	*N.*	tour	7

M

Mǎkè	馬克	马克	*N.*	German Marc	6s
mǎlù	馬路	马路	*N.*	road, avenue, street	3
mǎibuqǐ	買不起	买不起		cannot afford to buy	7
mǎidào	買到	买到	*V.C.*	to succeed in buying	7
mǎn	滿	满	*Adj.*	full	2
mǎnzài'érguī	滿載而歸	满载而归		to return with tremendous accomplishment	10
mén	門	门	*N.*	door	1
Měiguó yùntōngkǎ	美國運通卡	美国运通卡	*N.*	American Express card	6s
Měijīn	美金	美金	*N.*	US Dollar	6

Měiyuán	美元	美元	*N.*	US Dollar	6s
miáotiáo	苗條	苗条	*Adj.*	slim	9
miáoxiě	描寫	描写	*N.*	description, exposition	8
			V.	to describe	

N

ná	拿	拿	*V.*	to hold; take	2
náshǒucài	拿手菜	拿手菜	*N.*	best cooking	4
nándé	難得	难得	*Adv.*	seldom, rarely	4
nào	鬧	闹	*V.*	to make, cause, induce	5
niángāo	年糕	年糕	*N.*	new-year cake, rice cake	4
niánqīng	年輕	年轻	*Adj.*	young	4
nóngtián	農田	农田	*N.*	farmland; cropland	3
nǚháizi	女孩子	女孩子	*N.*	girl	9

O

ō	喔	喔	*Int.*	(used to indicate realization)	3
Ōuyuán	歐元	欧元	*N.*	Euro, currency used in the European Union	6s

P

pá	爬	爬	*V.*	to climb	10
pèiyuè	配樂	配乐	*V.O.*	to dub in background music	8s
piányi	便宜	便宜	*Adj.*	inexpensive	7
piàojià	票價	票价	*N.*	ticket price	8

Q

qǐngkè	請客	请客	*V.*	to act as the host, to treat	1
pò	破	破	*Adj.*	broken	1
pòfèi	破費	破费	*V.O.*	(a common courteous expression used by the gift receivers) to spend money; go to expenses	4
qíshí	其實	其实	*Adv.*	as a matter of fact, actually	7
qiān	千	千	*Num.*	thousand	6
qiānzhèng	簽證	签证	*N.*	visa	7
qiānzhèngkǎ	簽證卡	签证卡	*N.*	visa card	6s
qiáng	強	强	*Adj.*	better than, well off	8
qiáng	牆	墙	*N.*	wall	2
qiāo luó	敲鑼	敲锣	*V.*	to play the gong	2s
qiáo	橋	桥	*N.*	bridge	3s
qīnqi	親戚	亲戚	*N.*	relatives	7
qīng	輕	轻	*Adj.*	light	9

qīngsōng	輕鬆	轻松	*Adj.*	relieved, relaxed	8
qíngjié	情節	情节	*N.*	story; plot	8
qūzhé	曲折	曲折	*Adj.*	with twists and turns, complicated	10
qǔ	取	取	*V.*	to withdraw	6
qǔkuǎnjī	取款機	取款机	*N.*	banking machine	6
qǔkuǎnkǎ	取款卡	取款卡	*N.*	ATM card	6

R

rèqíng	熱情	热情	*Adj.*	warm-hearted, enthusiastic	5
Rénmínbì	人民幣	人民币	*N.*	Renminbi (name of currency used in Mainland China)	3
Rìyuán	日元	日元	*N.*	Japanese Yen	6s
rúguǒ	如果	如果	*Conj.*	if	7

S

sǎo	掃	扫	*V.*	to clean, sweep	1
shāngdiàn	商店	商店	*N.*	store	10
shǎoshùmínzú	少數民族	少数民族	*N.*	minority nationalities	7
shēnqǐng	申請	申请	*N.*	application	6
			V.	to apply	
shénqì	神氣	神气	*Adj.*	energetic; high-spirited; proud	2
shīmián	失眠	失眠	*N.*	insomnia	4s
			V.O.	to be unable to fall asleep	
shīmǔ	師母	师母	*N.*	(a honorific term used when addressing the teacher's wife)	4
shíchā	時差	时差	*N.*	time difference; jetlag	4
shìyìng	適應	适应	*V.*	to get used to	4
shòu	瘦	瘦	*Adj.*	thin, slim, skinny	9
shù	樹	树	*N.*	tree	1
shuāngxíngdào	雙行道	双行道	*N.*	two-way road	3s
shuìbuzháo	睡不著	睡不着	*V.*	cannot fall asleep	4
shuōhǎo le	說好了	说好了		to have agreement on	10
sījī	司機	司机	*N.*	driver	3
sǐ	死	死	*Adj.*	dead	1
			V.	to die	
sìjìrúchūn	四季如春	四季如春		to be like spring all year round	7
suīrán	雖然	虽然	*Conj.*	although	5

T

tā	它	它	*Pron.*	it	8
tánzòu	彈奏	弹奏	*V.*	to play, pluck; strike	2
tàng	燙	烫	*Adj.*	burning hot	4s
tèbié	特别	特别	*Adv.*	very; especially	8
tèdì	特地	特地	*Adv.*	specially	4

tèjì	特技	特技	*N.*	special technique	8
tǐzhòng	體重	体重	*N.*	body weight	9
tián	填	填	*V.*	to fill in/up	6
tiánshí	甜食	甜食	*N.*	sweet food	9
tǐng	挺	挺	*Adv.*	very	5
tóngyì	同意	同意	*V.*	to agree	8
tuán	團	团	*N.*	group	5

W

wàibì	外幣	外币	*N.*	foreign currency	6
wàitào	外套	外套	*N.*	coat	1
wán	完	完	*V.*	to finish	8
wànshìdákǎ	萬事達卡	万事达卡	*N.*	Master card	6s
wǎng	往	往	*Prep.*	toward	3
wǎngfǎnpiào	往返票	往返票	*N.*	round-trip ticket	7s
wǎngzhàn	網站	网站	*N.*	website	7
wàng	忘	忘	*V.*	to forget	1
wār	彎兒	弯儿	*N.*	turn, detour	3
wéishēngsù	維生素	维生素	*N.*	vitamin	4
wèidao	味道	味道	*N.*	taste	4
wǔtái	舞台	舞台	*N.*	(performance) stage	2
wùdiǎn	誤點	误点	*N.*	delay	5
			V.O.	to delay	

X

xīwàng	希望	希望	*V.*	to hope	10
			N.	hope	
xīyǐnrén	吸引人	吸引人	*Adj.*	appealing, attractive	8
xíguàn	習慣	习惯	*V.*	to be used to	4
xì	戲	戏	*N.*	play; drama	2
xiànjīn	現金	现金	*N.*	cash	6
xiànmù	羨慕	羡慕	*V.*	to envy	7
xiāng	香	香	*N.*	aroma	4
			Adj.	aromatic, good-smelling	
Xiānggǎng	香港	香港	*N.*	Hong Kong	7
xiāngjù	相聚	相聚	*V.*	to be together, get together	4
xiāngzi	箱子	箱子	*N.*	box, suitcase	1
xiàng	向	向	*Prep.*	toward	3
xiǎochī	小吃	小吃	*N.*	snack	5
xiǎochīdiàn	小吃店	小吃店	*N.*	snack store	3
xiǎotíqín	小提琴	小提琴	*N.*	violin	2s
xiǎoxīn	小心	小心	*Adj.*	be careful	1
xiǎoyìsi	小意思	小意思		not a big deal	4
xiàoguǒ	效果	效果	*N.*	effect	8

xiàohua	笑話	笑话	*N.*	joke	5
xiē	些	些	*M.W.*	some	4
xīndé	心得	心得	*N.*	what one has learned from work or study	8s
xīnshǎng	欣賞	欣赏	*V.*	to enjoy, appreciate	2s
Xīntáibì	新台幣	新台币	*N.*	Taiwan Dollar	6s
xìnyòngkǎ	信用卡	信用卡	*N.*	credit card	6
xíngli	行李	行李	*N.*	luggage, baggage	1
xìngqù	興趣	兴趣	*N.*	interest	8
xūyào	需要	需要	*V.*	to require	9
xún	旬	旬	*N.*	a period of ten days of a month	10

Y

ya	呀	呀	*Part.*	(used at the sentence end to soften the tone)	1
yánjiū bàogào	研究報告	研究报告	*N.*	research report	8
yánsè	顏色	颜色	*N.*	color	8
yǎnjīng	眼睛	眼睛	*N.*	eye	4
yǎnyuán	演員	演员	*N.*	actor or actress; performer	2
yàocǎo	藥草	药草	*N.*	medicinal herbs	4s
yàoshi	鑰匙	钥匙	*N.*	key	1s
yàoshì	要是	要是	*Conj.*	if	7
yīfu	衣服	衣服	*N.*	clothes	1
yìjiàn	意見	意见	*N.*	opinion	8s
yìyánwéidìng	一言為定	一言为定		It's a deal	2
yìzhí	一直	一直		straight	3
yìzhí	一直	一直	*Adv.*	always	7
yīn	陰	阴	*Adj.*	cloudy	5
yínháng	銀行	银行	*N.*	bank	6
yǐnshí	飲食	饮食	*N.*	food and drink, eating	9
Yīngbàng	英鎊	英镑	*N.*	British Pound	6s
yǐngzi	影子	影子	*N.*	shadow	8
yóngyuǎn	永遠	永远	*Adv.*	forever	4
yòngpǐn	用品	用品	*N.*	product	3
Yǒu péng zì yuǎnfāng lái, bú yì yuè hu?	有朋自遠方來，不亦樂乎？	有朋自远方来，不亦乐乎？		Isn't it pleasant to have friends coming from afar?	4
yòu	右	右	*Adj.*	right side	3
yuán	元	元	*M.W.*	dollar	6
yuánlái	原來	原来	*Adv.*	originally	7
yuèláiyuè......	越來越......	越来越......		more and more . . .	9
yuèqì	樂器	乐器	*N.*	musical instrument	2
yuèshī	樂師	乐师	*N.*	musician	2
Yúnnán	雲南	云南	*N.*	Yunnan, a province in the southwestern part of China	7

Z

zài	載	载	*V.*	to carry, transport	3s
zánmen	咱們	咱们	*N.*	we, us	1
zāng	髒	脏	*Adj.*	dirty	1s
zǎo	早	早	*Adj.*	(to emphasize long ago)	9
zhàn	站	站	*V.*	to stand	2
zhǎng	長	长	*V.*	to grow	4
zhuàng	撞	撞	*V.*	to collide with, hit, strike	1
zhànghù	帳户	账户	*N.*	account	6
zhǎo	找	找	*V.*	to seek, look for; to give (change)	3
zhǎodedào	找得到	找得到		to be able to find	7
zhàopiàn	照片	照片	*N.*	photograph, picture	2
zhe	著	着	*Part.*	(indicats continuous or stationary status)	2
zhěnglǐ	整理	整理	*V.*	to arrange, sort out	1
zhěngqí	整齊	整齐	*Adj.*	tidy	1s
zhīpiào	支票	支票	*N.*	check	6
zhídé	值得	值得	*Adj.*	worthwhile	5
zhíyuán	職員	职员	*N.*	staff, employee	6
zhǐshì	只是	只是	*Adv.*	just, simply	4
zhìzuò	製作	制作	*V.*	to produce	8s
zhōngtóu	鐘頭	钟头	*N.*	hour	9
zhōngyú	終於	终于	*Adv.*	finally, at last	5
zhǒng	種	种	*M.W.*	kind	6
zhòngyào	重要	重要	*Adj.*	important	9
zhōumò	週末	周末	*N.*	weekend	8
zhǔyào	主要	主要	*Adj.*	main, major	8
zhǔyi	主意	主意	*N.*	idea	1
zuòwèi	座位	座位	*N.*	seat	2
zhùyì	注意	注意	*V.*	to pay attention to	9
zhuānxīn	專心	专心	*Adj.*	be attentive, absorbed	2s
zhuǎn	轉	转	*V.*	to turn	3
zhuǎnjī	轉機	转机	*N.*	change planes; transfer	5
zhuāng	裝	装	*V.*	to install, assemble; load, pack	1
zhuàngguān	壯觀	壮观	*Adj.*	magnificent	10
zìdòng	自動	自动	*Adj.*	automatic	6
zìjǐ	自己	自己	*N.*	self	2
zǒngshì	總是	总是	*Adv.*	always	9
zuìhòu	最後	最后	*Adv.*	finally	10
zuǒ	左	左	*Adj.*	left side	3

英文索引 (英文索引) ENGLISH INDEX (LESSONS 1–10)

Each entry lists English meanings, traditional character, simplified character, Pinyin, part of speech, and lesson number.
Note: The letter "s" means that the entry occurs in the supplementary vocabulary to that lesson.

(a common courteous expression used by the gift receivers) to spend money; go to expenses	破費	破费	pòfèi	*V.O.*	4
(a honorific term used when addressing the teacher's wife)	師母	师母	shīmǔ	*N.*	4
(car) trunk	後車箱	后车箱	hòuchēxiāng	*N.*	3
(check) book	簿	簿	bù	*N.*	6
(indicats continuous or stationary status)	著	着	zhe	*Part.*	2
(measure word for buildings)	棟	栋	dòng	*M.W.*	3
(measure word for films, machines, or cars)	部	部	bù	*M.W.*	8
(performance) stage	舞台	舞台	wǔtái	*N.*	2
(to emphasize long ago)	早	早	zǎo	*Adj.*	9
(used at the sentence end to soften the tone)	呀	呀	ya	*Part.*	1
(used to indicate realization)	喔	喔	ō	*Int.*	3
(wooden) floor	地板	地板	dìbǎn	*N.*	1s

A

a period of ten days of a month	旬	旬	xún	*N.*	10
about	關於	关于	guānyú	*Prep.*	2s
about, with regard to	關於	关于	guānyú	*Prep.*	8
to accept	接受	接受	jiēshòu	*V.*	10
according to, based on	根據	根据	gēnjù	*Prep.*	10
account	帳戶	账户	zhànghù	*N.*	6
to act as the host, to treat	請客	请客	qǐngkè	*V.*	1
action movie	功夫片	功夫片	gōngfūpiān	*N.*	8
actor or actress; performer	演員	演员	yǎnyuán	*N.*	2
actor, actress	演員	演员	yǎnyuán	*N.*	8
to agree	同意	同意	tóngyì	*V.*	8
all included, altogether	俱全	俱全	jùquán		4
although	雖然	虽然	suīrán	*Conj.*	5

B

to book, make reservations	訂	订	dìng	*V.*	7
box, suitcase	箱子	箱子	xiāngzi	*N.*	1
bridge	橋	桥	qiáo	*N.*	3s
bright	亮	亮	liàng	*Adj.*	1s
brilliant, wonderful	精彩	精彩	jīngcǎi	*Adj.*	8
British Pound	英鎊	英镑	Yīngbàng	*N.*	6s
broken	破	破	pò	*Adj.*	1
burning hot	燙	烫	tàng	*Adj.*	4s

C

cannot afford to buy	買不起	买不起	mǎibuqǐ		7
cannot fall asleep	睡不著	睡不着	shuìbuzháo	*V.*	4
car fare	車費	车费	chēfèi	*N.*	3
carpet	地毯	地毯	dìtǎn	*N.*	1s
to carry, transport	載	载	zài	*V.*	3s
cash	現金	现金	xiànjīn	*N.*	6
to catch; catch up with	趕上	赶上	gǎnshàng	*V.C.*	5
centimeter	公分	公分	gōngfēn	*N.*	9s
certificate of deposit; fixed deposit	定期存款	定期存款	dìngqī cúnkuǎn	*N.*	6s
to change	換	换	huàn	*V.*	6
to change	變化	变化	biànhuà	*V.*	3
change				*N.*	
change planes; transfer	轉機	转机	zhuǎnjī	*N.*	5
check	支票	支票	zhīpiào	*N.*	6
to check	查	查	chá	*V.*	7
to clean, sweep	掃	扫	sǎo	*V.*	1
clean, tidy	乾淨	干净	gānjìng	*Adj.*	1s
to climb	爬	爬	pá	*V.*	10
to close	關上	关上	guānshàng	*V.*	1
clothes	服裝	服装	fúzhuāng	*N.*	2
clothes	衣服	衣服	yīfu	*N.*	1
cloudy	陰	阴	yīn	*Adj.*	5
coat	外套	外套	wàitào	*N.*	1
to collaborate by dividing up the work	分工合作	分工合作	fēngōnghézuò		1
to collide with, hit, strike	撞	撞	zhuàng	*V.*	1
color	顏色	颜色	yánsè	*N.*	8
computer	計算機	计算机	jìsuànjī	*N.*	3
consulate	領事館	领事馆	lǐngshìguǎn	*N.*	7s
to control	控制	控制	kòngzhì	*V.*	9
convenient	方便	方便	fāngbiàn	*Adj.*	6
convenient	方便	方便	fāngbiàn	*Adj.*	1s
cool, cold	涼	凉	liáng	*Adj.*	4

costume	服裝	服装	fúzhuāng	*N.*	8s
counter	櫃檯	柜台	guìtái	*N.*	6
cousin	表妹	表妹	biǎomèi	*N.*	8
credit card	信用卡	信用卡	xìnyòngkǎ	*N.*	6

D

day time	白天	白天	báitiān	*N.*	4
dead	死	死	sǐ	*Adj.*	1
to die				*V.*	
delay	誤點	误点	wùdiǎn	*N.*	5
to delay				*V.O.*	
demand deposit	活期存款	活期存款	huóqīcúnkuǎn	*N.*	6s
to deposit	存	存	cún	*V.*	6
description, exposition	描寫	描写	miáoxiě	*N.*	8
to describe				*V.*	
dexterous, agile, flexible	靈活	灵活	línghuó	*Adj.*	9
to develop	發展	发展	fāzhǎn	*V.*	3
development				*N.*	
direction	方向	方向	fāngxiàng	*N.*	5
direction	方向	方向	fāngxiàng	*N.*	3s
director	導演	导演	dǎoyǎn	*N.*	8
to direct (a film)				*V.*	
dirty	髒	脏	zāng	*Adj.*	1s
dollar	元	元	yuán	*M.W.*	6
don't	别	别	bié	*Aux.*	1
door	門	门	mén	*N.*	1
driver	司機	司机	sījī	*N.*	3
drum	鼓	鼓	gǔ	*N.*	2
to dub in background music	配樂	配乐	pèiyuè	*V.O.*	8s

E

effect	效果	效果	xiàoguǒ	*N.*	8
electronics	電子	电子	diànzǐ	*N.*	3
embassy	大使館	大使馆	dàshǐguǎn	*N.*	7s
emotion	感情	感情	gǎnqíng	*N.*	8
energetic, high-spirited	精神	精神	jīngshen	*Adj.*	4
energetic; high-spirited; proud	神氣	神气	shénqì	*Adj.*	2
to enjoy, appreciate	欣賞	欣赏	xīnshǎng	*V.*	2s
enough	夠	够	gòu	*Adj.*	6
to envy	羨慕	羡慕	xiànmù	*V.*	7
Euro, currency used in the European Union	歐元	欧元	Ōuyuán	*N.*	6s
even	連	连	lián	*Prep.*	8

everybody (a term to address people)	各位	各位	gèwèi	*Pron.*	3
exchange rate	匯率	汇率	huìlǜ	*N.*	6
exchange	兌換	兑换	duìhuàn	*N.*	6
to exchange				*V.*	
eye	眼睛	眼睛	yǎnjīng	*N.*	4

F

face	臉	脸	liǎn	*N.*	2
factual, objective	客觀	客观	kèguān	*Adj.*	8
farmland; cropland	農田	农田	nóngtián	*N.*	3
to feel, sense	感	感	gǎn	*V.*	8
to fill in/up	填	填	tián	*V.*	6
film editing	剪輯	剪辑	jiǎnjí	*M.W.*	8s
finally	最後	最后	zuìhòu	*Adv.*	10
finally, at last	終於	终于	zhōngyú	*Adv.*	5
to finish	完	完	wán	*V.*	8
flight	班機	班机	bānjī	*N.*	5
flight; flying	飛行	飞行	fēixíng	*N.*	5
floor; layer	層	层	céng	*M.W.*	1s
food and drink, eating	飲食	饮食	yǐnshí	*N.*	9
foot (British measurement)	呎	呎	chǐ	*N.*	9
foreign currency	外幣	外币	wàibì	*N.*	6
forever	永遠	永远	yóngyuǎn	*Adv.*	4
to forget	忘	忘	wàng	*V.*	1
form	表	表	biǎo	*N.*	6
form	單子	单子	dānzi	*N.*	6
French Franc	法郎	法郎	Fǎláng	*N.*	6s
full	滿	满	mǎn	*Adj.*	2
full	飽	饱	bǎo	*Adj.*	4

G

German Marc	馬克	马克	Mǎkè	*N.*	6s
to get used to	適應	适应	shìyìng	*V.*	4
girl	女孩子	女孩子	nǚháizi	*N.*	9
to go on a business trip	出差	出差	chūchāi	*V.O.*	3s
gray hair	白頭髮	白头发	báitóufa	*N.*	4
group	團	团	tuán	*N.*	5
to grow	長	长	zhǎng	*V.*	4
Guan Gong (name) a famous general in the Three Kingdoms	關公	关公	Guān Gōng	*N.*	2s
guide	導遊	导游	dǎoyóu	*N.*	7s
guitar	吉他	吉他	jítā	*N.*	2s

H

to hang	掛	挂	guà	*V.*	1
to have agreement on	說好了	说好了	shuōhǎo le		10
to have enough time to	來得及	来得及	láidejí		7
healthy	健康	健康	jiànkāng	*Adj.*	4
height, stature	個子	个子	gèzi	*N.*	9
help	幫助	帮助	bāngzhù	*N.*	10
hero	好漢	好汉	hǎohàn	*N.*	10
high	高	高	gāo	*Adj.*	6
history	歷史	历史	lìshǐ	*N.*	8
hoiliday	假日	假日	jiàrì	*N.*	3
to hold; take	拿	拿	ná	*V.*	2
home-made meal	家常便飯	家常便饭	jiāchángbiànfàn	*N.*	4
Hong Kong	香港	香港	Xiānggǎng	*N.*	7
Hong Kong Dollar	港幣	港币	Gǎngbì	*N.*	6
to hope	希望	希望	xīwàng	*V.*	10
hope				*N.*	
hospitable	好客	好客	hàokè	*Adj.*	5
hotel, hostel	旅館	旅馆	lǚguǎn	*N.*	3
hour	鐘頭	钟头	zhōngtóu	*N.*	9

I

idea	主意	主意	zhǔyi	*N.*	1
if	如果	如果	rúguǒ	*Conj.*	7
if	要是	要是	yàoshì	*Conj.*	7
important	重要	重要	zhòngyào	*Adj.*	9
inch (British measurment)	吋	吋	cùn	*N.*	9
inexpensive	便宜	便宜	piányi	*Adj.*	7
insomnia	失眠	失眠	shīmián	*N.*	4s
to be unable to fall asleep				*V.O.*	
to install, assemble; load, pack	裝	装	zhuāng	*V.*	1
interest	利息	利息	lìxī	*N.*	6
interest	興趣	兴趣	xìngqù	*N.*	8
interest rate	利率	利率	lìlǜ	*N.*	6
intersection	交叉口	交叉口	jiāochākǒu	*N.*	3
Isn't it pleasant to have friends coming from afar?	有朋自遠方來，不亦樂乎?	有朋自远方来，不亦乐乎?	Yǒu péng zì yuǎnfāng lái, bú yì yuè hu?		4
it	它	它	tā	*Pron.*	8
It's a deal	一言為定	一言为定	yìyánwéidìng		2

J

Japanese Yen	日元	日元	Rìyuán	*N.*	6s
joke	笑話	笑话	xiàohua	*N.*	5
just, simply	只是	只是	zhǐshì	*Adv.*	4

K

key	鑰匙	钥匙	yàoshi	*N.*	1s
kilogram	公斤	公斤	gōngjīn	*N.*	9s
kilometer	公里	公里	gōnglǐ	*N.*	3
kind	種	种	zhǒng	*M.W.*	6
knife	刀	刀	dāo	*N.*	2
Kunming, the capital city of Yunan province	昆明	昆明	Kūnmíng	*N.*	7

L

to land, descend	降落	降落	jiàngluò	*V.*	3
landlord	房東	房东	fángdōng	*N.*	1
large and high building	大廈	大厦	dàshà	*N.*	5
left side	左	左	zuǒ	*Adj.*	3
light	輕	轻	qīng	*Adj.*	9
to lose weight	減肥	减肥	jiǎnféi	*V.O.*	9
low	低	低	dī	*Adj.*	6
luggage, baggage	行李	行李	xíngli	*N.*	1

M

magnificent	壯觀	壮观	zhuàngguān	*Adj.*	10
to mail	寄	寄	jì	*V.*	6
main, major	主要	主要	zhǔyào	*Adj.*	8
to make payment	付款	付款	fùkuǎn	*V.O.*	10
to make, cause, induce	鬧	闹	nào	*V.*	5
to manage to find time	抽空	抽空	chōukòng	*V.O.*	7
Master card	萬事達卡	万事达卡	wànshìdákǎ	*N.*	6s
measure word (classifier) for an utensil which has a handle	把	把	bǎ	*M.W.*	2
measure word (modifier) for Chinese theatre performance	齣	出	chū	*M.W.*	2
medicinal herbs	藥草	药草	yàocǎo	*N.*	4s
messy	亂	乱	luàn	*Adj.*	1s
meter	公尺	公尺	gōngchǐ	*N.*	3
meter	公尺	公尺	gōngchǐ	*N.*	9s
minority nationalities	少數民族	少数民族	shǎoshùmínzú	*N.*	7

mirror	鏡子	镜子	jìngzi	*N.*	1
money	款	款	kuǎn	*N.*	6
more	更	更	gèng	*Adv.*	9
more and more . . .	越來越......	越来越......	yuèláiyuè......		9
to move backwards	倒	倒	dào	*V.*	1
Mount Huang, (the Yellow Mountain, a famous tourist attraction in Anhui Province of central China)	黃山	黄山	Huángshān	*N.*	10
musical instrument	樂器	乐器	yuèqì	*N.*	2
musician	樂師	乐师	yuèshī	*N.*	2

N

nearby	附近	附近	fùjìn	*N.*	1
new-year cake, rice cake	年糕	年糕	niángāo	*N.*	4
no wonder	怪不得	怪不得	guàibude		9
not (used in Classical Chinese)	非	非	fēi	*Adv.*	10
not a big deal	小意思	小意思	xiǎoyìsi		4
not very different, similar, about the same	差不多	差不多	chàbuduō	*Adv.*	6

O

of course	當然	当然	dāngrán	*Adv.*	6
office, agency	辦事處	办事处	bànshìchù	*N.*	7s
on that day	當天	当天	dāngtiān	*Adv.*	10
one-way road	單行道	单行道	dānxíngdào	*N.*	3s
one-way trip	單程	单程	dānchéng	*N.*	7s
opinion	意見	意见	yìjiàn	*N.*	8s
original, genuine, authentic	地道	地道	dìdao	*Adj.*	4
originally	本來	本来	běnlái	*Adv.*	3
originally	原來	原来	yuánlái	*Adv.*	7
other people	別人	别人	biérén	*N.*	5
ounce	盎司	盎司	àngsī	*N.*	9s
to overtake another car	超車	超车	chāochē	*V.O.*	3s

P

to paint, draw	畫	画	huà	*V.*	2
painting				*N.*	
passer-by	路人	路人	lùrén	*N.*	3
to pay attention to	注意	注意	zhùyì	*V.*	9
to open	開	开	kāi	*V.*	6
. . . percent (%)	百分之......	百分之......	bǎifēnzhi......	*Num.*	6

performance	表演	表演	biǎoyǎn	*N.*	2
to perform				*V.*	
to persist, persevere	堅持	坚持	jiānchí	*V.*	9
photograph, picture	照片	照片	zhàopiàn	*N.*	2
piano	鋼琴	钢琴	gāngqín	*N.*	2s
to place, put	擺	摆	bǎi	*V.*	2
to place, to put	放	放	fàng	*V.*	1
to plan	打算	打算	dǎsuàn	*V.*	7
plan				*N.*	
to plan	計畫	计划	jìhuà	*V.*	10
plan				*N.*	
plane ticket	機票	机票	jīpiào	*N.*	7
play; drama	戲	戏	xì	*N.*	2
to play (string musical instrument); to pull	拉	拉	lā	*V.*	2
to play (the drum); to hit	打	打	dǎ	*V.*	2
to play the flute	吹笛子	吹笛子	chuī dízi	*V.O.*	2s
to play the gong	敲鑼	敲锣	qiāo luó	*V.*	2s
to play, pluck; strike	彈奏	弹奏	tánzòu	*V.*	2
pound (measure word for weight measurement)	磅	磅	bàng	*M.W.*	9
probably	大概	大概	dàgài	*Adv.*	7
to produce	製作	制作	zhìzuò	*V.*	8s
product	用品	用品	yòngpǐn	*N.*	3
prosperous	繁榮	繁荣	fánróng	*Adj.*	5

R

reflections, thoughts	感想	感想	gǎnxiǎng	*N.*	8s
relatives	親戚	亲戚	qīnqi	*N.*	7
relieved, relaxed	輕鬆	轻松	qīngsōng	*Adj.*	8
Renminbi (name of currency used in Mainland China)	人民幣	人民币	Rénmínbì	*N.*	3
to rent	出租	出租	chūzū	*V.*	3
to require	需要	需要	xūyào	*V.*	9
research report	研究報告	研究报告	yánjiū bàogào	*N.*	8
to reserve a room	訂房間	订房间	dìng fángjiān	*V.O.*	7s
return trip	回程	回程	huíchéng	*N.*	7s
to return with tremendous accomplishment	滿載而歸	满载而归	mǎnzài'érguī		10
right side	右	右	yòu	*Adj.*	3
road, avenue, street	馬路	马路	mǎlù	*N.*	3
round-trip ticket	往返票	往返票	wǎngfǎnpiào	*N.*	7s
Russian Ruble	盧布	卢布	Lúbù	*N.*	6s

S

safe	安全	安全	ānquán	*Adj.*	10
savings	儲蓄	储蓄	chǔxù	*N.*	6
to save (money)				*V.*	
scene	場面	场面	chǎngmiàn	*N.*	8
seat	座位	座位	zuòwèi	*N.*	2
seat belt, safety belt	安全帶	安全带	ānquándài	*N.*	3
to seek, look for; to give (change)	找	找	zhǎo	*V.*	3
seldom, rarely	難得	难得	nándé	*Adv.*	4
self	自己	自己	zìjǐ	*N.*	2
shadow	影子	影子	yǐngzi	*N.*	8
short	矮	矮	ǎi	*Adj.*	9
to show (movies); to place	放	放	fàng	*V.*	8
sleepy, dozy	睏	困	kùn	*Adj.*	4
slim	苗條	苗条	miáotiáo	*Adj.*	9
snack	小吃	小吃	xiǎochī	*N.*	5
snack store	小吃店	小吃店	xiǎochīdiàn	*N.*	3
some	些	些	xiē	*M.W.*	4
southern part	南方	南方	nánfāng	*N.*	7
special technique	特技	特技	tèjì	*N.*	8
specially	特地	特地	tèdì	*Adv.*	4
staff, employee	職員	职员	zhíyuán	*N.*	6
stair	樓梯	楼梯	lóutī	*N.*	1s
to stand	站	站	zhàn	*V.*	2
store	商店	商店	shāngdiàn	*N.*	10
story	故事	故事	gùshi	*N.*	8
story; plot	情節	情节	qíngjié	*N.*	8
straight	一直	一直	yìzhí		3
street	街道	街道	jiēdào	*N.*	4
to succeed in buying	買到	买到	mǎidào	*V.C.*	7
to surpass	超過	超过	chāoguò	*V.*	9
sweet food	甜食	甜食	tiánshí	*N.*	9

T

Taiwan Dollar	新台幣	新台币	Xīntáibì	*N.*	6s
to take (a means of transportation)	搭乘	搭乘	dāchéng	*V.*	3
taste	味道	味道	wèidao	*N.*	4
to tell	告訴	告诉	gàosu	*V.*	10
the Great Wall	長城	长城	Chángchéng	*N.*	2
thin, slim, skinny	瘦	瘦	shòu	*Adj.*	9
thousand	千	千	qiān	*Num.*	6
ticket price	票價	票价	piàojià	*N.*	8

tidy	整齊	整齐	zhěngqí	*Adj.*	1s
to tie, fasten, buckle up	繫上	系上	jìshàng	*V.C.*	3
time difference; jetlag	時差	时差	shíchā	*N.*	4
times, -fold	倍	倍	bèi	*M.W.*	8s
tired, get tired of	累	累	lèi	*Adj.*	1
to toast, cheers	乾杯	干杯	gānbēi	*V.O.*	4
top	頂	顶	dǐng	*N.*	10
tour	旅遊	旅游	lǚyóu	*N.*	7
toward	往	往	wǎng	*Prep.*	3
toward	向	向	xiàng	*Prep.*	3
toward, to	對	对	duì	*Prep.*	8
traffic light	紅綠燈	红绿灯	hónglǜdēng	*N.*	3
travel agency	旅行社	旅行社	lǚxíngshè	*N.*	7
traveler, passenger	旅客	旅客	lǚkè	*N.*	3
tree	樹	树	shù	*N.*	1
to turn	拐	拐	guǎi	*V.*	3
to turn	轉	转	zhuǎn	*V.*	3
turn, detour	彎兒	弯儿	wār	*N.*	3
two-stringed bowed instruments	胡琴	胡琴	húqín	*N.*	2
two-way road	雙行道	双行道	shuāngxíngdào	*N.*	3s

U

to understand	瞭解	了解	liǎojiě	*V.*	8s
understanding				*N.*	
US Dollar	美金	美金	Měijīn	*N.*	6
US Dollar	美元	美元	Měiyuán	*N.*	6s

V

various, all kinds of	各種	各种	gèzhǒng	*Adj.*	2
very	挺	挺	tǐng	*Adv.*	5
very; especially	特别	特别	tèbié	*Adv.*	8
view, way of looking at things	看法	看法	kànfǎ	*N.*	8s
violin	小提琴	小提琴	xiǎotíqín	*N.*	2s
to visit	拜訪	拜访	bàifǎng	*V.*	7
visit				*N.*	
visa	簽證	签证	qiānzhèng	*N.*	7
visa card	簽證卡	签证卡	qiānzhèngkǎ	*N.*	6s
vitamin	維生素	维生素	wéishēngsù	*N.*	4

W

wall	牆	墙	qiáng	*N.*	2
warm-hearted, enthusiastic	熱情	热情	rèqíng	*Adj.*	5
we, us	咱們	咱们	zánmen	*N.*	1

寫字簿的生字 (写字簿的生字)
CHARACTERS IN THE CHARACTER BOOK

The following list shows the 260 characters that appear in the Character Book, grouped by the lesson in which they are first introduced. Students are required to memorize how to read and write these key characters to build up their literacy skills. The items and number of new characters introduced in each lesson are carefully selected and controlled, and are provided in the list.

繁體字版 Traditional Character Version

(1) 第一課 (27 characters)

倒 別 樹 撞 壞 呀 鏡 破 合 主 負 責 李 裝 掃 整 理 箱 衣 掛 累 死 附 忘 窗 套 咱

(2) 第二課 (31 characters)

牆 著 照 片 北 台 擺 各 種 器 演 表 鼓 拉 胡 琴 彈 奏 己 齣 戲 畫 臉 拿 刀 神 座
滿 眾 站 長

(3) 第三課 (36 characters)

往 降 落 全 繫 計 算 品 搭 乘 航 棟 交 叉 口 左 拐 直 里 展 變 化 農 田 成 喔 呎
山 燈 向 右 轉 彎 費 民 幣

(4) 第四課 (28 characters)

母 維 素 永 康 輕 特 涼 精 髮 眼 睛 花 適 差 睏 街 慣 味 香 俱 飽 便 相 聚 乾 亦 乎

(5) 第五課 (17 characters)

陰 終 於 誤 趕 情 津 界 團 鬧 笑 繁 榮 廈 雖 挺 值

(6) 第六課 (28 characters)

銀 帳 戶 存 款 取 利 率 儲 蓄 之 支 職 低 夠 單 填 千 元 金 寄 簿 卡 當 換 匯 兌
櫃

(7) 第七課 (23 characters)

寒 遊 社 訂 羨 慕 親 戚 原 抽 拜 訪 查 宜 季 數 族 果 簽 證 辦 概 及

(8) 第八課 (27 characters)

連 報 告 鬆 強 完 導 夫 它 節 引 古 代 故 彩 描 歷 史 趣 而 且 技 效 顏 週 末 價

(9) 第九課 (25 characters)

越 需 瘦 減 肥 堅 持 磅 怪 苗 孩 控 制 飲 食 注 甜 早 矮 呎 吋 超 靈 總 更

(10) 第十課 (18 characters)

希 望 旬 受 商 根 據 零 爬 頂 助 漢 訴 壯 曲 折 載 歸

简体字版 Simplified Character Version

(1) 第一课 (27 characters)

倒 别 树 撞 坏 呀 镜 破 合 主 负 责 李 装 扫 整 理 箱 衣 挂 累 死 附 忘 窗 套 咱

(2) 第二课 (31 characters)

墙 着 照 片 北 台 摆 各 种 器 演 表 鼓 拉 胡 琴 弹 奏 己 出 戏 画 脸 拿 刀 神 座 满 众 站 长

(3) 第三课 (36 characters)

往 降 落 全 系 计 算 品 搭 乘 航 栋 交 叉 口 左 拐 直 里 展 变 化 农 田 成 喔 呎 山 灯 向 右 转 弯 费 民 币

(4) 第四课 (28 characters)

母 维 素 永 康 轻 特 凉 精 发 眼 睛 花 适 差 困 街 惯 味 香 俱 饱 便 相 聚 干 亦 乎

(5) 第五课 (17 characters)

阴 终 于 误 赶 情 津 界 团 闹 笑 繁 荣 厦 虽 挺 值

(6) 第六课 (28 characters)

银 账 户 存 款 取 利 率 储 蓄 之 支 职 低 够 单 填 千 元 金 寄 簿 卡 当 换 汇 兑 柜

(7) 第七课 (23 characters)

寒 游 社 订 羡 慕 亲 戚 原 抽 拜 访 查 宜 季 数 族 果 签 证 办 概 及

(8) 第八课 (27 characters)

连 报 告 松 强 完 导 夫 它 节 引 古 代 故 彩 描 历 史 趣 而 且 技 效 颜 周 末 价

(9) 第九课 (25 characters)

越 需 瘦 减 肥 坚 持 磅 怪 苗 孩 控 制 饮 食 注 甜 早 矮 呎 吋 超 灵 总 更

(10) 第十课 (18 characters)

希 望 旬 受 商 根 据 零 爬 顶 助 汉 诉 壮 曲 折 载 归